The Management of Global Careers

Michael Dickmann
Vesa Suutari • Olivier Wurtz
Editors

The Management of Global Careers

Exploring the Rise of International Work

Editors
Michael Dickmann
Cranfield School of Management
Cranfield University
Cranfield, UK

Vesa Suutari
School of Management
University of Vaasa
Vaasa Finland

Olivier Wurtz
School of Management
University of Vaasa
Vaasa Finland

ISBN 978-3-319-76528-0   ISBN 978-3-319-76529-7   (eBook)
https://doi.org/10.1007/978-3-319-76529-7

Library of Congress Control Number: 2018936533

© The Editor(s) (if applicable) and The Author(s) 2018
This work is subject to copyright. All rights are solely and exclusively licensed by the Publisher, whether the whole or part of the material is concerned, specifically the rights of translation, reprinting, reuse of illustrations, recitation, broadcasting, reproduction on microfilms or in any other physical way, and transmission or information storage and retrieval, electronic adaptation, computer software, or by similar or dissimilar methodology now known or hereafter developed.
The use of general descriptive names, registered names, trademarks, service marks, etc. in this publication does not imply, even in the absence of a specific statement, that such names are exempt from the relevant protective laws and regulations and therefore free for general use.
The publisher, the authors, and the editors are safe to assume that the advice and information in this book are believed to be true and accurate at the date of publication. Neither the publisher nor the authors or the editors give a warranty, express or implied, with respect to the material contained herein or for any errors or omissions that may have been made. The publisher remains neutral with regard to jurisdictional claims in published maps and institutional affiliations.

Printed on acid-free paper

This Palgrave Macmillan imprint is published by the registered company Springer International Publishing AG part of Springer Nature.
The registered company address is: Gewerbestrasse 11, 6330 Cham, Switzerland

To my siblings, Klaus-Peter, Nikola, Dietger, Thomas—
for an exciting youth and thoughtful advice.
Michael Dickmann

To my children, Eveliina, Essi-Noora and Niko.
Vesa Suutari

To Adeline.
Olivier Wurtz

Acknowledgements

The authors would like to show their appreciation and admiration of Michael Harvey who sadly died during the writing of this book. Our thoughts and condolences go to his family and friends. He is already sorely missed.

The authors would also like to express their profound gratitude to Sheena Darby whose support made it possible to pull this book together.

Contents

1. **The Multiple Forms and Shifting Landscapes of Global Careers**   1
Michael Dickmann, Vesa Suutari, and Olivier Wurtz

2. **Typologies of Internationally Mobile Employees**   33
Maike Andresen, Michael Dickmann, and Vesa Suutari

3. **Contrasting Assigned Expatriates and Self-Initiated Expatriates: A Review of Extant Research and a Future Research Agenda**   63
Vesa Suutari, Chris Brewster, and Michael Dickmann

4. **Coaching of Global Careerists**   91
Raija Salomaa

5. **Career Success in Different Countries: Reflections on the 5C Project**   117
Jon Briscoe, Michael Dickmann, Tim Hall, Emma Parry, Wolfgang Mayrhofer, and Adam Smale

x   Contents

6   Managing Global Careerists: Individual, Organizational
and Societal Needs   149
Michael Dickmann and Maike Andresen

7   Individual Offshoring: An Emerging Trend
for Global Careers   183
Caroline Creven Fourrier and Sébastien Point

8   Inpatriate Career Profiles: A Historical Review
and Future Outlook   201
Miriam Moeller and Michael Harvey

9   The Role of Repatriation in and for Global Careers   223
Eren Akkan, Mila Lazarova, and B. Sebastian Reiche

10   A Typology of Dual-Career Expatriate (Trailing)
Spouses: The 'R' Profile   257
Yvonne McNulty and Miriam Moeller

11   Management of Work-Life Interface of Global
Careerists: Experiences Among Different
Types of International Professionals   291
Vesa Suutari, Liisa Mäkelä, and Olivier Wurtz

12   Compensating Global Careerists   319
Celia Zárraga-Oberty and Jaime Bonache

Index   341

Notes on Contributors

Eren Akkan is a PhD candidate in the Managing People in Organizations Department at IESE Business School, Spain. His research interests lie at the intersection of international management and organizational behaviour fields, and his studies concentrate on topics such as identities, motivations and careers of individuals who take on different types of global work. He has presented his research at the Annual Meeting of the Academy of Management, the Academy of International Business and the European Academy of Management. He is also an adjunct professor at the Ramon Llull University of La Salle, Spain.

Maike Andresen is Professor of Human Resource Management and Organisational Behaviour and Vice President for Research at University of Bamberg, Germany. Her primary research interests are in the area of international labour mobility, (global) career management, work flexibilization and management and organization development. She has contributed numerous peer-reviewed articles to leading academic journals including *European Management Review* and *Journal of Managerial Psychology* and to edited volumes and has published or edited ten books. She is the coordinator of the Horizon 2020 international research project "Global mobility of employees" (GLOMO) and is a member of the 5C project investigating careers across 30 countries.

Jaime Bonache is Professor of Management at Carlos III University of Madrid, Spain. He has also been Full Professor of International Human Resource Management at Cranfield School of Management (UK) and Full Professor of Human Resource Management at ESADE Business School (Spain). His research interests include expatriation and global mobility, international compensation and global people management. His academic publications include more than 30 articles in international journals, and he has written and edited 4 books. With a focus on international human resource management, he co-authored *Managing a Global Workforce*.

Chris Brewster had substantial industrial experience and earned his doctorate from the London School of Economics before becoming an academic. He is a part-time Professor of International Human Resource Management at Vaasa University in Finland; Henley Business School, University of Reading in the UK; Radboud University in the Netherlands; and ISCTE-Instituto Universitário de Lisboa in Portugal. He has been involved as author or editor in the publication of more than 30 books, more than 100 chapters in other books and well over 200 articles.

Jon P. Briscoe holds a DBA from Boston University and is Professor of Management at Northern Illinois University (NIU). Teaching courses including leadership, coaching and change management, he has received numerous teaching awards. Briscoe is a co-founder of the Cross-Cultural Collaboration on Contemporary Careers (5C Group) and a past president of the Careers Division in the Academy of Management. His key research concerns career management and cultural differences in careers. In addition he studies leadership, leadership development and values in organizations. He publishes regularly in scholarly journals such as *Journal of Vocational Behavior*, *Organizational Dynamics* and *Personnel Psychology*.

Caroline Creven Fourrier is a PhD student in the area of International Human Resources Management at EM Strasbourg Business School (Universite de Strasbourg, France). Since late 2014, she has researched individual offshoring as a new form of expatriation and its impact on company talent. She has also worked for more than ten years in international procurement, holding both global and regional roles. Her current responsibility is the management of the APAC regional procurement teams, based in Singapore.

Michael Dickmann is Professor of International Human Resources Management at Cranfield University's School of Management. Dickmann is also the Senior Editor-in-chief of *The International Journal of Human Resource Management*. His research focuses on human resource strategies, structures and processes of multinational organizations, international mobility and global careers. Dickmann has worked with many multinational corporations, humanitarian agencies, government and the United Nations.

Tim Hall is the Morton H. and Charlotte Friedman Professor of Management Emeritus in the Questrom School of Business at Boston University. He has held faculty positions at Yale, York, Michigan State and Northwestern Universities, as well as visiting positions at Columbia, Minnesota, the US Military Academy at West Point, Boston College, the University of Canterbury (NZ) and the Center for Creative Leadership. His research deals with careers, work-family dynamics and leadership development.

Michael Harvey (1944–2016) received his PhD from the University Arizona in 1976. After a distinguished academic career at Southern Methodist University, the University of Oklahoma and the University of Mississippi, Harvey returned to the UA. He was lauded for his scholarship and for his work with students. In addition to receiving numerous teaching awards, he was ranked third on a list of the most productive international business researchers globally.

Mila Lazarova holds a PhD from Rutgers University, USA, and is Associate Professor of International Business, Beedie School of Business, Simon Fraser University and the Canada Research Chair in Global Workforce Management. Her diverse research interests include global careers and the role of organizational career development and mobility practices in organizations; expatriate management, focusing on repatriation and the career impact of international assignments; work/life balance issues related to assignments; the changing role of the HR department; comparative human resource management and HR issues related to workplace integration of migrants. She is the co-author of *Essentials of International Human Resource Management*.

Liisa Mäkelä is a professor at the University of Vaasa, School of Management, Finland. Her research interests are a combination of management and work psychology. Mäkelä's research focuses on the international workforce and occupational well-being, career paths and work-life interface among international professionals. Leadership and gender issues are also part of her areas of interest. Her research article has appeared in international journals including Human Resource Management and International Journal of Human Resource Management and as book chapters. Mäkelä has also co-edited a book, Work and Family Interface in the International Career Context, and is a referee for several international journals.

xiv **Notes on Contributors**

Wolfgang Mayrhofer is a full professor and head of the Interdisciplinary Institute of Management and Organisational Behaviour, WU Vienna, Austria. He has previously held full-time positions at the University of Paderborn and at Dresden University of Technology, Germany. He conducts research in comparative international human resource management and leadership, careers, and systems theory and management and has received national and international awards for outstanding research and service to the academic community. Mayrhofer has widely published, serves as an editorial or advisory board member of several international journals and research centres and regularly consults with organizations in the for-profit and non-profit world.

Yvonne McNulty is a senior lecturer, School of Human Development and Social Services at Singapore University of Social Sciences, Singapore. She previously held academic appointments at Shanghai University and James Cook University Singapore. She has published over 100 academic articles, book chapters and conference papers on expatriates and expatriation. Her research has been extensively cited in the *New York Times, International Herald Tribune, Wall Street Journal, Financial Times*, BBC Radio and Economist Intelligence Unit. Her research interests include expatriate return on investment, expatriate families, expatriate divorce and the Hague Convention on International Child Abduction, expatriate entrepreneurs, expatriate crises and nontraditional expatriates.

Miriam Moeller is Senior Lecturer of International Business, UQ Business School, University of Queensland. She holds a PhD from the University of Mississippi. Her primary research interest focuses on the impact of globalization on human resource management practices and processes, with a special interest in the impact on the inpatriate staffing method. Her research is sensitive to global mobility as well as acculturative challenges. Her research article has appeared in the *Journal of International Business Studies, International Journal of Human Resource Management, Journal of World Business, International Journal of Intercultural Relations, International Business Review* and *Journal of Business Research*.

Emma Parry is Professor of Human Resource Management and Head of the *Changing World of Work* Group at Cranfield School of Management. Her research interests focus on the impact of the changing context on managing people, in particular the influence of national context, workforce demographics and technological advancement. She has published several books and numerous peer-reviewed journal articles in these areas. Parry is Editor in Chief of the

Notes on Contributors **xv**

International Journal of Human Resource Management, Academic Fellow of the Chartered Institute of Personnel and Development and an Honorary Fellow of the Institute for Employment Studies.

Sébastien Point lectures in the areas of human resources management and international management at EM, Strasbourg Business School, France. He is the Director of the Research Centre in Management called HuManiS. His research focuses on organizational discourse and the way human resources management is promoted in official discourses. Over the years, he has widely analysed corporate websites and annual reports. His analysis often provides comparisons at European level. He has widely published in international and French academic journals.

B. Sebastian Reiche holds a PhD from the University of Melbourne, Australia, and he is Associate Professor and Head of the Department of Managing People in Organizations at IESE Business School in Barcelona, Spain. His research focuses on international assignments and global work, international human resources management, knowledge transfer, employee retention and careers, global leadership and cross-cultural management and has appeared in leading academic journals such as *Journal of International Business Studies*, *Personnel Psychology*, *Journal of Management Studies*, *Academy of Management Discoveries*, *Human Relations*, *Human Resource Management* and *Journal of World Business*, among others.

Raija Salomaa completed her article-based PhD at the University of Vaasa, Department of Management, and her MA at the University of Turku, School of Languages and Translation. She has completed change management and work psychology studies at the Technical University of Helsinki. She holds an Evidence-Based Coaching Certificate from the Fielding Graduate University, USA, and is a Professional Certified Coach by International Coach Federation. Salomaa has presented at several international conferences and guest lectures on coaching and leadership development at some institutes of higher education. She works globally as an executive and a mentor coach and as a coaching skills trainer.

Adam Smale is Professor of Management at the University of Vaasa, Finland. His research interests focus on talent management, human resources management and careers and knowledge transfer in multinational corporations. He has published a number of articles in journals such as the *Journal of International Business Studies*, *Human Resource Management*, *Journal of World Business*,

xvi   Notes on Contributors

International Business Review and *The International Journal of Human Resource Management*. He sits on the editorial boards of *Human Resource Management Journal*, the *Journal of Organizational Effectiveness: People and Performance* and the *Nordic Journal of Business*.

Vesa Suutari is a professor at the School of Management, University of Vaasa, Finland, and has recently acted as Dean of the Faculty of Business Studies and Vice Rector of the University for seven years. He has published over 80 journal articles and chapters on topics such as European management cultures, expatriation, self-initiated expatriation, global leadership and global careers. He is one of the most cited researchers on expatriation in the world.

Olivier Wurtz is Assistant Professor of School of Management at the University of Vaasa, Finland. He holds a PhD in International Human Resource Management from HEC Paris. His article has appeared in *The Journal of International Business Studies* and *The International Journal of Human Resource Management*.

Celia Zárraga-Oberty is Associate Professor of Management at the Department of Business Administration, Carlos III University of Madrid, Spain. She holds a degree in industrial engineering and a PhD in Business Administration from the ULPGC. Her research interests are in the areas of knowledge management, international compensation, work teams and high performance work systems. Her articles have appeared in a variety of journals, including *Organization Studies, Human Resource Management Review, International Human Resource Management* and the *European Management Journal.*

List of Figures

Fig. 5.1	Heuristic framework on the antecedents and outcomes of career success. Source: The authors	125
Fig. 5.2	Financial security by country. Source: The authors	129
Fig. 5.3	Work-life balance by country. Source: The authors	130
Fig. 5.4	Financial success by country. Source: The authors	131
Fig. 5.5	Entrepreneurial by country. Source: The authors	131
Fig. 5.6	Importance of dimensions of career success for women and men (DACH-countries). Source: The authors	132
Fig. 5.7	Achievement in dimensions of career success for women and men (DACH-countries). Source: The authors	133
Fig. 5.8	Importance-achievement gap in dimensions of career success for women and men (DACH-countries). Source: The authors	134
Fig. 5.9	National income inequality and importance of financial achievement. Source: The authors	135
Fig. 7.1	A list of expatriation types. Source: The authors	189
Fig. 10.1	A typology of dual-career expatriate (trailing) spouses—the 'R' profile. Source: The authors	271
Fig. 12.1	Current types of global mobility within MNCs. Source: The authors (Bonache and Zárraga-Oberty 2016)	327

List of Tables

Table 2.1	Criteria for theories in the (empirical) sciences (Asendorpf and Neyer 2012)	37
Table 2.2	Types of internationally mobile employees as mentioned in literature	51
Table 2.3	Criteria used in literature to define IMEs	55
Table 5.1	Summary of the career success scale	127
Table 5.2	Country sample (by GLOBE cluster)	128
Table 6.1	Overview of the three international career paths	153
Table 6.2	Responsibilities regarding expatriate career management	155
Table 6.3	Key global mobility interfaces: regulatory compliance of individuals and organizations towards government	157
Table 6.4	Key global mobility interfaces: organizations and individuals interactions with society	159
Table 6.5	Key global mobility interfaces: the interaction of global careerists, their families and organizations	163
Table 6.6	Key global mobility interfaces: the interdependency of organizations and global careerists and the threat of competitors	165
Table 6.7	The expatriation cycle perspective: mutual dependency of global careerists and organizations	167
Table 7.1	Objectives of individual offshoring, international assignment and self-initiated expatriation	188

xix

xx   List of Tables

Table 7.2	Comparing individual offshoring to international assignment and self-initiated expatriation	194
Table 8.1	Inpatriate and expatriate differences	202
Table 10.1	Profile of participants ($n = 46$)	266
Table 12.1	Traditional expatriate compensation systems	322
Table 12.2	Summary	334
Table 12.3	The case of an assignee posted from *Alfa* to *Beta*	336

1

The Multiple Forms and Shifting Landscapes of Global Careers

Michael Dickmann, Vesa Suutari, and Olivier Wurtz

Dynamics of the Global Careers Landscape

"Every boring or mundane activity you experience at home is, when you move to a foreign country, suddenly transformed into an exciting adventure" according to Reannon Muth, a travel writer. Indeed, it has long been known that some of the key drivers for global careers are adventure, excitement and learning (Hippler 2009; Doherty et al. 2011). While global careers and these worldwide talent management and knowledge flows are key ingredients for organizational success (Scullion and Collings 2011), our understanding of international work and careers has dramatically advanced in the last decades. This book

---

M. Dickmann (✉)
Cranfield School of Management, Cranfield University, Cranfield, UK
e-mail: m.dickmann@cranfield.ac.uk

V. Suutari • O. Wurtz
School of Management, University of Vaasa, Vaasa, Finland
e-mail: vsu@uva.fi; owurtz@uva.fi

© The Author(s) 2018
M. Dickmann et al. (eds.), *The Management of Global Careers*,
https://doi.org/10.1007/978-3-319-76529-7_1

outlines a vast array of recent insights into global careers and charts this dynamic field in order to allow global careerists and their families, multinational corporations (MNCs) and other key stakeholders to make better informed decisions. In so doing, the book moves beyond the basic insights depicted above to reflect the huge diversity of global career contexts and actors.

The "exciting adventure" outlined above may not materialize in some situations and environments. Recent advances in our access and use of information, ease and lowered cost of travel and higher expectations in relation to what millennials expect from their working lives may mean that a move from Istanbul, Athens, Berlin or Paris to a shared service centre abroad results in a more administrative work embedded in a local city context that may not be seen as highly stimulating. Maybe this particular person has widely travelled and has experienced a phenomenon that *The Economist*, a news magazine, describes as many countries becoming relatively more similar. In turn, the relative "boredom" that a person can experience may be highly preferable in the eyes of the individual to an assignment in a hostile environment context (Dickmann et al. 2017) where one's life is at stake. The world has increased in volatility, uncertainty, complexity and ambiguity in recent years which can make working abroad more exciting but more difficult, increases the need for flexibility and may be more dangerous for international workers (Bader and Schuster 2015).

Khilji and Schuler (2017) argue that global labour markets, talent flows, people living abroad in the diaspora and repatriates are key factors in the competitiveness of countries and organizations. The continued globalization trend, larger expatriate numbers (Brookfield 2016) and stronger migration flows (Al Ariss 2010), often encouraged through the push factors of hostile environments, mean that the ranks of global careerists are swelling. There is a massive "brain circulation" (Saxenian 2005) ongoing in the world. It is important to understand these different international talent flows in terms of key drivers, career types and gestalt, work and family effects, management interfaces and outcomes in relation to global careers.

Types of International Experience

International work appears in many different forms. International work experiences have typically been studied through the focus on certain type of assignment/assignee group. For example, clearly most of the studies in the field have focused on analysing the nature of long-term assignments within MNCs and thus the experiences of assignees who work abroad over several years. Later, there has been increasing interest towards those people who have self-initiated their long-term international assignments, that is, they have not been sent abroad by any organizations but instead the individuals arrange a job abroad on their own. Clearly less research attention has been given to short-term assignments or commuter assignments though in practice those are seen to be increasingly popular within companies. In the next section, we will briefly introduce the specific features of different types of assignments as they appear in the literature. After this, we will also take a more long-term perspective on global careers that often consist of various international assignments of different kinds during one's career.

Assigned Expatriates (AEs)

Tharenou (2015) defines AEs as managers and professionals assigned or sent abroad by their employer, who supports and funds the move, to work on an assignment temporarily for a pre-set period of more than a year to achieve organizational goals. Organizational reasons for the use of global mobility and AEs include the filling of a local competency gap (maybe there are no adequate candidates on the local labour market), a drive to have a high level of corporate (reporting and planning issues, other standardized approaches) and cultural integration (attitudes and behaviours) around head office ideas and the global management of talent including leadership development (Edström and Galbraith 1977; Stahl et al. 2002). Further organizational drivers include other operational (knowledge transfer) and political considerations (getting rid of a local competitor) outlined in various writings (Tharenou 2015;

Dickmann and Baruch 2011). Of course, AEs have their own set of individual drivers to seek and accept working abroad. These include a large range of motives that have been outlined by various writers such as Dickmann et al. (2008) or Hippler (2009). Broadly speaking, individuals consider a large set of factors when deciding whether and where to work abroad. These fall into categories such as career and development, individual drivers such as a sense of adventure, family and friends, organizational inducements, national, regional and location-specific factors (Dickmann and Mills 2009).

Going on assignment on behalf of an organization typically creates a mutual or dual dependency between individuals (including their families) and their employers (Larsen 2004). When AEs are sent from the head office to a foreign subsidiary, in reality, much of the time when AEs go anywhere abroad, they tend to become a "bigger fish in a smaller pond" or, sometimes, simply a more colourful fish in the sea. They often experience objective career advantages such as more rapid promotion, better performance evaluations and higher pay (Doherty and Dickmann 2012; The RES Forum 2017) in the short and long term. Thus, they have often become more costly and more important to their organizations. In turn, they normally rely on their organizations more strongly in terms of physical moves to the new country, pre-departure preparation, post-arrival support, children's educational provision, housing, health care, tax and residence/working permit compliance and social security payments (The RES Forum 2016). Especially where AEs encounter highly different national contexts, extreme insecurity/terrorist threats and potential natural and human-caused disasters, the dependence of expatriates on their employers is likely to be very high (Bader et al. forthcoming).

To capture a large array of organizational activities to manage this dual dependency, Harris et al. (2003) developed the concept of expatriate cycle. This takes account of strategic and operational global mobility issues that are relevant before an AE is selected to work abroad, during and after the assignment. Dickmann and Baruch (2011) expand this discussion and centre it around global careers, the focus of our book. The focus of much (global) career writing has shifted to the individual careerist (Briscoe and Hall 2006; Gunz and Peiperl 2007; Sullivan and Baruch

2009). A lot of pertinent information is available to the reader and is, to an extensive extent, outlined in the following chapters of this book. Therefore, we will concentrate on a short depiction of organizational considerations and activities when managing their assignee populations.

Our discussion will focus on general global mobility considerations, resourcing, talent, career and performance management activities, reward and compliance issues as well as programme management, data analytics and global mobility technology approaches. While some of these issues are based on academic writings (Dowling et al. 2008; Dickmann and Baruch 2011), there are others that spring from the strong interest of the professional audience (see The RES Forum 2016, 2017).

General Global Mobility Considerations

It is argued that organizations need to consider their general assignment strategy and what they want to achieve with their global mobility activities (Edström and Galbraith 1977; Harris et al. 2003). It is clear that any international HR strategy—and by extension a global talent management and mobility approach—would benefit from an integration with the MNC's worldwide configuration of business strategy, structure, policies and practices (Bartlett and Ghoshal 1989; Dickmann and Müller-Camen 2006). Once the vertical alignment is achieved, the role of the global mobility (GM) function can be determined. Based on the ideas of Ulrich (1998), a number of GM department roles including strategic GM advisor, global talent manager, administrative GM expert and global people effectiveness expert have been suggested (The RES Forum 2015). With respect to global careers, organizations could clarify the diverse purposes of international assignments and link their career structures to those. For instance, leadership development-driven assignments would mean that the payback of these is in the very long term. Thus, AEs should stay in the organization for a long time so that the company can benefit fully. Thus, special long-term career planning including the assessment of what assignees are likely to be able to learn and use in future work and retention measures may be developed. In contrast, where AEs simply fill a skills gap, other career, reward, development and retention approaches may be utilized (Dickmann 2017). Attributing international work a high kudos is likely to be useful for both individuals and organizations as it increases the willingness of staff to work abroad and is mostly based on actual career progression for individuals who therefore are likely to benefit (Doherty and Dickmann 2009). Operational considerations of what firms can do to manage the general GM phase are manifold and too broad to discuss in detail. The reader can find 15 suggestions in a recent publication (The RES Forum 2017).

Resourcing, Talent, Career and Performance Management

It has long been known that GM resourcing is often haphazard and unsystematic. Harris and Brewster (1999) distinguish between formal and informal, open and closed GM selection and liken some corporate approaches to a coffee machine selection approach. Obviously, open advertising of global vacancies can increase the candidate pool and formal, sophisticated selection may increase the resourcing quality. With a focus on dual dependency and career concerns, the authors would like to advocate that understanding the underlying motivations of potential AEs is highly important as it may aid the identification of the right candidate, a more sophisticated selection approach and can inform a more tailored expatriation package. Resourcing can also benefit from psychometric or other assessments, the matching of the candidate's profile to the intercultural job demands (Baruch et al. 2013); the provision of realistic job, country and host team previews (e.g. through look-see visits); and the assessment of family and partner constraints with a view to individual obligations and expectations (Harvey 1997; Mäkelä et al. 2015; Mäkelä and Suutari 2011).

Many authors have argued for pre-departure and post-arrival training for expatriates and their families (Sparrow et al. 2004). While these often look at cultural and country differences, it would be useful to integrate novel and more challenging job demands into these. In addition, integrating the host team into any cultural training, that is, to prepare it for the newcomer and to sensitize it to cultural differences and how to handle

The Multiple Forms and Shifting Landscapes of Global Careers 7

these, seems to be less common but may improve team effectivity. In addition, enabling good interaction of expatriates, their families, host team members and citizens of the host country can help assignee adjustment (Dowling et al. 2008; Haslberger et al. 2013). Finally, pre-repatriation seminars and post-repatriation networking events may be helpful to successfully master the most difficult assignment (Hurn 1999).

This book provides the reader with many broad and in-depth insights into global careers so that a detailed discussion here is superfluous. Nevertheless, a short outline of what activities companies can undertake is developed below. First, we advocate that companies develop a career management approach that identifies a candidate's long-term career aspirations and plans to the organizational career management approach. In fact, we would advocate that organizations encourage and conduct longer-term career (scenario) planning that factors in the expatriate position and jobs upon return. In addition, global assignments should be designed in a way as to foster the acquisition of career capital that drives intelligent careers (DeFillippi and Arthur 1994; Inkson and Arthur 2001). Recent research has shown that the career capital and marketability of expatriates, both AEs and SIEs, is expanded and useful over the long term (Suutari et al. 2017; Dickmann et al. 2016). Other support mechanisms such as GM business sponsors and expatriate mentors (home and host based) can further refine a corporate global career approach.

For most assignments, performance management is conducted locally (with some exceptions in 'global' jobs or those where assignees report to the global centre). A key source of friction can therefore be that the AE originally gets assignment objectives from the sending unit and will then be performance reviewed and managed by the receiving unit where the original assignment goals may be less important. Therefore, authors have suggested a more integrated performance management system (Tarique et al. 2015: Chapter 13). Thus, integrating the primary assignment purpose into performance management and making sure that this purpose is also attractive for the host unit could improve assignment effectiveness. However, fundamental problems, such as where the primary purpose is to control and coordinate a host unit that values its autonomy and idiosyncratic processes, can remain.

Global Mobility Programme Compliance

Much of the work of GM professionals is centred around complying with local laws and regulations with regard to tax and social security issues. This is a highly important, dynamically developing and highly bureaucratic arena that has been comparatively neglected by academic researchers. Nevertheless, where companies disregard the laws and regulations that govern the payment of, say, corporate or individual tax, it becomes highly risky for them and may result in substantial fines, potential prison sentences and inhibitions for their operations in a host country. This may be the key reason why MNCs tend to be less price sensitive when outsourcing in these areas. In essence, they value quality of service provision over cost savings (The RES Forum 2016).

In addition, compliance may be defined more broadly in organizations and include the observance of all their internal GM approaches. Companies typically have diverse approaches, but these may include their logistical support during and after moves abroad—accommodation, health insurance, banking, schooling and so on—and/or their support to the assignee with local networking and learning activities.

Global Rewards

Rewards, again, are more highly discussed amongst GM professionals than academics. Professionals work day-to-day with concepts such as home-based pay (using "cost of living adjustments" calculations), host-based pay or other reward approaches. In addition, they are grappling with issues such as early return or partners/families that move to the host country not at the beginning of an assignment but later. Moreover, they are keenly interested in the motivational effects of their various global reward packages (often distinguishing between long-term, short-term, local-plus assignees, frequent business travellers, etc.) in order to increase the attractiveness of international work (Dowling et al. 2008). Some recommendations in the practitioner literature include that organizations strive for reward equity, minimize the exposure of individuals in relation to social security and taxation and to keep administrative complexity low

The Multiple Forms and Shifting Landscapes of Global Careers   9

(The RES Forum 2017). For the design of reward systems, HR professionals need to explore the attractiveness of their approaches in relation to different stakeholder groups, for example, families may have distinct needs from sole expatriates, people with caring responsibilities for their elder parents may seek more free time and travel support, assignees in hostile environments have higher security needs and, therefore, understand their drivers and value systems well (Dickmann et al. 2008). Moreover, the range of intrinsic rewards such as developmental opportunities and career choices need to be factored in when designing reward systems. In addition, some deferred assignment-linked compensation may be considered in order to retain repatriates.

Programme Management, Data Analytics and Technology

Programme management is not consistently defined in GM but can include activities such as assignment policy writing and ongoing management of expatriates by a global GM centre of excellence, global vendor management of outsourcing service providers, analysis and management of compliance issues (see above), compensation and salary review activities, assignee tracking for reporting purposes and assignment documentation. The scope of programme management, its interfaces with global talent management and local host organizations are likely to vary amongst MNCs, especially in relation to the various roles of GM departments, industry pressures and country spread. With respect to the use of technology and data analytics in GM work within MNCs, it is surprising how many firms still use predominantly stand-alone data storage systems (e.g. Excel) that are not integrated in a wider ERP system (Dickmann and Marsh 2017). There have been voices raised that suggest to compile and consolidate data more effectively, to enable firms to visualize their GM data better and analyse their information more in-depth as to enable more evidence-based GM decision making. This could, of course, extend to vendor management and other linkages to external stakeholders.

Above, we have briefly outlined the perspective of GM professionals when working with AEs. Next, we aim to explore the world of self-initiated assignments. When comparing the motives of AEs to those of

SIEs, the organization-sent individuals are typically more motivated by looking for new development possibilities and career development (Doherty et al. 2011; Andresen et al. 2014). These and other issues in relation to SIEs are further explicated below.

Self-Initiated Expatriates (SIEs)

Due to globalization, increasing amounts of individuals are looking for interesting international jobs on their own initiative and thus become a self-initiated expatriate (Suutari and Brewster 2000). Tharenou (2015) defines SIEs as "Managers and professionals who decide on their own initiate to search for a job abroad, self-fund their expatriation without organizational support, for a temporary but undefined time, likely from over a year up to a decade, for career professional, lifestyle, cultural and personal reasons, and usually employed on a host country contract there". In line with this, Andresen et al. (2014) specify three criteria that are needed to differentiate such SIEs from assigned expatriates: (1) among SIEs the initiative for the assignment comes from the individual who searches for international job possibilities (while among AEs the initiative comes from the employer organization); (2) among SIEs there is a new work contract partner, and (3) the final decision to employ the expatriate is made by a new contract partner, usually in the host country (while among AEs the decision is typically made in the home country).

It is common that at least among more highly educated assignees, both AEs and SIEs are looking for new experiences in an international context and have career and development-related motives for moving abroad (Suutari and Brewster 2000). Among SIEs, the motives such as family-related factors (Richardson 2006), overall lifestyle and location (Doherty et al. 2011) are typically in a more central role than among AEs. Also a poor employment situation in the home country is a more common motive among SIEs (Suutari and Brewster 2000).

It is also good to recognize that there are very different kinds of assignees among SIEs (Suutari and Brewster 2000) and that the motives of such subgroups may differ considerably from each other. For example, there are "young job seekers" who in the early stage of their career seek a job abroad and are thus a very different kind of group to that of internationally experienced senior managers within MNCs. It is also unlikely that companies will contemplate sending young people without professional experience to an international assignment abroad. Thus, for young people looking for new cross-cultural experiences, excitement and possibilities for growth and career prospects (Tharenou 2003), there is no other option than to self-initiate their move abroad. In turn, academic SIEs, who often did not have specific plans for moving abroad but rather talked with colleagues at conferences or had seen, accidentally, some job advertisement were driven by three dominant motivations: adventure/travel, life change and family reasons (Richardson and Mallon 2005).

For international organizations, SIEs offer an alternative recruitment channel for internationally mobile professionals but with clear lower levels of costs than typically for traditional expatriation. SIEs are usually recruited with local contracts, while expatriates are paid various kinds of extra allowances and insurances (Suutari and Brewster 2000). At the same time, the SIE population naturally expands the possible pool of candidates for international positions when it is sometimes difficult to find suitable professionals willing to move abroad for many years. When living abroad, SIEs are typically outside corporate support and training practices and thus have to make their arrangements and preparations on their own (Jokinen et al. 2008). However, this does not mean that SIEs would not need support practices such as cross-cultural training or induction sessions from their new employer. The opposite may be the case when they are less supported before the assignment. The empirical research on how HRM can support SIEs in their adjustment is fairly limited, but such support is typically recommended (Howe-Walsh and Schyns 2010).

The discussion of the management of SIEs is drastically different from the one on AEs for the very reasons that in most cases no particular managerial practices are arranged specifically for them. No dedicated management is applied towards them first because many practitioners are not fully aware of their existence. They are also often not conscious of them being real assets for the company requiring as such dedicated actions. Consequently, in most companies, these employees are not identified. They are lost among the bulk of local employees and are not identified as having particular common characteristics and as belonging to a special group. Therefore in most cases, companies are far from deploying specific practices to manage them as a group.

However, research has suggested some tools that should be applied to manage SIEs. They are presented in Chap. 3 from Vesa Suutari, Chris Brewster and Michael Dickmann. The first step is to identify them and customize management practices for them. This group has competencies and skills that are real assets for many companies. This call for a particular management of this group cannot be done without first an identification of this group (see Chap. 3). Considering attraction and retention, SIEs have to some extent different profiles from that of AEs, with different motivations for expatriating (Cerdin 2013; Suutari and Brewster 2000). In addition, the percentage of women who are SIEs is higher than amongst AEs, and self-initiated global workers are seen to have different personal characteristics such as being more educated or staying, on average, longer than AEs (Doherty et al. 2011). This suggests that companies should adjust their communication and branding activities in order to specifically target these professionals (Chap. 3).

Regarding compensation, the reward packages of SIEs could be rethought. In most cases SIEs sign a standard local contract that does not take into account their skills and competencies, such as language skills and cultural understanding. More strikingly, SIEs receive markedly lower salaries and benefits than expatriates even when compared to local-plus assignees (The RES Forum 2016). Next, supporting adjustment, notably with the cross-cultural training of SIEs, is rarely done but would most likely deliver a high return on investment due to the motivation of many SIEs to culturally learn. Strong drivers to work abroad, such as a sense of adventure and the willingness to explore the host country physically and socially, could be taken into account in order to motivate and retain SIEs. Finally, the work content and responsibilities could be also tailored to fit the skills and interests of SIEs, such as providing a significant component of interactions with locals and using their superior insights into their home countries as a work component in their jobs.

The Multiple Forms and Shifting Landscapes of Global Careers 13

Short-Term Expatriates

Short-term assignments (STAs) are typically defined as assignments lasting more than a few weeks (otherwise these would be extended business travel) but less than a year (Collings et al. 2015; The RES Forum 2016). Sometimes they are defined within companies as assignments lasting less than six months since in some countries foreign sojourns longer than half a year may create tax and social security changes to the individuals (Suutari et al. 2013). Though the evidence is limited, all available information seems to support the view that such STAs are becoming increasingly popular within companies (Collings et al. 2015). There are many reasons for such trends, that is, improved transportation and communication systems, cost containment initiatives, organizational networks and flexible intra-organizational coordination of global units (Harvey et al. 2010). The individual level of unwillingness to move abroad due to individual or family reasons may also be leading towards increasing the amount of STAs in which the possible negative impacts of mobility on the children or the career of the partner may be avoided. In comparison with long-term expatriates, the repatriation stage is typically less challenging—though not always without any problems (Starr 2009). Due to a short time scale, replacements for assignees may not be needed and the assignees may thus be able to return to their old jobs. Among project assignees, the STA is sometimes followed by another assignment due to the overall project nature of the work (Suutari et al. 2013).

STAs may attract assignees since those offer new cross-cultural experiences (Starr and Currie 2009). STAs also offer development possibilities when dealing with new kinds of job responsibilities in a new location and with foreign colleagues often having their own ways of doing the job. In that way, STAs embody a possibility to gather new experiences and offer a change to daily routines (Crowley-Henry and Heaslip 2014). They offer a possibility also for younger professionals to get international experience when they may not yet have access to longer-term assignments due to their limited professional experience (Collings et al. 2015; Starr and Currie 2009; Suutari et al. 2013). STAs typically develop language skills, cross-cultural skills and project management skills of assignees and offer a possibility to learn about foreign markets, technologies and products. Thus they are often used as a management development method (Crowne and Engle 2016; Harvey et al. 2010; Reiche et al. 2009). Some companies distinguish between generating cultural sensitivity for STAs and deeper cultural understanding for traditional, long-term assignees.

STAs may also create some challenges. The absence of the assignee from home places an additional burden on the partner and the children and can cause family stress (Meyskens et al. 2009; Starr and Currie 2009). The work during the assignment may be very intensive and cause a lot of development challenges when working in a new environment. This is likely to lead to stress and even burnout (Collings et al. 2007). The support and training from the company may be fairly limited due to short preparation times and limited length of assignments. This is likely to lead to the lack of depth of integration of assignees with the local workforce, with difficulties in working in cross-cultural teams and with the lack of adaptation to local culture. If proper replacement arrangements cannot be made at the home unit, there may be an extensive amount of unfinished work waiting at home after repatriation.

There has not been so much research concerning the management of STAs, but the available evidence is typically drawn from qualitative case studies (Tahvanainen et al. 2005; Suutari et al. 2013). For example, we know little about how STAs are staffed, what the selection criteria are, who gets chosen and who the key decision maker in the process is (Collings et al. 2015). Despite the clear preference of HRM specialists for more systematic processes with pre-selected pools of candidates, the reality is usually quite different (Suutari et al. 2013). The line mangers are in a central role, and often the selection process is very informal which may lead to a narrow range of candidates (Kang et al. 2016). Practical arrangements, such as travel and visa arrangements and accommodation, are often handled by the IHRM or global mobility department (Collings et al. 2015), while compliance with taxation as well as immigration regulations are often outsourced (The RES Forum 2016). General information about travel and health and safety in foreign countries is also provided (Collings et al. 2007).

The assignee typically continues on the same contract that they were on at home (Kang et al. 2016), but are most often adjusted through cost of living allowance calculations (The RES Forum 2016). In addition, STAs are typically awarded a *per diem* allowance (tax-free daily allowance) and a hardship allowance when deemed necessary. Also, the training and preparation of assignees is often very limited due to lack of time and informality of the process. Such a lack of systematic preparation may be negative for both organizational and individual outcomes (Collings et al. 2015). Because assignees typically move without their families, no family support (larger homes, schooling) is provided though the company may offer additional holiday leave and may finance flights home (The RES Forum 2016). In a case company reported by Suutari et al. (2013), the company had already started arranging visits and informal guidance for the whole family in order to reduce the problems involved. The repatriation process may not be much supported by the company, as the repatriation is expected to be an easy process due to the fairly short duration of the work abroad. In turn, Starr (2009) reported that unexpected repatriation problems appeared also among STAs and called for further research on the topic in order to understand the repatriation challenges and related support needs of STAs better.

International Commuters

International commuters can be defined as assignees travelling from their home locations to take a post in a foreign location on a weekly or biweekly basis (Mayrhofer et al. 2012). Employees thus have job responsibilities both in the home and host country, but they maintain their main residence in their home country and frequently travel between the two locations (Collings and Isichei 2017).

There are many reasons for the use of commuters such as skills and knowledge transfer, managerial control, project work and management development (Konopaske et al. 2009). Companies also perceive commuter assignments as a cheaper option than longer-term relocation as they do not have to pay for the move, children's schooling and so on. It also offers flexibility for both organization and the individual (Suutari and Brewster 2009). The employee is able to experience working in a new country without needing to fully integrate into its culture or give up their everyday life in their home country (Mäkelä et al. 2017). Due to such benefits, there has been an increase in the use of commuters within companies (Collings and Isichei 2017).

As with all types of international work, there are also challenges involved in commuter arrangements. By definition, commuters are living in two different locations which have a clear family impact due to the absence of the commuter. This impact, both on the partner and children, has hitherto been insufficiently explored. Also, there may be challenging tax, immigration and other legal issues involved in the process, and work schedules may be unpredictable and difficult to control (Collings and Isichei 2017). It also means that the commuter is travelling frequently and thus faces the extra travel-related burdens that all international business travellers encounter (see below).

International Business Travelers

Though the focus of the present book is on expatriation, it is also useful to briefly discuss the findings in relation to international business travellers (IBTs). Many kinds of international jobs typically involve international travel in international organizations that operate in global markets. This 'frequent flying' for work can be short trips of one or two days. However, extended business travel has become more popular and carries its own risks (The RES Forum 2018).

From the individual perspective, there are many motives encouraging professionals to seek jobs involving international travel. First, some individuals have a high international orientation meaning that they are overall interested in different cultures and thus interested in seeing the world and working with people from different cultures (Suutari and Taka 2004). Some travellers strive for new experiences, novelty and challenges or want to promote their career through having international experience. Such experiences have also been associated with increased social and professional status and a cosmopolitan identity (Gustafsson 2012).

In light of this, the high frequency of travelling and long duration of trips have been connected to health issues, such as sleeping problems, stress, burnout and overall challenges in getting the work done due to travel and work overload (Mäkelä et al. 2014, 2015; Mäkelä and Kinnunen 2016). Furthermore, frequent departures, the absence from daily family life and often a need for intensive working when at home often impact on the whole family (Saarenpää 2018). Due to such challenges resulting from international travelling, reliable high-quality travel management support is needed to avoid problems caused by extensive travelling. It has also been argued that travellers' control over their travel schedule is an important factor contributing to their well-being. It has a positive health and emotional impact when travellers have control over how much and when they travel (Jensen 2013). However, higher autonomy and control of IBTs is often in contrast with the aim of developing stricter travel policies which are targeted at cost savings. A further problem is that many business travellers are expected to work during their journeys and immediately after arrival. It is also important that the supervisors recognize the employees' needs for re-energizing and allow flexibility in working hours for recovery after trips that might have been highly stressful and wearing.

Global Careerists: A Longer-Term Career Perspective on International Careers

Due to the need of international organizations for internationally experienced professionals and managers, increasing numbers of individuals have more longer-term experiences of working in different kinds of international jobs in different countries and often also in different organizations. Sometimes such global careerists have had an international orientation from their early career and even education stage while others have grown that kind of orientation through their first international experiences which they found to be positive and developmental (Suutari 2003). After these first international experiences, global careerists have worked in different international jobs. Some of them continue from one international job to another one, while some of them want to repatriate back to their home country before accepting new international challenges. Such periods back in the home country naturally help in keeping domestic contacts and thus ease the process of repatriation after new assignments. In short, global careerists have repeated international experiences which may be a mix of short- and long-term assignments, self-initiated foreign work, cross-border commuting and extended international business travel (from a domestic or foreign base), over a long time.

Global careerists may also change their international work type during their career by being recruited by another local or international company in the host country (and thus changing their position from AE to SIE), or through localization if the assignment gets very long (i.e. change from the expatriate contract to local contract). Expatriate contracts are typically fixed-term arrangements. Therefore, new arrangements need to be made periodically which may similarly lead from AE status to short-term assignee status if working on a project. In addition, contractual changes may be induced by repatriation or the shift towards an international job involving frequent international travel. In order to better manage such global careers, we need a better understanding of the manifold variants of modern international careers (Baruch et al. 2013). As Collings et al. (2007) argue, a significant challenge for global mobility and HR managers is to develop a range of IHRM policies and practices tailored to the different types, objectives and different circumstances surrounding each type of assignment.

As an outcome of their long-term international experiences, internationally mobile professionals developed a strong global career identity (Suutari and Mäkelä 2007). Findings among managers with multiple IAs during their career show that such an identity consists of elements including awareness of their high levels of developed career capital, high levels of self-understanding and significant self-confidence. These can be attributed to their wide international experiences in different countries and often also across different organizations and jobs. After having such international and often in-depth work experiences, global careerists have a clearer understanding of their work values and career interests, know their market value and thus have a high level of confidence in their employability (Suutari et al. 2017). This is combined with an expanded

The Multiple Forms and Shifting Landscapes of Global Careers   19

job market perspective, that is, they see a global job market being open to them besides a traditional focus on host country possibilities. In addition, they show a strong emphasis on global networking activity increasing their job prospects. They are often highly committed to work in an international career context in the future and are interested in constantly looking for new challenges and developmental opportunities.

While much of the existing research indicates that the short-term career impacts of corporate assignments are often negative, in the longer term, the effect may be more positive (Doherty and Dickmann 2012; Suutari et al. 2017). It may be that international work experience improves the opportunity to obtain a top management position (Ng et al. 2005; Magnusson and Boggs 2006). However, having a background of multiple international jobs may not always lead to a fast track to the top of the organization. Multiple international assignments may slow down the process of getting access to the top level in the organization (Hamori and Koyuncu 2011) and related prolonged absence from the home country makes subsequent repatriation more difficult (Kraimer et al. 2009). Sometimes it is seen to be beneficial to stay close to key decision makers in order to avoid an "out of sight—out of mind" situation frequently discussed in the repatriation literature. Research indicates high turnover rates immediately after repatriation from assignments (Benson and Pattie 2008). This suggests it might often be necessary to change employer to find an organization that values international work experience more highly. In turn, the hierarchical career progress may not even be the key career goal of global careerists when they are more interested in the international nature of their work environment and in the constant learning and development opportunities working abroad offers (Suutari et al. 2012).

Nevertheless, it might be that the higher the number of international assignments and the longer the duration outside a global careerist's home country, the more problematic it may become to find an adequate job in the home country. More research is needed to explore the thrills and downturns of long-term global career journeys. This research should entail wider scale studies from different parts of the world in order to better understand the nature of long-term global careers in different cultural contexts.

20   M. Dickmann et al.

Global careerists are assets for companies; their international experiences provided them strong learning opportunities and developed their social capital (Cappellen and Jannssens 2005). They should therefore be identified by companies as talent and receive dedicated support and management (Suutari et al. 2014). One key element is that these employees value nonfinancial over financial rewards (Suutari et al. 2014; Dickmann et al. 2008). Commitment, turnover and retention, for instance, seem to be quite unrelated with financial elements of their package, but directly affected by nonfinancial elements (Tornikoski 2011). Support regarding family-related issues is one of the key supports that organization can provide. More generally, a total reward approach that does not focus only on monetary elements is needed (Tornikoski 2011).

Above, we have explored global careers through the lens of different types of global work, traditional long-term assignees, short-term expatriates, self-initiated foreign workers, international commuters, business travellers and global careerists. This book is devoted to an in-depth exploration of global careers. Below, we briefly outline the chapter contents and book structure.

Book Overview

This book first sheds light on those various global careerists; it presents in detail their specification and their similarities. It looks in particular at assigned expatriates, corporate expatriates, repatriates and individuals who have been working abroad and traces their development. It also further introduces how companies can manage these employees, how they can support, compensate and coach their global workers. This book also focuses on specific issues encountered by individuals in their global careers beyond the only work-related aspects; spouse and private life and work-life interface are analysed. It provides advice on how these can be handled. Furthermore, one key step of an international career, the return to the home country (whether definitive or temporary) is discussed. A wider perspective is also provided by considering the career success of global professionals around the world, based on a major international research project.

The Multiple Forms and Shifting Landscapes of Global Careers   21

In Chap. 2, Maike Andresen, Michael Dickmann and Vesa Suutari develop precise typologies of international mobile employees. They provide an extensive review of the types of international mobile employees mentioned in the literature and the various criteria used to categorize and order them. They further analyse and discuss in depth how these criteria should be used and what should be done in order to build and use scientifically relevant and empirically useful typologies. Their work is particularly meaningful in a rapidly changing world, in which some criteria and categories widely used yesterday may be much less appropriate tomorrow.

Vesa Suutari, Chris Brewster and Michael Dickmann, in Chap. 3, focus on two of the most common global career types: the assigned and the self-initiated expatriates. Since the seminal article on self-initiated expatriation (Suutari and Brewster 2000), which had a major role in the field by showing that expatriation is a multifaceted phenomenon that encompasses many very different types of experiences, a large amount of research has been undertaken to explore the differences and the similarities between these two types of expatriation. This chapter provides an historical perspective on expatriation, showing when it began and how it evolved along the ages and how the dichotomy between assigned and self-initiated expatriation emerged. Additionally, it provides a useful base to look at the future. It further reviews the similarities and the differences of these two types of global careerists regarding motives to engage in global careers. Towards the end, it provides detailed advice on how these expatriates should be managed.

Chapter 4 by Raija Salomaa shows how global careerists can be supported by coaching. Expatriates live through complex and challenging experiences, difficult in many ways, and coaching is consequently particularly meaningful for them. This chapter introduces coaching, explains the specificities of coaching in an international context and reviews the literature and the empirical evidence on coaching in an international setting. It explains, discusses and illustrates how coaching can be useful for both corporate and self-initiated expatriates. It shows, among others, how coaching can help individuals overcome the issues related to transition and facilitate the development of individuals abroad.

Then, in Chap. 5, John Briscoe, Michael Dickmann, Tim Hall, Wolfgang Mayrhofer and Adam Smale provide a wider perspective by exploring career success in different cultures. Based on the large international 5C project, they present key findings, compare career success in terms of achievement and of importance in various countries and highlight the influence that gender can have on career success in some countries. They also outline the empirical outcomes of this project in terms of advice for practitioners.

Michael Dickmann and Maike Andresen discuss how global careerists should be managed based on extensive analyses of their needs in Chap. 6. They expand on some of the overview information given in this chapter to show what organizations, but also global careerists themselves, can do to ensure positive outcomes to global experiences/careers. They outline different types of global careers and examine how these different types should be managed at the operative level (i.e. short-term) and at the strategic level (i.e. long-term). Their work also uses the lens of mobility interfaces—government, society, family and organization—and provides extensive recommendation of actions to each stakeholder of international careers (individual, families, organizations, government/society and competitors). Their analyses and advice are also displayed along the different steps of the expatriation cycle.

In the next chapter, Caroline Creven Fourrier and Sebastian Point introduce an emerging trend in terms of a type of global careerists, individual offshoring. This refers to permanent transfer with limited package and to do the same job as was previously done at home. They discuss in detail this developing case and explain why this is a growing trend. They advocate that offshoring can offset some issues related to classical expatriation and be a meaningful alternative to it.

In Chap. 8, Miriam Moeller and (the late) Michael Harvey build a historical review of inpatriation and provide a future outlook on the topic. They analyse the relationship between an inpatriate and the company and apply agency theory to shed light on their interaction. They discuss the issues that can arise in inpatriation and outline inpatriate career profiles. Finally they identify future trends and emphasize the need for more empirical data on repatriation.

The Multiple Forms and Shifting Landscapes of Global Careers   23

Chapter 9, by Eren Akkan, Mila Lazarova and Sebastian Reiche, examines repatriation and career decisions that are taken during this often uncertain and difficult period in a career. They analyse how key features of the previous expatriation are affecting this challenging phase. They also consider obstacles and facilitators that influence that period, such as the various possibly unmet expectations (including the financial ones), social resources and career capital. Career success during repatriation and self-initiated repatriates are also discussed.

Yvonne McNulty and Miriam Moeller explore "trailing spouses", dual global career couples, in Chap. 10. In order to better understand these spouses and based on empirical qualitative data, they show differences between them and build a typology of dual career partners, that is, the Ready, the Reborn, the Resentful and the Resigned. They discuss and provide advice on how the members of these different categories (of spouses and couples) should be managed based on their specificities.

In Chap. 11, Vesa Suutari, Liisa Mäkelä and Olivier Wurtz look at the work-life interface of global careerists. They analyse what work-life experiences and issues international business travellers, short-term assignees, assigned expatriates and self-initiated and experienced global careerist go through. They show that interactions between work and personal life are not systematically detrimental but can lead to mutual enrichment. Finally they provide customized recommendations on how the work-life interface of each type of global professional should be managed.

In Chap. 12, Celia Zàrraga-Oberty and Jaime Bonache discuss, review and provide advice on the compensations of global careerists. They analyse how the arrangements made to compensate expatriates are evolving from a traditional approach (home-country balance sheet), which suffers from many drawbacks, to a local/local-plus arrangement. They show how this trend is anchored and explained by several evolutions, like the change of the expatriate profiles. They detail how and why the developing arrangement is more attractive and relevant.

Taken as a whole, these chapters aim to provide the latest research perspective on key dimensions and key issues of international careers. Twenty-one international experts from 15 countries join forces to provide a global picture on global careers that can be used both for researchers in their endeavours to get a step ahead in our knowledge of these phenomena and for practitioners looking for academic knowledge and advice in their field. In so doing, we aim to augment the understanding of the multiple forms and shifting landscapes of global careers.

References

Al Ariss, Akram. 2010. Modes of Engagement: Migration, Self-Initiated Expatriation, and Career Development. *Career Development International* 15 (4): 338–358.

Andresen, Maike, Franziska Bergdolt, Jil Margenfeld, and Michael Dickmann. 2014. Addressing International Mobility Confusion—Developing Definitions and Differentiations for Self-Initiated and Assigned Expatriates as Well as Migrants. *The International Journal of Human Resource Management* 25 (16): 2295–2318.

Bader, Benjamin, and Tassilo Schuster. 2015. Expatriate Social Networks in Terrorism-Endangered Countries: An Empirical Analysis in Afghanistan, India, Pakistan, and Saudi Arabia. *Journal of International Management* 21 (1): 63–77.

Bader, Benjamin, Tassilo Schuster, and Michael Dickmann. forthcoming. Special Issue of *The International Journal of Human Resource Management*: Danger and Risk as Challenges for HRM: How to Manage People in Hostile Environments.

Bartlett, Christopher A., and Sumantra Ghoshal. 1989. *Managing Across Borders: The Transnational Solution*. Boston: Harvard Business School.

Baruch, Yehuda, Michael Dickmann, Yochanan Altman, and Frank Bournois. 2013. Exploring International Work: Types and Dimensions of Global Careers. *The International Journal of Human Resource Management* 24 (12): 2369–2393.

Benson, George S., and Marshall Pattie. 2008. Is Expatriation Good for My Career? The Impact of Expatriate Assignments on Perceived and Actual Career Outcomes. *The International Journal of Human Resource Management* 19 (9): 1636–1653.

Briscoe, Jon P., and Douglas T. Hall. 2006. The Interplay of Boundaryless and Protean Careers: Combinations and Implications. *Journal of Vocational Behavior* 69 (1): 4–18.

Brookfield. 2016. Global Mobility Trends Survey: Breakthrough to the Future of Global Talent Mobility. Accessed November 27, 2017. http://globalmobilitytrends.bgrs.com/download2016.html

Cappellen, Tineke, and Maddy Janssens. 2005. Career Paths of Global Managers: Towards Future Research. *Journal of World Business* 40 (4): 348–360.

Cerdin, Jean-Luc. 2013. Motivation of Self-Initiated Expatriates. In *Self-Initiated Expatriation: Individual, Organizational, and National Perspectives*, ed. Maike Andresen, Akram Al Ariss, and Matthias Walther, 59–74. London: Routledge.

Collings, David G., and Michael Isichei. 2017. The Shifting Boundaries of Global Staffing: Integrating Global Talent Management, Alternative Forms of International Assignments and Non-Employees into the Discussion. *The International Journal of Human Resource Management*: 1–23. https://doi.org/10.1080/09585192.2017.1380064.

Collings, David G., Anthony McDonnell, and Amy McCarter. 2015. Types of International Assignees. In *The Routledge Companion to International Human Resource Management*, ed. David G. Collings, Geoffrey T. Wood, and Paula M. Caligiuri, 259–274. London: Routledge.

Collings, David G., Hugh Scullion, and Michael J. Morley. 2007. Changing Patterns of Global Staffing in the Multinational Enterprise: Challenges to the Conventional Expatriate Assignment and Emerging Alternatives. *Journal of World Business* 42 (2): 198–213.

Crowley-Henry, Marian, and Graham Heaslip. 2014. Short-Term International Assignments. Military Perspectives and Implications for International Human Resource Management. *European Management Journal* 32 (5): 752–760.

Crowne, Kerrie Anne, and Robert L. Engle. 2016. Antecedents of Cross-Cultural Adaptation Stress in Short-Term International Assignments. *Organization Management Journal* 13 (1): 32–47.

DeFillippi, Robert J., and Michael B. Arthur. 1994. The Boundaryless Career: A Competency-Based Perspective. *Journal of Organizational Behavior* 15 (4): 307–324.

Dickmann, Michael. 2017. International Human Resource Management—Historical Developments, Models, Policies and Practices in MNCs. In *Contemporary Human Resource Management Text and Cases*, ed. Adrian Wilkinson, Tom Redman, and Tony Dundon, 5th ed., 258–292. Harlow: Pearson Education Ltd.

Dickmann, Michael, and Yehuda Baruch. 2011. *Global Careers*. London: Routledge.

Dickmann, Michael, Noeleen Doherty, Timothy Mills, and Chris Brewster. 2008. Why Do They Go? Individual and Corporate Perspectives on the Factors Influencing the Decision to Accept an International Assignment. *The International Journal of Human Resource Management* 19 (4): 731–751.

Dickmann, Michael, and Vicki Marsh. 2017. Data Mastery: A Key Global Mobility Challenge. *HR Zone.* Accessed November 23, 2017. https://www.hrzone.com/perform/business/data-mastery-a-key-global-mobility-challenge

Dickmann, Michael, and Tim Mills. 2009. The Importance of Intelligent Career and Location Considerations: Exploring the Decision to Go to London. *Personnel Review* 39 (1): 116–134.

Dickmann, Michael, and Michael Müller-Camen. 2006. A Typology of International Human Resource Management Strategies and Processes. *The International Journal of Human Resource Management* 17 (4): 580–601.

Dickmann, Michael, Emma Parry, and Nadia Keshavjee. 2017. Localization of Staff in a Hostile Context: An Exploratory Investigation in Afghanistan. *The International Journal of Human Resource Management*: 1–29. https://doi.org/10.1080/09585192.2017.1291531.

Dickmann, Michael, Vesa Suutari, Chris Brewster, Liisa Mäkelä, Jussi Tanskanen, and Christelle Tornikoski. 2016. The Career Competencies of Self-Initiated and Assigned Expatriates: Assessing the Development of Career Capital Over Time. *The International Journal of Human Resource Management.* https://doi.org/10.1080/09585192.2016.1172657.

Doherty, Noeleen, and Michael Dickmann. 2009. Exploring the Symbolic Capital of International Assignments. *The International Journal of Human Resource Management* 20 (2): 301–320.

Doherty, Noeleen T., and Michael Dickmann. 2012. Measuring the Return on Investment in International Assignments: An Action Research Approach. *The International Journal of Human Resource Management* 23 (16): 3434–3454.

Doherty, Noeleen, Michael Dickmann, and Timothy Mills. 2011. Exploring the Motives of Company-Backed and Self-Initiated Expatriates. *International Journal of Human Resource Management* 22 (3): 595–611.

Dowling, Peter J., Marion Festing, and Allen D. Engle. 2008. *International Human Resource Management: Managing People in a Multinational Context.* 5th ed. London: Thomson Learning.

Edström, Anders, and Jay R. Galbraith. 1977. Transfer of Managers as a Coordination and Control Strategy in Multinational Organizations. *Administrative Science Quarterly* 22 (2): 248–263.

Gunz, Hugh P., and Maury Peiperl. 2007. *Handbook of Career Studies.* Thousand Oaks: Sage Publications.

Gustafsson, Per. 2012. Travel Time and Working Time: What Business Travellers Do When They Travel, and Why? *Time & Society* 21 (2): 203–222.

Hamori, Monika, and Burak Koyuncu. 2011. Career Advancement in Large Organizations in Europe and the United States: Do International Assignments Add Value? *International Journal of Human Resource Management* 22 (4): 843–862.

Harris, Hilary, and Chris Brewster. 1999. The Coffee-Machine System: How International Selection Really Works. *International Journal of Human Resource Management* 10 (3): 488–500.

Harris, Hilary, Chris Brewster, and Paul Sparrow. 2003. *International Human Resource Management*. London: CIPD Publishing.

Harvey, Michael. 1997. Dual-Career Expatriates: Expectations, Adjustment and Satisfaction with International Relocation. *Journal of International Business Studies* 28 (3): 627–658.

Harvey, Michael, Helene Mayerhofer, Linley Hartman, and Miriam Moeller. 2010. Corralling the "Horses" to Staff the Global Organization of 21st Century. *Organizational Dynamics* 39 (3): 258–268.

Haslberger, Arno, Chris Brewster, and Thomas Hippler. 2013. The Dimensions of Expatriate Adjustment. *Human Resource Management* 52 (3): 333–351.

Hippler, Thomas. 2009. Why Do They Go? Empirical Evidence of Employees' Motives for Seeking or Accepting Relocation. *The International Journal of Human Resource Management* 20 (6): 1381–1401.

Howe-Walsh, Liza, and Birgit Schyns. 2010. Self-Initiated Expatriation: Implications for HRM. *International Journal of Human Resource Management* 21 (2): 260–273.

Hurn, Brian J. 1999. Repatriation—The Toughest Assignment of All. *Industrial and Commercial Training* 31 (6): 224–228.

Inkson, Kerr, and Michael B. Arthur. 2001. How to Be a Successful Career Capitalist. *Organizational Dynamics* 30 (1): 48–61.

Jensen, Maria Therese. 2013. Exploring Business Travel with Work-Family Conflict and the Emotional Exhaustion Component of Burnout as Outcome Variables: The Job Demands-Resources Perspective. *European Journal of Work and Organizational Psychology* 23 (4): 497–510.

Jokinen, Tiina, Chris Brewster, and Vesa Suutari. 2008. Career Capital During International Work Experiences: Contrasting Self-Initiated Expatriate Experiences and Assigned Expatriation. *International Journal of Human Resource Management* 19 (6): 979–998.

Kang, Haiying, Jie Shen, and John Benson. 2016. Not All Expatriates are the Same: Non-Traditional South Korean Expatriates in China. *International Journal of Human Resource Management* 28 (13): 1842–1865.

Khilji, Shaista E., and Randall S. Schuler. 2017. Talent Management in the Global Context. In *The Oxford Handbook of Talent Management*, ed. David G. Collings, Kamel Mellahi, and Wayne F. Cascio. Oxford: Oxford University Press.

Konopaske, Robert, Chet Robie, and John M. Ivancevich. 2009. Managerial Willingness to Assume Travelling, Short-Term and Long-Term Assignments. *Management International Review* 49 (3): 359–387.

Kraimer, Maria L., Margaret A. Shaffer, and Mark C. Bolino. 2009. The Influence of Expatriate and Repatriate Experiences on Career Advancement and Repatriate Retention. *Human Resource Management* 48 (1): 27–47.

Larsen, Henrik Holt. 2004. Global Career as Dual Dependency Between the Organization and the Individual. *Journal of Management Development* 23 (9): 860–869.

Magnusson, Peter, and David J. Boggs. 2006. International Experience and CEO Selection: An Empirical Study. *Journal of International Management* 12 (1): 107–125.

Mäkelä, Liisa, Barbara Bergbom, Jussi Tanskanen, and Ulla Kinnunen. 2014. The Relationship Between International Business Travel and Sleep Problems Via Work-Family Conflict. *Career Development International* 19 (7): 794–812.

Mäkelä, Liisa, and Ulla Kinnunen. 2016. International Business Travelers' Psychological Well-Being: The Role of Supportive HR Practices. *The International Journal of Human Resource Management*: 1–22. https://doi.org/10.1080/09585192.2016.1194872.

Mäkelä, Liisa, Ulla Kinnunen, and Vesa Suutari. 2015. Work-to-Life Conflict and Enrichment Among International Business Travellers: The Role of International Career Orientation. *Human Resource Management* 54 (3): 517–531.

Mäkelä, Liisa, K. Saarenpää, and Y. McNulty. 2017. International Business Travellers, Short-Term Assignees and International Commuters. In *Research Handbook of Expatriates*, ed. Yvonne McNulty and Jan Selmer, 276–298. Cheltenham: Edward Elgar.

Mäkelä, Liisa, and Vesa Suutari. 2011. Coping with Work-Family Conflicts in the Global Career Context. *Thunderbird International Business Review* 53 (3): 365–375.

Mayrhofer, Wolfgang, Astrid Reichel, and Paul Sparrow. 2012. Alternative Forms of International Working. In *Handbook of Research into International Human Resource Management*, ed. Günter K. Stahl, Ingmar Björkman, and Shad Morris, 2nd ed., 293–320. Cheltenham: Edward Elgar.

The Multiple Forms and Shifting Landscapes of Global Careers   29

Meyskens, Moriah, Mary Ann Von Glinow, William B. Werther, and Linda Clarke. 2009. The Paradox of International Talent: Alternative Forms of International Assignments. *The International Journal of Human Resource Management* 20 (6): 1439–1450.

Ng, Thomas W.H., Lillian T. Eby, Kelly L. Sorensen, and Daniel C. Feldman. 2005. Predictors of Objective and Subjective Career Success: A Meta-Analysis. *Personnel Psychology* 58 (2): 367–408.

Reiche, B. Sebastian, Anne-Wil Harzing, and Maria L. Kraimer. 2009. The Role of International Assignees' Social Capital in Creating Inter-Unit Intellectual Capital: A Cross-Level Model. *Journal of International Business Studies* 40 (3): 509–526.

Richardson, Julia. 2006. Self-Directed Expatriation: Family Matters. *Personnel Review* 35 (4): 469–486.

Richardson, Julia, and Mary Mallon. 2005. Career Interrupted? The Case of the Self-Directed Expatriate. *Journal of World Business* 40 (4): 409–420.

Saarenpää, Kati. 2018. Stretching the Borders: How International Business Travel Affects the Work–Family Balance. *Community, Work and Family* 21 (1): 1–16.

Saxenian, AnnaLee. 2005. From Brain Drain to Brain Circulation: Transnational Communities and Upgrading in China and India. *Studies in Comparative International Development* 40 (2): 35–61.

Scullion, Hugh, and Davide G. Collings. 2011. *Global Talent Management.* Abingdon: Routledge.

Sparrow, Paul, Chris Brewster, and Hilary Harris. 2004. *Globalizing Human Resource Management.* London: Routledge.

Stahl, Günter K., Edwin L. Miller, and Rosealie L. Tung. 2002. Toward the Boundaryless Career: A Closer Look at the Expatriate Career Concept and the Perceived Implications of an International Assignment. *Journal of World Business* 37 (3): 216–227.

Starr, Tina L. 2009. Repatriation and Short-Term Assignments: An Exploration into Expectations, Change and Dilemmas. *The International Journal of Human Resource Management* 20 (2): 286–300.

Starr, Tina L., and Graeme Currie. 2009. 'Out of Sight but Still in the Picture': Short-Term International Assignments and the Influential Role of Family. *The International Journal of Human Resource Management* 20 (6): 1421–1438.

Sullivan, Sherry E., and Yehuda Baruch. 2009. Advances in Career Theory and Research: A Critical Review and Agenda for Future Exploration. *Journal of Management* 35 (6): 1542–1571.

Suutari, Vesa. 2003. Global Managers: Career Orientation, Career Tracks, Life-Style Implications and Career Commitment. *Journal of Managerial Psychology* 18 (3): 185–207.

Suutari, Vesa, and Chris Brewster. 2000. Making their Own Way: International Experience Through Self-Initiated Foreign Assignments. *Journal of World Business* 35 (4): 417–436.

———. 2009. Beyond Expatriation: Different Forms of International Employment. In *Handbook of International Human Resource Management: Integrating People, Process and Context*, ed. Paul Sparrow, 131–150. Chichester: John Wiley.

Suutari, Vesa, Chris Brewster, Liisa Mäkelä, Michael Dickmann, and Christelle Tornikoski. 2017. The Effect of International Work Experience on the Career Success of Expatriates: A Comparison of Assigned and Self-Initiated Expatriates. *Human Resource Management*. https://doi.org/10.1002/hrm.21827.

Suutari, Vesa, Chris Brewster, Kimmo Riusala, and Salla Syrjäkari. 2013. Managing Non-Standard International Experience: Evidence from a Finnish Company. *Journal of Global Mobility* 1 (2): 118–138.

Suutari, Vesa, and Kristiina Mäkelä. 2007. The Career Capital of Managers with Global Careers. *Journal of Managerial Psychology* 22 (7): 628–648.

Suutari, Vesa, and Milla Taka. 2004. Career Anchors of Managers with Global Careers. *Journal of Management Development* 23 (9): 833–847.

Suutari, Vesa, Christelle Tornikoski, and Liisa Mäkelä. 2012. Career Decision Making of Global Careerists. *International Journal of Human Resource Management* 23 (16): 3455–3478.

Suutari, Vesa, Olivier Wurtz, and Christelle Tornikoski. 2014. How to Attract and Retain Global Careerists: Evidence from Finland. In *Global Talent Management: Challenges, Strategies, and Opportunities*, ed. Akram Al Ariss, 237–249. Heidelberg: Springer International Publishing.

Tahvanainen, Marja, Denice Welch, and Verner Worm. 2005. Implications of Short-Term International Assignments. *European Management Journal* 23 (6): 663–673.

Tarique, Ibraiz, Dennis R. Briscoe, and Randall S. Schuler. 2015. *International Human Resource Management: Policies and Practices for Multinational Enterprises*. London: Routledge.

Tharenou, Phyllis. 2003. The Initial Development of Receptivity to Working Abroad: Self-Initiated International Work Opportunities in Young Graduate Employees. *Journal of Occupational and Organizational Psychology* 76 (4): 489–515.

The Multiple Forms and Shifting Landscapes of Global Careers   31

————. 2015. Researching Expatriate Types: The Quest for Rigorous Methodological Approaches. *Human Resource Management Journal* 25 (2): 149–165.

The RES Forum Annual Report. 2015. *Global Mobility and the Global Talent Management Conundrum*, written by Michael Dickmann. RES Forum, UniGroup Relocation Network and Equus Software, London.

————. 2016. *Beyond Uniformity—A World of Opportunity*, 116 pages, written by Michael Dickmann. The RES Forum, Harmony Relocation Network and Equus Software, London.

————. 2017. *The New Normal of Global Mobility—Flexibility, Diversity and Data Mastery*, 122 pages, written by Michael Dickmann. The RES Forum, Harmony Relocation Network and Equus Software, London.

————. 2018. *Rethinking Global Mobility—Smart, Agile, Flawless, Efficient and Purposeful Design and Execution*, written by Michael Dickmann. The RES Forum, Harmony Relocation Network and Equus Software, London.

Tornikoski, Christelle. 2011. Fostering Expatriate Affective Commitment: A Total Reward Perspective. *Cross Cultural Management: An International Journal* 18 (2): 214–235.

Ulrich, Dave. 1998. A New Mandate for Human Resources. *Harvard Business Review* 76 (1): 124–134.

2

Typologies of Internationally Mobile Employees

Maike Andresen, Michael Dickmann, and Vesa Suutari

Introduction

International business needs require many employees to undertake international work. Companies that prefer to rely on experienced leaders in new markets often mobilize managers for a *long-term foreign assignment*. When technical workers realize a short-term project in a foreign subsidiary, they may be *assigned abroad for a short term*. In order to negotiate a contract with a foreign customer, employees may take an *international*

M. Andresen (✉)
University of Bamberg, Bamberg, Germany
e-mail: maike.andresen@uni-bamberg.de

M. Dickmann
Cranfield School of Management, Cranfield University, Cranfield, UK
e-mail: m.dickmann@cranfield.ac.uk

V. Suutari
School of Management, University of Vaasa, Vaasa, Finland
e-mail: vsu@uva.fi

© The Author(s) 2018
M. Dickmann et al. (eds.), *The Management of Global Careers*,
https://doi.org/10.1007/978-3-319-76529-7_2

business trip. Others may decide to *commute* between countries so as not to uproot family, either to meet a short-term business requirement abroad or because the employee lives in a different country than where the workplace is located. Other companies again require their employees to execute *mobile jobs* that involve on-the-job-mobility, for example, in the transport and logistic sector (e.g. truck drivers on long-distance routes, mariners) or the service sector (e.g. journalists, pilots, stewards) (Otto and Dalbert 2010). As the realm of international business grows and changes, so do the types of international work-related mobility that support it. Thus, internationally operating companies nowadays need to administer many different forms of international work.

When counting the number of internationally mobile employees (IMEs) and analysing the consequences of international mobility in order to improve the management of different kinds of IMEs, who counts as an expatriate (and its variants) is of crucial importance. Yet there is no consensus on a single definition of, for example, a "self-initiated expatriate" or a "migrant" (Anderson and Blinder 2015). Tharenou (2015), in a comparative review of the literatures on assigned expatriates (AEs), self-initiated expatriates (SIEs) and skilled immigrants, recently warned not to combine these conceptually distinct groups of globally mobile individuals, as doing so contaminates the results, posing a threat to the validity of our findings. In pursuit of exactness, preciseness and completeness, we find many authors who seek to define (new) types of IMEs based on an increasing number of criteria. We want to question the added value of doing so and formulate a plea for a sound theory of expatriation types.

Definitions and Typologies

When summarizing the literature on international mobility, we find a long list of types of internationally mobile employees. Briscoe et al. (2009) were one of the first to draw our attention to this terminological development by providing a valuable overview of terms used in research and practice. Appendix 1 gives an overview of different typologies of internationally mobile persons as mentioned in the literature.

Typologies of Internationally Mobile Employees   35

From our extended list of different types of internationally mobile persons (see Appendix 1), three things become apparent: (1) Numerous criteria are used to define types that refer to mobility, employment and conditions (see Appendix 2). This reflects the fact that typologies, by definition, are based on a limited number of theoretically meaningful dimensions (Doty and Glick 1994). However, depending on the theory or conceptual model used, the criteria usually differ between authors resulting in different types. (2) The criteria are, however, not used consistently across all typologies so that demarcations between types are not always distinct on the one hand and some overlaps exist on the other hand. (3) To describe one type of IME, a single criterion is sometimes used differently by authors, leading to contradictions, as we will show in the following chapter. (4) The major disadvantage of typologies is that empirical evidence running counter to theoretical specifications may not be strong enough to discover inherent weaknesses of the typology (Bailey 1994). Hence, in the following we aim to critically analyse existing typologies of internationally mobile employees including the criteria used.

This attempt to differentiate an increasing number of different types of IMEs is comparable to a double-edged sword. On the one hand, precise sampling allows scientists to derive precise implications for a specific sub-group of IMEs. Thus, practitioners get very clear answers to how to manage specific IMEs. On the other hand, a highly differentiated typology requires employers to develop a range of differentiated policies instead of standardized rules, involving organizational costs. Moreover, a differentiation of types also requires scientists to agree on criteria and definitions and to use these consistently. Strikingly, only very few authors in the field of expatriation disguise the specific items or selection criteria they used to specify their sample. This implies that studies that used the same term to designate their type of IME might in fact have different definitions in mind and have included different types in their sample, which again reduces the comparability of results between studies. Furthermore, the transferability of research results to other subgroups is open in view of a lack of replication studies with different subgroups.

In view of the increasing number of typologies and types of IMEs developed by researchers, this long list of criteria used to define types and the overlap in the definitions of these types as well as a lack of clarity, we seek preciseness and a sound theory of expatriation. Our goal is to use fewer criteria leading to general ("rough") types (see Andresen et al. 2014) that allow for clear sampling strategies in empirical research and the development of targeted policies in practice.

The Quest for Developing a Theory of International Employee Mobility

Overall, the numerous existing types of IMEs in literature and practice are a highly differentiated, practical system of statements about different forms of international mobility. Do we still need a scientific alternative in this case? Would it be an option to make existing typologies in research and practice a little more explicit by collecting *all types* of IMEs and fixing them in writing, comparable to the list in Appendix 1? Would that lead to a scientifically sound theory of expatriation and a useful typology?

We can only answer this question by first, establishing criteria for a science and then examining whether the ordinary typologies of IMEs (as presented in Appendix 1) meet these criteria of a science. Most sciences are at least entitled to satisfy the following quality criteria: General criteria include explicitness, consistency, completeness, parsimony, productivity and applicability (Asendorpf and Neyer 2012). Additional criteria are empirical anchoring and empirical testability (see Table 2.1):

In the following, we evaluate typologies of IMEs according to these criteria that characterize science. We refer to a selection of types (i.e. migrant, immigrant, SIE, AE) to illustrate our argument that these probably represent the majority of the existing types of IMEs.

Explicitness

Scientific terms, in our case types of IMEs, need to be explicitly defined so that they are understood in the same way by different scientists and, ideally, practitioners. The increasing number of types presented in literature (Arp et al. 2013; Baruch et al. 2013; McPhail et al. 2012; Tharenou

Table 2.1 Criteria for theories in the (empirical) sciences (Asendorpf and Neyer 2012)

Criteria	Explanation
General criteria	
Explicitness	The terms and statements of the typology are to be explicitly stated.
Consistency	The statements that can be derived from the typology shall not be contradictory.
Completeness	The statements of the typology shall explain all known phenomena of the subject matter of the typology.
Parsimony	The typology is intended to deal with as few basic concepts as possible.
Productivity	The typology is intended to create new research questions and thereby promote research.
Applicability	The typology should be applicable practically.
Additional criteria for empirical sciences	
Empirical anchoring	The concepts of the typology should refer directly or indirectly to observational data.
Empirical verifiability	The statements of the typology shall be verifiable based on observational data.

Source: The authors

2015) runs the risk of remaining vague (see McNulty and Brewster 2016 for a critique) and is used by different people in a similar but not identical way. For example, the term "migrant", as typical in economics, is sometimes assumed to refer to (a) permanent moves of (b) lower skilled labour (c) from developing countries (Al Ariss 2010). This definition contradicts the broader definition of migrants in sociology and economics that covers all qualification levels, see, for example, "highly skilled migrants" (Chaloff and Lemaître 2009), and includes both temporary and permanent mobility (Massey and Bartley 2006; Wiles 2008) from both developing and developed countries (Stilwell et al. 2004). Moreover, when researchers in the field of expatriate management are asked for a definition of an ordinary expatriate type, such as a "self-initiated expatriate", they have to think hard in order to reconstruct the most appropriate meaning. What does "self-initiated" mean? Strikingly, only very few definitions of SIEs explicitly address criteria of initiative (for an exception, see Andresen et al. 2014; see also Selmer et al. 2017 for a critique), and most authors do not present the items they used to identify SIEs in their sample.

Consistency

In research as well as in public statistics about international labour mobility, contradictory assertions are often found, as Anderson and Blinder (2015) critically point out. For example, "Migrants might be defined by foreign birth, by foreign citizenship, or by their movement into a new country to stay temporarily (sometimes for as little as a year) or to settle for the long-term." (Anderson and Blinder 2015: 3). Some definitions of migrants even include children who are born in or are nationals of the country they live in, but whose parents are foreign-born or foreign nationals (Anderson and Blinder 2015). It becomes obvious that none of these definitions are equivalent and distinct. Taking only the example of the term "migrant", contradictions in terms of length of stay (permanent versus temporary) and birth/citizenship become obvious. This raises the question: How far are research results and statistics comparable and transferable?

Moreover, the terms "immigrant" and "migrant" are sometimes used interchangeably among researchers (Tharenou 2015), while others distinguish immigrants (people who are or intend to be settled in their new country) from migrants (who are temporarily resident) (Anderson and Blinder 2015). McNulty and Brewster (2016), by contrast, suggest a contradictory definition of migrants as used in economics and politics by claiming that migrants move permanently to another country. This shows clear inconsistencies in the use of technical terms between, and sometimes even within, disciplines.

In addition, demarcations of migrants and immigrants from self-initiated expatriates are not unambiguous. So, Tharenou (2015) defines SIEs as persons who expatriate for a temporary but undefined time, whereas skilled (im)migrants are defined to expatriate "for the long-term usually to settle permanently" (Tharenou 2015: 162; Cerdin and Selmer 2014). This distinction is relativized by the explanation that "SIEs can also be 'immigrants' if a visa and residence permit are required" (Tharenou 2015: 150) and, thus, risks to be perceived as being inconsistent by some readers.

The inconsistent typologies of IMEs explain every state of affairs—unfortunately, they also can be used to explain the opposite state of affairs. Thus, in reality they explain nothing as they provide only *apparent* explanations. While we agree with McNulty and Brewster (2016) that a good theory of expatriation requires consistency, we claim that their limitation to the criterion of consistency is insufficient. Rather, sound theories need to fulfil additional criteria, as will be shown in the following.

Completeness

Theories should explain all that is already known. This is one of the strengths of the extensive typologies of internationally mobile employees that have been suggested in the past (Baruch et al. 2013; Briscoe et al. 2009; Appendix 1), because of the huge amount of types and criteria that can be used for a categorization of expatriates. With the numerous typologies that have been suggested by researchers almost all observable peculiarities can be explained (and named). This is, however, sometimes brought about by a lack of absence of contradiction. Suggested types become vague when we talk about transitions between types. The following example is meant to show ambiguities in existing types that appear when taking a life-course perspective: A couple intends to work and live in China. She manages to be assigned by her employer to China for four years. He accompanies his wife as the trailing spouse. One year after they settle, he starts looking for a job. He receives a job offer after a further year of applying for work. Thus, during this two-year period of unemployment, the husband holds migrant status, but is not an expatriate (Andresen et al. 2014). Does the husband become a self-initiated expatriate after these 24 months of unemployment and is he then losing migrant status? How much (proactive) initiative did he show or did he simply respond to the situation that his wife was assigned abroad? After the official ending of her assignment, the couple decide to continue to stay abroad for a temporary but undefined time. She applies for a new job and changes employer. Does she become a SIE although she has already lived in China for four years and thus did not self-initiate her expatriation for this specific step in her career? What does the self-initiation relate to?—to the decision to go abroad or to any decision to change employer during a stay abroad? After several prolongations of their stay, they finally look back at 15 years living and working in China. Did they both become immigrants in the meantime in view of their long-term stay and, if yes, at which point in time? A somewhat heretical question, do we need types and names for all of these tiny differences and if so, for what purpose?

In this vein, based on a systematic literature review, Andresen et al. (2014) define international migrants as individuals who move from one geographical point to another geographical point, crossing national borders, and change their dominant place of residence which is the centre of their life. An expatriate is a migrant who executes legal work abroad. While in the case of SIEs, the first key binding activity to move internationally is solely made by the individual who initiates the expatriation and the legal decision of employment is made by a new work contract partner, in the case of AEs, the first key binding activity to expatriate is taken by the organization and the legal decision of employment is made by the current work contract partner, usually in the home country.

Parsimony

Existing typologies of IMEs are extremely rich in basic coverage, because every type of international mobility is a basic concept (it is not derived from other basic assumptions). For example, Briscoe et al. (2009) distinguish between 20 different kinds of IMEs in their typology. There are, therefore, at least as many basic concepts as there are words to characterize international employment mobility properties. Such an abundance of basic assumptions cannot necessarily be justified by the complexity of the subject matter, as a glance at chemistry shows where the huge variety of substances can be attributed extremely economically to combinations of few elements. Even though such a drastic reduction regarding criteria and forms of international mobility may not be possible, the great number of almost synonymous features of different types appears far too uneconomical (Andresen et al. 2014). Long lists of types of IMEs based on numerous criteria massively violate the principle of parsimony.

Productivity

The existing extensive lists of types of IMEs constitute a rich reservoir of properties which offer almost unlimited possibilities for investigations into the function of certain properties and their couplings. However, there is a tension with the ability to combine insights from research as the existence of so many diverse definitions and specific international mobility types evokes the risk of spreading into narrow and non-interrelated research questions. One way to overcome this tension would be to distinguish between broad criteria that can be used to develop different foci. Highly productive approaches allow the accumulation and integration of research insights due to having an agreed set of fundamental criteria while at the same time opening up the possibility to employ diverse perspectives and to pursue a wide array of research questions when honing in *within* the different fundamental types.

Applicability

As we have seen, the strength of extensive typologies of IMEs lies in its simple, fast and robust applicability to ordinary problems in the field of international relocation. This is why extensive IME typologies prove themselves good despite the weaknesses mentioned above. However, a comprehensive typology based on numerous criteria may take more time to be applied, look complex and be harmed by overlaps between types. From a practitioner's point of view, categorizing employees in numerous different types in order to offer type-specific HR practices might not be applicable and economic.

Today's management research is also understood as an empirical science, which, like natural sciences, physics, chemistry and biology, is based on observational data and its statements can be confirmed or disproved by observation. In addition to the general criteria already discussed, empirical sciences must satisfy two supplementary criteria (see Table 2.1).

Empirical Anchoring

Body size is a property that can be observed directly. Attitudes, motivations and dispositions, by contrast, are not directly observable and measurable, but can only be derived from statements or behaviour. They are constructs "behind" the observable behaviours and should explain it. The intention to stay abroad is a construct that is intended to explain the observation that someone is showing particular or very little relocation mobility behaviour. Constructs need to be linkable to observational data (the empirical indicators of the construct). The measurement procedure is also called the operationalization of the construct.

Are ordinary typologies of IMEs empirically anchored? At first sight, this seems to be the case, because typologies were partly determined based on directly observable properties (e.g. educational level), but mostly derived from behaviours (e.g. motives) of IMEs. However, one of the main problems of these ordinary typologies is that only very few requirements are imposed on the conditions under which researchers may conclude from observations of behaviours on types of international mobility. Interestingly, more than 100 articles about SIEs have been published, but no agreed-on operationalization of "self-initiation" has been presented yet, let alone that similar criteria have been used to identify SIEs, making the study results more or less incomparable. In consequence, the requirements regarding SIEs' behaviour to be observed are imprecise. Is it sufficient that people have changed employers when going abroad? What does that say about their initiative?

Thus, ordinary typologies of IMEs risk being insufficiently anchored empirically. In particular, the imprecise definition of behavioural regularity regarding the initiative suggests a circular closure in the definition of SIEs; from a one-time behaviour, it is concluded to be a mobility type, which is then used to explain regular behaviour. For example: "Why is Anna a self-initiated expatriate? Because she showed personal initiative when going abroad." However, the fact that she self-initiated her expatriation does not imply that Anna *in general* shows personal initiative. Rather, a *general* personal initiative would require that Anna regularly shows initiative, that is, throughout her relocation process as well as in her work. This would need to be proven by observations based on numerous incidents. In other words, there is an observable risk that researchers and practitioners overgeneralize from a one-time behaviour (e.g. a self-initiated expatriation) to a generally high trait (e.g. personal initiative) of a certain type of IMEs (Vance 2005).

Empirical Verifiability

Empirical sciences are expected to be empirically testable. More specifically, their statements are expected to be empirically confirmable or disprovable. To this end, they must be formulated clearly so that such a test is possible. The lack of explicitness and the insufficient empirical anchoring of many characteristics of ordinary types of IMEs complicate such a test because any statement can be immunized against a refutation by appropriate modification of the explanation.

The following examples illustrate the mechanism of suitable modifications in explanations of ordinary types of IMEs: "Anna has been categorized as migrant in official statistics, because she moved abroad in order to stay temporarily in the host country. Looking back, Anna has been staying in the host country for 20 years. Does this mean that describing her as migrant is wrong? To immunize against this potential criticism, one explanation could be that Anna changed her mind whilst abroad and now intends to stay permanently (and, thus, became an immigrant only later-on). If this is not the case, another explanation could be used by arguing that she stuck to her initial plan to stay temporarily, but prolonged her stay again and again. Finally, if this is disproved, one could again argue that Anna privately wanted to stay permanently, but was not sure whether she would pass immigration requirements upon relocation and, thus, indicated a conservative plan." In this example, one explanation is replaced by another explanation and as it does not prove to be plausible, again another explanation can be sought to justify the initial classification as migrant.

Since explanations and predictions of single IME types are arbitrarily modifiable and, thus, avoid any refutation, this also applies to IME typologies as a whole. If you cannot refute single types as the conditions are quite broad, then it is clear that the whole typology cannot be refuted. This is the greatest weakness of many typologies from an empirical point of view.

Further Reflection on These Typologies

This section outlines first some of the practical drawbacks of not having agreed, consistent global types of IMEs. Second, it will investigate the tension between a broad and agreed typology and further specific research interests and will suggest a way forward.

Given the more than three dozen different forms of IMEs identified (Appendix 1), the space in this chapter is insufficient to discuss the effects of definitional shortcomings on all of these. Instead, we will concentrate on a few global career types. Taking the example of AEs, those company-sent global careerists who have been covered most in the literature, we can start to explore the impact of the lack of a widely accepted, high-quality definition on the recommendations for individuals and organizations. Using the four phases of the expatriation cycle as depicted in Dickmann and Baruch (2011), an array of issues, questions and shortcomings are raised.

Global Mobility Strategies, Structures and Policies and Individuals

Organizations determine the underlying goals and configurations of their international mobility (IM) often geared to traditional AEs. Several ways to design IM strategies and to structure their global mobility departments are possible (RES Forum 2015). Where companies have a highly integrated international HR approach (a global or transnational configuration according to Bartlett and Ghoshal 2002; Dickmann and Müller-Camen 2006), it is likely that they have many control and coordination and knowledge transfer assignments (Dowling et al. 2013; Edström and Galbraith 1977). In addition, it can be seen that firms now distinguish between developmental and business needs assignments, with the latter commanding a more generous expatriation package (RES Forum 2017). AEs are often treated in the literature as if their employers initiated the first key binding activity in the drive to fill a position abroad. However, when staff urge their employer to send them abroad, that is, the expatriate themselves undertake the first key binding step (Andresen et al. 2014; Heckhausen 2012), this could have an impact on the reward package that the organization offers. In turn, individuals have their own sets of individual drivers that influence their decision to (seek) work abroad (Doherty et al. 2011; Hippler 2009). Contrasting these with the (organizational) assignment goals, the host context and family situation would give important information to the design of expatriation packages and how difficult (or easy) it might be to persuade particular expatriation candidates to work in a specific job in a determined country. Overall, going beyond the binary distinction of who initiates foreign work (organization-individual) to capture the rich motivational patterns and drivers of global careerists could yield important insights as to the design of global mobility strategies and reward approaches. Other distinctions within the category of AEs, for example, whether these are assigned to their home country, the head office of the organization, to hostile, insecure environments and so on, would give additional nuancing to the IM approaches of organizations.

Selection by the Organization, Negotiation and Predeparture Preparation

The literature on how to select appropriate candidates for working abroad is wide-ranging and covers a broad spectrum of factors including psychological (Caligiuri 2013), family (Harvey 1995), political (Dickmann and Baruch 2011; Ferner et al. 2004), cultural (Black and Stephens 1989; Haslberger et al. 2013), performance (Dowling et al. 2013) and specific location (Dickmann 2012) elements. Clearly, each of the different perspectives incorporates a set of diverse recommendations. Thus, organizational policies could be refined based on an array of different recommendations. Again, understanding the drivers of individuals better, their cultural and work competency stretch to their host environment would be useful for organizations to shape their selection processes so that they can go beyond the "coffee machine selection" approach (Harris and Brewster 1999). In addition, clearly distinguishing AEs who return to a country they have lived in (ex-host country nationals), understanding the elements of their work (AEs who are also frequent business travellers, reward expatriates, just-in-time workers who lack the time to prepare, etc.) could give valuable insights. In turn, not distinguishing the richness of the AE population will lead to highly generic recommendations. Individuals, in contrast, will want to understand the importance and pressure to fill a position, the success elements of the work that may be linked to improved careers (Dickmann et al. 2016; Suutari et al. 2017), and, crucially, may want to contrast their own drivers with the short- and long-term attractiveness of the expatriation sojourn in order to shape their negotiation strategy and predeparture preparation. Thus, it would be important not just to refine our definitions of IM patterns but also those that relate to the job on offer, the host environment and the career (and other) benefits that are associated with working abroad for a particular organization.

Working Abroad—Unequal Contractual Agreements and HR Management

Employers tend to strive for fair, equal and consistent treatment of their staff in order not to break their psychological contract and to encourage motivation and commitment (Conway and Briner 2005). However, the absence of clear definitions of who is an international traveller or commuter, who is on a short- or long-term assignment or when (if at all) to convert an assignment contract into a local plus arrangement leads to unfair treatment of IMEs. It is well known (RES Forum 2015, 2016, 2017) that these different categories of global work are associated with highly distinctive contracts that specify different financial reward levels as well as highly different benefits (travel, accommodation, health insurances, support measures). Moreover, while short- and long-term assignment policies are normally centrally defined (which ensures a higher degree of equal treatment and fairness), international travellers are often flying under the radar screen of IM departments, and their higher costs are borne by travel budgets while there are few financial incentives. By not officially categorizing frequent flyers as global careerists, organizations tend to treat them highly differently from AEs breaching their own principles of equality and fairness.

While we argue to increase the fairness of global work compensation, it does not mean one size fits all. It would be useful for MNCs to take account of the specific circumstances of the work abroad. Organizations should tailor their international development approaches in relation to the underlying needs of the work abroad, the host context and the interests of the IMEs, be they officially assignees, frequent travellers or cross-border commuters. It is not as if organizations do not take account of the job demands or security aspects of foreign postings. However, if research would be able to distinguish a range of different elements in relation to the individual's and the organization's needs, it would be able to create deeper insights and nuance their recommendations. In addition, while many of the career aspects of AEs have been explored, there is considerable uncertainty about the career outcomes of other forms of international mobility, especially those where the work abroad is rolled into a general career system as with frequent flyers or virtual international workers. In contrast, much of performance management when working abroad is conducted through local hosts using the general organizational HR system. It is rare that the strains of expatriate challenges or other issues used for the classification of assignment type such as intention to return are formally taken account of in performance appraisals.

Repatriation and Review of Outcomes

Individual and organizational motivations and goals in relation to the foreign sojourn should be evaluated upon repatriation. However, the general definition of global careerists has so far led to little more than this generic recommendation. If the definitions were more precise, they would allow us to specifically look at whether assignment goals such as development, control and coordination, knowledge transfer, skills filling and so on were fulfilled by the individual. In turn, they would also facilitate an assessment of the key drivers of assignees. To some extent, predominantly in the areas of career, development and marketability, this has been explored in general for SIEs and AEs (Dickmann et al. 2016; Suutari et al. 2017). However, they have not been connected to the specific organizational assignment objectives. In addition, research into the immediate and long-term outcomes of other forms of global mobility could be expanded.

Overcoming the Tensions Between Broad Types and Specific Research

We have argued that the existing typologies and associated definitions should be improved in order to allow us to advance research into IMEs. The key challenges include, first, it is currently often impossible to combine insights from different authors as they are using different definitions for certain types of IMEs and different operationalizations. Indeed, the overlap of criteria, for example, both AEs and SIEs are supposed to repatriate (Tharenou 2015), and a temporal dimension during which global workers can change "status", for example, from AE to SIE, creates ambiguous distinctions to immigration and may lead to confusion. One way around it may be to make a choice regarding temporal dimensions that relates the type of global worker to a time span (e.g. at the time of moving across national borders or the most recent status in relation to the research). Second, and related, the quality of the general criteria used to define and categorize diverse forms of global work could be improved. Above, we have outlined the current drawbacks of global career typologies in terms of explicitness, consistency, completeness, parsimony, productivity, empirical anchoring and verifiability. The effect of this lack of definitional quality is that the applicability of our practical insights is limited and may have to be reconsidered in terms of its operational and personal value as well as the inherent limitations.

Overall, typologies of global careerists are living with a tension. One way to advance the field, as we have suggested, would be to define the types more explicitly, to create a consistent and complete overview which would allow us to explore new research questions and to practically apply the findings. However, the challenge in relation to combining the research insights in a parsimonious way is readily apparent. Thus, we suggest concentrating on less elaborate typologies that are based only on a few criteria and use broad types to subsequently develop research investigating issues within these. One of the examples of such an approach is that of Andresen and her co-authors (Andresen et al. 2014) who use a small number of criteria to distinguish between an array of foreign work forms such as AEs, SIEs, assigned travellers and self-initiated travellers. When global workers relocate across national borders and change their dominant place of residency, their approach looks at the legality of work (distinguishing migrants and expatriates), who initiates the first binding activity (distinguishing between AEs and SIEs) and whether the person has changed organizations (e.g. intra-organizational SIEs vs inter-organizational SIEs). The advantage of such a typology is that it is easy to apply across a range of research scenarios, that it can be empirically verified and that it leaves out a range of criteria (e.g. intention to stay) that may not be relevant for many research studies.

Thus, in a first step, types of international mobility need to be described in a comprehensive way. This might be informed by an interdisciplinary discussion where insights from sociology, psychology, migration studies, ethnography and so on can be used to build a better description of the many types of IMEs. In a second step we would suggest to condense the core descriptors in order to arrive at parsimony. An example of this process can be found in Andresen and her colleagues (2014). In practice, selecting the adequate types to research will be linked to the specific perspective of the scientific study and the purpose pursued. Therefore, step one allows a more integrated and comprehensively exhaustive approach (aiding consistency in the field) while step two factors in the pragmatic needs and specific interests of researchers.

In addition, we outlined above that a clear delineation of types of international mobility will allow organizations to design, evaluate and refine tailored global mobility activities to certain mobile employee groups before, during and after working abroad. Key is often to understand the diverse drivers, interests, backgrounds and experiences that expatriates and other foreign workers have and to utilize these insights to develop targeted global mobility approaches. Using more systematic typologies allows not just single organizations to create distinct global mobility approaches; it would also enable them to learn better from the experiences of other organizations and to apply scientific research to their own globally mobile employee groups.

Conclusions and Recommendations for Future Work

As has been shown above, current research in expatriation suffers from the fact that terms are not adequately defined, or terms are defined, but used in a different way by others researching the same phenomenon (McNulty and Brewster 2016) or suffer from some overlap. Thus, it is time to develop an empirically based theory of expatriates that describes peculiarities of mobility types based on criteria such as international mobility intention, behaviour and experience.

All descriptions need to be empirically anchored and statements must be empirically verifiable. We have suggested two steps that would ensure researchers work in a comprehensive, integrated and yet parsimonious way. In addition, the concept of peculiarity has to be specified in three respects. Firstly, this means that the characteristics of types are stable in time and the degree of stability must be quantifiable (days, months, years?). Secondly, peculiarity means that the property under consideration varies between people, not between any people, but between those working for similar kinds of organizations, because it makes no sense to confuse differences in international mobility with organizational differences. Thirdly, extreme features should be excluded because their stability and explanation are often different from those of normal variants of international mobility patterns.

Both researchers and practitioners could profit from a parsimonious typology differentiating only a few types using a coherent set of criteria.

Appendix 1

Table 2.2 Types of internationally mobile employees as mentioned in literature

- *Assigned expatriate or international assignee*: "Employees who are supported by their employers to legally work in a country outside their country-of-origin generally for a duration of more than one year and usually less than five years." (Brewster et al. 2017)

- *Boomerang*: "These are individuals who have emigrated and are hired by firms in their original home country to return home or are foreigners with experience in the country, who have returned home and are now hired to come back to the foreign country." (Briscoe et al. 2009)

- *Business expatriate*: People who are organizationally and legally employed and stay abroad for a certain intended length of time (temporary or permanent) as non-citizens of this host country. (McNulty and Brewster 2016)

- *Corporate or organizational expatriate*: "Those who are dispatched by their home companies to international posts." (Peltokorpi and Froese 2009)

- *Corporate or organizational self-initiated expatriate*: A person "who independently initiate mobility abroad within their own organisation under its sponsorship, support and knowledge." (Tharenou 2015)

- *Domestic internationalist*: "Employees who never leave home but conduct international business with customers, suppliers, and colleagues in other countries (via telephone, email, fax, or even snail mail)." (Briscoe et al. 2009)

- *Ex-host country national*: Nationals who return home, after having lived abroad for an extensive period of time. (Tung and Lazarova 2006)

- *Expatriate*: People working outside their own country for what they anticipate will be a limited period of time. (Brewster et al. 2017)

- *Flexpatriate*: Persons whose "work assignments are characterized by a continuation of their current work position in their domestic country combined with work projects in different international destinations, commutes to divers [sic!] cultural settings, assignments on short notice with and flexible travel. On the personal side assignments beyond flexpatriates' domestic country do not involve relocating a home or family." (Mayerhofer et al. 2011)

- *Foreign executives in local organizations*: "FELOs can be viewed as SIEs or, more generally, expatriates (...) who work at executive level, in local organisations, in distant countries." (Arp et al. 2013)

- *Global careerist*: "Internationally oriented professionals with a long-term global career involving different types of international work during their careers." (Brewster et al. 2017)

(continued)

Table 2.2 (continued)

- *Global or international itinerants*: Persons who may remain outside their home country for substantial parts of their career. (Banai and Harry 2004)
- *Global manager*: Persons "who are senior executives whose careers during the course of a working life cover frequent (e.g. three or more) international assignments and positions with one or several employers." (Tharenou 2015)
- *Globetrotter*: Person who regularly or frequently travels to different places around the world.
- *Immigrant (legal/illegal/asylum)*: "(a) traditional TCNs, employees who are hired to work in a foreign subsidiary but whose home of citizenship is another country, thus they become immigrants to the country of the subsidiary; (b) people hired by the parent firm (either in-country or as new immigrants and brought into the country) to work in the parent country." (Briscoe et al. 2009)
- *Inpatriate/impatriate*: Persons "who are host or third country nationals the parent company transfers to its headquarters on a semi- or permanent basis usually for development, often to return to manage a subsidiary in their home country." (Tharenou 2015)
- *Intern (or temporary immigrant)*: "These are workers brought into a firm's home country to work for short (six months to two years) periods as interns or trainees, used especially to fill in for labor shortages." (Briscoe et al. 2009)
- *International business traveller*: People travelling "frequently to different parts of their company or to clients or prospective clients for visits ranging from days to weeks depending on the task required of them." (Brewster et al. 2017)
- *International commuter or cross-border*: "Employees who live in one country (home countries) but who work in another (host) country and regularly commute across borders to perform aspects of their work. They may live at home in one country yet commute on a daily or weekly basis to another country to work." (Briscoe et al. 2009)
- *International volunteer*: Individual with specialist expertise undertaking an international work assignment with specific development objectives. (Fee and Gray 2011)
- *Just-in-time expatriate*: "These are *ad hoc* or contract expatriates who are hired from outside the firm as they are needed and just for one assignment." (Briscoe et al. 2009)

- *Localized employee*: "Often referred to as localization, this normally refers to the situation where an employee is sent to work in a foreign country but hired as a local employee (with some allowances to get over there). This may be because they really want to work in that country, often because they marry a local spouse or for some other reason want to spend the rest of their careers in that location. It may also involve an international assignee who is concerted to permanent local status once the assignment period is over." (Briscoe et al. 2009)
- *Migrant*: "People moving from their original home country to another country in the expectation that they will spend the rest of their lives in the new country." (Brewster et al. 2017)
- *Outsourced employee*: "(…) the MNE decides to pay someone else (in another country) for the services of an "employee" or group of employees. (…) global employment companies (…) provide a few employees or whole staffs for overseas locations." (Briscoe et al. 2009)
- *Permanent cadre or globalist*: "These are employees who spend essentially their whole careers in international assignments, moving from one locale to another." (Briscoe et al. 2009)
- *Retirement expatriate*: "This refers to the hiring of a firm's retirees for short-term foreign assignments." (Briscoe et al. 2009)
- *Returnee*: "These are emigrants who are hired (or selected, if already employed by the firm) to return to their home countries to work for the firm there." (Briscoe et al. 2009)
- *Reward or punishment assignee*: "These are employees who are late in their careers and who are either given a desirable foreign assignment to enjoy and to pad their pensions for when they retire in a couple of years (pay is higher on foreign assignments) or are sent to a difficult locale or undesirable assignment as a way to sideline them to finish out their careers, rather than have to discipline or terminate them because of marginal performance." (Briscoe et al. 2009)
- *Second-generation expatriate*: "These are naturalized citizens (immigrants who have become citizens) and are sent on foreign assignments to countries other than their countries of birth. The assumption is that, since they have lived through the "expatriate" experience once, they should be better able (than those without this experience) to handle it the second time." (Briscoe et al. 2009)
- *Secondee overseas*: Overseas secondments are fixed-term placements that usually occur between organizations in different countries, with the expectation that the secondee will return to the sending organization. "In a secondment, the initiative to be mobile often comes from the individual." (Thorn 2009)

(*continued*)

Table 2.2 (continued)

- *Self-initiated expatriate or self-initiated foreign worker*: "People working abroad for what they intend to be a limited, even if quite long in some cases, period, who have made their own way to the country on their own initiative." (Brewster et al. 2017)
- *Short-term (international) assignee*: "Person assigned abroad for a period of less than a year (usually less than six months) where the expatriate, even if they have a family, leaves them behind and goes on their own." (Brewster et al. 2017)
- *Sojourner*: Sojourners are temporary visitors to a foreign country. (Cox 1988)
- *Stealth assignee*: "International assignees who are relocated by their managers without ever informing HR (that is, they 'fly under the radar'), so that they do not show up in the records, benefits, and support systems used to manage such employees." (Briscoe et al. 2009)
- *Virtual global employee or virtual international employee*: "This is the situation where all or most of the work is performed across borders via electronic media: teleconferences, email, telephone, videoconferences, fax, etc." (Briscoe et al. 2009)
- *Skilled (im)migrant*: "Managerial, professional and technical persons usually holding at least a bachelor's degree gained in their home country and a skilled occupation, who self-initiate migration for the long-term usually to settle permanently in a new country for reasons of economic motivation, career progress, lifestyle, establishment of better lives and living conditions, and/or family and relationships, either migrating through employer sponsorship of a job in the new country or independently by a skilled migration programme seeking to gain employment once there." (Tharenou 2015)

Appendix 2

Table 2.3 Criteria used in literature to define IMEs

Mobility	Geographical mobility (individual perspective)	• to the expatriate's original home country • to country outside the expatriate's country-of-origin • to "new" country
	Geographical mobility (organizational perspective)	• to a firm's home/parent country • to foreign subsidiary • to a parent company's headquarters • to a (local) organization abroad
	Organizational mobility	• within the organization • between organizations
	Career-related mobility	• late in the career; mid-career • early career
	Duration	• temporary (few days, weeks, months, few to many years) versus permanent (for the rest of an individual's career/life) • intended/anticipated versus actual length of time
	Frequency of travelling	• commuting; frequent/regular travelling • one-time relocation (home, family)
	Occurrence	• one singular mobility • frequent mobility • long-term global career
	Kind of mobility	• physical mobility • virtual collaboration
	Planning horizon	• on short notice • long-term preparation period
	Variance (geographically)	• one country • variety of countries
	Variance (organizationally)	• one versus several employers • one versus different parts of the company • to (prospective) clients for visits
Employment	Contract partner	• continuation of current work contract with parent organization in home country • hired as a local employee
	Legality	• legal employment • illegal employment
	Level/job role	• (senior) executive, manager, professional, specialist, technical person, worker, intern, trainee
	Organizational membership	• international mobility as one step in a longer-lasting organizational career • membership limited to one foreign stay (ad hoc/contract expatriates)
	Task	• assignment • work project
	Employment status	• organizationally employed • self-employed • retiree • unemployed

(continued)

Table 2.3 (continued)

Conditions	Citizenship/origin	• non-citizen of the host country/foreigners • foreigner who became citizen of the host country/naturalized citizen • third-country national • host-country national
	Educational level	• at least a bachelor's degree • others
	Educational (non-) residents	• degree gained in their home country • degree gained in their host country
	Employee's emotional attachment	• to home country • to host country
	Initiation	• employee independently initiates mobility abroad • employer initiates mobility abroad
	Motives	• organization (e.g. fill in for labour shortages, reward, punishment, development, often to return to manage a subsidiary in the expatriate's home country) • individual (e.g. international orientation, marriage to a local spouse, economic motivation, career progress, lifestyle, establishment of better lives and living conditions and/or family relationships, seeking employment elsewhere)
	Relocation of family	• yes versus no
	Staffing approach	• ethnocentric • polycentric • regiocentric • geocentric
	Support/sponsorship	• high to low/missing support/sponsorship • by domestic and/or foreign employer • with(out) informing HR • independently (by a skilled migration programme)
	Taxation	• in home country • in host country
	Visa status	• work permit • status depends on immigration policies • visa

References

Al Ariss, Akram. 2010. Modes of Engagement: Migration, Self-Initiated Expatriation, and Career Development. *Career Development International* 15 (4): 338–358. https://doi.org/10.1108/13620431011066231.

Typologies of Internationally Mobile Employees 57

Anderson, Bridget, and Scott Blinder. 2015. *Who Counts as a Migrant? Definitions and their Consequences*, 4th Revision. http://www.migrationobservatory.ox.ac.uk/wp-content/uploads/2016/04/Briefing-Who_Counts_as_a_Migrant.pdf

Andresen, Maike, Franziska Bergdolt, Jil Margenfeld, and Michael Dickmann. 2014. Addressing International Mobility Confusion—Developing Definitions and Differentiations for Self-Initiated and Assigned Expatriates as Well as Migrants. *International Journal of Human Resource Management* 25 (16): 2295–2318. https://doi.org/10.1080/09585192.2013.877058.

Arp, Frithjof, Katherine Hutchings, and Wendy A. Smith. 2013. Foreign Executives in Local Organisations: An Exploration of Differences to Other Types of Expatriates. *Journal of Global Mobility: The Home of Expatriate Management Research* 1 (3): 312–335. https://doi.org/10.1108/JGM-01-2013-0006.

Asendorpf, Jens B., and Franz J. Neyer. 2012. *Psychologie der Persönlichkeit*. 5th ed. Heidelberg: Springer.

Bailey, Kenneth D. 1994. *Typologies and Taxonomies: An Introduction to Classification Techniques*. Thousand Oaks, CA: Sage.

Banai, Moshe, and Wes Harry. 2004. Boundaryless Global Careers: The International Itinerants. *International Studies of Management and Organization* 34 (3): 96–120.

Bartlett, Christopher A., and Sumantra Ghoshal. 2002. *Managing Across Borders: The Transnational Solution*. Boston: Harvard Business Press.

Baruch, Yehuda, Michael Dickmann, Yochanan Altman, and Frank Bournois. 2013. Exploring International Work: Types and Dimensions of Global Careers. *The International Journal of Human Resource Management* 24 (12): 2369–2393. https://doi.org/10.1080/09585192.2013.781435.

Black, J. Stewart, and Gregory K. Stephens. 1989. The Influence of the Spouse on American Expatriate Adjustment and Intent to Stay in Pacific Rim Overseas Assignments. *Journal of Management* 15 (4): 529–544.

Brewster, Chris, Michael Dickmann, Liisa Mäkelä, and Vesa Suutari. 2017. Managing Global and Migrant Workers. In *Human Resource Management: A Global and Critical Perspective*, ed. Robin Kramar and Jawad Syed, 2nd ed., 359–378. London: Palgrave Macmillan.

Briscoe, Dennis, Randal Schuler, and Lisbeth Claus. 2009. *International Human Resource Management*. 3rd ed. London: Routledge.

Caligiuri, Paula. 2013. *Cultural Agility: Building a Pipeline of Successful Global Professionals*. San Francisco: John Wiley & Sons.

Cerdin, Jean-Luc, and Jan Selmer. 2014. Who is a Self-Initiated Expatriate? Towards Conceptual Clarity of a Common Notion. *International Journal of Human Resource Management* 25 (9): 1281–1301.

Chaloff, Jonathan, and Georges Lemaître. 2009. Managing Highly-Skilled Labour Migration: A Comparative Analysis of Migration Policies and Challenges in OECD Countries. *OECD Social, Employment and Migration Working Papers*, No. 79. Paris: OECD Publishing. https://doi.org/10.1787/225505346577

Conway, Neil, and Rob B. Briner. 2005. *Understanding Psychological Contracts at Work: A Critical Evaluation of Theory and Research.* Oxford: Oxford University Press.

Cox, John L. 1988. The Overseas Student: Expatriate, Sojourner or Settler? *Acta Psychiatrica Scandinavica* 78 (S344): 179–184. https://doi.org/10.1111/j.1600-0447.1988.tb09019.x.

Dickmann, Michael. 2012. Why Do They Come to London? Exploring the Motivations of Expatriates to Work in the British Capital. *Journal of Management Development* 31 (8): 783–800. https://doi.org/10.1108/02621711211253240.

Dickmann, Michael, and Yehuda Baruch. 2011. *Global Careers.* London: Routledge.

Dickmann, Michael, and Michael Müller-Camen. 2006. A Typology of International Human Resource Management Strategies and Processes. *International Journal of Human Resource Management* 17 (4): 580–601. https://doi.org/10.1080/09585190600581337.

Dickmann, Michael, and Vicki Marsh. 2017. Data Mastery: A Key Global Mobility Challenge. HR Zone. Accessed November 23, 2017.

Dickmann, Michael, Vesa Suutari, Chris Brewster, Liisa Mäkelä, Jussi Tanskanen, and Christelle Tornikoski. 2016. The Career Competencies of Self-Initiated and Assigned Expatriates: Assessing the Development of Career Capital Over Time. *The International Journal of Human Resource Management*: 1–25. https://doi.org/10.1080/09585192.2016.1172657.

Doherty, Noeleen, Michael Dickmann, and Timothy Mills. 2011. Exploring the Motives of Company-Backed and Self-Initiated Expatriates. *The International Journal of Human Resource Management* 22 (3): 595–611. https://doi.org/10.1080/09585192.2011.543637.

Doty, D. Harold, and William H. Glick. 1994. Typologies as a Unique Form of Theory Building: Toward Improved Understanding and Modeling. *Academy of Management Review* 19 (2): 230–251. https://doi.org/10.5465/AMR.1994.9410210748.

Dowling, Peter J., Marion Festing, and Allen Engle. 2013. *International Human Resource Management*. 6th ed. London: Cengage Learning.

Edström, Anders, and Jay R. Galbraith. 1977. Transfer of Managers as a Coordination and Control Strategy in Multinational Organizations. *Administrative Science Quarterly* 22 (2): 248–263.

Fee, Anthony, and Sidney J. Gray. 2011. Fast-Tracking Expatriate Development: The Unique Learning Environments of International Volunteer Placements. *The International Journal of Human Resource Management* 22 (3): 530–552. https://doi.org/10.1080/09585192.2011.543631.

Ferner, Anthony, Phil Almond, Ian Clark, Trevor Colling, Tony Edwards, Len Holden, and Michael Muller-Camen. 2004. Dynamics of Central Control and Subsidiary Autonomy in the Management of Human Resources: Case-Study Evidence from US MNCs in the UK. *Organization Studies* 25 (3): 363–391.

Harris, Hilary, and Chris Brewster. 1999. The Coffee-Machine System: How International Selection Really Works. *International Journal of Human Resource Management* 10 (3): 488–500. https://doi.org/10.1080/095851999340440.

Harvey, Michael G. 1995. The Impact of Dual-Career Families on International Relocations. *Human Resource Management Review* 5 (3): 223–244. https://doi.org/10.1016/1053-4822(95)90003-9.

Haslberger, Arno, Chris Brewster, and Thomas Hippler. 2013. The Dimensions of Expatriate Adjustment. *Human Resource Management* 52 (3): 333–351. https://doi.org/10.1002/hrm.21531.

Heckhausen, Heinz. 2012. *Motivation and Action*. Hamburg: Springer Science & Business Media.

Hippler, Thomas. 2009. Why Do They Go? Empirical Evidence of Employees' Motives for Seeking or Accepting Relocation. *The International Journal of Human Resource Management* 20 (6): 1381–1401. https://doi.org/10.1080/09585190902909889.

Massey, Douglas S., and Katherine Bartley. 2006. The Changing Legal Status Distribution of Immigrants: A Caution. *International Migration Review* 39 (2): 469–484. https://doi.org/10.1111/j.1747-7379.2005.tb00274.x.

Mayerhofer, Helene, Angelika Schmidt, Linley Hartmann, and Regine Bendl. 2011. Recognising Diversity in Managing Work Life Issues of Flexpatriates. *Equality, Diversity and Inclusion: An International Journal* 30 (7): 589–609. https://doi.org/10.1108/02610151111167043.

McNulty, Yvonne, and Chris Brewster. 2016. Theorizing the Meaning(s) of 'Expatriate': Establishing Boundary Conditions for Business Expatriates. *International Journal of Human Resource Management* 28 (1): 27–61. https://doi.org/10.1080/09585192.2016.1243567.

McPhail, Ruth, Ron Fisher, Michael Harvey, and Miriam Moeller. 2012. Staffing the Global Organization: "Cultural Nomads". *Human Resource Development Quarterly* 23 (2): 259–276. https://doi.org/10.1002/hrdq.21133.

Otto, Kathleen, and Claudia Dalbert. 2010. New Challenges for Human Resource Management: Readiness to Perform a Mobile Job and Its Antecedents. *International Journal of Human Resource Management* 21 (4): 600–614. https://doi.org/10.1080/09585191003612109.

Peltokorpi, Vesa, and Fabian J. Froese. 2009. Organizational Expatriates and Self-Initiated Expatriates: Who Adjusts Better to Work and Life in Japan? *The International Journal of Human Resource Management* 20 (5): 1096–1112. https://doi.org/10.1080/09585190902850299.

RES Forum. 2015. *The RES Forum Annual Report: Global Mobility and the Global Talent Management Conundrum*, Report authored by M. Dickmann. RES Forum, UniGroup Relocation Network and Equus Software, 108 pages, London.

———. 2016. *The RES Forum Annual Report 2016: Beyond Uniformity—A World of Opportunity*, Report authored by M. Dickmann. The RES Forum, Harmony Relocation Network and Equus Software, 116 pages, London.

———. 2017. *The RES Forum Annual Report 2017: The New Normal of Global Mobility—Flexibility, Diversity & Data Mastery*, Report authored by M. Dickmann. The RES Forum, Harmony Relocation Network and Equus Software, 120 pages, London.

Selmer, Jan, Maike Andresen, and Jean-Luc Cerdin. 2017. Self-Initiated Expatriates. In *Research Handbook of Expatriates*, ed. Yvonne McNulty and Jan Selmer, 187–201. Cheltenham, UK: Edward Elgar.

Stilwell, Barbara, Khassoum Diallo, Pascal Zurn, Marko Vujicic, Orvill Adams, and Mario Dal Poz. 2004. Migration of Health-Care Workers from Developing Countries: Strategic Approaches to its Management. *Bulletin of the World health Organization* 82 (8): 595–600.

Suutari, Vesa, Chris Brewster, Liisa Mäkelä, Michael Dickmann, and Christelle Tornikoski. 2017. The Effect of International Work Experience on the Career Success of Expatriates: A Comparison of Assigned and Self-Initiated Expatriates. *Human Resource Management*. https://doi.org/10.1002/hrm.21827.

Tharenou, Phyllis. 2015. Researching Expatriate Types: The Quest for Rigorous Methodological Approaches. *Human Resource Management Journal* 25 (2): 149–165.

Thorn, Kaye. 2009. The Relative Importance of Motives for International Self-Initiated Mobility. *Career Development International* 14 (5): 441–464. https://doi.org/10.1108/13620430910989843.

Tung, Rosalie L., and Mila Lazarova. 2006. Brain Drain Versus Brain Gain: An Exploratory Study of Ex-Host Country Nationals in Central and East Europe. *International Journal of Human Resource Management* 17 (11): 1853–1872. https://doi.org/10.1080/09585190600999992.

Vance, Charles M. 2005. The Personal Quest for Building Global Competence: A Taxonomy of Self-Initiating Career Path Strategies for Gaining Business Experience Abroad. *Journal of World Business* 40 (4): 374–385.

Wiles, Janine. 2008. Sense of Home in a Transnational Social Space: New Zealanders in London. *Global Networks* 8 (1): 116–137. https://doi.org/10.1111/j.1471-0374.2008.00188.x.

3

Contrasting Assigned Expatriates and Self-Initiated Expatriates: A Review of Extant Research and a Future Research Agenda

Vesa Suutari, Chris Brewster, and Michael Dickmann

Introduction

Expatriation in Historical Perspective

The history of a concept has important implications for the way that knowledge is constructed and the assumptions that develop. Academic fields are built on the foundations of the strengths (and weaknesses) of the early pioneers, and the trajectory of the field develops from those

---

V. Suutari (✉)
School of Management, University of Vaasa, Vaasa, Finland
e-mail: vsu@uva.fi

C. Brewster
Henley Business School, University of Reading, Reading, UK
e-mail: c.j.brewster@henley.ac.uk

M. Dickmann
Cranfield School of Management, Cranfield University, Cranfield, UK
e-mail: m.dickmann@cranfield.ac.uk

© The Author(s) 2018
M. Dickmann et al. (eds.), *The Management of Global Careers*,
https://doi.org/10.1007/978-3-319-76529-7_3

insights and those flaws, even if eventually it goes well beyond them. To advance we need, first, to acknowledge the base upon which our current understandings and knowledge have been built, then to fix any problems inherent in that base.

People have always moved around the Earth, and expatriation (from the Latin *ex-patria*: out of country) has existed from the time when there were countries or other unified administered areas (such as city states, feudal regions) for people to expatriate from. Some of these journeys were to nearby territories, but some involved journeys that, given the difficulties of travel in those days, can seem almost incredible: empires sent emissaries to far-flung lands, and religious history is full of stories of missionaries sent by the church to achieve their objectives amongst 'strangers' (Oberholster and Doss 2017; Walker et al. 1985). The Silk Road (or in fact roads) from China through many different countries to the edge of Europe dates back almost two millennia (Boulnois 2004). The giant East India companies set up in the Netherlands and Britain to trade with the Far East were established well over 400 years ago (Stening 1994).

During these times, national boundaries were rather fungible. The formal introduction of passports as a requirement to cross borders was established during and after the First World War (Marrus 1985). The term 'expatriate' was first used in the seventeenth century, and since then, it has had a very broad definition. An 'expatriate' is someone living outside their native country (Oxford Dictionary of English 2015) or someone who has been sent or exiled abroad (Collins Dictionaries 2011). According to Green (2009: 308) it is a contradictory concept whereby 'The meaning of expatriation … varies depending on who is initiating the act, the state or the individual, and whether or not it is voluntary. The state banishes; the subject can choose to depart'.

For much of the last century, 'expatriate' was typically used to describe Westerners who lived abroad for varying lengths of time (Cleveland et al. 1960; Copeland and Griggs 1985), including artists, writers, musicians, colonial administrators and those with some kind of mission such as teachers, NGO workers, students, interns or volunteers: it was mainly used as a synonym for what are now commonly referred to as 'migrants'.

If they were in employment, they received standard rates with little uplift for living abroad other than adjustments so that they were no worse off than if they had stayed at home (diplomats, United Nations workers, etc.), or they received local terms and conditions (Bickers 2010; Cohen 1977; Earnest 1968). Recent attempts have been made to reintroduce this wider definition into the management literature (Al Ariss and Syed 2011; Andresen et al. 2014; Dumont and Lemaitre 2005). Using this approach it has been suggested that the number of expatriates is high, perhaps over 200 million (Clarke et al. 2017).

The business literature began to recognize the importance of internationalization during the last century (Coase 1937; Dunning 1958; Kolde and Hill 1967). Between 1970 and 2005, the number of multinational corporations (MNCs) grew from 7000 to 70,000, with the same rate of growth expected to continue for the next 30 years (Salt 2008). Almost inevitably, the literature gradually began to focus on people being moved abroad for (private, public or third sector) business reasons.

It was in the 1950s before the early academic research into business expatriates began. As studies investigated American companies expanding abroad, there developed an associated literature exploring the challenges related to managing 'overseas executives' (Howell and Newman 1959; Wallace 1959). Around the 1960s the first studies examined these executives' intercultural experiences (Lysgaard 1955; Oberg 1960), relevant success factors (Kiernan 1963), issues associated with how they transferred knowledge (Negandhi and Estafen 1965), their careers (Gonzalez 1967) and how they were selected (Borrmann 1968; Triandis 1963) and compensated (Schollhammer 1969). There were also studies of expatriates in non-corporate settings, such as aid organizations (Taylor 1968), the Peace Corps (Hapgood 1968) and the military (Campbell 1969).

The following decade saw articles examining why companies used expatriates (Baker and Ivancevich 1971), their satisfaction (Ivancevich and Baker 1970) and their communities (Cohen 1977) and further work on their selection (Miller 1973) and their compensation (Foote 1977; Reynolds 1972). There were the first studies of the expatriates themselves—their success and failure characteristics (Baker and Ivancevich 1971; Lanier 1979; Miller 1972), their repatriation concerns (Gama and

Pedersen 1977; Heenan 1970; Murray 1973) and assignment outcomes (Miller 1975; Misa and Fabricatore 1979). Other work looked at their training needs (Jones 1975) and at their decision-making criteria when undertaking an international assignment (Mincer 1978). There was the first article examining gender roles (Adler 1979). Interest spread. There were articles reporting research into Japanese multinational enterprises or MNEs (Peterson and Schwind 1977; Yoshino 1976).

Expatriate researchers in the 1980s and 1990s followed these early beginnings, reporting on both the human resource management policies MNEs used in relation to their expatriates (Mendenhall et al. 1987; Peterson et al. 1996) and on the expatriates themselves (Black and Gregersen 1991; Feldman and Thomas 1992; Torbiorn 1982; Tung 1988).

All of these early papers took their data from the MNEs themselves and largely 'subcontracted' construct definition to the employers—if they were included under that heading in the employers' databases, then they were assigned expatriates (AEs). The weaknesses of this approach became clear when Suutari and Brewster (2000), using comprehensive database not drawn from employers, identified different types of expatriates going abroad on their own initiative in different stages of their career and introduced the term self-initiated foreign expatriates (SIEs). The study thus expanded the work by Inkson et al. (1997) who analyzed the experiences of 'young people heading overseas for a prolonged period of travel, work and tourism' to get overseas experience (called OE) which was a common phenomenon in New Zealand and Australia. Since then there has been a plethora of studies examining SIEs and a burst of activity attempting to identify 'new' categories of expatriate, often through the mechanism of renaming existing categories (McNulty and Brewster 2016). This creates a lack of construct clarity and a lack of construct validity, and these are important if we are to advance understanding. Here, therefore, we adopt the definition of expatriates as: 'legally working individuals who reside temporarily in a country of which they are not a citizen in order to accomplish a career-related goal, being relocated abroad either by an organization, by self-initiation or directly employed within the host-country' (McNulty and Brewster 2016).

It can be seen that we are linking our definition of expatriates to employment—if they are not working, then these people are not subject to any form of international human resource management or careers and hence are outside our scope. Within this overall definition, we separate out AEs, defined as those who meet the preceding definition but are sent to their new country by their employing organization—including those loaned to another employer by their own organization such as football players or experts going to regulatory bodies, usually with enhanced terms and conditions and the possibility of returning to their home country in a position with the same organization on completion of the assignment. In turn, SIEs, defined as those who secured their employment in a new country through their own initiative, are generally on standard or local employment conditions.

To explore these issues, we adopt the following format for this chapter. We first discuss the motives of both AEs and SIEs for international work. Second, the nature of careers and jobs of AEs and SIEs are analyzed. Third, we discuss the outcomes of expatriation for different types of expatriates. After that we will explore the management of such expatriates. Finally, we will draw some conclusions and discuss future research needs.

Motives for International Work Among AEs and SIEs

Even in early expatriate studies that were focused on AEs (Miller and Cheng 1978), it was reported that personal interest related to internationalism played an important role alongside financial benefits in the motives for moving abroad. Later studies identified the search for new challenges, possibilities for development and career progress as other important factors (Stahl et al. 2002; Bossard and Peterson 2005). Hippler (2009) concludes that four motives appear most consistently in the literature and in his own research: career prospects, development of job-related skills, financial benefits and internationalism. In a study of why AEs and SIEs move to London, Dickmann (2013) found six key categories that impact on the decision to work abroad. The key influences on the decision to go were career and development considerations, individual interests and drivers such as a desire for adventure, concerns about family and friends, the assessment of monetary and non-monetary organizational incentives, host country context (including nature, history, climate and security) and specific location considerations taking account of host in-country variations.

When discussing the motives of SIEs, it is important to note that SIEs form a very diverse group and thus motives vary (Suutari and Brewster 2000). There have been some studies among students and young graduates with the findings indicating that the major reasons for taking international jobs were excitement, cross-cultural experiences, growth, meeting new and different people and also future career prospects (Tharenou 2003). Early international experiences through education increase the likelihood of seeking a job in the same location afterwards (Baruch et al. 2007). Whilst companies rarely send inexperienced employees as AEs to international assignments, young people seem keen to go abroad on their own initiative as SIEs. Due to their early career stage, young people are also more commonly motivated by simply finding a job, especially when the home country job markets may offer fewer possibilities (Suutari and Brewster 2000). They also reported professional development and career progress as more important motives than SIEs in general.

There have also been studies of the motives of SIEs working in specific sectors. For example, the internationalization of higher education has led to increasing interest amongst academic SIEs (Richardson and Mallon 2005; Selmer and Lauring 2010). These academics have been found to have three dominant motivations: adventure/travel, life change and family, although financial reasons were significant in a number of cases (Richardson and Mallon 2005). SIEs also often find work in the not-for-profit sector, where motivation is often values-based (Doherty et al. 2011) and includes dedication to a cause (Cerdin and Le Pargneux 2010). The motives of SIEs working within international organizations such as the European Union and the United Nations have been found to differ to some extent from the average SIEs since they regard economic benefits, personal interest towards internationalization and new experiences as slightly more important motives (Suutari and Brewster 2000; Dickmann and Cerdin 2016). Sometimes the motive of the SIEs is directly linked to their family situation through a dual career situation, that is, SIEs have gone abroad due to the assignment of their spouse and then found a job for themselves in order to continue their own career. This is much easier in regions such as the European Union, where work permits are not necessary for member states citizens and active policies exist to encourage mobility (Doherty et al. 2010).

Oberholster et al. (2013) have analyzed the expatriate motivation in religious and humanitarian non-profit organizations and found that altruism (consisting of opportunities to make a difference, a sense of calling to help others and the meaningfulness of the assignment) is the most important underlying reason for accepting work abroad. This was followed by an interest in international experiences and family reasons. According to Fee and Karsaklian (2013), international voluntary workers are increasingly also motivated by more self-directed and pragmatic outcomes such as adventure and excitement or professional and personal development.

Overall, whilst the motives for international work are quite similar among AEs and SIEs, the different groups stress different aspects. For example, Doherty et al. (2011) found that career factors were seen as important by both AEs and SIEs, while location and the host country reputation were particularly important for SIEs. Lifestyle is a very important career anchor for both AEs and SIEs but is more important for SIEs (Cerdin and Le Pargneux 2010; Doherty et al. 2011). Overall, family-related concerns play a central role among SIEs who have less company-related motives to take into account in their decision-making (Richardson 2006). At the same time, SIEs are likely to be less strongly motivated by the job than AEs though it is important for both groups (Cerdin 2013). However, this finding does not apply to the humanitarian expatriates. Further, push factors such as a desire to escape the economic environment of their home country or to escape personal problems emerge more commonly among SIEs than AEs.

The Nature of Careers and Jobs of AEs and SIEs

Though both AEs and SIEs have international careers, the logic of such careers is to some extent different. As SIEs search for their job abroad on their own, their assignment implies normally a movement between different organizations simultaneously with the move across national borders. AEs, by definition, move within the boundaries of one organization. Consequently, AEs regard their assignment as part of their organizational career, while SIEs tend to follow an individualized career path (Andresen et al. 2013). AEs are thus mostly supported in their career moves by HRM professionals and the international assignment policies of the MNCs. SIEs not only look for their job on their own but also handle all the transfer complications themselves. Here again, the type of SIE matters—those going to work for international organizations will have support from the EU or the UN or whichever body they have got a job with. Other SIEs and often trailing partners find a job after their arrival in a new country (Peltokorpi 2008), although they often also search for jobs abroad before they depart their home country. They may start with locations they find attractive or where they are familiar with the language or culture or that are closer to their home country and thus easier to move into than more distant and difficult locations (Suutari and Brewster 2000). The number of AEs in turn is frequently reduced within MNCs in more developed societies and often also with the more established business operations of MNCs in these countries, while new operations in more undeveloped locations or organizational business units require more extensive use of expatriates.

On average, SIEs often work in lower hierarchical positions in organizations (Jokinen et al. 2008; Doherty et al. 2011) and so may have less challenging tasks than AEs (Suutari and Brewster 2000). However, the variation in the jobs held by SIEs is wide due to the diversity of the SIE group. Because of a lack of social connections in the new country, job seeking may not be an easy task for self-initiated expatriates, and thus SIEs are exposed to potential underemployment which may influence their motivation and career (Lee 2005). It is also more common among AEs to work for big international MNCs than among SIEs (Jokinen et al. 2008).

It would seem that there are more women in the SIE category than in the AE category and that often they are younger than the typical AEs so less likely to move with their family (Doherty et al. 2011). When companies send their employees abroad, they are usually professionally more experienced, whilst among SIEs there are different kinds of people from very early career stages up to senior international professionals who have had long-term international careers within many organizations (Suutari and Brewster 2000).

SIEs tend to have longer international careers than AEs and have a greater interest in considering more permanent global careers (Suutari and Brewster 2000; Doherty et al. 2011). While MNCs typically limit the maximum lengths of international assignments (e.g. to three or five years after which the expatriate is encouraged to leave that country), SIEs often have no such time limitations in their local contracts. Due to their international orientation and sometimes also to limited possibilities after the assignment, the proportion of SIEs who have already worked abroad earlier tends to be higher than that of AEs (Jokinen et al. 2008). Similarly, in a longer-term follow-up study by Suutari et al. (2018), it appeared that a significantly higher proportion of AEs than SIEs had repatriated back to their home country.

Repatriation agreements sometimes guarantee at least a similar level of job after the repatriation as before the assignment and AEs typically repatriate back to their home country in a similar or higher position within the same company. SIEs left their employer when moving abroad and thus usually have to find a new job in a new employer organization on return. It is therefore not surprising that SIEs, overall, intend to change organizations more than AEs (Biemann and Andresen 2010). In that sense, in general, the careers of SIEs are more independent of organizational borders than those of AEs, although the evidence is that they do not fit easily into the predicted 'boundaryless' or 'protean' career mindsets (Suutari et al. 2016). If their jobs after the repatriation are not satisfying and the overall treatment of repatriation is not managed well, AEs too tend to start thinking about career options in external job markets. However, while there is evidence that the repatriate retention of AEs is lower than for their non-expatriated peers during the first year after return, the cumulative long-term retention effects seem to be similar (Doherty and Dickmann 2012).

What Are the Outcomes of Expatriation for Different Types of Expatriates?

One important question concerning expatriation in its different forms relates to the impacts of assignments on the individuals both in the short and longer term. This discussion links naturally with the previous discussion of the motives individuals have for moving abroad. It also raises organizational issues, that is, what are the benefits of expatriation for the organizations in the longer run?

One of the main motives for expatriation was personal development and growth through facing new challenges. From this angle, the outcome appears to be positive. Various expatriate studies report extensive development taking place during assignments. This applies both to assigned and self-initiated expatriates (Dickmann et al. in press; Jokinen et al. 2008; Kraimer et al. 2009; McNulty 2013). The differences in starting point between assignees may impact to some extent on the development of AEs in comparison to SIEs. For example, given the stronger career and work-related motivation of AEs and their, on average, higher status and position, it is likely that AEs gain more organizational and business knowledge through their foreign work (Shaffer et al. 2012). Because of their social connections within the MNC, AEs are also seen to be more likely to build better business contacts both at the head office and at their local operating unit (Farh et al. 2010). In line with this reasoning, Dickmann et al. (in press) report that AEs developed more organizational knowledge and knowing whom career capital (i.e. relationships that can be beneficial to one's work and career) whilst working abroad than SIEs did. However, in most areas, the extent of development was similar among both types of expatriates, indicating that all kinds of expatriates developed themselves while working abroad. Of course, all expatriates get international experience and develop related international competences. The level to which they are able to utilize such competences depends on their future careers, which we discuss next.

From the perspective of career progress, the findings are quite mixed and the literature often suggests that the career impacts of international work are not as positive as AEs expect (Shaffer et al. 2012). It is quite common for AEs to leave their employer soon after repatriation (Kraimer

Contrasting Assigned Expatriates and Self-Initiated Expatriates...   73

et al. 2012). However, some studies on career progression at high hierarchical levels indicate that international work experience has a positive impact on career success (Ng et al. 2005; Magnusson and Boggs 2006). Hamori and Koyuncu (2011) found that while the path to the top of the corporate ladder in large organizations may not be faster for executives who had international work experience, larger organizations often had former expatriates as CEOs. More research is needed to refine our picture of the career success of SIE and AE executives.

It is also important to note that as SIEs tend to stay abroad longer, their social connections in the home country easily become weaker (Mäkelä and Suutari 2013). This is often true in particular with regard to their organizational contacts, since as self-initiated expatriates they left their employer when moving abroad while most AEs still have connections back to their home country colleagues and the headquarters of the company (Dickmann and Doherty 2010). On the other hand, it has also been reported that SIEs' international work experience increases both their chances of promotion with their current employer and their marketability in the external market (Richardson and Mallon 2005). SIEs also tend to build stronger connections with locals, and such connections may be used when seeking new jobs abroad. The latest evidence indicates that, among matched samples of highly educated business professionals, the career impacts of international assignments were found to be similar among SIEs and AEs (Suutari et al. 2018). The only significant difference was that AEs got more jobs offers (and more often those were internal) than SIEs, presumably as a consequence of their better networks within the organization that sent them abroad.

Over a longer term both AEs and SIEs saw their international marketability as having increased and being higher than their home country marketability, particularly so for SIE (Suutari et al. 2018). If we combine this observation with the fact that high numbers of expatriates are interested in future international jobs, it is not surprising that a high proportion of both AEs and SIEs experience multiple foreign assignments (Stahl and Cerdin 2004; Jokinen et al. 2008).

The financial impact of international assignments is naturally closely connected with the level of the position which the expatriate holds both abroad and after repatriation. Since AEs often work in more senior organizational roles abroad and receive more generous assignment packages that raise their standard of living compared to SIEs who usually have local contracts with fewer benefits (Dickmann 2016), the salary impacts differ between the groups. Positive salary impacts are found in some studies of AEs (Daily et al. 2000; Carpenter et al. 2001; Ramaswarmi et al. 2016), but there is less information about SIEs. Clearly more evidence is needed both on the career progress and salary impacts of international experience.

If we analyze the impacts of international assignments from the organizational perspective, then several observations can be made. First the overall development of expatriates abroad and their new international experience provide organizations with important talent that should be included in their talent management programmes (Cerdin and Brewster 2014). There is an indication that global mobility professionals are aware of this and that some work actively to increase linkages of global mobility and talent management within organizations (Dickmann 2015). International assignments are recognized as being among the best possible management development methods. In turn, the observation that many repatriates are unhappy with their treatment after the assignment and thus leave the organization or at least seriously consider doing so is bad news. This raises the question of how SIEs and AEs are (and should be) managed by their employers.

Management of International Assignees: AEs vs SIEs

There is far more evidence on how AEs are being managed compared to SIEs (Doherty and Dickmann 2013). Summaries of recommendations of how AEs are or should be managed, often linked to the expatriate cycle (Harris et al. 2003), can be found in diverse publications (Dickmann 2017; Dickmann and Baruch 2011). Based on the discussion above, we are looking at the individual, organizational or wider contextual differences between the two types of international workers to explore the implications for the management of SIEs.

Targeting the Recruitment and Selection of SIEs

It is clear that due to their home country insights and language skills, SIEs and AEs can be highly attractive employees for organizations that can utilize them in jobs where these capabilities are useful. Since SIEs are more holistically oriented, putting less emphasis on career progression and professional development and more on individual factors such as adventure seeking or personal challenge (Cerdin 2013; Doherty et al. 2011) means that employer branding and attraction strategies could stress different messages when aiming either at an (internal) audience of AEs or an external audience of SIEs or staff who may go on an international assignment in the future. Job aspects that show diverse situations or challenges could be emphasized by corporations. However, the scant evidence available shows that major German and French companies often do not mention global career opportunities on their websites (Point and Dickmann 2012). In addition, SIEs are often seen to be highly educated and be more likely to be women compared to AEs. Given that SIEs are financing and organizing their stay abroad themselves, it is argued that they are more interested in lower cost moves to secure environments (Andresen et al. 2013; Dickmann and Cerdin 2016), with some exceptions in the not-for-profit sector. SIEs tend to have established a local network before they go abroad which may be used by organizations to attract foreign candidates to work for them. Overall, it is not only the attraction mechanisms but also the selection and job matching criteria that could factor in the different background, drivers and behaviours of SIEs.

Rethinking the Package Design of SIEs

The difference of monetary incentives and administrative support of AEs in comparison to SIEs is stark. First, AEs tend to earn substantially more than their peers on 'normal', local contracts. While contracts vary substantially, observers have consistently pointed out hefty expatriation premiums (Doherty and Dickmann 2012; Dowling et al. 2013; Oltram et al. 2013). Some research points to a large variety of additional payments and support, including housing allowances, hardship payments, home leave flights and extra vacation days, family educational support and so on (Dowling et al. 2013). Even the 'local plus' contracts, where AEs who want to stay in their host country sign on to a local contract, have certain perks included, most likely paid private schooling for expatriates' children (Dickmann 2016). In turn, most SIEs sign a standard local contract, and thus their contract does not include such extra benefits. Given the potentially highly useful SIE competencies—beyond language capabilities they have an in-depth understanding of their home culture, institutions, legal frameworks and have country-of-origin social networks—employers may consider giving them extra incentives to stay in the organization or to refresh their contacts and insights. This could include sponsored home trips or considerations to compensate some of the social security differences from which SIEs may suffer. This could increase the engagement levels of SIEs. Alternatively, companies could develop a more flexible system of where people live and work.

Strengthening the Current Cross-Cultural Training and Adjustment Support for SIEs

While even AEs often do not get much predeparture training (Harris et al. 2003; Doherty and Dickmann 2012) and little cross-cultural adjustment support, SIEs are highly unlikely to get in-country cultural training (Haslberger and Vaiman 2013). While some of the drivers of SIEs are closely connected to learning about and exploring their host country, and due to the fact that they seem to have a larger non-company host social network, it might be concluded that less adjustment support is needed for SIEs than AEs. Also, SIEs stay longer in the host country (Mäkelä and Suutari 2013) and have more time to adjust. Nevertheless, offering some cultural training and local mentor/coaching networks may help SIEs especially during their initial time in country. Cultural understanding, especially the cognitive and behavioural components of adjustment (Haslberger et al. 2013), may be supported through such initiatives.

Tailoring HR Policies and Practices to Distinguish Between AEs and SIEs

There are many HRM activities that affect AEs and SIEs. In relation to training and development, SIEs tend to be new to the organization and are likely to benefit more than AEs from host organization induction sessions and support for international in-company networking. In addition, SIEs are more likely to be female, so activities that support women in management (and other areas of activities) such as the work associated with the Female FTSE 100 (Vinnicombe et al. 2015) may have positive effects. In addition, we have seen that SIEs are more often on lower hierarchical levels which have an impact on the types of capabilities associated with in-job success. Sensitive and responsive training and development offers enhance the chances of increased performance. Given that SIEs are highly self-driven individuals and are, on average, guided by a set of more holistic drivers—including a higher interest to interact with locals and to experience wide facets of the host environment—there are implications for work content, job assignments and for how to manage SIEs (Doherty and Dickmann 2012, 2013). Interaction with host country nationals and local content of work that leads to learning are likely to be highly valued by SIEs.

Developing Organizational Repatriation Approaches for SIEs

SIEs are a population of workers who have a range of cross-cultural insights and skills by the time they return home. A stream of research has shown that they, like AEs, have benefitted tremendously from their international sojourn in terms of enduring career capital development and high external marketability (Suutari et al. 2018; Dickmann et al. in press). It seems likely that MNCs would be well advised to work towards retaining SIEs who want to leave their host country, provided that the organization has sizeable operations in the country that they are moving to. One of the ways this could be achieved is simply to support their move financially. However, the issue is actually much broader. If organizations started to treat SIEs (once they are their employees) similar to AEs in terms of tailored career support and position finding, then they are much more likely to find vacancies and home country opportunities. In addition, they may provide some of the reintegration support that may be needed even more by SIEs who, on average, stay much longer abroad. Overall, this would increase the chances of SIEs staying with their organization and in some sense becoming AEs on their way home. While this clearly happens informally in some cases, large MNCs may be well advised to develop more equitable policy approaches.

This section has argued that SIEs have the potential to be highly valuable to organizations at a price, that is, their package while working abroad, which is substantially lower than that of AEs (Dowling et al. 2013). We have suggested, to start with, the differences that distinguish SIEs from AEs to develop HRM policies and practices in terms of recruitment and selection, training and development, career and performance management as well as repatriation approaches that are sensitive to their unique backgrounds, interests and demographics, in order to attract, develop, utilize and retain SIEs better.

Conclusions and Recommendations for Future Work

In this chapter we have systematically contrasted the similarities and differences in the motivations to work abroad, the nature of careers and jobs, outcomes of working abroad and the management of AEs and SIEs. After approximately half a century of expatriate research, there is already much known in relation to 'traditional expatriation', even though the field is prone to changes and authors are finding new perspectives and new sub-groups. Systematic exploration of the SIE phenomenon, initiated more than one and a half decades ago, while beyond its infancy, still harbours many opportunities for exciting insights.

Amongst these opportunities are the fields that this chapter has chartered. For instance, with respect to the drivers of international work, we have yet to explore why and how motivations change over time. Of course, there are many angles that could be investigated within the motivational arena such as the impact of life and career stages on individuals, gender and other diversity patterns, host country characteristics and so on. Within the psychological and sociological perspectives, broad well-being issues may be investigated. For instance, SIEs have to cope with a lot of insecurity and uncertainty (Richardson 2006). Understanding their coping strategies and the effect of SIE work on well-being would be important. In addition, the findings on underemployment of SIEs and migrants may be further explored, and links to job satisfaction, attachment to their host country and employer, intention to return or even happiness may be investigated.

The second large section of this chapter looked at the careers and jobs of international workers. There is some work using the intelligent career framework (DeFillippi and Arthur 1994). The intelligent career is a modern career concept that explores three ways of knowing. Knowing how are the skills, knowledge and abilities that help individuals in their careers. Knowing whom is the reputation of individuals in the minds of others and their social contacts and networks that can further their careers. Knowing why consists of the motivations and drivers of individuals that give them energy to pursue a career journey and to succeed in the world of work. Individual careerists are advised to invest in these three ways of knowing (Inkson and Arthur 2001). With reference to global careers, some emerging long-term studies show positive impacts for both AEs and SIEs (Suutari et al. 2018; Dickmann et al. in press). Going beyond quantitative studies, tracing the development, transfer and utilization of career capital in different contexts and understanding the various influencing factors in depth (for instance, through qualitative studies), over time, is still underexplored.

Our third section looked at outcomes of global work. Especially in relation to SIEs, the picture is still highly fragmented and partial. Often, SIEs have been treated predominantly as a 'homogenous entity'. Understanding the impact of differences—educational, age, gender, nationality, hierarchical—would be highly important to be able to improve the exploration of influences on outcomes and sub-group patterns.

The fourth section of this chapter discussed the management of global workers. While we have some insights (albeit not perfect) in relation to AEs, the evidence of how SIEs are managed is sparse. Many of the suggestions we developed on how to manage SIEs better are logical inferences, and high-quality investigations are needed. These could, for instance, take an action research approach in which researchers cooperate with MNCs to put tailored SIE approaches in relation to their sourcing, management, development, careers and retention into practice. In addition, better information regarding the monetary and non-monetary packages of SIEs over time would be highly welcome. Moreover, the organizational context—industry, size of firm, host team, hierarchy of job, transnationality and so on—will be important to factor into the research to better understand links.

Above, we have argued that an in-depth understanding of differences in SIE (and AE) sub-groups would be highly beneficial (Dorsch et al. 2013). The nearer researchers get to a more holistic picture, the better this is likely to be. Understanding location characteristics and their impact on SIEs and AEs (Dickmann 2013; Doherty et al. 2010) is another piece of the puzzle. The impact of host country characteristics such as security, location, tolerance and acceptance of the host country population are likely to shape many outcomes of global mobility. We are all persuaded that improving our insights into global mobility remains a worthy and exciting aim.

References

Adler, Nancy. 1979. Women as Androgynous Managers: A Conceptualization of the Potential for American Women in International Management. *International Journal of Intercultural Relations* 3 (4): 407–436.

Al Ariss, Akram, and Jawad Syed. 2011. Capital Mobilization of Skilled Migrants: A Relational Perspective. *British Journal of Management* 22 (2): 286–304.

Andresen, Maike, Akram Al Ariss, and Matthias Walther, eds. 2013. *Self-Initiated Expatriation. Individual, Organizational, and National Perspectives.* London: Routledge.

Andresen, Maike, Franziska Bergdolt, Jil Margenfeld, and Michael Dickmann. 2014. Addressing International Mobility Confusion—Developing Definitions and Differentiations for Self-Initiated and Assigned Expatriates As Well As Migrants. *International Journal of Human Resource Management* 25 (16): 2295–2318.

Baker, James, and John Ivancevich. 1971. The Assignment of American Executives Abroad: Systematic, Haphazard, or Chaotic? *California Management Review* 13 (3): 39–44.

Baruch, Yehuda, Pawan S. Budhwar, and Neresh Khatri. 2007. Brain Drain: Inclination to Stay Abroad After Studies. *Journal of World Business* 42 (1): 99–112.

Bickers, Robert. 2010. *Settlers and Expatriates: Britons Over the Seas*. Oxford: Oxford University Press.

Biemann, Torsten, and Maike Andresen. 2010. Self-Initiated Foreign Expatriates Versus Assigned Expatriates. Two Distinct Types of International Careers? *Journal of Managerial Psychology* 25 (4): 430–448.

Black, J. Steward, and Hal B. Gregersen. 1991. The Other Half of the Picture: Antecedents of Spouse Cross-Cultural Adjustment. *Journal of International Business Studies* 22 (3): 461–477.

Borrmann, Werner. 1968. The Problem of Expatriate Personnel and Their Selection in International Enterprises. *Management International Review* 8 (4/5): 37–48.

Bossard, Annette B., and Richard B. Peterson. 2005. The Repatriate Experience as Seen by American Expatriates. *Journal of World Business* 40 (1): 9–28.

Boulnois, Luce. 2004. *Silk Road: Monks, Warriors and Merchants on the Silk Road*. Hong Kong: Odyssey Publications.

Campbell, Robert D. 1969. United States Military Training for Cross-Cultural Interaction. *Office of Naval Research*, June.

Carpenter, Mason, Gerard Sanders, and Hal Gregersen. 2001. Bundling Human Capital with Organizational Context: The Impact of International Assignment Experience on Multinational Firm Performance and CEO Pay. *Academy of Management Journal* 44 (3): 493–511.

Cerdin, Jean-Luc. 2013. Motivation of Self-Initiated Expatriates. In *Self-Initiated Expatriation: Mastering the Dynamics*, ed. Maike Andresen, Akram Al Ariss, and Matthias Walther, 59–74. London: Routledge.

Cerdin, Jean-Luc, and Chris Brewster. 2014. Talent Management and Expatriation: Bridging Two Streams of Research and Practice. *Journal of World Business* 49 (2): 245–252.

Cerdin, Jean-Luc, and Marie Le Pargneux. 2010. Career Anchors: A Comparison Between Organization-Assigned and Self-Initiated Expatriates. *Thunderbird International Business Review* 52 (4): 287–299.

Clarke, Lisa, Corbin Akhentoolove, and Betty Jane Punnett. 2017. Expatriates to and from Developed and Developing Countries. In *The Research Handbook of Expatriates*, ed. Yvonne McNulty and Jan Selmer, 133–147. London: Edward Elgar.

Cleveland, Harland, Cerard Mangone, and John Adams. 1960. *The Overseas Americans*. New York, NY: McGraw-Hill.

Coase, R.H. 1937. The Nature of the Firm. *Economica* 4 (16): 386–405.

Cohen, Erik. 1977. Expatriate Communities. *Current Sociology* 24 (3): 5–133.

Collins Dictionaries. 2011. *Collins English Dictionary*. Glasgow, UK: Collins.

Copeland, Lennie, and Lewis Griggs. 1985. *Going International: How to Make Friends and Deal Effectively in the Global Marketplace*. New York: Random House.

Daily, Catherine, S. Trevis Certo, and Dan R. Dalton. 2000. International Experience in the Executive Suite: The Path to Prosperity. *Strategic Management Journal* 21 (4): 515–523.

DeFillippi, Robert, and Michael Arthur. 1994. The Boundaryless Career: A Competency-Based Perspective. *Journal of Organizational Behavior* 15 (4): 307–324.

Dickmann, Michael. 2013. Why Do They Come to London? Exploring the Motivations of Expatriates to Work in the British Capital. *Journal of Management Development* 31 (8): 783–800.

———. 2015. *The RES Forum Annual Report: Global Mobility and the Global Talent Management Conundrum*. RES Forum, UniGroup Relocation Network and Equus Software, 108 pages, London.

———. 2016. *The RES Forum Annual Report 2016: Beyond Uniformity—A World of Opportunity*. RES Forum, Harmony Relocation Network and Equus Software, 116 pages, London.

———. 2017. International Human Resource Management. In *Contemporary Human Resource Management, Text and Cases*, ed. Adrian Wilkinson, Tom Redman, and Tony Dundon, 5th ed., 258–292. London: Prentice Hall.

Dickmann, Michael, and Yehuda Baruch. 2011. *Global Careers*. London: Routledge.

Dickmann, Michael, and Jean-Luc Cerdin. 2016. Exploring the Development and Transfer of Career Capital in an International Governmental Organization. *The International Journal of Human Resource Management*. Published online October 5, 2016. http://www.tandfonline.com/doi/abs/10.1080/09585192.2016.1239217

Dickmann, Michael, and Noeleen Doherty. 2010. Exploring Organizational and Individual Career Goals, Interactions and Outcomes of Developmental International Assignments. *Thunderbird International Review* 52 (4): 313–324.

Dickmann, Michael, Vesa Suutari, Chris Brewster, Liisa Mäkelä, Jussi Tanskanen, and Christelle Tornikoski. in press. The Career Competencies of Self-Initiated and Assigned Expatriates: Assessing the Development of Career Capital Over Time. *The International Journal of Human Resource Management*. Published online May 4. http://www.tandfonline.com/doi/abs/10.1080/09585192.2016.1172657

Doherty, Noeleen, and Michael Dickmann. 2012. Measuring the Return on Investment in International Assignments: An Action Research Approach. *International Journal of Human Resource Management* 23 (16): 3434–3454.

———. 2013. Self-Initiated Expatriation: Drivers, Employment Experience and Career Outcomes. In *Self-Initiated Expatriation: Mastering the Dynamics*, ed. Maike Andresen, Akram Al Ariss, and Matthias Walther, 122–142. London: Routledge.

Doherty, Noeleen, Michael Dickmann, and Timothy Mills. 2010. Mobility Attitudes and Behaviours Among Young Europeans. *Career Development International* 15 (4): 378–400.

———. 2011. Exploring the Motives of Company-Backed and Self-Initiated Expatriates. *The International Journal of Human Resource Management* 22 (3): 595–611.

Dorsch, Michael, Vesa Suutari, and Chris Brewster. 2013. Research on Self-Initiated Expatriation: History and Future Directions. In *Self-Initiated Expatriation. Individual, Organizational, and National Perspectives*, ed. Maike Andresen, Akram Al Ariss, and Matthias Walther, 42–58. London: Routledge.

Dowling, Peter, Marion Festing, and Allen Engle. 2013. *International Human Resource Management*. 6th ed. London: Cengage Learning.

Dumont, Jean-Christophe, and Georges Lemaitre. 2005. *Counting Immigrants and Expatriates in OECD Countries: A New Perspective*. Accessed October 3, 2017. http://www.oecd-ilibrary.org/social-issues-migration-health/counting-immigrants-and-expatriates-in-oecd-countries_521408252125

Dunning, John. 1958. *American Investment in British Manufacturing Industry*. London: George Allen and Unwin.

Earnest, Ernest. 1968. *Expatriates and Patriots: American Artists, Scholars and Writers in Europe*. Durham, NC: Duke University Press.

Farh, Crystal, Kathryn Bartol, Debra Shapiro, and Jiseon Shin. 2010. Networking Abroad: A Process Model of How Expatriates form Support Ties to Facilitate Adjustment. *Academy of Management Review* 35 (3): 434–454.

Fee, Anthony, and Elaine Karsaklian. 2013. Could International Volunteers be Considered Ethical Consumers? A Cross-Discipline Approach to Understanding Motives of Self-Initiated Expatriates. In *Talent Management of Self-Initiated Expatriates: A Neglected Source of the Global Talent,* ed. Vlad Vaiman and Arno Haslberger, 88–116. Basingstoke: Palgrave Macmillan.

Feldman, Daniel, and David Thomas. 1992. Career Management Issues Facing Expatriates. *Journal of International Business Studies* 23 (2): 271–293.

Foote, Marion. 1977. Controlling the Cost of International Compensation. *Harvard Business Review* 55 (6): 123–132.

Gama, Elizabeth, and Paul Pedersen. 1977. Readjustment Problems of Brazilian Returnees from Graduate Studies in the United States. *International Journal of Intercultural Relations* 1 (4): 46–59.

Gonzalez, Richard. 1967. *The United States Overseas Executive: His Orientations and Career Patterns.* East Lansing, MI: Michigan State University.

Green, Nancy. 2009. Expatriation, Expatriates, and Expats: The American Transformation of a Concept. *American Historical Review* 114 (2): 307–319.

Hamori, Monika, and Burak Koyuncu. 2011. Career Advancement in Large Organizations in Europe and the United States: Do International Assignments Add Value? *International Journal of Human Resource Management* 22 (4): 843–862.

Hapgood, David. 1968. *Agents of Change: A Close Look at the Peace Corps.* Boston, MA: Little, Brown and Co..

Harris, Hilary, Chris Brewster, and Paul Sparrow. 2003. *International Human Resource Management.* CIPD Publishing.

Haslberger, Arno, Chris Brewster, and Thomas Hippler. 2013. The Dimensions of Expatriate Adjustment. *Human Resource Management* 52 (3): 333–351.

Haslberger, Arno, and Vlad Vaiman. 2013. Self-Initiated Expatriates: A Neglected Source of the Global Talent Flow. In *Talent Management of Self-initiated Expatriates: A Neglected Source of the Global Talent,* ed. Vlad Vaiman and Arno Haslberger, 1–15. Basingstoke: Palgrave Macmillan.

Heenan, D. 1970. The Corporate Expatriate: Assignment to Ambiguity. *Columbia Journal of World Business* 5 (3): 49–54.

Hippler, Thomas. 2009. Why Do They Go? Empirical Evidence of Employees' Motives for Seeking or Accepting Relocation. *International Journal of Human Resource Management* 20 (6): 1381–1401.

Howell, Margaret, and Sidney Newman. 1959. How We Should Train for Overseas Posts. *Thunderbird International Business Review* 1 (1): 21–22.

Inkson, Kerr, and Michael Arthur. 2001. How to Be a Successful Career Capitalist. *Organizational Dynamics* 30 (1): 48–61.

Inkson, Kerr, Michael Arthur, Judith Pringle, and Sean Barry. 1997. Expatriate Assignment Versus Overseas Experience: Contrasting Models of International Human Resource Development. *Journal of World Business* 32 (4): 351–368.

Ivancevich, John, and James Baker. 1970. A Comparative Study of the Satisfaction of Domestic United States Managers and Overseas United States Managers. *Academy of Management Journal* 13 (1): 69–77.

Jokinen, Tiina, Chris Brewster, and Vesa Suutari. 2008. Career Capital During International Work Experiences: Contrasting Self-Initiated Expatriate Experiences and Assignees Expatriation. *International Journal of Human Resource Management* 19 (6): 979–998.

Jones, Lyndon. 1975. Training in the Jungle—CALTEX Style. *Education + Training* 17 (1/2): 45–48.

Kiernan, Paul. 1963. What It Takes to Be a Successful International Manager. *Thunderbird International Business Review* 5 (4): 1–4.

Kolde, Endel, and Richard Hill. 1967. Conceptual and Normative Aspects of International Management. *Academy of Management Journal* 10 (2): 119–128.

Kraimer, Maria, Margaret Shaffer, and Mark Bolino. 2009. The Influence of Expatriate and Repatriate Experiences on Career Advancement and Repatriate Retention. *Human Resource Management* 48 (1): 27–47.

Kraimer, Maria, Margaret Shaffer, David Harrison, and Ren Hong. 2012. No Place Like Home? An Identity Strain Perspective on Repatriate Turnover. *Academy of Management Journal* 55 (2): 399–420.

Lanier, A.R. 1979. Selecting and Preparing Personnel for Overseas Transfers. *Personnel Journal* 58 (3): 160–163.

Lee, Chay Hoon. 2005. A Study of Underemployment Among Self-Initiated Expatriates. *Journal of World Business* 40 (2): 172–187.

Lysgaard, S. 1955. Adjustment in a Foreign Country: Norwegian Fulbright Grantees Visiting the United States. *International Social Sciences Bulletin* 7: 45–51.

Magnusson, Peter, and David Boggs. 2006. International Experience and CEO Selection: An Empirical Study. *Journal of International Management* 12 (1): 107–125.

Mäkelä, Kristiina, and Vesa Suutari. 2013. Social Capital of Traditional and Self-Initiated Expatriates. In *Talent Management of Self-Initiated Expatriates: A Neglected Source of the Global Talent*, ed. Vlad Vaiman and Arno Haslberger, 278–303. Basingstoke: Palgrave Macmillan.

Marrus, Michael. 1985. *The Unwanted: European Refugees in the Twentieth Century*. New York, NY: Oxford University Press.

McNulty, Yvonne. 2013. Are Self-Initiated Expatriates Born or Made? Exploring the Relationship Between SIE Orientation and Individual ROI. In *Talent Management of Self-initiated Expatriates: A Neglected Source of the Global Talent*, ed. Vlad Vaiman and Arno Haslberger, 30–58. Basingstoke: Palgrave Macmillan.

McNulty, Yvonne, and Chris Brewster. 2016. Theorizing the Meaning(s) of 'Expatriate': Establishing Boundary Conditions for Business Expatriates. *International Journal of Human Resource Management* 28 (1): 27–61.

Mendenhall, Mark, Edward Dunbar, and Gary Oddou. 1987. Expatriate Selection, Training and Career-Pathing: A Review and Critique. *Human Resource Management* 26 (3): 331–345.

Miller, Edwin. 1972. The Selection Decision for an International Assignment: A Study of the Decision Maker's Behavior. *Journal of International Business Studies* 3 (2): 49–65.

———. 1973. The International Selection Decision: A Study of Some Dimensions of Managerial Behavior in the Selection Decision Process. *Academy of Management Journal* 16 (2): 239–252.

———. 1975. The Job Satisfaction of Expatriate American Managers: A Function of Regional Location and Previous International Work Experience. *Journal of International Business Studies* 6 (2): 65–73.

Miller, Edwin, and Joseph Cheng. 1978. A Closer Look at the Decision to Accept an Overseas Position. *Management International Review* 18 (3): 25–33.

Mincer, Jacob. 1978. Family Migration Decisions. *Journal of Political Economy* 86 (5): 749–773.

Misa, K.F., and J.M. Fabricatore. 1979. Return on Investment of Overseas Personnel. *Financial Executive* 47: 42–46.

Murray, J. 1973. International Personnel Repatriation: Culture Shock in Reverse. *MSU Business Topics* 21 (3): 59–66.

Negandhi, Anant, and Bernard Estafen. 1965. A Research Model to Determine the Applicability of American Management Know-How in Differing Cultures and/or Environments. *Academy of Management Journal* 8 (4): 309–318.

Ng, Thomas, Lillian Eby, Kelly Sorensen, and Daniel Feldman. 2005. Predictors of Objective and Subjective Career Success: A Meta-Analysis. *Personnel Psychology* 58 (2): 367–408.

Oberg, Kalervo. 1960. Cultural Shock: Adjustment to New Cultural Environments. *Practical Anthropology* 7 (4): 177–182.

Oberholster, Abraham, Ruth Clarke, Mike Bendixen, and Barbara Dastoor. 2013. Expatriate Motivation in Religious and Humanitarian Non-Profit-Organizations. *Journal of Global Mobility* 1 (1): 7–27.

Oberholster, Braam, and Cheryl Doss. 2017. Missionary (Religious) Expatriates. In *The Research Handbook of Expatriates*, ed. Yvonne McNulty and Jan Selmer, 316–334. London: Edward Elgar.

Oltram, Victor, Jaime Bonache, and Chris Brewster. 2013. A New Framework for Understanding Inequalities Between Expatriates and host Country Nationals. *Journal of Business Ethics* 115 (2): 291–310.

Oxford Dictionary of English, 3rd ed. 2015. Oxford: Oxford University Press.

Peltokorpi, Vesa. 2008. Cross-Cultural Adjustment of Expatriates in Japan. *International Journal of Human Resource Management* 19 (9): 1588–1606.

Peterson, Richard, John Sargent, Nancy Napier, and Won S. Shim. 1996. Corporate Expatriate HRM Policies, Internationalization, and Performance in the World's Largest MNCs. *Management International Review* 36 (3): 215–230.

Peterson, Richard, and Hermann Schwind. 1977. A Comparative Study of Personnel Problems in International Companies and Joint Ventures in Japan. *Journal of International Business Studies* 8 (1): 45–55.

Point, Sébastien, and Michael Dickmann. 2012. Branding International Careers: An Analysis of Multinational Corporations' Official Wording. *European Management Journal* 30 (1): 18–31.

Ramaswarmi, Aarti, Nancy M. Carter, and George F. Dreher. 2016. Expatriation and Career Success: A Human Capital Perspective. *Human Relations* 69 (10): 1959–1987.

Reynolds, C. 1972. Career Paths and Compensation in MNCs. *Columbia Journal of World Business* 7 (6): 77–87.

Richardson, Julia. 2006. Self-Directed Expatriation: Family Matters. *Personnel Review* 35 (4): 469–486.

Richardson, Julia, and Mary Mallon. 2005. Career Interrupted? The Case of the Self-Directed Expatriate. *Journal of World Business* 40 (4): 409–420.

Salt, Bernard. 2008. *The Global Skills Convergence: Issues and Ideas for the Management of an International Workforce*. Switzerland: KPMG.

Schollhammer, H. 1969. Compensation of International Executives. *Michigan State University Business Topics* 17 (1): 19–30.

Selmer, Jan, and Jakob Lauring. 2010. Self-Initiated Academic Expatriates: Inherent Demographics and Reasons to Expatriate. *European Management Review* 7 (3): 169–179.

Shaffer, Margaret, Maria L. Kraimer, Yu-Ping Chen, and Mark C. Bolino. 2012. Choices, Challenges, and Career Consequences of Global Work Experiences: A Review and Future Agenda. *Journal of Management* 38 (4): 1282–1327.

Stahl, Günter, and Jean-Luc Cerdin. 2004. Global Careers in French and German Multinational Corporations. *Journal of Management Development* 23 (9): 885–902.

Stahl, Günter, Edwin Miller, and Rosalie Tung. 2002. Toward the Boundaryless Career: A Closer Look at the Expatriate Career Concept and the Perceived Implications of an International Assignment. *Journal of World Business* 37 (3): 216–227.

Stening, Bruce. 1994. Expatriate Management: Lessons from the British in India. *The International Journal of Human Resource Management* 5 (2): 385–404.

Suutari, Vesa, and Chris Brewster. 2000. Making Their Own Way: International Experience Through Self-Initiated Foreign Assignments. *Journal of World Business* 35 (4): 417–436.

Suutari, Vesa, Michael Dickmann, Chris Brewster, and Liisa Mäkela. 2016. Expatriation and the Boundaryless Career—Empirical Evidence. Paper presented at the *European Academy of Management Conference*, Paris, France, June 1–4.

Suutari, Vesa, Chris Brewster, Michael Dickmann, Liisa Mäkelä, and Christelle Tornikoski. 2018. The Effect of International Work Experience on the Career Success of Expatriates: A Comparison of Assigned and Selfinitiated Expatriates. *Human Resource Management* 57 (1): 37–54. https://doi.org/10.1002/hrm.21827.

Taylor, A.J.W. 1968. The Selection of N.Z. Volunteers for Service Abroad: An Appraisal of the First Five Years. *Personnel Psychology* 21 (3): 345–357.

Tharenou, Phyllis. 2003. The Initial Development of Receptivity to Working Abroad: Self-Initiated International Work Opportunities in Young Graduate Employees. *Journal of Occupational and Organizational Psychology* 76 (4): 489–515.

Torbiorn, I. 1982. *Living Abroad: Personal Adjustment and Personnel Policy in the Overseas Setting*. New York, NY: Wiley.

Triandis, H.C. 1963. Factors Affecting Employee Selection in Two Cultures. *Journal of Applied Psychology* 47 (2): 89–96.

Tung, Rosalie. 1988. Career Issues in International Assignments. *Academy of Management Perspectives* 2 (3): 241–244.

Vinnicombe, Susan, Elena Doldor, Ruth Sealy, Patricia Pryce, and Caroline Turner. 2015. *The Female FTSE Board Report 2015*. Cranfield: Cranfield University. Accessed October 3, 2017. https://www.cranfield.ac.uk/som/expertise/changing-world-of-work/gender-and-leadership/female-ftse-index

Walker, Williston, Richard Norris, David Lotz, and Robert Handy. 1985. *A History of the Christian Church*. 4th ed. New York, NY: Scribner.

Wallace, W.J. 1959. How to Maintain Productive Working Relationships with Overseas Managers. *Thunderbird International Business Review* 1 (2): 17–18.

Yoshino, M. 1976. *Japan's Multinational Enterprises*. Cambridge, MA: Harvard University Press.

4

Coaching of Global Careerists

Raija Salomaa

Introduction

Today, coaching has become a global phenomenon that is practised all over the world. Its growth has followed the trends of globalization, international mergers and acquisitions and the growing diversity in the workplace (Tompson et al. 2008). In addition, given the steady increase in academic coaching literature over recent years, coaching is evolving into a scholarly field in its own right (Bachkirova et al. 2016), who posit that coaching has matured to a point where it might be deemed an emerging profession. However, as a relatively new area of scholarship, coaching is generally seen as an under-explored and under-researched human resource development-related practice requiring further examination and discovery (Ellinger et al. 2011). The majority of the empirical studies and the meta-analytic studies (Jones et al. 2015; De Meuse et al. 2009; Sonesh et al. 2015; Theeboom et al. 2014) conducted to date indicate that coaching is

---

R. Salomaa (✉)
Crossnomads, Tuusula, Finland
e-mail: raija.salomaa@crossnomads.com

© The Author(s) 2018
M. Dickmann et al. (eds.), *The Management of Global Careers*,
https://doi.org/10.1007/978-3-319-76529-7_4

an effective tool for improving and developing individuals and their organizations (Bartlett et al. 2014; Jones et al. 2015). Indeed, it has been argued that two key benefits of coaching for organizations are the development of the talent pool and organizational capacity and talent retention and improvement in morale (Dagley 2006). Moreover, coaching is known to enhance leadership skills in several ways (Kombarakaran et al. 2008). There is also increasing evidence that coaching has positive effects on, for example, individual well-being and performance (Theeboom et al. 2014).

However, although coaching is widely used, there is no consensus on its definitions or contents (Athanasopoulou and Dopson 2015). For the purpose of this chapter, coaching is understood to be "a human development process of an international assignee that involves structured interaction and the use of appropriate strategies, tools and techniques in an international context. It is aimed at promoting desirable and sustainable change for the benefit of the coachee and, potentially, for other stakeholders" (modified from Bachkirova et al. 2010: 1). This chapter integrates recent knowledge from coaching, international coaching and international mobility and offers a view on the cross section of these fields. Its aim is to provide an overall picture of coaching's role as a *support* and *development* intervention for different types of expatriates.

Expatriates are individuals who live and work abroad and can be categorized in two groups: "assigned" or corporate expatriates and "self-initiated" expatriates (Andresen et al. 2014). Assigned expatriates typically refer to employees who are sent abroad by their company, whereas self-initiated expatriates are individuals who undertake their international work experience with little or no organizational sponsorship and often with less favourable local work contracts (Biemann and Andresen 2010; Suutari and Brewster 2000). Self-initiated expatriates relocate to a country of their choice to pursue cultural, personal and career development experiences (Jokinen et al. 2008; Shaffer et al. 2012). The duration of expatriation varies from less than a year to long-term assignments. Furthermore, an increasing number of expatriates pursue so-called global careers, which Mäkelä and Suutari (2009: 992) have defined as careers "involving multiple international relocations including various positions and assignments." These global careerists can be either corporate expatriates sent abroad by their organizations or self-initiated expatriates.

International human resource management literature shows that multinational companies search for individuals who can manage effectively in the complex, challenging, changing and ambiguous global business environment (Caligiuri and Bonache 2016), and there is also considerable evidence that organizations face formidable talent challenges. Furthermore, when individuals work in challenging international environments, they need flexibility and related competencies that can be transferred to various contexts. It is known that international assignments (IAs) are the most powerful strategy for developing global leaders and that IAs are very challenging experiences for individuals (Suutari and Mäkelä 2007). For these reasons, coaching has been recommended as a support and development intervention both in the talent management (Al Ariss et al. 2014) and expatriation literatures (Mendenhall 2006; Selmer 1999). Although coaching research in the international context is still scarce, there is an evolving body of empirical research showing that coaching is an efficient support and development approach in the expatriate context (Abbott 2006; Herbolzheimer 2009; McGill 2010; Salomaa 2015; Salomaa and Mäkelä 2017). In addition, coaching is argued to provide support in adjusting to the frequent, yet often unexpected, role transitions and career changes (Parker 2016), typical in the context of global mobility.

This chapter is structured as follows: first, coaching in general is introduced; second, the unique features and challenges evolving from the global mobility context are discussed; and third, aspects of coaching in an international context are considered and empirical research on expatriate coaching is reviewed. Then the coaching experiences of two different kinds of expatriates are presented. Finally, the chapter ends with some concluding words and ideas for future research.

Coaching

As stated earlier, although there have been many attempts to define coaching, there is no one unique definition for executive coaching. The International Coach Federation (ICF), the world's largest professional association for coaches, defines coaching as "partnering with clients in a thought-provoking and creative process that inspires them to maximize their personal and professional potential" (International Coach Federation 2018). According to ICF coaches honor the client as the expert in his or her life and work and believe every client is creative, resourceful and whole. Regardless of the definition of coaching offered, they all share common characteristics (Parker 2016). Typically, there is an emphasis on collaborative goal setting as well as on learning through coaching. It is understood to be a systematic process, aimed at fostering the ongoing self-directed learning and growth of the coachee (Grant and Stober 2006). Indeed, it is typically considered to be a set of behaviours that enables individuals to learn and develop, as well as to improve their skills and enhance their performance (Ellinger and Kim 2014). Bartlett et al. (2014) posit that relationship, goals, performance and learning are the keywords used most often in defining executive coaching.

Coaching is known to be a cross-disciplinary approach that has its roots in psychology, management, learning theory and theories of human and organizational development, philosophy and sport. In general, the literature on executive coaching has differentiated coaching from other helping interventions such as mentoring (Abbott et al. 2006; Feldman and Lankau 2005). In comparison to mentoring, coaching is more formal in nature and is based on an equal relationship between coach and coachee. Typically, a mentor has held a similar role to the mentee, and mentoring is characterized by giving advice, whilst the professional coach's expertise lies in facilitating learning and development using a variety of techniques.

With regard to the coaching process, the stakeholders in executive coaching typically include the coach, the coachee and the organization. Executive coaching is often funded by the organization and requested, usually, by the coachee's manager or HR professional (Athanasopoulou and Dopson 2015), and organizational support of the coachee has been found to be important to coaching success (Hooijberg and Lane 2009; Salomaa 2015). The executive coaching process is typically described in the literature as consisting of different steps. For example, Feldman and Lankau (2005) describe it as consisting of data gathering, feedback, implementation of the coaching intervention and evaluation. In general, coaches work with two forms of feedback: feedback that is generated externally to the coachee and feedback that is generated internally when coachees engage in self-reflection and self-appraisal. Developing the coachee's reflective and reflexive capability is a means of developing self-awareness for the coachee (Maxwel 2016). Instruments typically employed in executive coaching include an assessment of an individual's emotional intelligence and 360-degree feedback and an assessment that involves soliciting feedback from one's immediate work circle including subordinates, peers and supervisors. The length of the executive coaching process is usually predefined and is short-term in nature, although there is some variation in the research findings concerning the duration and content (Athanasopoulou and Dopson 2015). During the coaching process, the coach typically uses open-ended questions, active listening, summaries and reflections, all of which are aimed at stimulating the self-awareness and personal responsibility of the coachee (Passmore and Fillery-Travis 2011). In this sense, coaching can be seen as an ongoing activity, using an interactive learning process to increase the executive's awareness of the impact of behaviour on performance. Executive change involves identifying the patterns of experience and behaviour that affect goal attainment, creating a fresh perspective of these patterns by reframing and rehearsing new behaviours (Kombarakaran et al. 2008).

In summary, the field of coaching research is maturing but still needs a larger evidence-base. As contextual factors have been found to be of importance in coaching (Abbott and Salomaa 2016), different kinds of expatriates may have different kinds of coaching needs evolving from the challenging context of global mobility.

The Context of Global Mobility

This section describes the unique features and challenges arising from the context of global mobility and which impact, for example, the coaching needs of expatriates. In general, there is a growing understanding of the complexity of the global mobility field in terms of variation in types of expatriates, other types of international experiences, types of organizations and desired objectives. The field is characterized by diversity (Brewster et al. 2014). Today, almost half of company-assigned expatriates are relocating from non-headquarters, and the most frequently cited reasons for sending expatriates abroad include filling a managerial gap, building international management experience and career development. Organizations are focusing on creating a pipeline of future leaders with global management experience. Consequently, IAs can be seen as a significant route to career enhancement because international experience is perceived as an essential leadership competency (Brookfield Global Mobility Trends Survey 2016).

It is known that effectively managing expatriation and repatriation is a significant challenge for organizations (Cerdin and Brewster 2014; Shaffer et al. 2012). Indeed, research indicates that expatriation is a costly and risky investment with many challenges for the expatriates and for the employing organizations. Although it is known that managers value an IA for the opportunity it brings for skills acquisition, personal development and career enhancement, there are several transition points that prompt perceptions of high uncertainty and risk for expatriates (Haslberger and Brewster 2009).

Much of the research on expatriation has been focused on adjustment. This is a multifaceted concept that refers to the degree of psychological comfort with various aspects of a new cultural setting. It consists of individual factors, job factors, organizational factors and nonwork factors, as well as factors related to repatriation (Black et al. 1991). This conceptual model implies that factors that reduce uncertainty facilitate adjustment and vice versa. Research on expatriates indicates that assignees are confronted with a variety of work role and situational stressors, arising from both the organization and the foreign culture (Shaffer et al. 2012; Takeuchi 2010). For example, there is evidence that international assignees may carry out tasks that are more demanding and at a higher organizational level than their duties in the home country (Suutari and Brewster 2000). Further, expatriate jobs are often characterized by a high level of autonomy and without much local support or help from the headquarter staff due to distance and unfamiliarity with the specific context. Moreover, global travel, which is typically an essential component of international jobs, has been shown to increase physical, emotional and intellectual stress (Shaffer et al. 2012). Furthermore, assignees have to overcome various barriers such as gender bias among female expatriates, obtaining work permits and so on. One of the greatest concerns for corporate assignees is managing the repatriation transition and issues such as opportunities for using the skills acquired abroad, career advancement and career opportunities for their spouse (Shaffer et al. 2012). In addition, an assignment may be a challenge for the whole family, not only for the expatriate, and several work-family conflicts have been reported (Mäkelä and Suutari 2011). Family concerns have been found to be the primary reason for the refusal of individuals to accept foreign assignments and for their failure (McNulty 2015).

In addition, studies show that international assignees face several paradoxes (Osland 2000; Osland and Osland 2005). For example, there are paradoxes concerning the relationship with the other culture. When an assignee becomes comfortable in another culture, it involves sacrificing, albeit often unconsciously, aspects of self-identity associated with his or her own culture. A basic dilemma for expatriates is determining how much of one's identity must be relinquished and how much of the other culture's values must be acquired in order to be acculturated. Indeed, several scholars have reported that identity transformations take place during IAs and that these are challenging for individuals because they affect their sense of self and their subsequent attitudes and behaviours towards their organization (Kohonen 2007; Muir 2014; Näsholm 2011). Moreover, several paradoxes concerning job-related role conflict also exist. For example, the role of an expatriate manager confers considerable power, but at the same time the manager is dependent upon subordinates for their knowledge of the local culture, business practices and, for example, politics (Osland and Osland 2005; Shaffer et al. 2012). However, paradoxes can be viewed as developmental experiences, as development occurs when assignees overcome obstacles. Further, Dragoni et al.'s study (2014, cited in Caligiuri and Bonache 2016) indicates that exposure to cultural novelty provides assignees with a set of cultural contrasts through which they can develop more elaborated cognitive structures that represent more advanced levels of professional competencies.

In summary, the above discussion on various challenges faced by expatriates indicates that there are different kinds of support needs in which coaching can be helpful for both corporate and self-initiated expatriates. Moreover, the life of expatriates is often characterized by various changes such as onboarding to a new role and moving to a new location or returning home. Coaching has been argued, among other things, to be valuable in different kinds of transitions, because it helps individuals to manage not only the external career change in terms of a different role, status or position but also the internal impact of a career transition with the associated challenges of motivation, identity and emotional management (Parker 2016). Also, the developmental role of coaching is important because assignees need to acquire self-awareness, new skills and attitudes in order to be successful in their jobs. Given that the international environment affects the coachees, it certainly also impacts the coaching, and therefore the next chapter focuses on what is currently known about international coaching.

International Coaching

The existing literature on international coaching has mainly focused on cultural aspects of coaching. Given that work is increasingly conducted across borders in a highly interconnected world, all coaching assignments are in some way cross-cultural. Typically, cross-cultural coaching occurs when the context is in some way cross-, multi- or intercultural (Abbott and Salomaa 2016). Culture has recently emerged in the executive coaching literature as an aspect that needs to be actively considered in the executive coaching process (Athanasopoulou and Dopson 2015). Often the terms international, multicultural, global and cross-cultural coaching are utilized interchangeably. Booysen (2015) has suggested that cross-cultural coaching is a meaning-making process in which the coach helps the coachee to surface and address deeply held beliefs and behaviours arising from cognitive schemas and frameworks. In this process, a particular focus is on working with schemas shaped by culture and identity construction that underlie beliefs and behaviours that inhibit a coachee's performance in his/her current context. Further, Milner et al. (2013) have suggested that the intercultural component of coaching, in terms of the coaching topic, should be distinguished from the intercultural component, in terms of the players, within the coaching process.

The field of international coaching has been largely influenced by intercultural management theories and intercultural research, which have provided frameworks upon which coaches can draw. An understanding of cultural dimensions and values and awareness of one's own cultural assumptions are commonly stated as requirements for coaches working in the international context (Abbott and Salomaa 2016; Van Nieuwerburgh 2016). Rosinski (2003, 2010) was the first to combine cultural theories with coaching by utilizing Milton Bennett's (1993) approach. This approach includes stages such as denial of differences, defence against difference, minimization of difference, acceptance of difference, adaptation to difference and integration of difference. Rosinski developed Bennett's ideas further by adding a stage entitled "leverage difference." He also created an assessment questionnaire, the "Cultural Orientations Framework," which may be beneficial in cross-cultural coaching. In addition, approaches such as complexity theory, systems thinking and theories of adult development have been recommended as frameworks for coaches working internationally (Abbott and Salomaa 2016).

However, coaching engagements that concentrate only on culture are not useful, because there may also be other contextual factors impacting the coaching relationship (Abbott 2010). Empirical papers show that even where the context is cross-cultural, coaching can evolve to cover other issues beyond merely the cross-cultural. Indeed, from the outset, the coaching intervention may focus on, for example, leadership development, regardless of the cross-cultural context (Salomaa 2015; Salomaa and Mäkelä 2017). Indeed, coaching approaches that integrate culture into a holistic approach to individual and organizational change are finding favour, one of them being the "integral model" of Ken Wilber (Abbott 2010). In this framework the coachee is a participant in a whole system that includes culture, systems and the social context of their situation, and the different dimensions of the framework are interconnected. Recently, the concepts of "cultural intelligence," the capability for consciousness and awareness during intercultural situations (Ng et al. 2009), and the "Global Mindset," a construct consisting of psychological, social and intercultural capital (Javidan et al. 2010), have also been utilized in some theoretical and empirical coaching papers (Abbott et al. 2013; Booysen 2015). It is notable that most of the authors discussing coaching in an international context point out the danger of stereotyping individuals based on generalizations derived from a national culture

(Abbott et al. 2013). In addition, there are some publications discussing and exploring coaching in a special country context, for example, in China, Hong Kong and in Malaysia (Gallo 2015; Gan and Chong 2015; Lam 2016) or generally in Asia (Nangalia and Nangalia 2010). Given that coaching is argued to be a Western concept (Lam 2016), these publications discuss how it is being perceived and adapted by local coaches and coachees. In general, the number of cross-cultural coaching papers has increased recently in peer-reviewed journals, the majority of them being empirical papers studying cross-cultural coaching from the coach's perspective.

One of the developing areas of international coaching is research on expatriate coaching. Although coaching is recommended for international assignees (Booysen 2015), expatriate coaching research is not well developed. For example, it is not clear how earlier assignments impact the coaching needs of different kinds of assignees. Most of the texts concerning expatriate coaching have been theoretical. Many authors have taken the lenses of adjustment and discussed the benefits of coaching compared to traditionally used development and support interventions such as mentoring and training for expatriates (Abbott et al. 2006; Chmielecki 2009). With regard to training, Mendenhall (2006) suggests that traditional training programmes cannot anticipate, in terms of content covered, the multitude and variety of potential cross-cultural challenges encountered during an assignment. He therefore recommends coaching as the preferred approach for leadership development in the expatriate context, as it is highly individualized, focuses on the present, is confidential and offers a freedom to learn driven by the coachee and his or her specific needs and preferences. Indeed, given the many different forms of international work, coaching is a highly flexible developmental form. Subsequently, a number of texts on expatriate coaching have presented theoretical models (Abbott and Stening 2009) for how coaching may support expatriates in different phases of the assignment cycle, or how expatriate coaching may support couples' adjustment (Miser and Miser 2009). In addition, the literature has also explored the coaching of third culture kids (Burrus 2009a), and female expatriates (Burrus 2009b).

A literature review yielded a total of five empirical studies written in the English language with a focus on expatriate coaching (conference papers not included). Three are PhD dissertations (Abbott 2006; Herbolzheimer 2009; McGill 2010), and two are papers published in peer-reviewed journals (Salomaa 2015; Salomaa and Mäkelä 2017). The key findings of these studies are discussed next.

The first study (Abbott 2006) was a case study of fifteen coached expatriates in Central American and explored how their acculturation was facilitated through coaching. Using an action research methodology, the results indicated that coaching improved both job performance and satisfaction of the expatriates. The study showed that coaching encouraged expatriates to operate from a basis of trust in professional cross-cultural relationships. Coaching also clarified personal values and facilitated reflective thinking, allowing expatriate managers to step back from their complex situations and to better understand themselves and their context. Further, coaching provided a medium to transfer knowledge from other contexts into the local situations, and, from a cultural perspective, it promoted leveraging individual and group differences. The second study (Herbolzheimer 2009) was China-specific and aimed to explore the existing situation with regard to expatriate coaching and to examine its potential. Thirty-one semi-structured interviews were analysed using global and circular analysis. This study showed that coaching could provide support for expatriates and replace or supplement intercultural training and that it could facilitate attitude and behaviour change. Further, it suggested that coaching could accelerate the assignee's effectiveness by developing a comprehensive set of competencies that facilitate a smoother, more effective and healthier handling of the long-term assignment, both in professional and private regard. According to this study coaching contributes to the development of expatriates as persons, executives and international staff.

The third study (McGill 2010) was the first exploration of executive coaching for international managers of a single organization. The participants were a mixture of Western assignees and non-Western host-country nationals in China. This action research study indicated that executive coaching enhanced leadership development, increased happiness and confidence and reduced stress. It provided evidence that coaching increases expatriates' emotional intelligence capabilities of self-awareness, emotional control, communication strategies, self-reflection and empathy. The study further found that executive coaching outcomes and performance could be moderated by the relationship between coach and client and the impact of culture on the coach and the coached managers. The study suggests that coaches may be able to improve the effectiveness of coaching by developing a greater understanding of the role of the host-country's culture and the international human resource issues of international assignments.

The fourth study (Salomaa 2015) investigated which factors impact the success of expatriate coaching by utilizing twenty five semi-structured interviews, an interpretative phenomenological analysis and Wilber's integral coaching framework (Bachkirova et al. 2010). The study provided evidence that the degree to which the coaching process could be adapted to the needs of the expatriate, and the coachability of the coachee (the openness and willingness to be coached) impacted coaching success. In addition, international experience, including knowledge of the language, culture and business environment, and the ability to challenge behaviour were found to be critical attributes for expatriate coaches in terms of coaching success. This study also highlighted the impact of coaching language on coaching success in several ways. Other aspects underpinning a successful expatriate coaching assignment included a coaching friendly managerial leadership style of the sponsoring organization, a clear contract with objectives and an evaluation of the coaching process. The paper also suggested that there are several layers to the processes involved in the coaching of expatriates and that different coaching needs evolve during the coaching process. Thus, national or organizational culture, for example, is only one of the factors at play.

The fifth study (Salomaa and Mäkelä 2017) explored the development of career capital (Inkson and Arthur 2001), a concept comprising of three knowing capabilities, for expatriates through coaching by utilizing a narrative analysis on stories of six coached expatriates. It highlighted the development of identity construction and indicated that coaching boosted motivation levels in the challenging global environment. Moreover, the study showed that coaching enhanced the development of all three (knowing-how, -why, -whom) career capital capabilities and that career capital development also happened in areas that were not prioritized or even expected when coaching was started. Furthermore, the study suggested that adoption of the career capital concept as a practical tool for coaches would be beneficial.

The limitations of expatriate coaching are portrayed in several ways in the literature. For example, Abbott et al. (2006) suggest the following limitations: non-responsiveness to coaching on the part of some managers; the risk of a dependent relationship developing between the coach and the coachee that might, in fact, inhibit adjustment; the timing of coaching early on in the assignment, which is often the most stressful period for an expatriate, may not be the most appropriate; and the lack of skilled coaches in some developing countries. Herbolzheimer (2009) also discusses several limitations, such as the high cost of coaching and lack of commitment on the part of the coachee. Moreover, the amount of time associated with the coaching process has been found to be a barrier to the adoption of coaching. Further, requests for expatriate coaching may be limited by a lack of knowledge about coaching. Although expatriate coaching could supplement or replace cross-cultural training and other support interventions, HR representatives are not familiar with coaching, nor have the power to implement it. In addition, coaching may be seen as a "career killer," because some expatriates may think that receiving coaching might be a reason for not being promoted. Herbolzheimer (2009) also argues that HR professionals find it challenging to find qualified coaches. As coaching is not a registered profession, the market is full of various kinds of service providers offering their services under the umbrella of "coaching." While McGill (2010) argues, based on his study in China, that executive coaching has great potential for supporting and developing both Western and non-Western international managers, he also suggests that the fact that coaching has been derived from Western concepts and practices may limit its adoption in Chinese or Asian cultures. Further, if the coaching language is English and coachees are both Westerners and host-country nationals, this may unfairly benefit Western managers over local non-Western managers.

As an illustration of how coaching functions as a means for support and development for different kinds of expatriates, two stories of coached assignees are presented next. These are based on interviews about coaching experiences and were modified from a conference paper (Salomaa and

Mäkelä 2015). The first story (Peter) represents the experiences of a corporate expatriate on his first and second IA, whereas the second story (Michael) is a story of a self-initiated expatriate with extensive international experience.

Peter's Story

Peter, an American general manager, who was on his first IA in Japan, perceived the new environment as a challenge, and his motivation to start coaching was strongly related to the need to learn about Japanese culture, which was very dissimilar to his own culture.

> … moving to Japan, it was my first expat experience […] so the trigger there [to start coaching] was to understand Japanese culture from a foreigner's point of view.

However, it became clear that Peter's development during his assignment shaped the coaching process over time and changed his needs towards coaching from cultural issues to leadership development. Peter appeared to be satisfied with his coach's support. Through coaching, Peter learned a great deal about Japanese culture and was able to be more effective in conversations with Japanese individuals. For instance, he acquired knowledge of how to use Japanese metaphors, typical in the Japanese business jargon, that were very useful for him in his day-to-day work. By developing cross-cultural leadership skills through coaching, he learned how to lead his team more efficiently:

> What he [the coach] was able to really do that was useful, was to introduce the kind of cultural pitfalls and traps that I might fall into and also to give me the tools I needed to get the most out of my team.

Besides the original goals and the development he expected from coaching, Peter related that he had also learned other skills, such as new techniques to focus his mind and clarify his thinking. Peter was able to adopt a new way of doing business and leading people. He discovered the power of asking questions.

Even though the original reason for starting coaching was related to how to behave and perform in a foreign culture, Peter and his coach worked on several other perspectives as well. Peter's assignment in Japan was full of hardships, during which his motivation suffered badly. His coach challenged him to move beyond his comfort zone, and this approach was very positive for Peter's motivation to persevere. The foreign Japanese environment and his inability to understand the language sapped Peter's strength. For example, he needed to use a translating device to be able to follow and lead meetings. Peter described his normal working day to be "like sitting in front of a very loud television with a very loud earphones playing something different in his ear." Coaching helped Peter to put things into perspective so that he was able to solve problems and boosted his energy levels. Peter also worked with his coach on issues such as his role in the organization, why his conforming was beneficial for the organization and how the assignment impacted his career. Peter confirmed that coaching provided him with the understanding of the bigger picture. Coaching also supported his identity construction in two ways. First, it helped him to define his identity as a leader within the organization, and second, it assisted him in understanding who he was in a foreign country.

After three years in Japan, Peter had his second international assignment and expatriated to Korea where he started a new coaching process with a new Korean coach. In Peter's story, the reason for hiring a new coach was not explicitly explained, but interpretation of his story clearly reveals that he was expecting to receive support for his learning and development, similar to that he had received in Japan. In particular, it is likely that Peter wanted an effective start in his job in a new location and wanted to develop his skills, learn some specific issues about the local culture and gain understanding about how to communicate effectively. In describing his first coaching experience, Peter emphasized that they only focused specifically on the local culture for a short time before moving on to wider leadership issues. He clearly expected a similar kind of process with his new coach in Korea.

This time, however, Peter's high expectations of coaching were not met. Even though Peter said that his capabilities concerning cultural issues developed with the help of his coach in Korea, he criticized the coaching process as being more like cultural training, with the coach having her own agenda. Many of the topics could have been learned directly from books. He compared this new coaching relationship unfavourably to his previous, deep coaching discussions that were focused on his needs and developed him in more versatile ways than he had originally expected. For instance, Peter said:

> That [coaching process in Japan] was quite a different experience to the coaching I do now [...]She [the coach in Korea] is doing a lot more cultural training courses and she's tried to evolve it into leadership training [...] it became clear that it wasn't really working out that well but I was getting a lot out of the cultural side of it.

Peter seemed to expect more comprehensive support for his development and appeared to be very disappointed when he did not receive this from his second coach.

Peter's story makes clear that expatriates' needs for coaching change. In this particular case, Peter needed support for different issues during his second assignment in Korea, compared to his first expatriation experience in Japan, even though he perhaps did not recognize this clearly himself. He reflected:

> I've been able to take a lot of that [what I learned in Japan] here, into Korea.

Peter's story illustrates that the skills developed during a first international assignment can be more transferable than the expatriate himself understands. It is important that the coaching needs of an assignee are reviewed carefully before starting a coaching process, particularly with expatriates who have earlier international experience. In addition, cultural approaches in coaching need to be integrated with other coaching methodologies and not be used as a stand-alone approach. This is important in order to avoid frustration and perceptions of misuse of resources and time. Also, the selection of a coach with suitable skills appears to be a vital part of a successful coaching experience. Peter's story exemplifies how coaching can support the development of a senior level manager on his first and second assignment with little previous experience of expatriation. Although acquiring coaching skills were not among the goals of the process, Peter also learned to coach others. Peter's story further illustrates how coaching needs may evolve over time.

Michael's Story

Michael, a German, and a truly global careerist, had worked for several years in the USA and for shorter periods in many other countries. At the time of the interview, he had lived for five years as a self-initiated expatriate in Finland and worked as a senior manager. Michael reported that international assignments had "become a part of his DNA." His coaching started because he wanted to learn coaching skills and because he was mentally stuck and misaligned with his values. Michael had hired (without the support of his employing company) two external, professional coaches who worked with him one after another.

Michael highlighted several skills that he gained through coaching. For example, through experiencing coaching himself, Michael understood better the structure of a coaching process. Further, he learned actual coaching skills: listening, asking questions, quieting one's mind, being non-judgmental and open to another individual's ideas, showing emotional intelligence and developing his coaching to help others. He also learned to coach himself. Michael said that, from his point of view, these coaching skills are portable capabilities.

> …I learned this coaching aspect and I can enlarge this learning to others and be a better colleague, but also act as a coach to them. And, I think the other thing is, something that I extended, I focus on even more now, is quieting my mind and listening carefully. So the listening skills are another key, let's say asset that coaching has reintroduced to myself.

Through coaching Michael adopted the idea that he could work across the different departments within his company and by doing so, develop himself in various ways. Michael was able to learn about tasks and processes that were beyond his own area of expertise, and he gained a much wider understanding of the different ways the business could be built by different departments in the organization.

...I volunteered to work on two projects in our sustainability department, although it is not part of my job description. [...] This helped me understand what they are trying to achieve.

As an engineer Michael had always trusted the analytical perspective. During his coaching processes, he learned to better understand his own weaknesses and strengths, and he was also able to recognize the importance of feelings and emotions. This development enabled Michael to enjoy his life in a new way, and it also gave him new resources to fulfil his role more ably.

Most shocking part for me was really the aspect of values and bringing sort of the emotional side of the brain into play, not just the analytical data-driven decision-making part, but you know, if you are not happy, you would not–perform-well-kind-of-thing was a real revelation for me and gave me a lot additional ammunition for my work.

Michael was able to clarify his own values, understand what was important to him, and, thus, he was able to envision his future and make a plan to achieve it. He also gained the confidence and self-belief needed to perform the required actions. Michael discussed his identity and how coaching was helping him to better know who he was and what he wanted to accomplish.

Even though it was not his original intention to have coaching discussions about cross-cultural issues, Michael also gained new cross-cultural skills and understanding. He understood that he had strived to be someone other than who he truly was. He realized that cultural differences were connected to his values and started to behave in a more authentic way.

Further, Michael said that coaching helped him to understand the importance of the existing relationships and networks of which he was part. He started to be more active in maintaining his relationships, both in the work and personal life spheres. Michael noted:

I would say that the actual coaching exercise reintroduced me to very important concept of nourishing, meaning keeping active, your network of friends and colleagues.

Additionally, by working across different departments, Michael's social networks within the company extended. He started to share his business expertise outside his own organization and began, as a volunteer, to contact young entrepreneurs and offer them his help.

Michael's story is an example of how coaching can support and develop a truly global careerist in several ways. As desired, he was able to develop his coaching skills. He was also able to develop many other skills and increase his understanding of unanticipated areas.

In summary, the studies reviewed and the two preceding stories illustrate that coaching in the expatriate context functions as an efficient support intervention in versatile ways, for example, by reducing stress and by enhancing coping mechanisms for different kinds of challenges. In addition, coaching boosts motivation, accelerates learning and helps to develop both the leadership and cross-cultural skills needed in the global business environment.

Conclusions and Recommendations for Future Work

Coaching across cultures and borders is a highly contextual field (Abbott and Salomaa 2016). When looking at the existing international coaching literature, there seems to be an overemphasis on cultural aspects. Empirical studies are still scarce. It is therefore important to further explore the unique features of and differences between domestic and international coaching. The existing studies do, however, suggest that coaching is an advantageous support and development intervention for expatriates because it can be adjusted to meet various needs and contexts. Given that assignees confront role, identity and career transitions, it would be valuable to study the way in which coaching supports individuals in these transformations. Further, as global leadership competencies in general have been found to be critical in the context of global careers, coaching's contribution to their development warrants further study. Given that the organizational expatriates are generally receiving better support than self-initiated expatriates, SIEs in particular could benefit from coaching. It is also important to understand how the previous international experiences of global careerists impact their subsequent coaching needs and processes. Research on expatriate coaching would benefit from a focus on repatriation. Furthermore, given that published studies examining the use of language in international coaching literature are, to date, non-existent, and given that language-sensitive research has gained momentum (Piekkari and Tietze 2011), this is becoming an important area for future study.

References

Abbott, Geoffrey N. 2006. Exploring Evidence-Based Executive Coaching as an Intervention to Facilitate Expatriate Acculturation: Fifteen Case Studies. PhD diss., Australian National University.

———. 2010. Cross- Cultural Coaching: A Paradoxical Perspective. In *The Complete Handbook of Coaching*, ed. Elaine Cox, Tatiana Bachkirova, and David Clutterbuck, 324–340. London: Sage.

Abbott, Geoffrey N., Kate Gilbert, and Philippe Rosinski. 2013. Cross-Cultural Working in Coaching and Mentoring. In *The Wiley-Blackwell Handbook of The Psychology of Coaching and Mentoring*, ed. Jonathan Passmore, David B. Peterson, and Theresa Freire, 483–500. Chichester: John Wiley and Sons.

Abbott, Geoffrey N., and Raija Salomaa. 2016. Cross-Cultural Coaching: An Emerging Practice. In *The Sage Handbook of Coaching*, ed. Tatiana Bachkirova, Gordon Spence, and David Drake, 453–469. Los Angeles: Sage.

Abbott, Geoffrey N., and Bruce W. Stening. 2009. Coaching Expatriate Executives: Working in Context Across the Affective, Behavioural and Cognitive Domains. In *The Routledge Companion to International Business Coaching*, ed. Michael Moral and Geoffrey Abbott, 181–202. London and New York: Routledge.

Abbott, Geoffrey N., Bruce W. Stening, Paul W.B. Atkins, and Anthony M. Grant. 2006. Coaching Expatriate Managers for Success: Adding Value Beyond Training and Mentoring. *Asia Pacific Journal of Human Resources* 44 (3): 295–317.

Al Ariss, Akram, Wayne F. Cascio, and Jaap Paauwe. 2014. Talent Management: Current Theories and Future Research Directions. *Journal of World Business* 49 (2): 173–179.

Andresen, Maike, Franziska Bergdolt, Jil Margenfeld, and Michael Dickmann. 2014. Addressing International Mobility Confusion—Developing Definitions and Differentiation for Self-Initiated and Assigned Expatriates as

Well as Migrants. *International Journal of Human Resource Management* 9 (4): 525–548.

Athanasopoulou, Andromachi, and Sue Dopson. 2015. *Developing Leaders by Executive Coaching: Practice and Evidence.* Oxford: OUP.

Bachkirova, Tatiana, Elaine Cox, and David Clutterbuch. 2010. Introduction. In *The Complete Handbook of Coaching.* London: Sage.

Bachkirova, Tatiana, Gordon Spence, and David Drake. 2016 "Introduction." In *The Sage Handbook of Coaching,* edited by Tatiana Bachkirova, Gordon Spence and David Drake, 419–435. London: Sage.

Bartlett, James E., II, Robert V. Boylan, and Jimmie E. Hale. 2014. Executive Coaching: An Integrative Literature Review. *Journal of Human Resource and Sustainability Studies* 2 (4): 188–195.

Bennett, Milton J. 1993. Towards Ethnorelativism: A Developmental Model of Intercultural Sensitivity. In *Education for the Intercultural Experience,* ed. R.M. Paige, 2nd ed., 21–71. Yarmouth, ME: Intercultural Press.

Biemann, Torsten, and Maike Andresen. 2010. Self-Initiated Foreign Expatriates Versus Assigned Expatriates: Two Distinct Types of International Careers? *Journal of Managerial Psychology* 25 (4): 430–448.

Black, J. Stewart, Mark Mendenhall, and Gary Oddou. 1991. Toward a Comprehensive Model of International Adjustment: An Integration of Multiple Theoretical Perspectives. *Academy of Management Review* 16 (2): 291–317.

Booysen, Lize A.E. 2015. Cross-Cultural Coaching. In *The Center for Creative Leadership Handbook of Coaching in Organizations,* ed. Douglas Riddle, Emily Hoole, and Elizabeth Gullette, 241–287. Jossey-Bass.

Brewster, Chris, Jaime Bonache, Jean-Luc Cerdin, and Vesa Suutari. 2014. Exploring Expatriate Outcomes. *The International Journal of Human Resource Management* 25 (14): 1921–1937. https://doi.org/10.1080/09585192.2013 .870284.

Brookfield Global Mobility Trends Survey. 2016. Accessed November 5, 2016. http://globalmobilitytrends.brookfieldgrs.com

Burrus, Katrina. 2009a. Coaching Managers in Multinational Companies: Myths and Realities of the Global Nomadic Leader. In *The Routledge Companion to International Business Coaching,* ed. Moral Michel and Geoffrey Abbott, 230–237. London: Routledge.

———. 2009b. Coaching Women Managers in Multinational Companies. In *The Routledge Companion to International Business Coaching,* ed. Michel Moral and Geoffrey Abbott, 218–229. London: Routledge.

Caligiuri, Paula, and Jaime Bonache. 2016. Evolving and Enduring Challenges in Global Mobility. *Journal of World Business* 51 (1): 127–141.

Cerdin, Jean-Luc, and Chris Brewster. 2014. Talent Management and Expatriation: Bridging Two Streams of Research and Practice. *Journal of World Business* 49 (2): 245–252.

Chmielecki, Michal. 2009. Coaching Modern Day Nomads. *Journal of Intercultural Management* 1 (2): 135–146.

Dagley, Gavin. 2006. Human Resources Professionals' Perceptions of Executive Coaching: Efficacy, Benefits and Return on Investment. *International Coaching Psychology Review* 1 (2): 34–45.

De Meuse, Kenneth P., Guangrong Dai, and Robert J. Lee. 2009. Evaluating the Effectiveness of Executive Coaching: Beyond ROI? *Coaching: An international Journal of Theory, Research and Practice 2* (2): 117–134.

Dragoni, Lisa, Oh. In-Sue, Paul E. Tesluk, Ozias A. Moore, Paul VanKatwyk, and Joy Hazucha. 2014. Developing Leaders' Strategic Thinking Through Global Work Experience: The Moderating Role of Cultural Distance. *Journal of Applied Psychology* 99 (5): 867–882.

Ellinger, Andrea D., Alexander E. Ellinger, Daniel G. Bachrach, Yu-Lin Wang, and Ays Banu Emadag Bas. 2011. Organizational Investments in Social Capital, Managerial Coaching, and Employee Work-related Performance. *Management Learning* 42 (1): 67–85.

Ellinger, Andrea D., and Sewon Kim. 2014. Coaching and Human Resource Development: Examining Relevant Theories, Coaching Genres, and Scales to Advance Research and Practice. *Advances in Developing Human Resources* 16 (2): 127–138.

Feldman, Daniel C., and Melanie J. Lankau. 2005. Executive Coaching: A Review and Agenda for Future Research. *Journal of Management* 31 (6): 829–848.

Gallo, Frank T. 2015. *The Enlightened Leader: Lessons from China on the Art of Executive Coaching*. Bingley: Emerald Group Publishing.

Gan, Chew Gan, and Chin Wei Chong. 2015. Coaching Relationship in Executive Coaching: A Malaysian Study. *Journal of Management Development* 34 (4): 476–493.

Grant, Anthony M., and Dianne Stober. 2006. Introduction. In *Evidence Based Coaching Handbook: Putting Best Practices to Work for Your Clients*, ed. Dianne R. Stober and Anthony M. Grant, 1–14. Hoboken: Wiley and Sons.

Haslberger, Arno, and Chris Brewster. 2009. Capital Gains: Expatriate Adjustment and the Psychological Contract in International Careers. *Human Resource Management* 48 (3): 379–397.

Herbolzheimer, Anna. 2009. Coaching Expatriates. The Practice and Potential of Expatriate Coaching for European Executives in China. PhD diss., Kassel University.

Hooijberg, Robert, and Nancy Lane. 2009. Using Multisource Feedback Coaching Effectively in Executive Education. *Academy of Management Learning and Education* 8 (4): 483–493.

Inkson, Kerr, and Michael B. Arthur. 2001. How to Be a Successful Career Capitalist. *Organizational Dynamics* 30 (1): 48–61.

International Coach Federation (ICF). 2018. Accessed March 14, 2017. https://www.coachfederation.org/

Javidan, Mansour, Leaetta Hough, and Amanda Bullough. 2010. *Conceptualizing and Measuring Global Mindset*: Development of the Global Mindset Inventory.* Glendale, AZ: Thunderbird School of Global Management.

Jokinen, Tiina, Brewster Chris, and Suutari Vesa. 2008. Career Capital during International Work Experiences: Contrasting Self-Initiated Expatriate Experiences and Assigned Expatriation. *The International Journal of Human Resource Management* 19 (6): 979–998.

Jones, Rebecca J., Stephen A. Woods, and Yves R.F. Guillaume. 2015. The Effectiveness of Workplace Coaching: A Meta-Analysis of Learning and Performance Outcomes from Coaching. *Journal of Occupational and Organizational Psychology* 89 (2): 249–277. https://doi.org/10.1111/joop.12119.

Kohonen, Eeva. 2007. Essays on the Consequences of International Assignments on Expatriates' Identity and Career Aspirations. PhD diss., University of Vaasa.

Kombarakaran, Francis A., Julia A. Yang, Mila N. Baker, and Pauline B. Fernandes. 2008. Executive Coaching: It Works! *Consulting Psychology Journal: Practice and Research* 60 (1): 78–90.

Lam, Pansy. 2016. Chinese Culture and Coaching in Hong Kong. *International Journal of Evidence Based Coaching and Mentoring* 14 (1): 57–73.

Mäkelä, Kristiina, and Vesa Suutari. 2009. Global Careers: A Social Capital Paradox. *The International Journal of Human Resource Management* 20 (5): 992–1008.

Mäkelä, Liisa, and Vesa Suutari. 2011. Coping with Work-Family Conflicts in the Global Career Context. *Thunderbird International Business Review* 53 (3): 365–375.

Maxwel, Alison. 2016. The Use of Feedback for Development in Coaching: Finding the Coach's Stance. In *The Sage Handbook of Coaching*, ed. Tatiana Bachkirova, Gordon Spence, and David Drake, 310–328. London: Sage Publications.

McGill, John Owens, IV. 2010. The Impact of Executive Coaching on the Performance Management of International Managers in China. PhD diss., University of Sydney.

McNulty, Yvonne. 2015. Till Stress Do Us Part: The Causes and Consequences of Expatriate Divorce. *Journal of Global Mobility: The Home of Expatriate Management Research* 3 (2): 106–136.

Mendenhall, Mark E. 2006. The Elusive, Yet Critical Challenge of Developing Global Leaders. *European Management Journal* 24 (6): 422–429.

Milner, Julia, Esther Ostmeier, and Ronald Franke. 2013. Critical Incidents in Cross-Cultural Coaching: The View from German Coaches. *International Journal of Evidence Based Coaching and Mentoring* 11 (2): 19–32.

Miser, Andrew L., and Martha F. Miser. 2009. Couples Coaching for Expatriate Couples. In *The Routledge Companion to International Business Coaching*, ed. Michel Moral and Geoffrey N. Abbott, 203–217. Oxon: Routledge.

Muir, Melinda J. 2014. The Career Narratives of Professional Self-initiated Expatriate Women Living and Working in Beijing, China. DBA thesis, Southern Cross University.

Nangalia, Lina, and Ajay Nangalia. 2010. The Coach in Asian Society: Impact of Social Hierarchy on the Coaching Relationship. *International Journal of Evidence Based Coaching and Mentoring* 8 (1): 51–66.

Näsholm, Malin. 2011. Global Careerists' Identity Construction: A Narrative Study of Repeat Expatriates and International Itinerants. PhD diss., University of Umeå.

Ng, K.Y., Linn Van Dyne, and Soon Ang. 2009. From Experience to Experiential Learning: Cultural Intelligence as a Learning Capability for Global Leader Development. *Academy of Management Learning and Education* 8 (4): 511–526.

Osland, Joyce S. 2000. The Journey Inward: Expatriate Hero Tales and Paradoxes. *Human Resource Management* 39 (2, 3): 227–238.

Osland, Joyce S., and Asbjörn Osland. 2005. Expatriate Paradoxes and Cultural Involvement. *International Studies of Management and Organization* 35 (4): 91–114.

Parker, Polly. 2016. Coaching for Role Transitions/Career Change. In *The Sage Handbook of Coaching*, ed. Tatiana Bachkirova, Gordon Spence, and David Drake, 419–435. London: Sage.

Passmore, Jonathan, and Anette Fillery-Travis. 2011. A Critical Review of Executive Coaching Research: A Decade of Progress and What's to Come. *Coaching: An International Journal of Theory, Practice and Research* 4 (2): 70–88. https://doi.org/10.1080/17521882.2011.596484.

Piekkari, Rebekka, and Susanne A. Tietze. 2011. World of Languages: Implications for International Management Research and Practice. *Journal of World Business* 46 (3): 267–269.

Rosinski, Philippe. 2003. *Coaching across Cultures: New Tools for Leveraging National, Corporate and Professional Differences*. London: Nicholas Brealey Publishing.

———. 2010. *Global Coaching: An Integrated Approach for Long-Lasting Results*. London: Nicholas Brealey Publishing.

Salomaa, Raija. 2015. Expatriate Coaching: Factors Impacting Coaching Success. *Journal of Global Mobility* 3 (3): 216–243.

Salomaa, Raija, and Liisa Mäkelä. 2015. Expatriates' Experiences Concerning Coaching as a Part of their Career Capital Development. Paper presented at the HRD Conference for the Academy of Management, Cork, Ireland, June.

———. 2017. Coaching for Career Capital Development: A Study of Expatriates' Narratives. *The International Journal of Evidence Based Coaching and Mentoring* 15 (1): 114–132.

Selmer, Jan. 1999. Career Issues and International Adjustment of Business Expatriates. *Career Development International* 4 (2): 77–87.

Shaffer, Margaret, Maria L. Kraimer, Yu-Ping Chen, and Marck C. Bolino. 2012. Choices, Challenges, and Career Consequences of Global Work Experiences: A Review and Future Agenda. *Journal of Management* 38 (4): 1282–1327.

Sonesh, Shirley C., Chris W. Coultas, Christina N. Lacerenza, Shannon L. Marlow, Lauren E. Benishek, and Eduardo Salas. 2015. The Power of Coaching: A Meta-Analytic Investigation. *Coaching: An International Journal of Theory, Research and Practice* 8 (2): 73–95.

Suutari, Vesa, and Chris Brewster. 2000. Making Their Own Way: International Experience Through Self-Initiated Foreign Assignments. *Journal of World Business* 35 (4): 417–436.

Suutari, Vesa, and Kristiina Mäkelä. 2007. The Career Capital of Managers with Global Careers. *Journal of Managerial Psychology* 22 (7): 628–648.

Takeuchi, Riki. 2010. A Critical Review Of Expatriate Adjustment Research Through a Multiple Stakeholder View: Progress, Emerging Trends, and Prospects. *Journal of Management* 36 (4): 1040–1064.

Theeboom, Tim, Bianca Beersma, and Annelies E.M. van Vianen. 2014. Does Coaching Work? A Meta-Analysis on the Effects of Coaching on Individual Level Outcomes in an Organizational Context. *The Journal of Positive Psychology* 9 (1): 1–18.

Tompson, Holly B., Bear Donna, J. Dennis, Mark Vickers, Judy London, and Carol L. Morrison. 2008. *Coaching: A Global Study of Successful Practices: Current Trends and Future Possibilities 2008–2018*. New York: American Management Association.

Van Nieuwerburgh, Christian. 2016. Interculturally Sensitive Coaching. In *The Sage Handbook of Coaching*, ed. Tatiana Bachkirova, Gordon Spence, and David Drake, 439–452. Los Angeles: Sage.

5

Career Success in Different Countries: Reflections on the 5C Project

Jon Briscoe, Michael Dickmann, Tim Hall, Emma Parry, Wolfgang Mayrhofer, and Adam Smale

Introduction

Left Behind: Career Studies and the Rise of International Work

Career studies have, at best, partly kept pace with the enormous rise of international work. While on virtually all accounts such as volume of international business transactions, importance of organizations operating across national and cultural boundaries or individuals pursuing an international or global career indicators point towards growth, the body of career-related research on this has not grown to the same extent. With

---

J. Briscoe (✉)
Department of Management, College of Business, Northern Illinois University, DeKalb, IL, USA
e-mail: jpbriscoe@niu.edu

M. Dickmann • E. Parry
Cranfield School of Management, Cranfield University, Cranfield, UK
e-mail: m.dickmann@cranfield.ac.uk; emma.parry@cranfield.ac.uk

© The Author(s) 2018
M. Dickmann et al. (eds.), *The Management of Global Careers*,
https://doi.org/10.1007/978-3-319-76529-7_5

the exception of expatriation and its various facets such as classic expatriation (Bader et al. 2016), self-initiated expatriation (Andresen et al. 2013) or migration (Solimano 2010), systematic research about various aspects of careers in different countries and cultures, in particular in a comparative sense (Lazarova et al. 2012), has only started to emerge.

A substantial body of knowledge about careers as such exist (see the overviews in, e.g. Arthur et al. 1989; Gunz and Peiperl 2007; Gunz et al. 2018 [in press]). Fed by a great variety of disciplines ranging from developmental psychology via management studies to labour economics and sociology, research efforts focusing on organization and management careers (OMC) have produced substantial insight on individuals' careers and the aspects linked to condition, space and time (Gunz and Mayrhofer 2018 [in press]). Often tracked back to the Chicago School of Sociology and the work of Hughes (1937) and his colleagues on a great variety of topics ranging from high-status professions such as medical doctors to careers more on the fringe of society such as taxi hall dancers (Cressey 1932), jackrollers (Shaw 1930), professional thieves (Sutherland 1937) or hobos (Anderson 1923), the existing body of knowledge is particularly strong in terms of career success and its influencing factors (Gunz and Heslin 2005; Heslin 2005a; Ng et al. 2005; Ng and Feldman 2014).

Looking at the research in this area reveals, however, a familiar picture in many areas of management studies: the research focuses on a comparatively small set of countries and uses concepts originating from North America with a strong explicit or implicit universality assumption. With regard to the former, much of career studies focuses on WEIRD countries,

---

T. Hall
Questrom School of Business, Boston University, Boston, MA, USA
e-mail: dthall@bu.edu

W. Mayrhofer
WU Vienna, Wien, Austria
e-mail: Wolfgang.Mayrhofer@wu.ac.at

A. Smale
University of Vaasa, Vaasa, Finland
e-mail: Adam.smale@uwasa.fi

that is, *W*estern, *e*ducated, *i*ndustrialized, *r*ich and *d*emocratic. While this has its merits, it also constitutes a severe limitation since it leaves out large parts of the world where we know little, if anything, about careers, career success and factors influencing careers. Another element of the emerging picture arguably is even more worrying. Underlying much of the existing research are theories, frameworks and operationalizations that come from a narrow set of countries, most often the USA, and implicitly or explicitly claim universal applicability. Examples include conceptualizations of career transitions (Louis 1980) or career success measures such as the widely used career success scale by Greenhaus et al. (1990). They represent an etic, that is, a general, non-structural and objective, view (Morris et al. 1999) on careers that give preference to 'outside' views instead of also looking at and analysing a phenomenon through the eyes of the respective local actors.

In a related field, human resource management, systematic efforts to comparatively study HRM policies and practices had already started in the early 1990s (Hegewisch and Brewster 1993), and comparative HRM is now a well-established field (Brewster and Mayrhofer 2012; Brewster et al. 2018 [in press]). In career studies, similar developments are only now starting to occur. In the mid-noughties, there was very little systematic and comparative information available on how people in different countries and cultures view different aspects of careers. Roughly a decade ago, initial efforts for a more comprehensive view on careers and career success across the globe took shape in the form of the 5C project (www.5C. careers) and started to bear its first fruit (Briscoe et al. 2012a, b; Chudzikowski et al. 2009; Shen et al. 2015). Building on this, the current effort of 5C targets a more comprehensive and emic view of different aspects of careers across the globe.

Our chapter focuses on the issue of career success in different countries based on the development of the 5C project. Before presenting major findings both in conceptual and empirical terms and taking stock about what we currently know in this area and outline promising avenues for future research, we outline efforts for a more emic view, that is, an approach focused on understanding careers more from a perspective that explores elements, their functioning and their interactions from an internal perspective. To this we turn next.

Digging Deep: Towards an Emic View on Careers

The 5C project started with rather traditional WEIRD goals at first. The groups three co-founders (Jon Briscoe, Douglas T. Hall and Wolfgang Mayrhofer) at first agreed to look at the protean or self-directed (Hall 1976, 2002) careers across cultures, wondering if such a career was indeed relevant across the globe. Fortunately, upon investigating research methods and reflecting upon alternatives, they arrived at a more emic approach. Realizing that documenting the reliability and variability of a construct created in the Northeastern United States (the protean career) was of little utility, they instead opted for an 'N-way' approach (Brett et al. 1997) in which the countries, research participants and researchers themselves each contribute to the theory and knowledge being formed. This demanded an approach in which the research participants' voice and circumstances were heard.

Initial Steps

Collaborating as a growing group, 5C decided to look at two broad areas of careers—career success and career management (management from the individual's perspective). We knew that how people attach meaning to their careers was important and would likely vary, in part, due to national culture. We were also interested in how culture as well as other contextual factors such as rate of economic change, access to education and degree of diversity might impact how individuals managed their career. We thus focused on career transition(s) as an important event that could reveal career management behaviours in context.

In terms of method, the semi-structured interview was our preferred approach in order to offer flexibility in exploring interviewee experiences and forming initial frameworks (Patton 1990). But who to interview? We decided after careful discussion to focus on three occupations (loosely speaking): nurses, business people and blue-collar workers. These groups were not precisely similar in terms of professional or informal realities across countries but at least the tasks were standardized. We reasoned further that the relative structure of each occupation would highlight important contrasts in how career actors networked, received validation, defined career success and so on.

Beyond occupation we tried where possible to balance genders and to address age. We wanted people to have at least two years of work experience so as to have gained career perspective, but from there we divided our sample into early (first ten years of career) and late (last ten years of career) career stages, seeking maximum contrast in how they managed their careers and defined career success.

In terms of country-level sampling, we chose to use Schwartz's cultural values framework (2006). We felt that Schwartz's methods for establishing his framework were superior to others (Hofstede 1991; Trompenaars and Hampden-Turner 1997) but that he also offered something unique—a division of countries into cultural regions. This made sampling countries a much easier project. The GLOBE framework (House et al. 2004) offers similar advantages and has some redundancies with Schwartz's work, but it was not readily available at the time we began our research (we have since incorporated it in later research stages). Schwartz outlined seven cultural regions: Africa/Middle East, Confucian Asia, Eastern Europe, English Speaking, Latin America, South Asia and Western Europe. Israel was considered as not fitting into any of these categories precisely. Using the Schwartz framework, we chose 11 countries for our qualitative interviews: Austria, China, Costa Rica, Israel, Japan, Malaysia, Mexico, Serbia, South Africa, Spain and the United States of America (USA). We wanted to have at least one country in each cultural region; in some cases we were able to obtain more than one.

After the interviews were conducted and transcribed, they were coded by each particular country team, and initial codes were developed around the general themes of career success, career transitions and contextual factors that impacted these themes. Representatives for country teams met to explain and question these tentative conclusions. Following on from the coding discussion, a coding guide was created with participation from all teams, based on their agreement about common themes. Then all teams used the coding guide and recoded their data. The derived data concerned career transitions (and their management) as well as meanings of career success.

Broad Findings

Looking first at career transitions, the 5C research revealed that both individual differences (e.g. mastery versus performance orientation) as well as social and macro contexts shaped the nature of how people coped with career change (Briscoe et al. 2012a, b). For example, at an individual level, business people were more likely to perceive themselves as driving career transitions, whereas nurses were the least likely. At a macro level, countries characterized by more hierarchy in Schwartz's (2006) framework were less likely to see transitions as self-driven, but those high in egalitarianism (i.e. favouring equality in all people) were more likely. Also, countries lower in uncertainty avoidance (Hofstede 1991) were more likely to attribute career transitions to individual factors.

Perhaps more interesting than the general associations just reviewed were the contextual factors that emerged in individual county samples. Countries undergoing drastic transitions due to political or economic developments such as China, Serbia and South Africa showed marked contrasts between the older and younger generations. The experience of an older worker in China, for example, was perceived as almost completely out of one's control, whereas younger workers felt a significant degree of autonomy.

Taking a closer look at five countries in terms of perceived career transition attributions and triggers (Austria, China, Serbia, Spain and the USA), 5C found that Western European and US participants were more likely to attribute career transitions to internal causes, while external context was seen as a stronger cause of career transitions in China, with Serbia sharing some features of both polarities (Chudzikowski et al. 2009). Overall, some of the key contextual factors that shape and frame career transitions were legal/political, education, socio-economic status, gender, race, age and generation.

Career success was also studied in depth in the qualitative phase of our research (Demel et al. 2012). Initially, three broad categories of career success emerged from our coding scheme: person (e.g. learning and development), job (e.g. performing one's role), and interaction with the environment (e.g. work-life balance). The most frequently perceived meanings of career success were achievement, satisfaction and job/task characteristics. Achievement was often depicted as an objective sort of success, satisfaction as subjective success and job/task characteristics could be either subjective or objective. Concerning influences upon their career success, over half of the research participants cited the context in which they were working, personal history, personal traits and motivations as key.

A further round of data analysis (Shen et al. 2015) also focused upon achievement, satisfaction and job/task characteristics but added learning and development as another 'universal' meaning of career success—indicating that it was found in each sample. This study also looked at 'contextualist' meanings of career success that were found or amplified in some countries but not others. For example, 'making a difference' was more important in Malaysia, South Africa and the USA, whereas survival and security was pronounced in China, Costa Rica and Mexico. The authors used this contextualist versus universalist aspect of career success and juxtaposed it with traditional versus agentic career orientations on the individual level. In addition, they discussed differentiation versus standardization in terms of HRM strategy. In doing so they outlined how multinational and international HRM can emphasize the more common meanings of career success but also cater to local populations where the differences are distinct and call for specific national rather than cross-national approaches.

Casting the Net Wide: Conceptual and Empirical Developments

The qualitative research phase described in the previous section provided some interesting initial insights into the different meanings of career and career success, as well as the role of context in shaping career attitudes and behaviours. The insights from this qualitative study led to a more encompassing endeavour involving both developing a heuristic framework and large-scale quantitative surveys building on it. Whilst seeking to test the generalizability of some of the findings of the qualitative phase, the quantitative phase had a narrower approach—focusing primarily on issues related to career success.

The primary research question that this stage focused on was: 'How do people in different countries perceive career success?' However, beyond the 'how' question, we were also interested in the many 'why' questions. Why do people view career success the way they do? Are these views better explained by structural societal explanations such as culture, economies, educational levels and generations, or by individual factors, for example, self-directed career behaviours, personality and gender? And why does career success matter? Are views of career success associated with, for example, higher levels of work engagement, objective career success or overall life satisfaction? In terms of their interaction, which contextual factors (societal, organizational) moderate the relationships between the antecedents, meanings and outcomes of career success?

Figure 5.1 presents the heuristic framework which informed much of the thinking around the quantitative research design.

Measuring Career Success

The central focus on meanings of career success was important partly due to the limitations in extant research in this area. Despite major conceptual contributions dealing with careers in general and career success in particular, the literature has concentrated on only a few broad distinctions, for example, 'objective vs. subjective' or 'satisfaction vs. salary'. Since Hughes (1937) studied the corporation, there has been a concern with subjective versus objective career experiences. Since salary and promotion can be objectified and quantified, they have often been turned to as proxies for career success. In 1976, Hall documented a new 'protean' career that was less concerned with objectified career paths and more concerned with the individual's idiosyncratic psychological and career success. Derr's career success map (1986) and Schein's career anchors (1978) are other examples of concerted efforts to capture the subjective forms of career success.

Despite this, existing measures of career success have failed to identify its true nature or to acknowledge its multidimensionality. For example, the commonly cited career satisfaction scale from Greenhaus et al. (1990) does not specify the source of the satisfaction. Following the suggestion

Career Success in Different Countries: Reflections on the 5C...

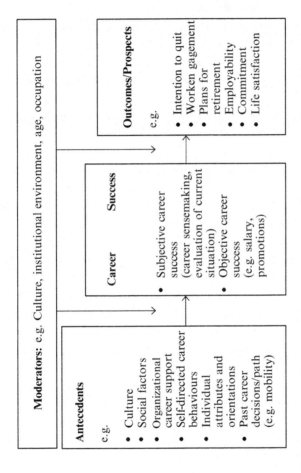

Fig. 5.1 Heuristic framework on the antecedents and outcomes of career success. Source: The authors

of Heslin (2005b) and others, scales have since been developed that account for the more subjective sources of career success meanings (Dries et al. 2008; Dries 2011; Shockley et al. 2015). However, these have been measured and examined within a single culture, and thus their cross-cultural robustness has not been tested.

Indeed, most theoretical and empirical research on career success has been based on a perspective dominated by looking at WEIRD countries. This contributes to the fact that up until now career research has not fully integrated the multi-layered richness and diversity of views on career success that individuals around the globe possess and, as such, has failed to take into account the importance of national context in our understanding of career success.

In order to address the above limitations, it was felt that a new career success scale was needed to enable the comparison of career success across countries. The 5C collaboration thus set about developing a scale (Briscoe et al. 2014) which was rooted in the initial qualitative research described above. After developing robust theoretical categories from an innovative combination of card sorting and cultural domain analysis (Borgatti 1998), a confirmatory factor analysis revealed that these categories of career success were present in countries in each of the GLOBE clusters (delineated in the global study of leadership by House et al. 2004). Using a sample of over 18,000 respondents from 30 countries and testing across four occupational categories (see below), the scale validation exercise arrived at the following seven dimensions of career success that were valid and culturally invariant across all of the GLOBE clusters: *learning and development, work-life balance, positive impact, positive work relationships, financial security, financial success* and *entrepreneurship* (see Table 5.1).

A further contribution of this scale is that it measures career success in terms of the value (what we refer to as *importance*) that people place on different aspects of their careers, as well as their degree of satisfaction (or *achievement*) with the level of success they have reached. This distinction acknowledges the fact that people can be driven by certain aspirations without feeling fulfilment in that respect and vice versa may experience fulfilment along a certain dimension to which they attach relatively little importance (Argyris 1982; Katz and Kahn 1978). Both aspects of career success can be applied to each of the seven dimensions

Table 5.1 Summary of the career success scale[a]

Dimension of career success	Example item
Learning and development	Doing work that gives me the opportunity to learn
Work-life balance	Achieving a satisfying balance between work and family life
Positive impact	Contributing to the development of others
Positive work relationships	Getting positive feedback from supervisors
Financial security	Being able to provide for my family financially
Financial success	Steadily making more money
Entrepreneurship	Owning my own company

Source: The authors based on Briscoe et al. 2014 and Mayrhofer et al. 2016
[a]For the complete career success scale and full list of items, please contact the authors

and thus can be compared and/or used to measure the gap between the perceived importance and achievement of career success. Some examples of this kind of analysis are provided below.

Multi-country Data Collection

Using this validated scale and other existing scales representing the antecedents and outcomes in our framework (see Fig. 5.1), we proceeded to gather research in multiple countries. One goal was to include at least two countries from each of the GLOBE cultural clusters to ensure that all the clusters were represented in our sample. Another target was to include data from at least 30 countries since that would provide a sufficient number of observations at the country level to perform multilevel analyses. This cross-cultural research collaboration required a long process of recruiting academic collaborators, establishing group norms, coordinating data collection efforts and addressing a variety of linguistic, ethical, methodological and practical challenges (see Easterby-Smith and Malina 1999; Thomas et al. 2009; for a discussion of some of these issues in cross-cultural research teams). While data collection is still ongoing at the time of writing, data has been collected from 30 countries (see Table 5.2).

128   J. Briscoe et al.

In each country a convenience sample was used. Past career research has tended to focus on managerial and professional careers, neglecting the careers of blue-collar, skilled labour. Therefore, we targeted at least 100 employees for each of the four broadly defined occupational groups: managers, professionals (defined as those in occupations which usually require degree level education), sales/clerical workers and skilled labour. Survey questions were back-translated from English (Brislin 1970) where acceptable translations of scales were not yet available. Surveys were pre-tested in each country and adjusted for factors such as respondent fatigue.

Empirical Insights

Some of the early findings on career success are presented below. For the purposes of this chapter, we have chosen to provide three examples of analyses: first, a comparison of career success conceptualizations by country; second, an analysis of gender differences within a particular region (Germany, Austria and Switzerland—DACH); and third, an analysis of the impact of a macro-level factor (income equality) on conceptualizations of career success. The purpose of this is to illustrate the utility of the 5C data as well as to provide a flavour of some of the initial findings.

Table 5.2 Country sample (by GLOBE cluster)

GLOBE cluster	Countries
Confucian Asia	China, Japan, South Korea
Southern Asia	India, Philippines
Sub-Saharan Africa	Malawi, Nigeria
Latin America	Argentina, Brazil, Mexico, Colombia
Middle East	Pakistan, Turkey
Anglo	Australia, UK, USA
Nordic Europe	Finland, Norway
Latin Europe	Italy, Portugal
Eastern Europe	Estonia, Greece, Russia, Serbia, Slovakia, Slovenia
Germanic Europe	Austria, Belgium, Germany, Switzerland

Source: The authors

Career Success Conceptualizations by Country

To examine career success conceptualizations across countries, descriptive data from ten countries have been selected, one from each of the ten GLOBE clusters. The countries are: China (Confucian Asia), India (Southern Asia), Argentina (Latin America), Finland (Nordic Europe), USA (Anglo), Italy (Latin Europe), Nigeria (Sub-Saharan Africa), Russia (Eastern Europe), Germany (Germanic Europe) and Pakistan (Middle East). A simple comparison between these countries in terms of the average scores for career success importance and achievement for some of the career success dimensions are reported together with a short commentary. The scale for importance was 1 = not at all important to 5 = very important and for achievement: 1 = strongly disagree to 5 = strongly agree. The charts below show the average rating for importance and achievement in each country for four of the scales. These four were chosen as an illustration of the country differences.

For the majority of countries, *financial security* was seen as the most important dimension of career success, especially in the USA (4.8) and Nigeria (4.8). Whilst one might expect to see notable differences in importance and achievement in developing and transition economies such as Nigeria, Russia and China, these differences are not much smaller than in the USA and Italy (Fig. 5.2).

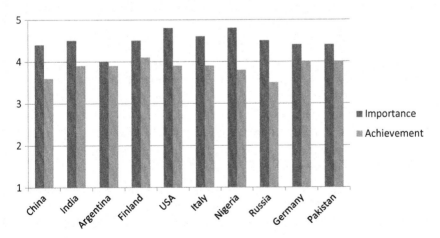

Fig. 5.2 Financial security by country. Source: The authors

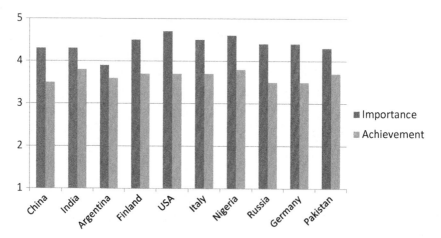

Fig. 5.3 Work-life balance by country. Source: The authors

Work-life balance follows financial security as generally the second most important dimension of career success for most countries. However, this dimension (together with financial success) produced some of the largest gaps between importance and achievement. Interestingly, there are few big differences between countries with perhaps the exception of Argentina (Fig. 5.3).

Compared to financial security and work-life balance, we see much more variance in the importance attached to *financial success*. We also see more between-country variance in the importance of financial success than its perceived achievement. There were large differences between the levels of importance and achievement in several countries, in particular Nigeria (4.7 vs. 3.5), Russia (4.2 vs. 3.1), China (4.2 vs. 3.2) and the USA (4.3 vs. 3.3) (Fig. 5.4).

As one would expect, for most dimensions of career success, people's levels of perceived achievement are almost always below that of importance since importance comprises an aspirational element. The *Entrepreneurial* dimension of career success, however, behaves differently in many countries (e.g. Finland, the USA and Germany). This might be partly due to the rather low overall importance attached to entrepreneurial career success (least important of all seven dimensions), where one

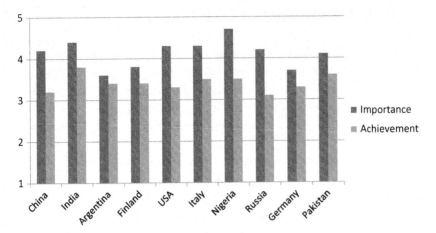

Fig. 5.4 Financial success by country. Source: The authors

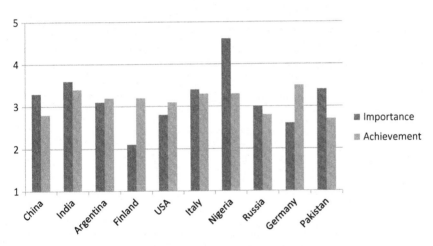

Fig. 5.5 Entrepreneurial by country. Source: The authors

explanation could be that such modest aspirations are easier to surpass. Another could be that certain aspects of being entrepreneurial (e.g. being self-employed and running your own business) are more straightforward to assess (Fig. 5.5).

Gender Differences Within the DACH Region

Next we turn to look at career success in a specific region of the world, the German-language countries Austria, Germany and Switzerland ('DACH-countries') that are on the one hand quite similar but nevertheless show clear fine differences. This makes them a good test bed for looking at similarities and differences in closely related contextual settings.

Using the seven dimensions of career success and looking at both importance and achievement as well as men and women, the following picture emerges. In terms of importance, work-life balance and financial security rank highest with entrepreneurship, positive impact and financial achievement lowest (Fig. 5.6). In this regard, there are no substantial differences between women and men.

With regard to achieving the various dimensions of career success, financial security, positive work relationships and learning and development score highest (Fig. 5.7). Again, there are hardly any noticeable differences between women and men.

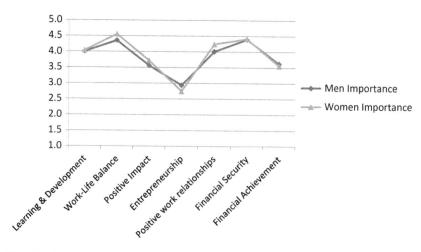

Fig. 5.6 Importance of dimensions of career success for women and men (DACH-countries). Source: The authors

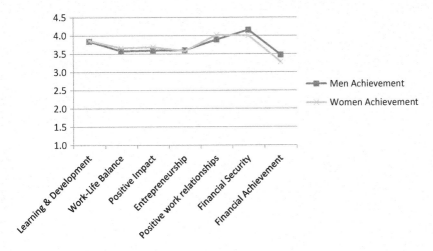

Fig. 5.7 Achievement in dimensions of career success for women and men (DACH-countries). Source: The authors

Looking at the expectation-realization gap, one can see clearly that there is the greatest negative gap in the area of work-life balance for both women and men. Vice versa, with regard to entrepreneurship, a low level of importance is far exceeded by actual achievement for both sexes (Fig. 5.8).

Overall, for both women and men importance and achievement of the seven dimensions of career success follow a pretty similar pattern. A more in-depth comparative analysis of the three countries reveals that again there are remarkable parallels between the three countries with hardly any noticeable differences.

Macro-Level Influences on Conceptualizations of Career Success

An additional effort of 5C research addresses the effects of factors at the societal level on career views. Following previous calls for a better integration of these macro-factors, first explorations show that this seems to be a promising route for better understanding commonalities and

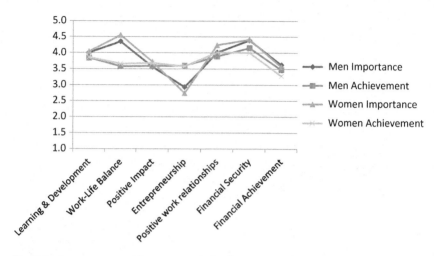

Fig. 5.8 Importance-achievement gap in dimensions of career success for women and men (DACH-countries). Source: The authors

differences in career views. One example for this kind of undertaking is the analysis of the effects of national income inequality on the importance of various career success dimensions. Looking at 18 countries across three continents—Americas (Argentina, Mexico), Asia (India, Japan, Pakistan, Korea), Europe (Austria, Belgium, Germany, Greece, Finland, Italy, Norway, Portugal, Russia, Serbia, Slovenia, Switzerland)—one can see that in countries with stronger income inequality, financial achievement is a more important aspect of subjective career success (Fig. 5.9).

Taking Stock: The Global Picture of Careers

In this section, we outline what we currently know, based on scholarly work in this area aiming at better understanding of what happens globally in terms of careers and muse about the extent to which this knowledge adds value to practitioners' activities, for example, in HRM, career counselling, coaching and national policy making.

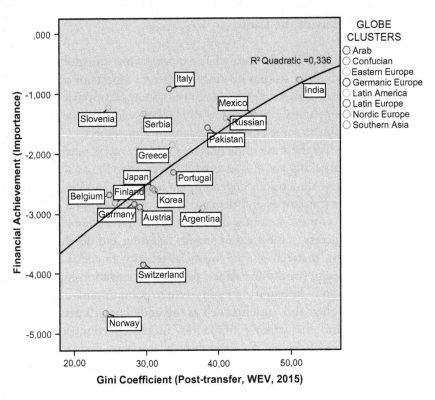

Fig. 5.9 National income inequality and importance of financial achievement. Source: The authors

Established Insights and Future Research

Although comparative career studies is a nascent area with a lot of work still ahead, one can identify at least three areas where both some insight and a broad idea of future research have been developed. They consist of exploring the lay of the land and developing a descriptive world map, following developments over time in terms of how individual careers and organizational career management in different countries, cultures and institutional contexts develop, and explaining relationships and developments both cross-sectional and over time. We will briefly address these issues in turn.

Exploring the Lay of the Land

In terms of empirical insight into what happens across the globe career wise, we have a bulk of studies looking at different aspects of careers in various countries. However, as argued above, systematic approaches that allow a sound comparative view are few and far between. Still, we are currently able to point to some emerging insights in this respect.

First, it seems like there are some universal underlying dimensions that people use when talking about a successful career. Individuals score very differently on these dimensions depending on respective specifics such as individual career trajectories and demand levels, profession and cultural and institutional context. Yet, they draw on the seven identifiable dimensions of career success in the areas of growth (learning and development, entrepreneurship), material output (financial security, financial achievement) and life design (work-life balance, positive work relationships, positive impact). Second, the empirical results seem to point towards a peculiar duality. On the one hand, insights such as the underlying dimensions of career success and the striking similarities in related countries point towards a substantial degree of universalism in this area. Factors such as the strong force of the capitalist economic logic, global media community transporting (largely 'Western') views of career and career success via cinema, TV and streaming services contribute to a certain kind of uniformity. On the other hand, both at the individual and the collective level we see substantial differences, too. This indicates that there are important factors that lead to individual differentiation. Hence, it becomes crucial to further analyse the interplay between various factors in order to better understand the forces pushing towards 'standardization' and 'differentiation' of career views, respectively. Third, despite a growing body of knowledge, we still know very little about basic 'facts and figures' in other regions of the world outside WEIRD countries', in particular large parts of Africa, Middle East, South East Asia and (parts of) South America.

Against this backdrop, further exploring the lay of the land and developing a descriptive world map with regard to conceptualizations of careers, views on career success and career-related HRM policies and practices become a crucial issue. Ideally, the respective data *collection* efforts go beyond safari research and ad hoc collaboration and target countries and regions beyond WEIRD countries. With regard to data *analysis*, focusing on descriptive analyses showing commonalities and differences and making this knowledge broadly accessible for both academia, organizational practitioners such as HRM specialists, policy makers and the broader public becomes a priority.

Following Developments Over Time

The existing data is the result of cross-sectional snapshots. Analyses based on this data are valuable by all means, but also limited. While it allows insight into the respective status quo, it is devoid of following developments over time. Both at the individual and the collective level, this is far from ideal. The time dimension built into careers and the resulting dynamics call for data that allows tracking the developments over the individual life course. In a similar vein, at the collective level these efforts allow to detect changes within and between national, institutional and cultural contexts and consequently to uncover stasis, convergence or divergence when comparing the relative positioning of national, cultural and institutional contexts (for a similar effort in HRM, see, e.g. Mayrhofer et al. 2004, 2011).

Explaining Relationships and Developments Over Time

Descriptively analysing the situation in various countries, cultures and institutional settings as well as tracking developments over time contributes to our insight into careers. In addition, sound empirical data and descriptive analyses provide the basis for answering the 'why' question of commonalities and differences as well as changes over time by using good theory that allows a guided in-depth analysis of why the observed commonalities and differences occur. Various theoretical schools are available and offer suitable theoretical concepts already used in other areas of comparative analysis. Besides the widespread use of cultural theories (Hofstede 1980; Trompenaars and Hampden-Turner 1997; House et al. 2004), one can mention neo-institutional theories (Greenwood et al. 2008; Thornton et al. 2012) focusing on the institutional setting within which individual careers and organizational career systems take place, or behavioural economic theories trying to combine insights from classical economics and behavioural approaches, in particular from sociology and psychology.

Applied Value

The applied value of the 5C research, the creation of a career world map and the ability to distinguish country (and country-cluster) patterns can be discussed looking at the levels of individual, team, organization and policy maker.

Individual Level

The 5C work has yielded seven dimension of career success in a culturally invariant scale: learning and development, work-life balance, positive impact, positive work relationships, financial security, financial success and entrepreneurial. These dimensions are investigated distinguishing importance and achievement.

The act of filling out the 5C questionnaire can trigger an intensive engagement with one's career success values, aspirations and behaviours. In combination with the survey feedback, individuals can reflect more deeply on their career strategies and actions and may formulate new career plans.

In addition, an emerging career world map allows individuals to understand the predominant career attitudes in their own country which can lead to a reflection vis-à-vis potential contrasts with their own career success values or organizational context. A deeper understanding of one's own personal and professional context can lead to superior career planning.

Group/Team Level

The emerging 5C world map (www.5C.careers) gives country-level data of career success values in combination with macro-level economic and sociological data. This leads to potentially useful applications at the group/team level.

Where all individuals in a team fill out the 5C questionnaire, an in-depth picture of the career values and aspirations will emerge. Team leaders and coaches can use this to reflect the fit of individuals to their current positions and engage in active career planning.

In addition, the overall picture may allow leaders and coaches to reflect on the role distribution within the team and adjust their management accordingly. For instance, individuals who value entrepreneurial activities highly may be more likely to be given projects that need entrepreneurial-minded staff. In addition, leaders may find it important to understand how individuals view work-life balance importance and achievement when drawing up job descriptions and distributing posts and activities.

Organizational Level

The 5C data adds new insights which are especially valuable for organizations operating in 'non-WEIRD' countries. While HR decisions are likely to be most affected, some strategic approaches can also benefit from the 5C insights.

Where MNCs expand into other countries, they have a choice of a range of configurations (Bartlett and Ghoshal 1998; Dickmann and Muller-Camen 2006) that determine the degree of international standardization and integration of (HR) policies. The 5C data shows that macro-economic factors such as inequality predict the importance attached to financial achievement and should, therefore, be factored into the design of reward systems. Different importance of entrepreneurism and work-life balance considerations will also constrain the ability of firms to highly standardize all their HR approaches across different countries, thus influencing strategic HR decisions to integrate people management approaches globally.

Factoring in 5C data could also assist in shaping decisions in HR policy areas. 5C has, among others, set out to understand the linkages of individuals' views on career success to work engagement and objective career success as measured by salary and hierarchical advancement. Understanding individuals' career values and aspirations better can inform talent sourcing strategies. The (local) corporate branding initiatives as well as selection approaches may be fine-tuned to attract (and choose) the best talent for an organization given its specific country location, context and corporate strategy. Given the individual and group level discussion above, it is clear that HR professionals would also benefit from using the 5C data in the design of overall career structures in organizations as well specific career planning for individuals. Job and work design implications should also be analysed. Gender and age patterns may also be used to design people management approaches in organizations. Lastly, performance management and reward strategies are generally aimed at motivating staff to exert effort on behalf of the organization and to do 'the right things in the right way'. 5C data would allow companies to understand the general career values that individuals hold in a country (and specifically in their organization if they choose to apply the 5C instrument broadly in their enterprise). Attitudes towards work-life balance, financial security and financial success as well as the other dimensions could be used as an input into the design of performance management and reward systems.

Policy Maker Level

Given that career success is likely to have a link to broader outcomes such as work engagement, employability or life satisfaction, policy makers are likely to be able to use the 5C data for a range of decisions. The seven dimensions of the career success scale are each in themselves important sources of information. Three are outlined as examples.

Differences in *learning and development* importance and achievement—especially when analysed in relation to other factors such as skills shortages in the economy, gender and age as well as occupational data—give important indication about the strive for (lifelong) learning and how difficult it might be to motivate individuals to fill particular skills shortages. Government policies, such as the UK's apprenticeship levy that came into effect in 2017, may then be developed that aim at strengthening lifelong professional development.

The degree of preference (and achievement) of individuals for *entrepreneurship*, in particular to own their own companies, can give important information with regard to how to design and shape industrial policy, especially in relation to small and medium-sized companies and the administrative and financial burdens of incorporating and running these organizations. Given that intrapreneurism is also often sought by companies, a high level of entrepreneurial orientation may be an attraction factor for foreign direct investment.

The importance and achievement of *financial security* can also be crucial information for governments who use their fiscal policies and social security systems to tax individuals and organizations and then to reallocate funds. Unemployment benefits and other social security spending are intimately related to individuals' feelings of how they are able to provide for their families. This may be particularly relevant in precarious or low-paid jobs or when the 'breadwinner' is out of work. Distribution policies and the Gini coefficient are shaped by many influences, and the need for financial security could be one of these.

It is not difficult to see that the 5C data can have even more application, for instance, through improved insights into work-life balance preferences or the attitudes to strive for a positive impact at work. The discussion about the applied value of the 5C research has only been able to give a brief glimpse into the broad array of fields in which the data could be used. As the 5C project matures, many more practical uses are likely to emerge.

More Than a Look into the Crystal Ball: Promising Future Avenues

As we think about major issues for research in contemporary careers, one of the most pressing is studying ways to help people make changes in their careers that will help them adapt to what Johansen (2012) calls the 'VUCA' environment (Volatile, Uncertain, Complex and Ambiguous.) This turbulent world is made so by many powerful forces in the institutional environment: political, economic, military, social, religious, technological and so on. Whether we are focusing on the needs of immigrants who, either voluntarily or involuntarily, have left an established career in their home countries and now find themselves in a totally new living and working environment, or on the plight of another kind of refugee, those

142   J. Briscoe et al.

who have lost their jobs and been shunted aside because of obsolete skills or high wages that cannot compete with those of workers in another part of the world, or people who would like to switch jobs or retire but are unable to find a way to do so, we are dealing with the need for major career change. In this section we will examine major research issues that must be addressed in the future if we want people to become more effective in acquiring new, current skills, as well as new attitudes and self-perceptions that would let them be more comfortable with the turbulent and demanding forces in the VUCA world.

Two specific career needs that people need to develop in a VUCA world are identity learning and adaptability (Hall 2002). By identity awareness we mean the ability to take perspective on one's self-identity and to be able to develop personal clarity about it (e.g. awareness of one's values, needs, capabilities, career goals, etc.). Identity learning and change occur through behaviour changes and experiments (Ibarra 2003; Pratt et al. 2006; Pratt 2012). This process involves taking risks, trying out new behaviours, receiving feedback and self-reflection. Argyris (1993) called this process 'double-loop learning', which means that the person takes in feedback and reflects not only on the outcomes of his or her behaviour but more fundamentally on his or her original purpose and sense of identity. We need more studies of ways this double-loop process might operate, as well as how it might produce both a greater sense of identity awareness and increased ability to engage in self-directed change, that is, greater adaptability.

One of the most understudied areas in career research is how far people can increase these identity learning and adaptability skills in their later career, as in the case of older workers who need to keep up with changing technologies and ways of working. Older workers are often the target of organizational cutbacks, and given the discrimination that often exists against this group, it can be difficult for them to find re-employment. One way to combat this issue would be for HR specialists to find ways to help older employees develop a more flexible, mobile career, with frequent moves and ongoing training, with the aim of maintaining high employability. Employability has been found to be a strong asset for unemployed workers in finding new employment (McArdle et al. 2007). There are numerous possibilities for good action research studies on innovative HR programmes for facilitating later career mobility. A good model here is the recent research being undertaken in Belgium, where government policy provides entitlements for career counselling for its citizens (Verbruggen et al. 2017; Dries 2011).

Similar talent development strategies could also be helpful for individuals and organizations in improving retirement practices. More focus on late career development could also include the encouragement of workers to begin thinking and planning for retirement, including options for phased approaches, with a gradual move from reduced work load to eventual retirement. An example here would be Kim's (2013) study of the changing work identity narratives as they age (adjusting, progressing and regressing). Research such as this could give the organization more options for managing its workforce, as well as for employees in realizing their career aspirations and financial life planning needs in later life.

Beyond the individual level, the interplay between various contextual factors and careers are an important element both from a comparative and a single country angle. This is a field that offers the potential for major advances in understanding how factors and developments from the macro-level affect individual careers. This not only includes a 'static' and 'snapshot' view of various factors such as income inequality, gender equality, demographic composition or national educational portfolio. In addition, developments over time in these areas and the potential consequences of different national trajectories do play an important role.

References

Anderson, Nels. 1923. *The Hobo. The Sociology of the Homeless Man*. Chicago, IL: University of Chicago Press.
Andresen, Maike, Akram Al Ariss, and Matthias Walther, eds. 2013. *Self-Initiated Expatriation. Individual, Organizational, and National Perspectives*. London and New York: Routledge.
Argyris, Chris. 1982. *Reasoning, Learning, and Action: Individual and Organizational*. San Francisco, CA: Jossey-Bass.
———. 1993. *Knowledge for Action: A Guide to Overcoming Barriers to Organizational Change*. San Francisco, CA: Jossey-Bass.

Arthur, Michael B., Douglas T. Hall, and Barbara S. Lawrence, eds. 1989. *Handbook of Career Theory*. Cambridge: Cambridge University Press.

Bader, Benjamin, Tassilo Schuster, and Anna K. Bader. 2016. *Expatriate Management: Transatlantic Dialogues*. Frankfurt and New York: Springer.

Bartlett, Christopher A., and Sumantra Ghoshal. 1998. *Managing Across Borders: The Transnational Solution*. 2nd ed. Boston: Harvard Business School Press.

Borgatti, Stephen P. 1998. Elicitation Methods for Cultural Domain Analysis. In *The Ethnographer's Toolkit*, ed. Jean Schensul and Margaret LeCompte, vol. 3. Walnut Creek: Altamira Press.

Brett, Jeanne M., Catherine H. Tinsley, Maddy Janssens, Zoe I. Barsness, and Anne L. Lytle. 1997. New Approaches to the Study of Culture in Industrial/ Organizational Psychology. In *New Perspectives on International Industrial/ Organizational Psychology*, ed. P. Christopher Earley and Miriam Erez, 75–129. San Francisco, CA: The New Lexington Press/Jossey-Bass.

Brewster, Chris, and Wolfgang Mayrhofer, eds. 2012. *Handbook of Research on Comparative Human Resource Management*. Cheltenham: Edward Elgar.

Brewster, Chris, Wolfgang Mayrhofer, and Elaine Farndale, eds. 2018. *Handbook of Research on Comparative Human Resource Management*. 2nd ed. Cheltenham: Edward Elgar. In press.

Briscoe, Jon P., Katherina Chudzikowski, and Julie Unite. 2012a. Careers Transitions: Windows into the Career Experience in 11 Country Contexts. In *Careers Around the World*, ed. Jon P. Briscoe, Douglas T. Hall, and Wolfgang Mayrhofer, 88–117. New York and London: Routledge Taylor and Francis Group.

Briscoe, Jon P., Douglas T. Hall, and Wolfgang Mayrhofer. 2012b. Careers Around the World. In *Careers Around the World*, ed. Jon P. Briscoe, Douglas T. Hall, and Wolfgang Mayrhofer, 3–14. New York and London: Routledge Taylor and Francis Group.

Briscoe, Jon P., R. Kaše, Nicky Dries, Anders Dysvik, Unite Julie, K. Övgü Çakmak-Otluoğlu, Ifedapo Adeeye, et al. 2014. A Cross-Culturally Generated Measure of Career Success: Results of a Three-Stage Study. In *Best Paper Proceedings of the 74th Annual Meeting of the Academy of Management*, ed. J. Humphreys. Philadelphia, PA: Academy of Management.

Brislin, Richard W. 1970. Back-Translation for Cross-Cultural Research. *Journal of Cross-Cultural Psychology* 1 (3): 185–216.

Career Success in Different Countries: Reflections on the 5C... 145

Chudzikowski, Katherina, Barbara Demel, Wolfgang Mayrhofer, Jon P. Briscoe, Julie Unite, B. Bogićević Milikić, Douglas T. Hall, Mireia L. Heras, Yan Shen, and Jelena Zikic. 2009. Career Transitions and Their Causes: A Country-Comparative Perspective. *Journal of Occupational and Organizational Psychology* 82 (4): 825–849.

Cressey, Paul G. 1932. *The Taxi-Dance Hall. A Sociological Study in Commercialized Recreation and City Life*. Chicago, IL: The University of Chicago Press.

Demel, Barbara, Yan Shen, Mireia L. Heras, Douglas T. Hall, and Julie Unite. 2012. Career Success Around the World: Its Meaning and Perceived Influences in 11 Countries. In *Careers Around the World*, ed. Jon P. Briscoe, Douglas T. Hall, and Wolfgang Mayrhofer, 59–87. New York and London: Routledge Taylor and Francis Group.

Derr, C. Brooklyn. 1986. *Managing the New Careerists: The Diverse Career Success Orientations of Today's Workers*. San Francisco, CA: Jossey-Bass.

Dickmann, Michael, and Michael Muller-Camen. 2006. A Typology of International Human Resource Management Strategies and Processes. *International Human Resource Management Journal* 17 (4): 580–601.

Dries, Nicky. 2011. The Meaning of Career Success: Avoiding Reification Through a Closer Inspection of Historical, Cultural, and Ideological Context. *Career Development International* 16 (4): 364–384.

Dries, Nicky, Roland Pepermans, and Olivier Carlier. 2008. Career Success: Constructing a Multidimensional Model. *Journal of Vocational Behavior* 73 (2): 254–267.

Easterby-Smith, Mark, and Danusia Malina. 1999. Cross-Cultural Collaborative Research: Toward Reflexivity. *Academy of Management Journal* 42 (1): 76–86.

Greenhaus, Jeffrey H., Saroj Parasuraman, and Wayne M. Wormley. 1990. Effects of Race on Organizational Experiences, Job Performance Evaluations, and Career Outcomes. *Academy of Management Journal* 33 (1): 64–86.

Greenwood, Royston, Christine Oliver, Kerstin Sahlin, and Roy Suddaby, eds. 2008. *The SAGE Handbook of Organizational Institutionalism*. London: Sage.

Gunz, Hugh, and Peter A. Heslin. 2005. Reconceptualizing Career Success. *Journal of Organizational Behavior* 26 (2): 105–111.

Gunz, Hugh P., Mila B. Lazarova, and Wolfgang Mayrhofer, eds. 2018. *The Routledge Companion to Career Studies*. Milton Park: Routledge. In press.

Gunz, Hugh, and Wolfgang Mayrhofer. 2018. *Career and Organization Studies. Facilitating Conversation Across Boundaries with the Social Chronology Framework*. Cambridge: Cambridge University Press. In press.

Gunz, Hugh, and Maury Peiperl, eds. 2007. *Handbook of Career Studies*. Los Angeles: Sage.

Hall, Douglas T. 1976. *Careers in Organizations*. Santa Monica: Goodyear.

———. 2002. *Careers In and Out of Organizations*. Thousand Oaks, CA: Sage.

Hegewisch, Ariane, and Chris Brewster, eds. 1993. *European Developments in Human Resource Management*. London: Kogan Page.

Heslin, Peter A. 2005a. Experiencing Career Success. *Organizational Dynamics* 34 (4): 376–390.

———. 2005b. Conceptualizing and Evaluating Career Success. *Journal of Organizational Behavior* 26 (2): 113–136.

Hofstede, Geert. 1980. *Culture's Consequences. International Differences in Work-Related Values*. Newbury Park: Sage Publications.

———. 1991. *Cultures and Organizations—Software of the Mind*. London: McGraw-Hill.

House, Robert J., Paul J. Hanges, Mansour Javidan, Peter W. Dorfman, and Vipin Gupta, eds. 2004. *Culture, Leadership, and Organizations: The GLOBE Study of 62 Societies*. Thousand Oaks, CA: Sage.

Hughes, Everett C. 1937. Institutional Office and the Person. *American Journal of Sociology* 43 (3): 404–413.

Ibarra, Herminia. 2003. *Working Identity—Unconventional Strategies for Reinventing Your Career*. Harvard: Harvard Business School Press.

Johansen, Robert. 2012. *Leaders Make the Future: Ten Leadership Skills for an Uncertain World*. San Francisco, CA: Berrett-Koehler Publishers.

Katz, Daniel, and Robert L. Kahn. 1978. *The Social Psychology of Organizations*. 2nd ed. New York: Wiley.

Kim, N. 2013. Work Transition, Work Identity Change, and Age: Where Do I Come From? Who Am I? Where Am I Going? PhD diss., Carroll School of Management, Boston College.

Lazarova, Mila, Françoise Dany, and Wolfgang Mayrhofer. 2012. Careers: A Country-Comparative View. In *Handbook of Research on Comparative Human Resource Management*, ed. Chris Brewster and Wolfgang Mayrhofer, 298–321. Cheltenham, UK and Northampton, MA: Edward Elgar.

Louis, Meryl R. 1980. Career Transitions: Varieties and Commonalities. *Academy of Management Review* 5 (3): 329–340.

Mayrhofer, Wolfgang, Chris Brewster, Michael Morley, and Johannes Ledolter. 2011. Hearing a Different Drummer? Convergence of Human Resource Management in Europe—A Longitudinal Analysis. *Human Resource Management Review* 21 (1): 50–67.

Career Success in Different Countries: Reflections on the 5C... 147

Mayrhofer, Wolfgang, Jon P. Briscoe, Douglas T. Hall, Michael Dickmann, Nicky Dries, Anders Dysvik, Robert Kaše, Emma Parry, and Julie Unite. 2016. Career Success Across the Globe—Insights from the 5C Project. *Organizational Dynamics* 45 (3): 197–205.

Mayrhofer, Wolfgang, Michael Morley, and Chris Brewster. 2004. Convergence, Stasis, or Divergence? In *Human Resource Management in Europe. Evidence of Convergence?* ed. Chris Brewster, Wolfgang Mayrhofer, and Michael Morley, 417–436. London: Elsevier/Butterworth-Heinemann.

McArdle, Sarah, Lea Waters, Jon P. Briscoe, and Douglas T. Hall. 2007. Employability During Unemployment: Adaptability, Career Identity and Human and Social Capital. *Journal of Vocational Behavior* 71 (2): 247–264.

Morris, Michael W., Kwok Leung, Daniel Ames, and Brian Lickel. 1999. Views from Inside and Outside: Integrating Emic and Etic Insights about Culture and Justice Judgment. *Academy of Management Review* 24 (4): 781–796.

Ng, Thomas W.H., Lillian T. Eby, Kelly L. Sorensen, and Daniel C. Feldman. 2005. Predictors of Objective and Subjective Career Success: A Meta-Analysis. *Personnel Psychology* 58 (2): 367–408.

Ng, Thomas W.H., and Daniel C. Feldman. 2014. Subjective Career Success: A Meta-Analytic Review. *Journal of Vocational Behavior* 85 (2): 169–179.

Patton, Michael Q. 1990. *Qualitative Evaluation and Research Methods*. Newbury Park, CA: Sage.

Pratt, Michael G. 2012. Rethinking Identity Construction Processes in Organizations: Three Questions to Consider. In *Constructing Identity In and Around Organizations*, ed. Majken Schultz, Steve Maguire, Ann Langley, and Haridimos Tsoukas, 22–29. Oxford: Oxford University Press.

Pratt, Michael G., Kevin W. Rockmann, and Jeffrey B. Kaufmann. 2006. Constructing Professional Identity: The Role of Work and Identity Learning Cycles in the Customization of Identity Among Medical Residents. *Academy of Management Journal* 49 (2): 235–262.

Schein, Edgar H. 1978. *Career Dynamics: Matching Individual and Organizational Needs*. Vol. 24. Reading, MA: Addison-Wesley.

Schwartz, Shalom H. 2006. A Theory of Cultural Value Orientations: Explication and Applications. *Comparative Sociology* 5 (2–3): 137–182.

Shaw, Clifford R. 1930. *The Jack-Roller. A Delinquent Boy's Own Story*. Chicago, IL: The University of Chicago Press.

Shen, Yan, Barbara Demel, Julie Unite, Jon P. Briscoe, Douglas T. Hall, Katharina Chudzikowski, Wolfgang Mayrhofer, et al. 2015. Career Success Across Eleven Countries: Implications For International Human Resource Management. *International Journal of Human Resource Management* 26 (13): 1753–1778.

Shockley, Kristen M., Heather Ureksoy, Ozgun B. Rodopman, Laura F. Poteat, and Timothy R. Dullaghan. 2015. Development of a New Scale to Measure Subjective Career Success: A Mixed-Methods Study. *Journal of Organizational Behavior* 37 (1): 128–153.

Solimano, Andrés. 2010. *International Migration in the Age of Crisis and Globalization: Historical and Recent Experiences.* Cambridge: Cambridge University Press.

Sutherland, Edwin H. 1937. *The Professional Thief.* Chicago: University of Chicago Press.

Thomas, Robyn, Janne Tienari, Annette Davies, and Susan Meriläinen. 2009. Let's Talk about "Us" A Reflexive Account of a Cross-Cultural Research Collaboration. *Journal of Management Inquiry* 18 (4): 313–324.

Thornton, Patricia H., William Ocasio, and Michael Lounsbury. 2012. *The Institutional Logics Perspective: A New Approach to Culture, Structure and Process.* Oxford: Oxford University Press.

Trompenaars, Fons, and Charles Hampden-Turner. 1997. *Riding the Waves of Culture: Understanding Cultural Diversity in Business.* 2nd ed. London: Nicholas Brealey.

Verbruggen, Marijke, Nicky Dries, and Koen Van Laer. 2017. Challenging the Uniformity Myth in Career Counseling Outcome Studies: Examining the Role of Clients' Initial Career Counseling Goals. *Journal of Career Assessment* 25 (1): 159–172.

6

Managing Global Careerists: Individual, Organizational and Societal Needs

Michael Dickmann and Maike Andresen

Introduction

Most of the typologies in literature model international work experience as a single career step in work life. In doing so, they omit a long-term career perspective including multiple career moves in different foreign countries as are typical for so-called global careers (Mäkelä and Suutari 2009). To manage these global careers successfully, detailed knowledge about individual, organizational and societal needs is necessary. However, only few research studies about global careerists exist to date.

There is a multitude of expectations that organizations have towards global careerists, and, in turn, these global careerists have an array of expectations towards key stakeholders, most prominently their employers

---

M. Dickmann (✉)
Cranfield School of Management, Cranfield University, Cranfield, UK
e-mail: m.dickmann@cranfield.ac.uk

M. Andresen
University of Bamberg, Bamberg, Germany
e-mail: maike.andresen@uni-bamberg.de

© The Author(s) 2018
M. Dickmann et al. (eds.), *The Management of Global Careers*,
https://doi.org/10.1007/978-3-319-76529-7_6

but also local teams, their families and the broader society. This chapter uses a multiple dependency perspective to outline a range of factors that impact on the global careerist. It will develop an overview of what individuals (the global careerist, her/his family, local teams and superiors) and organizations (the global mobility department, the employer) can do to increase the chances of positive outcomes of global careers. The chapter will also distinguish between diverse perspectives on outcomes and reflect on concepts of 'return on investment'.

To better understand the working and living conditions of global careerists and to successfully manage their careers, we first present their specific characteristics and challenges concerning their career aspirations and typical career patterns. Second, we suggest a set of differentiated expatriate career management practices including necessary career planning and related career guidance and support practices.

Defining Global Careerists

In contrast to the typical single international movements of many expatriates, more permanent global careers with frequent international relocations are becoming increasingly important in international business (Mäkelä and Suutari 2009, 2011; Suutari 2003; Suutari and Mäkelä 2007; Suutari and Taka 2004). The global manager's career usually includes a sequence of moves in different locations and positions (Cappellen and Janssens 2005) and does not necessarily follow fixed career paths predetermined by organizations. They pursue an international career for a longer term by changing between domestic and international assignments without focusing on some specific country or even some specific cultural area (Suutari 2003).

On the basis of a sample of 202 German managers, Andresen and Biemann (2013) derived a taxonomy of international career patterns of managers, including three patterns of global careers, namely: the international organizational career, the international boundaryless career and the transnational career. Managers following an international organizational and a transnational career pattern correspond largely to the group of global managers as described by Suutari (2003), (Mäkelä and Suutari

2009, 2011), who have had three or more international assignments in two or more countries and worked for either one or several employers. The three patterns as identified by Andresen and Biemann (2013) are characterized as follows.

Global careerists following an *international organizational career* pattern work most of the time for the same employer, usually in larger organizations, both in the home country and several times abroad (two to three assignments on average) and thus follow a 'bounded career'. Being highly career-oriented, they exhibit the highest objective career success in terms of salary, number of subordinate employees and hierarchical level reached as compared to the other two patterns. This career success, however, is achieved at the expense of comparably the longest working hours (see also Mäkelä and Suutari 2011), and the subjective career success is not higher in this group. *International organizational careerists* do not identify their international experience itself as a central career lever, but their repatriating to the headquarters in their home country between assignments in order not to miss the connection (Andresen and Biemann 2013).

Global careerists belonging to the *international boundaryless career* pattern change employers several times during their international career. Banai and Harry (2004) identified a similar group of employees that they labelled 'international itinerant'. However, this career pattern has its cost in that the objective career success is comparably low in this group. Similarly, Jokinen et al. (2008) found self-initiated expatriates (SIEs), which correspond to the international boundaryless career, to operate often at a lower organizational level than assigned expatriates (AEs), which, in turn, correspond to international organizational careerists. The limited career progress and hierarchical advancement could be explained by the fact that they purposely accumulate less company-specific knowledge and focus instead on knowledge that is transferable between organizations and/or strive less for status and hierarchical ranks (Andresen and Biemann 2013; Banai and Harry 2004).

To conclude, these two types of global careerists differ with regard to their career concepts (Arthur and Rousseau 1996): the *international organizational career* reflects a traditional career concept with a career in only one organization and career success being based on pay, promotion and status (Sullivan 1999). By contrast, individuals in the *international boundaryless career* work in multiple organizations and industries. Although objective career success can be comparably lower, subjective career success is not, which indicates that they could measure career success rather through the meaningfulness of their work, while career centrality is relatively similar in both groups (Andresen and Biemann 2013).

Transnational careerists spend almost their whole work life abroad with one employer who may assign them to many different places, resulting in the highest spatial mobility and see an international career as being most important for achieving promotion, income, challenging tasks and a rich private life. Although *transnational careerists* value the international experience, their career orientation is not notably high, and the perceived objective career success is the lowest among the three global career patterns. Their subjective career success being comparably higher than of those global careerists belonging to the other two career patterns suggests that *transnational careerists* sacrifice their external success in favour of a more inspiring and interesting job or a job environment that is more in line with their goals and capabilities (Andresen and Biemann 2013). This attitude is exemplary for the protean career where the individual's definition of success is internal, subjective success (Hall and Chandler 2005; Suutari and Mäkelä 2007).

Table 6.1 gives an overview of the three international career paths of global careerists presented and their characteristics.

Managing Global Careerists: The Need to Differentiate Between the Operative and Strategic Levels in Expatriate Management

With expatriation becoming an increasingly common part of a manager's and executive's career (Daily et al. 2000; Richardson and McKenna 2002), expatriate career management issues become one of the main challenges for international HR professionals. However, research on the specifics of international careers is typically limited to the effect of *one separate* international assignment on the career, after repatriation to the

Managing Global Careerists: Individual, Organizational... 153

Table 6.1 Overview of the three international career paths

	Number of international work experiences	Initiator of foreign work experience	External v internal mobility
International organizational career	Two to three foreign moves	Organizationally initiated only	Internal international mobility employer change
International boundaryless career	Several international foreign moves	Predominantly self-initiated	Predominantly external international mobility coupled with a change of employer
Transnational career	Very high number of international moves	Predominantly organizationally initiated	Predominantly internal international mobility coupled without frequent employer change

Source: The authors, adapted from Andresen and Biemann (2013)

home country, leading to homogeneous recommendations for HR practice and responsibilities (Suutari 2003). Thus, expatriate management does not take sufficient account of more *permanent global careers*, as described above, that are becoming increasingly important in international business (Mäkelä and Suutari 2009, 2011; Suutari 2003; Suutari and Mäkelä 2007; Suutari and Taka 2004).

The differences between these three types of career patterns of global careerists suggests the need for a *differentiation* with regard to expatriates' career management by organizations (1) into an operative and a strategic level as well as (2) for different types of global careerists. The operative aspect relates to questions connected to each single international move and concerns the government, societal, family and organizational interface. Depending on the type of global career, it makes sense to give more or less and a different kind of support to certain expatriates. The strategic level concerns the management of global careerists' talent in the long term by the organization, that is, over a global manager's entire career span. For example, at a strategic level it makes sense to assign different jobs to internationally mobile managers of different career patterns.

Thus, contrary to current practice (Deloitte 2008; Sparrow et al. 2004), organizations are advised to offer separate expatriation policies, that is, not only at the operative level but also at a strategic level, and to assign responsibilities for the expatriate career management at both levels either to the corporate or local HR department, the line management or the expatriates themselves. Yet, expatriation management continues to be the area of HR that is most centrally determined (Brewster et al. 2002), suggesting a comparably low differentiation of responsibilities between the HR function at headquarters or the international subsidiary, line management and expatriates themselves. Table 6.2 summarizes expatriate management tasks at the operative and strategic level and the respective responsibilities that we will explain below.

Operative Expatriate Management: Management Responsibilities Regarding Each Single International Move

One of the major functions in international human resource management concerns the management of each single expatriate movement, including expatriates' recruitment, preparation, relocation, placement, integration, rewarding, appraisal, promotion and the repetition of this process for repatriation (Baruch and Altman 2002). In view of the importance of the psychological contract that has been stressed recently by various researchers (Andresen and Göbel 2011; Haslberger and Brewster 2009), not only the content of the expatriate management practices at an organizational level but also the responsibilities regarding expatriate liaison and support and in the sense of contact persons at an individual level need to be aligned to different types of global careerists in order to closely tailor initiatives to expatriate needs (Andresen and Göbel 2011; Bonache et al. 2007).

Larsen (2004) described the interface between individual global careerists and organizations as one of mutual dependency. This is certainly correct with respect to international organizational and transnational careers where the organization helps the individual to move and to gain

Managing Global Careerists: Individual, Organizational... 155

Table 6.2 Responsibilities regarding expatriate career management

Expatriate management tasks	Career pattern		
	International organizational career	International boundaryless career	Transnational career
Operative expatriate management (short term, per assignment)			
Government interface	Home HR	Global careerist	Host HR
Societal interface	Home/host HR	Global careerist/host HR	Host HR
Family interface	Global careerist/ home HR	Global careerist	Global careerist/ host HR
Organizational interface	Home HR	Global careerist/host HR	Host HR
Strategic expatriate management (long term, entire global career)			
HR planning (outgoing)	Home HR	Global careerist	Host HR
Resourcing and placement	Home HR/line management	Global careerist	Host HR/line management
Training and development	Home/host HR	Host HR	Host HR
Performance appraisal	Home/host HR/line management	Host HR/line management	Host HR/line management
HR planning (return/ subsequent stay abroad	Home HR/line management	Global careerist/ home HR	Host HR/line management
Re-entry processes	Home HR	Global careerist	
Primary responsibility	*Home country and host countries*	*Global careerist*	*Host countries*
Expatriate management metaphor	*'spring' (expatriate management at HQ lets people go and brings them back)*	*'pilot' (local HR department helps expatriates to find their way, who need to steer their career themselves)*	*'baton' (passing on the baton, i.e., expatriate management responsibilities between local HR units)*

Source: The authors, adapted from Andresen and Biemann (2013)

156 M. Dickmann and M. Andresen

all necessary residence and work permits, supports their family in their search for schools and so on. But even individuals who go abroad under their own steam (the self-initiated or international boundaryless careerists) are likely to be initially more reliant on the support of their employers once they have found work. In turn, the company-supported careerists are often more important to their employers as they take on more central roles in subsidiaries or are the key person that links back to the head office or the assignee's country of origin. The latter point also applies to international boundaryless careerists. Our chapter expands this mutual dependency idea by identifying four key sets of interfaces which are centred around the individual-organizational dependency. However, in each there are more dependencies and interactions identified. These four key global mobility interfaces are outlined below.

The Government Interface: Regulatory Compliance of Individuals and Organizations

A German proverb outlines 'Von der Wiege bis zur Bahre—Formulare, Formulare' (From the cradle to the grave—forms, forms). It is certainly true that moving from one country to another triggers the need to arrange and adhere to a lot of governmental (and sometimes city) regulations such as pertaining to visas, residence permits, work permits or taxation for individuals. On the face of them, these government regulations are directed at the individual and therefore, apply to all forms of global mobility. Individuals are well advised to understand all these legal regulations for the work abroad and their implications for the long term. For instance, complying with and navigating successfully the bi- and multinational agreements with respect to taxation and long-term social security issues will be crucial for expatriates and their families (see Table 6.3). But the government-individual interface is often managed by organizations. MNCs often invest much time, effort and money to help their expatriates to successfully master compliance demands (RES Forum 2014, 2015). Not only do companies feel that this is one of the key roles of their global mobility (GM) functions, their work can be characterized by attempting to avoid risk and their willingness to invest in high-quality

Table 6.3 Key global mobility interfaces: regulatory compliance of individuals and organizations towards government

Individual considerations and actions	Organizational considerations and actions	Government and administrative considerations and implications
Legal compliance and social security: • Apply for residence and work permits and other necessary legal documents (most often in coordination with employer). • Explore the host effects and compliance demands of working in the host country in terms of taxation and social security. • Plan the long-term social security (and on-going tax) home implications of working in the host location (including long-term pension implications). • Understand bi- and multi-lateral agreements between governments in relation to taxation and social security (if assistance is not provided by employer).	*Legal compliance and social security:* • Gain residence permits and work permits for all international assignees and business travellers. • Provide good support for yearly taxation and other local/cross-border administrative and compliance issues. • Give financial and tax counselling, advice and help for time after return/next move. • Monitor own and service provider activities and gain expatriate feedback during the assignment. • Understand and abide by the rules in relation to maximum numbers of foreign employees. • Understand bi- and multi-lateral agreements between governments in relation to taxation and social security. • Abide by government monitoring and reporting standards.	*Legal regulations and social security:* • Residence permits and visa regulations. • Tax treatment of foreign workers. • Legal regulations with respect to maximum percentage of expatriates working in particular industries. • Fair and equal treatment of foreigners within the legal system. • Ability of families to unite with the employed global careerist. • General legal distance (e.g., gendered rights such as women's ability to drive, work, etc.).

Source: Adapted from the RES Forum Annual Report 2017: The New Normal of Global Mobility—Flexibility, Diversity & Data Mastery, 122 pages, The RES Forum, Harmony Relocation Network and Equus Software, London; own additions

outside service providers for visa and taxation issues. In addition, they are likely to work hard to also achieve corporate tax compliance and to abide by the monitoring and reporting standards set by governments, (federal) states and local administrations. The penalties for non-compliance can be severe, including high fines or the revocation of the operating licence. In addition, corporate reputation is at stake.

Table 6.3 outlines a range of interactions between the three parties, that is, individuals, organizations and government. Other sources (Dickmann and Baruch 2011; Dowling et al. 2013; RES Forum 2016) provide more in-detail information regarding the various demands and (re-)actions of the actors.

In terms of the three global career paths identified, it is clear that those where the initiator of the foreign work experience is the organization (predominantly for international organizational and transnational careers), the MNC/international entity is likely to engage in more government interaction on behalf of the individual or provide more support and information. In turn, where the global careerist is self-initiated (predominantly the international boundaryless worker), the onus is much more on the individual to comply with the wide sets of relevant regulations.

The Societal Interface: Cultural Adjustment and Security Considerations of Individuals and Organizations

There is a large and often long-standing literature regarding cultural intelligence (Earley and Ang 2003; Templer et al. 2006) and cultural adjustment (Black and Gregersen 1991). For instance, Haslberger et al. (2013) have explored the concept of cultural adjustment, arguing that there are cognitive, behavioural and emotional dimensions and processes that individuals go through when living abroad. Table 6.4 outlines some individual considerations and actions that aid cultural adjustment. Given the extensive suggestions about what personal, personality, job and contextual factors are conducive to successful cultural adjustment (Caligiuri 2013; Dickmann and Baruch 2011), the table concentrates on some generic activities that individuals can undertake. We also make clear that the obvious interface (individual with society) can also be moderated by

Table 6.4 Key global mobility interfaces: organizations and individuals interactions with society

Individual considerations and actions	Organizational considerations and actions	Societal considerations and implications
General location:	*General location:*	*Social and security:*
• Determine level of language proficiency and difficulty in language acquisition.	• Evaluate the attractiveness of the country destination for global careerists with respect to nature, culture, history, art, climate and communicate this to candidates.	• Security situation general and vis-à-vis foreigners (including counterterrorism).
• Evaluate the attractiveness of the country destination with respect to nature, culture, history, art, climate, etc.	• Explore transport links within the country and 'back home'.	• Crisis and emergency tasks forces and cooperation with MNCs and other organizations.
Specific location:	*Specific location:*	
• Identify the pros and cons of the specific assignment location (city, town, village) with respect to issues such as host hospitality, friendliness, openness.	• Understand the security situation and draw up support and security measures if necessary.	
• Assess education, health and security situation in specific location.	• Assess education, health and security situation in specific location.	

(continued)

Table 6.4 (continued)

160

Individual considerations and actions	Organizational considerations and actions	Societal considerations and implications
Cultural adjustment:	*Cultural adjustment:*	*Culture*
• Work actively to adjust to the host culture: –Prepare for culture shock. –Understand cultural differences (cognitive adjustment). –Develop and implement adequate behaviours (behavioural adjustment). –Appreciate and celebrate the positive sides of cultural differences (emotional adjustment). • Use every reasonable opportunity to interact with locals (and experienced expatriates), learn about the host culture and practise new behaviours as well as verify new cultural insights.	• Encourage local national employees to provide support to new global careerists and families. • Collect and provide information regarding social, religious, sport and cultural organizations and enable global careerists and their families to join these. • Develop social support networks. • Provide an Employee Assistance Programme (EAP) for people experiencing culture shock or other issues and train local managers to recognize symptoms. • Provide cultural awareness and cultural training programmes.	• General cultural distance to country-of-origin individuals. • Cultural and social openness, tolerance of host nation.

Source: Adapted from the RES Forum Annual Report 2017: The New Normal of Global Mobility—Flexibility, Diversity & Data Mastery, 122 pages, The RES Forum, Harmony Relocation Network and Equus Software, London, own additions

organizations. Amongst the activities that organizations can design are cultural awareness training and the provision of realistic (pre-departure and some post-arrival) information about the host environment. In addition, the organization can work with the host unit, and especially with the host team the assignee is embedded in to encourage their support. In turn, the state or host cities/towns can develop policies and approaches that encourage integration, tolerance and multi-culturalism (Andresen et al. 2012). These initiatives can seek active collaboration with organizations.

Beyond culture, a number of facets of the country and specific location, such as language spoken, history, art, climate and so on, will be evaluated by individuals in their decision to work abroad (Dickmann and Cerdin 2014). Organizations will be concerned about supply chains, transport links, taxation rates and so on. For some of these elements, such as the language spoken and the assignee's knowledge of the local language, there are interfaces such as where organizations offer formal tuition.

Many states are experiencing volatility, uncertainty, complexity and ambiguity in relation to the context that organizations operate in. Especially, the security situation in hostile environments is of great concern to individuals, organizations and governments (Doherty et al. 2011; Bader et al. in press). Organizations and governments are often actively working on approaches to fight terrorism and to mitigate the risks to individuals (Halibozek et al. 2007; Sageman 2011). In turn, individuals living as foreigners in the hostile environment will be acutely aware of personal risks, and it is known that this has a strong influence on their decision to live abroad (Dickmann et al. 2017; Doherty et al. 2011). Organizations react to dangers and potential crises by drawing up contingency plans (RES Forum 2015), preparing their expatriates for the dangers that they are facing through terrorism seminars or considering staff localization strategies (Dickmann et al. 2017).

All three international career paths outlined are affected by the societal context of the country and specific location that expatriates work in. Where the individuals are company-sent, they might get more support in terms of pre-departure preparation and crisis response training and planning compared to when individuals are self-initiated. Nevertheless,

162   M. Dickmann and M. Andresen

given that many organizations in hostile environments plan crisis reaction in a way to include locals and those on local contracts (RES Forum 2015), international boundaryless careerists can also have a strong interface to their organizations and, of course, to their host society.

The Family Interface: Care, Educational and Dual-Career Considerations of Individuals and Organizations

Notwithstanding that family members obviously also go through a process of cultural adjustment and that they are also affected by security and other context-related concerns, this set of considerations looks predominantly at family, partner and friend issues that are triggered when an individual moves abroad. The key interface is between expatriates and their families. The work of Michael Harvey (1985, 1997) and others (McNulty 2012; McNulty and De Cieri 2011; Richardson 2006) has given much nuance in terms of practical family and career concerns. Table 6.5 gives a broad overview of some of the key topics, including children's education, expatriates' wide care responsibilities to family members and dual-career issues.

Many of the critical discussions in relation to adequate health provision, the choice (and finance) of good schools, coping with the care responsibilities of the expatriates' parents (or other family members) and career prospects/activities of the trailing partner will be held within the expatriates' families. As such, flexibility, creativity, adaptability, willingness to learn, proactivity and self-confidence within these families are highly important for the acceptance of work abroad and the ability to successfully cope with challenges (Andresen et al. 2012; Dickmann and Baruch 2011; McNulty and Selmer 2017). However, organizations have an impact on these discussions and decisions. In terms of care decisions, they often offer to pay high-quality schooling or some flights back home in terms of visiting relatives (Dowling et al. 2013; RES Forum 2016). In addition, a part of their reward package is often an offer to pay for the educational activities of the trailing partner. In fact, this support for work-related activities for partners can also include the payment for executive search consultants, sponsorship of job-seeking activities or even the

Table 6.5 Key global mobility interfaces: the interaction of global careerists, their families and organizations

Individual considerations and actions	Family considerations and actions	Organizations' considerations and implications
Care responsibilities and education: • Understand the interests and challenges of trailing partners and family members. • Find a good-quality school that helps children to realize their potential while enabling them to fit back into the home country education system upon return. • Develop solutions to other obligations such as care responsibilities for elderly parents and other family members. • Encourage family members in the host country to interact and to achieve cultural adjustment. *Dual-career issues:* • Work towards finding a meaningful solution to dual-career issues and encourage host country activities of partners. • Consider joint planning that may involve switching career focus between partners over time.	*Care responsibilities and education:* • Gain clarity with regard to schooling and general interest. • Explore the psychological and physical challenges that a move abroad might entail—distance to friends, favourite sports activities that may be less possible to pursue, other hobbies and their implications from the move abroad. *Dual-career issues:* • Work towards finding a meaningful solution to dual-career issues and encourage host country activities of partners. • Look at substitution possibilities and activities. • Evaluate whether remote working and business travel may be feasible. • Consider joint planning that may involve switching career focus between partners over time.	*Care responsibilities and education:* • Give support for other important interests related to key family needs. • Develop a flexible approach (potentially akin to a cafeteria system) where international assignees can choose their benefits (e.g., if they need more travel in order to visit sick relatives). *Dual-career issues:* • Consider the needs of trailing partners and develop approaches (potentially in cooperation with other foreign firms) that enable employment in organizations, further education, charitable work, etc. • Consider monetary compensation/payments to family and partners to enable substitution activities such as further education.

Source: Adapted from the RES Forum Annual Report 2017: The New Normal of Global Mobility—Flexibility, Diversity & Data Mastery, 122 pages, The RES Forum, Harmony Relocation Network and Equus Software, London; own additions

provision of in-house positions. Further recommendations are outlined in Table 6.5.

Because the discussions are primarily intra-family and are less dependent on the form of international career path (organization- or individual-initiated), the decisions are likely to be centred around a wide array of similar interests. These are likely to vary with the diverse situations of the families. However, for self-initiated expatriates (i.e., mainly the international boundaryless careerists), the support of the organization is likely to be largely absent so that own activities and the labour-market chances of the trailing partner may be even more important for the decision to move abroad than for organization-sponsored assignees. Whereas organizational international careerists should be supported by the home organization, transnational careerists will be more strongly connected to the host organization due to their frequent changes of employers and should get support from the local HR department. However, the main responsibility of the family interface needs to be borne by the global careerists themselves.

The Organizational Interface: Individuals and Their Employers on the Journey Along the Expat Cycle and the Threat of Competitors

Most of the recent academic literature has concentrated on a range of issues that expatriates are facing and that organizations should consider, manage and evaluate. One of the most useful frameworks to analyse these is the expatriation cycle (Dickmann and Baruch 2011; Harris et al. 2003) that charts the journey of an international assignee from pre-departure (resourcing, negotiation, logistical and administrative support) to foreign work (training and development, careers, performance management, rewards) to return (repatriation, value assessment, exit considerations).

Table 6.6 explores the key mutual dependencies of individuals and their organizations while outlining the threat of competitors which might be attractive to the global careerist. The section of individual considerations explores the broad decision factors of individuals when exploring whether to accept to work for their current employer abroad or to seek a

Table 6.6 Key global mobility interfaces: the interdependency of organizations and global careerists and the threat of competitors

Individual considerations and actions	Organizational considerations and actions	Competitors' considerations and implications
Key life and career factors:	*Broad strategic considerations and general approach:*	*Strategic work and resource competition:*
• Identify the global careerist's key life and career drivers.	• Design and implement adequate International HR Management (IHRM) configuration to support global corporate strategy.	• Develop and enhance a clear corporate strategy and employer branding in order to increase attractiveness as employer of choice.
• Explore whether and to what extent the most important life and career drivers will be supported through working abroad.	• Explore best role of GM department.	
	• Clarify diverse purposes of global careers within the organization and specify those in relation to career opportunities/global moves.	• Define preference regarding internal and external resourcing and explore implications in relation to an aggressive approach of employees of competitors if they are deemed to have desirable insights and competencies.
• Assess the importance of the key life and career drivers in the decision whether to seek or accept working abroad.	• Create coherent global career approaches—they may be simply thinking in terms of careers rather than international mobility.	
• Make a judgement about what the impact of working abroad will be on the global careerist's long-term career and life plan.	• Assess the value of global work ex ante.	
	Principles and general approaches:	
• Evaluate whether the rewards of working abroad (those that others have experienced in the past) are attractive.	• Stick to your word: enact senior management promises in relation to global work.	• Consider a strategy that aims to hire global assignees in their host location.
	• Give global work high kudos to increase its attractiveness.	
	• Seek cooperation and agreement between global careerist (and family), home and host.	• Explore industry patterns—what are the typical GM approaches (including nontraditional forms of international work) amongst your competitors? Is an alternative approach superior?
• Assess dependents' situation (elderly parents/children) whether a move abroad would be feasible at the moment of intended expatriation.	• Provide adequate reward systems and incentives for all key stakeholders—home, host and global careerist.	
	• Work towards high levels of security and a high quality of crisis reaction capability in an increasingly volatile, uncertain, complex and ambiguous world.	
• Critically evaluate the benefits and costs of working abroad for the global careerist as well as his/her family and friends during and after the assignment.	• Factor in diversity aspects such as supporting women assignees, inpatriates and expatriates from emerging market and other countries, age and sexual orientation diversity in global mobility.	
	• Set up sophisticated and integrated GM programme technology that allows assignee tracking and key information gathering for compliance purposes. Ideally, develop high-quality data analytics to improve GM decision making.	
	• Select GM service vendors that are reliable, low risk, effective and cost-efficient.	
	• Use sophisticated GM data analytics to visual pertinent information and improve decision making.	
	• Analyse value of GM: how it is being created, how is it to be leveraged, who can exploit the created value and how can it be assessed?	

Source: Adapted from the RES Forum Annual Report 2017: The New Normal of Global Mobility—Flexibility, Diversity & Data Mastery, 122 pages, The RES Forum, Harmony Relocation Network and Equus Software, London; own additions

position with a new employer in a different country. Key life and career factors are investigated, including the prospective expatriate's long-term career drivers and plans, key life interests, family issues, location judgements and reward considerations. While naturally some of the factors such as governmental regulations, societal context and family and partner pressures are impacting on the decisions, the key considerations in this interface are in relation to the broad 'package' that the organization can offer. This package will include immediate benefits but also long-term prospects such as career movements after return and the reputational and network effects that are associated with working abroad in the organization.

The organizational considerations are broad. Starting with design considerations in relation to the organizational configuration (Dickmann and Müller-Camen 2006) and the associated purposes of GM (Edström and Galbraith 1977; Minbaeva and Michailova 2004) can create a range of roles for GM departments (RES Forum 2015). The principles and general approaches of organizational GM work are related to focus, consistency and attractiveness of international work (Dickmann and Baruch 2011; Doherty and Dickmann 2009). A large number of considerations for intra-organizational effectiveness (including the navigation of differences between home and host country unit and the willingness of departments to flexibly receive repatriates) are part of the challenges of GM departments. In addition, tracking expatriates for reporting and compliance issues as well as gathering and using data to assess the value of expatriation in order to improve GM decision making falls under the remit of GM management. Indications are that there is still much room for improvement in terms of data quality and predictive analytics (RES Forum 2017).

Table 6.7 also outlines the gestalt of the GM package in order to be attractive for diverse segments of the organization. This does not simply stop at monetary and non-monetary rewards as it should also include considerations of diversity aspects (age, gender, other). For instance, GM work would benefit from incorporating some of the lessons from gender research as to how to make work more flexible and attractive to women (Tharenou 2008; RES Forum 2016) or understand the effect of age and

Table 6.7 The expatriation cycle perspective: mutual dependency of global careerists and organizations

	Individual considerations and actions	Organizational considerations and actions
Resourcing	*Development and career considerations:* • Identify job challenge and autonomy levels in relation to growth mindset and personal preferences. • Assess the ability to learn and grow career capital in relation to the specific job and likely career progression after return. *Rewards:* • Evaluate the attractiveness of monetary rewards in relation to the specific posting. • Assess the provision of non-monetary rewards when considering the host situation and home country context. • Prepare for and conduct negotiations. *Other factors:* • Explore other pertinent decision factors such as general and specific location factors, family and partner factors, other key drivers (see this table).	*Resourcing process:* • Conduct sophisticated selection factoring in personality factors, soft competencies, performance and potential. • Involve partner in selections and consider extended family responsibilities. • Provide 'look-see visits', enabling realistic job, local team and country previews. • Conduct negotiations within the parameter of the global mobility reward policy. *Resourcing criteria and information:* • Assess motivation for the international work. • Match candidate's profile to inter-cultural job demands. • Use psychometric and other instruments and give feedback to candidate and partner regarding cross-cultural strengths and weaknesses. • Evaluate family constraints with a view to social obligation and individual expectations. • Evaluate the propensity of the candidate and the candidate's family to accept certain types of risks.

(continued)

Table 6.7 (continued)

	Individual considerations and actions	Organizational considerations and actions
Training and development	*T&D planning:* • Work towards being part of the global, home and host talent management planning.	*T&D planning and job design:* • Give discretion in the job. • Design positions so that it encourages systematic development of professional, personal and leadership skills.
	On-the-job: • Use the expanded job and position discretion to gain leadership experience. • Plan to use all opportunities to work across borders within the organization and with suppliers and customers. • Volunteer, if appropriate, to work in global projects.	*On-the-job:* • Enable interaction with repatriates from assignment regions/areas. • Provide team-building initiatives together with new teams. • Provide (where useful) extensive briefings to local employees regarding role and function of assignee. • Enable interaction with other expatriates and global careerists in assignment regions/areas (also from other companies).
	Off-the-job: • Undertake targeted training and development activities that benefit the current and future jobs. • Take part in cross-cultural training.	*Off-the-job:* • Provide rigorous training for increased job demands. • Provide inter-cultural training (pre-departure and post-arrival) and language classes. • Give post-arrival cultural training and briefings. • Include spouse/partner in the training. • Provide repatriation seminars on the emotional response.

Career issues	Career planning:	Career system and planning:
	• Plan for the next move well in advance to avoid the career wobble. • Review actual career-relevant international experiences and factor these into own career planning. Career capital: • Work towards acquiring career-relevant skills, knowledge and abilities. • Build (and preserve) international, local and home networks and use the potentially increased reputation from international work. • Utilize the increased motivation from living in another country.	• Link selection to global careerist's long-term career plan and organizational career management (avoid 'out of sight, out of mind' syndrome). • Design support mechanisms such as business sponsors, formal and informal networks, shadow career planning. • Conduct re-entry planning. • Operate a mentor system/international work sponsor system. Career capital: • Provide learning opportunities/stretch jobs. • Foster the acquisition of knowing-how, knowing-why and knowing-whom career capital.

(continued)

Table 6.7 (continued)

	Individual considerations and actions	Organizational considerations and actions
Performance management	*Home and host country integration:* • Ensure that assignment-specific objectives have a business link so that they are valued by the home and host country. • Work towards discussing the primary purpose of each assignment (developmental, control, coordination, skills-filling) in the performance appraisal. *Performance management linkages:* • With respect to own career vision, ensure to integrate AMO (ability, motivation, opportunity) in the performance management process.	*Home and host country integration:* • Use a globally integrated performance management system to encourage comparability. • Find a balance between local and global objectives. • Ensure that assignment-specific objectives are meaningful and attractive to local operating units and appraisers. • Embed the primary purpose of the assignments (developmental, control, coordination, skills-filling) in the performance management and appraisal. *Performance management linkages:* • Link performance management to development, career and succession planning.
Logistical, administrative	*Relocation process:* • Don't rely entirely on employer: take an active interest in the moves abroad (incl. housing, transport). • Cooperate with employer (if it offers these services) in terms of finding adequate schooling, banking, medical services. • Understand the key social customs, rights and limitations of foreign nationals living in the host country.	*Relocation process:* • Provide effective administrative support in relation to the international mobility framework, compensation and benefit questions. • Provide good logistical support and high-quality guidance in terms of moving abroad, accommodation (abroad and at home), health insurance, banking, schooling, return visits, etc. • Monitor own and service provider pre-assignment activities and gain expatriate feedback for improvements.

Rewards	Monetary and non-monetary rewards:	Reward system design:
	• Understand own key long-term drivers and negotiate in relation to these: factor in intrinsic motivations in relation to long-term interests. • Get clarity regarding base pay, assignment-linked incentives and benefits. Potentially negotiate these. • Negotiate to gain a business sponsor or mentor for the assignment. • Explore family-related benefits—schooling, health, home travel, educational allowances, crisis response—and potentially negotiate these. • Don't forget the post-assignment implications of resettlement help, bridging pay, etc.	• Create a perception of reward equity: create salary transparency and avoid large pay differentials between locals and global careerists as well as within the expatriate population. • Minimize social security and tax exposure to both global careerists and organizations. • Understand the implications of diverse primary goals on individual and organizational benefits. • Understand individual motivations in negotiations. • Consider rewards for developing an international perspective: worldwide network, global skills, abilities and knowledge. • Provide deferred assignment-linked compensation for repatriates.

(continued)

Table 6.7 (continued)

	Individual considerations and actions	Organizational considerations and actions
Repatriation	*Planning for work issues:* • Start pre-return planning well in advance of the intended assignment end date. • Identify a (number of) position that global careerist would like to occupy after return. • Network with key people in the destination unit and gain their support. *Planning for family and return issues:* • Conduct planning to integrate family return—accommodation, schooling, health, etc. • Prepare for reverse culture shock.	*Planning for work issues:* • Identify a destination position that would fit to the general career and development plan of the global careerist. • Assure that the next step also links to the successor and high-potential planning of the organization. • Check the attractiveness of the destination position with the global careerist. Consider promotion of returnee. • Coordinate with the receiving unit and leadership. • Potentially set up meetings and interviews of global careerist with receiving unit. *Further support:* • Provide relocation support to the family. • Consider tie-over pay and job finding support for partner.

Exit	*Marketability, disruption and opportunities:*	*Fairness process and loss limitation:*
	• For voluntary and involuntary moves: negotiate a fair exit deal. • Assess internal and external career options (and financial/family implications) for the long term and reflect on own protean career drivers. • Think about marketability and the transfer and utilization of international capabilities and networks. • Assess wider issues such as additional life disruption, learning opportunities, work-life balance issues, etc., associated with the move to another employer and develop an approach to master these.	• Create a fair process and a fair separation deal if competitive pressures or unforeseen circumstances (reorganizations, disinvestments) pressurize the organization to make repatriates redundant. • Reduce risks with respect to negative comments within (internet-based) social networks. • Retain contact if people may return to the organization or may become ambassadors for it.

Source: Adapted from the RES Forum Annual Report 2017: The New Normal of Global Mobility—Flexibility, Diversity & Data Mastery, 122 pages, The RES Forum, Harmony Relocation Network and Equus Software, London; own additions

generations on international careers (RES Forum 2017; Wechtler et al. 2015). In contrast, the competition does not sleep. Table 6.7 shows some of the activities that competitors can undertake to increase their attractiveness and employer brand in the market. This might, for instance, encompass a strategy to hire in-country expatriates in their host locations in order to save relocation and cultural learning/adjustment costs.

Whereas the home HR department is the key actor regarding the organizational interface of international organizational careerists, the respective host HR department takes over this role in the case of international boundaryless and transnational careerists. Moreover, self-management is decisive for international boundaryless global careerists.

Strategic Expatriate Career Management: Long-Term Management Responsibilities Regarding Entire Global Careers

Table 6.7 gives a wealth of detail and recommendations for actions at the strategic level charting the long-term career of a global careerist and concentrating on the individual—organizational interface as the competitors' threat is normally more meta-level. The reader will find such a large number of recommendations for key actors. We will focus our discussion on the three distinct types of global career paths and the strategic responsibilities as outlined in Table 6.2.

The *international organizational career* path is especially interesting for companies that aim at the development of a pool of highly qualified managers with international competencies, who will be able to manage global integration and coordination activities. Thus, these global careerists should be steered from the headquarters. Due to their change between national and international work periods, they need to be involved in their employers' long-term personnel planning, including concrete repatriation plans with definite and suitable job assignments for returnees where they can use the new skills and knowledge they have acquired while abroad. Additionally, companies need to communicate how the overseas assignment relates to the global careerists' overall career plan and to continuously manage the psychological contract between employer and expatriate to be able to retain them in the long term. The expatriate management department at the headquarters acts like a spring, letting people go and also bringing them back (Andresen and Biemann 2013).

Transnational careerists can fulfil tasks in several different foreign subsidiaries, such as the setup of new offices or plants worldwide. Although transnational careerists rarely work at the headquarters, corporate HRM should take over the responsibility for keeping personal contact and take care of their international professional development on a strategic level. Decisions about operational issues, including HR planning, recruitment and placement, training and development needs and performance appraisal, in contrast, should be made on a local level in the different countries. Hence, the HR departments in the local subsidiaries pass on the baton (Andresen and Biemann 2013).

International boundaryless careerists are well suited for projects that require international savvy, but are managed at the regional level. International boundaryless careerists are typically hired locally, and their career is co-managed by themselves and the local HR department. Because of their high international and organizational mobility and comparably low embeddedness, these expatriates best fit to projects of a limited duration. In order to get access to this type of global careerist and still meet their career expectations, organizations are advised to build up networks with other companies, though typically smaller, to develop a network labour market (Biemann and Andresen 2010). The local HR departments are comparable to maritime pilots who help internationally mobile managers to find their way, but the expatriates need to steer their career themselves (Andresen and Biemann 2013).

Conclusions

Research on the specifics of international careers is limited to the effect of *one separate* international assignment on the career after repatriation to the home country leading to homogeneous recommendations for *operational* HR practice and responsibilities. With the increase of global careerists, who pursue an international career for a longer term by changing between domestic and international assignments without focusing on some specific country or even some specific cultural area, expatriate management needs to take a *long-term* perspective and be leveraged at the *strategic level*. This rethinking involves planning how to share the *responsibilities* between home and host country HR departments, line management and the global careerists themselves.

At the *operational level*, the four key areas of interfaces in GM aim to provide a fresh, yet broad, perspective on key relationships and expatriation considerations. While it is impossible to be all encompassing in our treatment (there have been many books and articles written about the topic, none of which was collectively exhaustive), we aim to explicate the key influences that drive stakeholders' decisions in the field. While there are naturally some spill-over effects from one area to another, we have been able to go beyond the two-party mutual dependency perspective restricted to individuals and their employers to incorporate other main stakeholders. Factoring in these broader interests and developments should enable all parties to make better GM decisions in the future.

At the *strategic level*, the three career patterns of global careerists advise developing differentiated practices that imply a higher specialization of activities and programmes, for example, by assigning different jobs to internationally mobile managers of different career patterns or by giving more support to certain expatriates. Most importantly, the taxonomy suggests that separate expatriation policies for different career patterns make sense and that the responsibilities for the expatriate career management should be differentiated according to different career patterns and taken over by either the corporate or local HR department, line management, or the expatriates themselves. Note that the responsibility for the planning of several career management tasks (e.g., training and development) is not identical with its actual execution. In practice, by contrast, 82 per cent of the 70 medium-sized German companies surveyed by Deloitte in 2008 operate expatriation centrally at the headquarters, and a differentiation of expatriation policies according to various mobility patterns is only given in 22 per cent of the companies (Deloitte 2008). Similarly, Sparrow et al. (2004) showed that in close to 60 per cent of the international companies surveyed, the worldwide corporate HR managers are responsible for expatriation management.

References

Andresen, Maike, Akram Al Ariss, and Matthias Walther, eds. 2012. *Self-Initiated Expatriation: Individual, Organizational, and National Perspectives.* New York, NY: Routledge.

Andresen, Maike, and Torsten Biemann. 2013. A Taxonomy of Global Careers: Identifying Different Types of International Managers. *International Journal of Human Resource Management* 24 (3): 533–557. https://doi.org/10.1080/09585192.2012.697476.

Andresen, Maike, and Markus Göbel. 2011. Governance of Psychological Contracts Via Reciprocity: The Case of International Expatriation Management. In *Emerging Themes in International Management of Human Resources*, ed. Philip G. Benson, 187–210. Charlotte, NC: Information Age Publishing.

Arthur, Michael B., and Denise M. Rousseau. 1996. Introduction: The Boundaryless Career as a New Employment Principle. In *The Boundaryless Career—A New Employment Principle for a New Organizational Era*, ed. Michael B. Arthur and Denise M. Rousseau, 3–20. Oxford: Oxford University Press.

Bader, Benjamin, Tassilo Schuster, and Michael Dickmann. in press. Special Issue of *International Journal of Human Resource Management*: Danger and Risk as Challenges for HRM: How to Manage People in Hostile Environments.

Banai, Moshe, and Wes Harry. 2004. Boundaryless Global Careers. *International Studies of Management & Organization* 34 (3): 96–120.

Baruch, Yehuda, and Yochanan Altman. 2002. Expatriation and Repatriation in MNCs: A Taxonomy. *Human Resource Management* 41 (2): 239–259.

Biemann, Torsten, and Maike Andresen. 2010. Self-initiated Foreign Expatriates Versus Assigned Expatriates: Two Distinct Types of International Careers? *Journal of Managerial Psychology* 25 (4): 430–448.

Black, J. Stewart, and Hal B. Gregersen. 1991. Antecedents to Cross-Cultural Adjustment for Expatriates in Pacific Rim Assignments. *Human Relations* 44 (5): 497–515.

Bonache, Jaime, Chris Brewster, and Vesa Suutari. 2007. Knowledge, International Mobility, and Careers. *International Studies of Management and Organization* 37 (3): 3–15.

Brewster, Chris, Hilary Harris, and Paul Sparrow. 2002. *Globalising HR: Executive Briefing.* London: Chartered Institute of Personnel and Development.

Caligiuri, Paula. 2013. *Cultural Agility: Building a Pipeline of Successful Global Professionals*. Oxford: John Wiley & Sons.

Cappellen, Tineke, and Maddy Janssens. 2005. Career Paths of Global Managers: Towards Future Research. *Journal of World Business* 40 (4): 348–360.

Daily, Catherine M., S. Trevis Certo, and Dan R. Dalton. 2000. International Experience in the Executive Suite: The Path to Prosperity? *Strategic Management Journal* 21 (4): 515–523.

Deloitte (2008). Entsendungsmanagement im Wandel. *Human Capital Advisory Services*. Report written by Uwe Bohdal. Frankfurt: Deloitte Consulting GmbH.

Dickmann, Michael, and Yehuda Baruch. 2011. *Global Careers*. London: Routledge.

Dickmann, Michael, and Jean-Luc Cerdin. 2014. Boundaryless Career Drivers—Exploring Macro-Contextual Factors in Location Decisions. *Journal of Global Mobility: The Home of Expatriate Management Research* 2 (1): 26–52.

Dickmann, Michael, and Michael Müller-Camen. 2006. A Typology of International Human Resource Management Strategies and Processes. *International Journal of Human Resource Management* 17 (4): 580–601.

Dickmann, Michael, Emma Parry, and Nadia Keshavjee. 2017. Localization of Staff in a Hostile Context: An Exploratory Investigation in Afghanistan. *The International Journal of Human Resource Management*. Published Online 2 February 2017. https://doi.org/10.1080/09585192.2017.1291531. Special Issue on *Hostile Environments*.

Doherty, Noeleen, and Michael Dickmann. 2009. Exploring the Symbolic Capital of International Assignments. *The International Journal of Human Resource Management* 20 (2): 301–320.

Doherty, Noeleen, Michael Dickmann, and Timothy Mills. 2011. Exploring the Motives of Company-Backed and Self-Initiated Expatriates. *The International Journal of Human Resource Management* 22 (03): 595–611.

Dowling, Peter J., Marion Festing, and Allen D. Engle. 2013. *International Human Resource Management*. 6th ed. London: Cengage Learning.

Earley, P. Christopher, and Soon Ang. 2003. *Cultural Intelligence: Individual Interactions Across Cultures*. Stanford, CA: Stanford University Press.

Edström, Anders, and Jay R. Galbraith. 1977. Transfer of Managers as a Coordination and Control Strategy in Multinational Organizations. *Administrative Science Quarterly* 22 (2): 248–263.

Halibozek, Edward, Andrew Jones, and Gerald L. Kovacich. 2007. *The Corporate Security Professional's Handbook on Terrorism*. Oxford: Elsevier Inc..

Hall, Douglas T., and Dawn E. Chandler. 2005. Psychological Success: When the Career is a Calling. *Journal of Organizational Behavior* 26: 155–176.

Harris, Hilary, Chris Brewster, and Paul Sparrow. 2003. *International Human Resource Management*. London: CIPD Publishing.

Harvey, Michael G. 1985. The Executive Family: An Overlooked Variable in International Assignments. *Thunderbird International Business Review* 27 (3): 15–16.

Harvey, Michael. 1997. Dual-Career Expatriates: Expectations, Adjustment and Satisfaction with International Relocation. *Journal of International Business Studies* 28 (3): 627–658.

Haslberger, Arno, and Chris Brewster. 2009. Capital Gains: Expatriate Adjustment and the Psychological Contract in International Careers. *Human Resource Management* 48 (3): 379–397.

Haslberger, Arno, Chris Brewster, and Thomas Hippler. 2013. The Dimensions of Expatriate Adjustment. *Human Resource Management* 52 (3): 333–351.

Jokinen, Tiina, Chris Brewster, and Vesa Suutari. 2008. Career Capital During International Work Experiences: Contrasting Self-Initiated Expatriate Experiences and Assigned Expatriation. *International Journal of Human Resource Management* 19 (6): 979–998.

Larsen, H. Holt. 2004. Global Career as Dual Dependency Between the Organization and the Individual. *Journal of Management Development* 23 (9): 860–869.

Mäkelä, Kristina, and Vesa Suutari. 2009. Global Careers: A Social Capital Paradox. *International Journal of Human Resource Management* 20 (5): 992–1008.

Mäkelä, Liisa, and Vesa Suutari. 2011. Coping With Work-Family Conflicts in the Global Career Context. *Thunderbird International Business Review* 53 (3): 365–375.

McNulty, Yvonne. 2012. 'Being Dumped in to Sink or Swim': An Empirical Study of Organizational Support for the Trailing Spouse. *Human Resource Development International* 15 (4): 417–434.

McNulty, Yvonne, and Helen De Cieri. 2011. Global Mobility in the 21st Century. *Management International Review* 51 (6): 897–919.

McNulty, Yvonne, and Jan Selmer, eds. 2017. *Research Handbook of Expatriates*. Cheltenham: Edward Elgar Publishing.

Minbaeva, Dana B., and Snejina Michailova. 2004. Knowledge Transfer and Expatriation in Multinational Corporations: The Role of Disseminative Capacity. *Employee Relations* 26 (6): 663–679.

RES Forum. 2014. *Key Trends in Global Mobility.* Report authored by M. Dickmann, RES Forum, UniGroup Relocation Network and Equus Software, 102 pages, London.

———. 2015. *The RES Forum Annual Report: Global Mobility and the Global Talent Management Conundrum.* Report authored by M. Dickmann, RES Forum, UniGroup Relocation Network and Equus Software, 108 pages, London.

———. 2016. *The RES Forum Annual Report 2016: Beyond Uniformity—A World of Opportunity.* Report authored by M. Dickmann, The RES Forum, Harmony Relocation Network and Equus Software, 116 pages, London.

———. 2017. *The RES Forum Annual Report 2017: The New Normal of Global Mobility—Flexibility, Diversity & Data Mastery.* Report authored by M. Dickmann, The RES Forum, Harmony Relocation Network and Equus Software, 120 pages, London.

Richardson, Julia. 2006. Self-Directed Expatriation: Family Matters. *Personnel Review* 35 (4): 469–486.

Richardson, Julia, and Steve McKenna. 2002. Leaving and Experiencing: Why Academics Expatriate and How They Experience Expatriation. *Career Development International* 7 (2): 67–78.

Sageman, Marc. 2011. *Leaderless Jihad: Terror Networks in the Twenty-First Century.* Philadelphia, PA: University of Pennsylvania Press.

Sparrow, Paul, Chris Brewster, and Hilary Harris. 2004. *Globalising Human Resource Management.* London: Routledge.

Sullivan, Sherry E. 1999. The Changing Nature of Careers: A Review and Research Agenda. *Journal of Management* 25 (3): 457–484.

Suutari, Vesa. 2003. Global Managers: Career Orientation, Career Tracks, Life-style Implications and Career Commitment. *Journal of Managerial Psychology* 18 (3): 185–207.

Suutari, Vesa, and Kristiina Mäkelä. 2007. The Career Capital of Managers with Global Careers. *Journal of Managerial Psychology* 22 (7): 628–648.

Suutari, Vesa, and Milla Taka. 2004. Career Anchors of Managers with Global Careers. *Journal of Management Development* 23 (9): 833–847.

Templer, Klaus J., Cheryl Tay, and N. Anand Chandrasekar. 2006. Motivational Cultural Intelligence, Realistic Job Preview, Realistic Living Conditions Preview, and Cross-Cultural Adjustment. *Group & Organization Management* 31 (1): 154–173.

Tharenou, Phyllis. 2008. Disruptive Decisions to Leave Home: Gender and Family Differences in Expatriation Choices. *Organizational Behavior and Human Decision Processes* 105 (2): 183–200.

Wechtler, Heidi, Alexei Koveshnikov, and Cecile Dejoux. 2015. Just Like a Fine Wine? Age, Emotional Intelligence, and Cross-Cultural Adjustment. *International Business Review* 24 (3): 409–418.

7

Individual Offshoring: An Emerging Trend for Global Careers

Caroline Creven Fourrier and Sébastien Point

An Emerging Individual Offshoring Strategy: A Case Study

In 2014, a multinational company headquartered in Switzerland hiring more than 20,000 employees announced the progressive relocation of several activities (supply, production, finance and various support functions) to three different locations, all outside of its home country: Hungary, India and the UK.

Surprisingly, this decision to relocate more than 200 employees did not impact low qualified activities but positions held by people with Bachelor, Masters and even PhD degrees. The goal of this relocation was to reduce the high labour cost where the company is headquartered (Switzerland).

The labour cost of working in Switzerland was considered high. In addition, the burden on the company was increased for the following reasons:

C. Creven Fourrier (✉) • S. Point
EM Strasbourg Business School, University of Strasbourg, Strasbourg, France
e-mail: crevencaroline@yahoo.fr; point@unistra.fr

© The Author(s) 2018
M. Dickmann et al. (eds.), *The Management of Global Careers*,
https://doi.org/10.1007/978-3-319-76529-7_7

183

- Company reports were in US dollar. This meant that the strong Swiss Franc increased the labour cost in the profit and loss statement of the company.
- Switzerland having a relatively small market, sales were not able to absorb the cost generated by the employees paid in Swiss Francs.

Given that the company did not want to risk reducing the level of quality of the services provided so far to its offshoring functions, the choice of these particular offshoring locations underlines two dimensions: (1) attractiveness and (2) high level of education (schools, company pool).

For a cost reduction-based decision, destinations such as the UK and Hungary would not have been considered. Moreover, for process-driven activities such as information systems (IS), India had already proven its efficiency in the past: good quality service associated with low workforce costs. In the same vein, for the finance department (moderately standardized activities), Hungary, as a growing European economy, offered a sufficient talent pool and a sustainable education system to be an attractive destination. For less standardized activities (supply roles for instance), the UK was found to be a good compromise (education level coupled with significantly less costly workforce). Other advantages such as limited tax pressure were also taken into consideration.

The company offered a specific financial package to the relocated employees. The overall package comprised of:

- *Compensation*: set as per the company's benchmark for the country/town of relocation.
- *Pension*: inclusion in the company's country pension plan.
- *Health*: health cover if mandatory as per country laws.
- *Relocation*: move entirely funded by the company for the employees and their families (packing/unpacking, disassembling/assembling of furniture, Customs forms).
- *Housing search*: support to find accommodation (including pre-visit), but no funding/allowance for the cost of living in the house is provided.

- *School search*: support to find an adequate school (including pre-visit), but no funding/allowance for the cost of education is provided.
- *Cultural training*: a one hour session with a consultant knowledgeable about the culture of the host country is provided.

The main goal of the company was to move positions abroad (delocalizing positions but not necessarily individuals) with an attempt to retain global talents. Therefore, delocalized positions, when staffed by foreigners, will attract different assignment packages geared towards local contracts.

The international human resource management (IHRM) literature tends to develop various forms of international contracts (see Dickmann and Baruch 2011 for an exhaustive review) in order to increase retention post expatriation and limit the challenges linked to repatriation (Mayerhofer et al. 2004). Nevertheless, to date and to our knowledge, this case study emphasizes a new form of expatriation[1] rarely highlighted in the literature and somehow quite similar to classic expatriation: 'individual offshoring'. This new form of international assignment offers a relatively limited benefit package in comparison to the classic expatriation. In other words, as highlighted in the case study, individual offshoring aims at performing the exact same job abroad with a permanent geographical relocation. Nevertheless, it encompasses less attractive packages compared to other forms of international assignments (IAs). It also offers no guarantee of return and it does not take the family into consideration even though this is considered as important in the expatriation literature (Dickmann and Baruch 2011; Al Ariss and Crowley-Henry 2013).

Nowadays, an emerging trend is to permanently relocate global talents with less favourable financial conditions. Therefore, the goal of this chapter is to investigate the reasons why individual offshoring emerges as a new and alternative form of expatriation in multinational companies (MNCs). This chapter investigates the concept of individual offshoring

---

[1] We refer in this chapter to the definition of 'expatriation' as per Mayerhofer et al. (2004) which divides expatriation into four different types among which international assignment is defined as a time-limited relocation of the employee and his/her family abroad for a duration of more than one year and with a contract entailing various types of additional benefits.

and is structured as follows: the first part investigates the extent to which individual offshoring varies from other forms of expatriation, outlining the difference between organizational and individual offshoring, whereas the second part researches the pros and cons of individual offshoring.

Offshoring Individuals Compared to Other Forms of Expatriation

From Organizational to Individual Offshoring

Offshoring has been almost exclusively researched from an organizational perspective (Salt 1988; Dunning 1993; Mahroum 2000; Jennex and Adelakun 2003; Stack and Downing 2005; Farrell 2005; Couto et al. 2006; Bunyaratavej et al. 2007). From this organizational perspective, offshoring is defined as the relocation of (or part of) company's activities (a function or a department), while all entities remain fully owned by the firm (Lewin et al. 2009; Hutzschenreuter et al. 2011; Manning 2014; Gooris and Peeters 2014). Offshoring aims to be a cost-effective strategy linked to activities and/or subfunctions. Even though the offshoring literature highlights a shift from an organizational to a more human-impact concept (Farrell and Laboissière 2005; Lewin et al. 2009; Massini et al. 2010), it is rarely associated with career development.

Given that companies strive for a reduction of costs and simultaneously an access to highly qualified personnel (Lewin and Peeters 2006), most of them encourage a reorganization of their business via offshoring and/or outsourcing of some subfunctions and/or activities to lower cost locations (Mudambi and Venzin 2010). In the past, offshoring and/or outsourcing concerned almost exclusively blue-collar activities as well as standardized activities such as IT, finance/accounting or contact centres (Lewin and Peeters 2006). More recently, offshoring or outsourcing also targeted activities traditionally accomplished by white-collar workers with higher degrees (Bachelor, Masters or PhD), working in human resources or procurement departments (Manning et al. 2008) undertaking less specified and less process-driven activities.

Individual Offshoring: An Emerging Trend for Global Careers **187**

There is a key difference among those two aspects of offshoring: organizational offshoring aims to offshore a department or a team (i.e. driving the change for a group of people), while individual offshoring relates to individuals. For employees, offshoring can be seen as the permanent relocation of individuals to offshore locations. According to Lewin et al. (2009: 2), 'the outsourcing of manufacturing activities to low-cost countries is widely practiced and well understood.' Over the last decade, offshoring has evolved from a 'risky strategy to a routine business decision' (Dossani and Kenney 2007: 779). We found that offshoring opportunities for white-collar workers are far less documented and researched (James 2005; Larsen et al. 2011).

The goal for the company is to perform the same activity at a lower total cost while gaining sustainability in its employee pool (Mahoney 2005; Boudreau and Ramstad 2005a, b; Stahl et al. 2007; Beechler and Woodward 2009; McDonnell et al. 2010). It avoids the challenges of more traditional international assignments in which companies often fail to retain individuals upon their return (Lewis 2009). Similar to expatriation, people are sent abroad. However, instead of considering the development of the individual, the job position is moved with its incumbents. From an individual perspective, offshoring emerges as a new type of expatriation.

How Individual Offshoring Differs from Other Forms of Expatriations

Two major types of expatriation can be found in the literature: classic expatriation which is when the organization takes the initiative, that is, sends assigned expatriates (AEs), and self-initiated expatriation (SIE) which is exclusively when an individual takes the initiative (Peiperl et al. 2014; Suutari and Brewster 2000). The former is career orientated while the latter results more from personal opportunities (Howe-Walsh and Schyns 2010). We consider individual offshoring as a subset of AE as it is organization-initiated. It diverges from classic expatriation which involves a temporary move including a comprehensive package (Dickmann and Baruch 2011). It also has some similarities with SIE given that it involves a long-term or permanent relocation (Al Ariss et al. 2014; Crowley-Henry et al. 2016).

There are various supported and improved local contracts. The content of the package varies depending of the level of need of the company (initiating the mobility). The more the company needs an individual to relocate abroad, the better the benefit package and the higher the room for negotiation by the employee (Dickmann and Baruch 2011; Duvivier and Peeters 2011).

In the vein of Manning et al. (2008), Dickmann and Baruch (2011), Adler and Bartholomew (1992) and the Brookfield International Assignment Report (2014), we compared the objectives of organizational offshoring, international assignments and self-initiated expatriation to better understand how individual offshoring can foster talent management (Table 7.1). However, one might keep in mind that the SIE objectives are in essence individual objectives, while those of AEs are considering both the individual and the organization's objectives. Still, the analysis emphasizes that the objective of an IA and of individual offshoring are largely overlapping (e.g. fill a technical skill gap, build international management experience/career development, build worldwide business

Table 7.1 Objectives of individual offshoring, international assignment and self-initiated expatriation

	International assignment	Self-initiated expatriation	Individual offshoring
Objectives	Fill a technical skill gap	Adventure, drive for cultural learning, escape, etc.	Fill a technical skill gap
	Build international management experience/career development	Financials/ purchasing power	Build international management experience/career development
	Build worldwide business acumen	Career building	Build worldwide business acumen
	Develop local business relationships (create and/or control)		Develop local business relationships (create and/or control)
	Technology transfer		Cross country cultural awareness
	Transfer corporate culture		

Source: The authors

Individual Offshoring: An Emerging Trend for Global Careers

acumen, develop local business relationships) while the retention risk (post relocation) is lower in the case of individual offshoring. Obviously, some staff may not accept being relocated on the local terms offered, and some may leave for another employer while in the host country.

Taking into consideration Mayerhofer et al.'s (2004) work, one way to retain expatriates is by multiplying the potential expatriation experiences (Fig. 7.1, although the reader should note that this is not an exhaustive list, simply an expansion).

To Mayerhofer et al. (2004) original piece of work, we have added one additional expatriation type, 'individual offshoring,' and also a specification of whether individuals are more likely to have a job change or not. In the offshoring cases it is likely that there is a physical relocation abroad with the family. The difference between traditional short- and long-term assignments lies in the type of activity the individual will perform in the new, foreign location. For individual offshoring, the role is normally the same (any changes would not be in relation to the move abroad but in relation to 'normal' operational considerations). Thus,

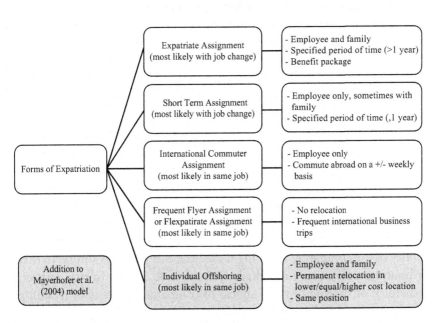

Fig. 7.1 A list of expatriation types. Source: The authors

typically only the location changes. From a theoretical point of view, the country could be a lower/equal/higher cost location compared to the country of origin. However, in reality, offshoring often seeks to reduce costs and to increase access to local employees so the location normally offers a reduced total labour cost. However, this may come from a reduced tax pressure but not necessarily, nor exclusively, from the wage difference between the home and host country. For Mayerhofer et al. (2004), leveraging various forms of expatriation allows the company to gain flexibility while managing cost.

Pros and Cons of Individual Offshoring

An Efficient Low-Cost Alternative to Traditional International Assignments

The Brookfield report (2014) suggests that international assignees are promoted faster and change employers more often (which cause a retention issue). However, international assignments are still considered a good way to globally develop (careers) and retain employees (Brookfield 2014; Lewis 2009; Mayerhofer et al. 2004). In that context, individual offshoring may be a low-cost strategy to retain those individuals the company seek to develop internationally. In contrast, international assignments remain very expensive (Doherty and Dickmann 2012; Brookfield 2014) and often fail to meet the retention objectives (Brookfield 2014). Sending employees abroad, especially if on local contracts, remains a smart way for companies to brand their investment into their staff's development, with a specific emphasis on the international and multicultural exposure (Point and Dickmann 2012).

As far as SIEs are concerned in terms of talent management and retention, the SIE population tends to be more volatile which limits the possibility of the companies retaining them. The SIE profile is similar to that of boundaryless career individuals (Peiperl et al. 2014). In that respect, individual offshoring can also appear to companies as a way of retaining their employees. Indeed, those employees willing to offshore demonstrate a level of commitment and loyalty higher than SIEs.

Failure in International Assignments: A Reason to Move Towards Individual Offshoring?

Overall the annual unit cost of an international assignment is extremely high: several surveys in the literature published 20 years ago already estimated the cost to be between 3 to 4 times the annual gross salary (Zetlin 1994) or put it at $250K a year (Hiltrop and Janssens 1990). Today, the cost of an international assignment is still estimated at approximately twice the total salary cost of any given employee (Doherty and Dickmann 2012).

For an IA to be considered successful, the employee needs to show good performance during the assignment as well as to remain in the company upon repatriation (and to continue to perform (Dickmann and Baruch 2011).

As highlighted in the literature, about 30–40 per cent of former international assignees leave the company within two years after return to their home country (Dowling et al. 1994; Stroh 1995; Baruch and Altman 2002). This may be explained by the high level of benefit package the assignee received whilst abroad. When the transition is not well managed and an appealing career plan not offered, once back in his/her home country, the disillusion can be significant and can lead to the departure of the former expatriate. In addition, an international assignee's attraction on the labour market is likely to have grown tremendously thanks to the international exposure, making it easier to find a position outside of the company (Inkson et al. 1997). Consequently, the success of an IA does not only lie in its preparation and its progress but also in its repatriation and the assignee's re-adaptation back to the home country (Doherty and Dickmann 2012; Suutari et al. 2017; Haslberger et al. 2013).

Given the significant cost of an IA, it is safe to assume that companies will prefer to send 'high performers' abroad. As a consequence the attrition of those former international assignees on their return hurts the company twice: (1) a poor return on a very costly investment and (2) a loss of high performers, which could damage the future growth prospect of the company (Baruch et al. 2013; Dickmann and Baruch 2011).

Companies can avoid facing these two disadvantages by choosing an individual offshore contract as the relocation is permanent. There is no repatriation back to the home country, avoiding the stage that has proven to be so unsuccessful for many IAs.

The Other Side of the Coin: Some Challenges of Individual Offshoring

However, it is clear that individual offshoring also has some drawbacks. From the individual perspective, it is not clear how attractive offshoring would be to uproot oneself and one's family. Thus, many individuals may not choose to accept an offshoring contract. For instance, moving operations from Western Europe or North America to lower salary countries such as India, Pakistan, Ukraine, Hungary, Mexico and other parts of Middle America may result in salaries and benefits being substantially lower, the education systems not being aligned or lower quality and overall the broader environment (health provision, security, etc.) being perceived as much less attractive. In addition, those individuals who do accept an offshoring contract might leave their employers during their work abroad if they can find a better (local or expatriate) offer resulting in replacement and training costs for the sending organization. There are some well-known environments such as the Pacific Rim in China, where labour turnover is particularly high.

Locations for Individual Offshoring: Any Difference with Classic Expatriation and/or Self-Initiated Expatriation?

Individual offshoring is entirely dependent upon the organizational offshoring location. According to AT Kearney (2004), if low- or medium-cost locations remain the main countries of destination for organizational offshoring, the top 25 countries of developed and high-cost countries such as Singapore (the fourth most expensive location worldwide as per Mercer's 2015 ranking[2]) are now appearing on the offshoring location list as well.

---

[2] https://www.uk.mercer.com/newsroom/2015-quality-of-living-survey.html

This contributes to the argument that a reduction of costs, especially labour cost, is not the sole driver nor is it necessarily predominant for offshoring activities and individuals. The reality of high-cost location in AT Kearney's (2004) report also supports the argument of a trend for sourcing employees (and talent mainly) globally rather than relocating solely to reduce labour costs. Organizational offshoring has a new objective of creating a footprint in countries where the company wishes to attract talent either internally (relocation) or externally (recruitment from the local talent pool).

Hutzschenreuter et al. (2011) confirm the findings of Lewin and Peeters (2006) and Manning et al. (2008) that service level improvement, reduced competitive pressures (the cost aspects) and access to qualified personnel are key drivers for companies to relocate offshore some of their activities. It applies equally to the organizational as well as to the individual side of offshoring.

Conclusion

This chapter emphasizes a new form of expatriation emerging in multinational companies: individual offshoring. The concept of individual offshoring (whereby an employee is asked to perform the exact same activity in a different location with lower financial advantages) is intrinsically linked to organizational offshoring with its emergence facilitated by the failure of international assignments to fulfil its retention objectives, to attract local talent and/or to manage costs effectively.

Globalization as it has evolved over the last few decades has given way to a variety of expatriation contracts that are deemed to fill the strategic needs of the firms at a given point in time. Individual offshoring is an emerging form of international assignment focusing more on the job position rather than individuals.

Having understood the 'why' of the emergence of individual offshoring, we also compiled (in more detail) how this new form of global career varies or is similar to the more traditional international assignment contract or self-initiated expatriation initiative (Table 7.2).

Table 7.2 Comparing individual offshoring to international assignment and self-initiated expatriation

Contract details	Adapted from	International assignment	Self-initiated expatriation	Individual offshoring
		Howe-Walsh and Schyns 2010, Peterson et al. 1996 and PricewaterhouseCoopers 2005	Al Ariss et al. 2014; Al Ariss et al. 2014	This chapter
	Initiation	Company	Self	Company
	Predeparture preparation/training (culture, language)	Company	Self	Company
	Time perspective	Limited	No specific limit	No limit
	Job security prior expatriation	Yes	Yes or No	Yes
	Extra compensation package	Yes	No	No
	Support in nonwork issues (schooling, spouse, housing)	Yes	No	No
	Fill a managerial skill gap/manage across cultures	Explore/seeking adventure/understand culture	Fill a managerial skill gap/manage across cultures	

Objectives	Fill a technical and/or managerial skill gap	Individual drivers: adventure, cultural learning, escape, etc.	Fill a technical skill gap
	Build international management experience/ career development	Financials/purchasing power	Build international management experience/career development
	Build worldwide business acumen	Career building	Build worldwide business acumen
	Develop local business relationships (create and/or control)		Develop local business relationships (create and/or control)
	Technology transfer		Cross country cultural awareness
	Transfer corporate culture		
		Baruch et al. 2013	
Retention perspectives	Retention problems upon repatriation most acute but less severe in host country	Retention risks in the host country include the adventure drivers of SIEs and their willingness to embark on boundaryless careers	Repatriation is not intended, so little problems in company-planned repatriation. However, those who want to return might leave the company to go home

Source: The authors

Individual offshoring is emerging as a new form of expatriation. Together with the current developments in process automatization and artificial intelligence, this raises the issue that relocation is about to concern any kind of work and education level. Thus, individual offshoring does not necessarily take place in low-cost locations. In other words, cost mitigation is only one element among others that will drive the business decision to relocate activities.

This new type of expatriation might also encourage researchers to further explore this new form of expatriation. Many questions remain open, such as whether the employees who accept the relocation in the first place are non-talent or a company's critical talent for tomorrow's growth. Or, when successfully managed (i.e. when employees agree to relocate to the offshored location), does the individual offshoring contract tend to be more successful than an international assignment for retaining employees?

We have argued that offshoring leads to more successful retention as it avoids the repatriation stage. Only further research will show whether our propositions are valid. Obviously, our understanding would benefit from detailed investigation into the various forms of offshoring. In addition, research should explore the array of advantages and disadvantages associated with this new form of expatriation. High-quality studies are urgently needed in order to illuminate this emerging, important global work field.

References

Adler, Nancy J., and Susan Bartholomew. 1992. Managing Globally Competent People. *Executive* 6 (3): 52–65.

Al Ariss, Akram, and Marian Crowley-Henry. 2013. Self-Initiated Expatriation and Migration in the Management Literature: Present Theorizations and Future Research Directions. *Career Development International* 18 (1): 1–34.

Al Ariss, Akram, Yusuf Sidani, and Sophie D'Armagnac. 2014. Le Management International Des Talents Dans Une Perspective Institutionnelle: Les Conflits de Logique Dans Les Pays Du Golfe. *Management International* 19 (4): 168–183.

Al Ariss, Akram, Wayne F. Cascio, and Jaap Paauwe. 2014. Talent Management: Current Theories and Future Research Directions. *Journal of World Business* 49 (2): 173–179. https://doi.org/10.1016/j.jwb.2013.11.001.

Baruch, Yehuda, and Yochanan Altman. 2002. Expatriation and Repatriation in MNCs: A Taxonomy. *Human Resource Management* 41 (2): 239–259.

Baruch, Yehuda, Michael Dickmann, Yochanan Altman, and Frank Bournois. 2013. Exploring International Work: Types and Dimensions of Global Careers. *The International Journal of Human Resource Management* 24 (12): 2369–2393.

Beechler, Schon, and Ian C. Woodward. 2009. The Global 'War for Talent'. *Journal of International Management* 15 (3): 273–285.

Boudreau, John W., and Peter M. Ramstad. 2005a. Talentship, Talent Segmentation, and Sustainability: A New HR Decision Science Paradigm for a New Strategy Definition. *Human Resource Management* 44 (2): 129–136.

———. 2005b. Where's Your Pivotal Talent? *Harvard Business Review* 83 (4): 23–24.

Brookfield. 2014. 2014 Global Mobility Trends Survey. *Zhurnal Eksperimental'noi i Teoreticheskoi Fiziki* 81.

Bunyaratavej, Kraiwinee, Eugene D. Hahn, and Jonathan P. Doh. 2007. International Offshoring of Services: A Parity Study. *Journal of International Management* 13 (1): 7–21.

Couto, Vinay, Mahadeva Mani, Arie Y. Lewin, and Carine Peeters. 2006. The Globalization of White-Collar Work The Facts and Fallout of Next-Generation Offshoring. *Booz Allen Hamilton*: 1–13.

Crowley-Henry, M., Edward O'Connor, and Akram Al Ariss. 2016. Portrayal of Skilled Migrants' Careers in Business and Management Studies: A Review of the Literature and Future Research Agenda. *European Management Review.* http://onlinelibrary.wiley.com/doi/10.1111/emre.12072/abstract

Dickmann, Michael, and Yehuda Baruch. 2011. *Global Careers.* New York: Routledge.

Doherty, Noeleen Teresa, and Michael Dickmann. 2012. Measuring the Return on Investment in International Assignments: An Action Research Approach. *The International Journal of Human Resource Management* 23 (16): 3434–3454.

Dossani, Rafiq, and Martin Kenney. 2007. The Next Wave of Globalization: Relocating Service Provision to India. *World Development* 35 (5): 772–791.

Dowling, Peter, Randall S. Schuler, and Denice E. Welch. 1994. *International Dimensions of Human Resource Management.* Belmont, CA: Wadsworth.

Dunning, J. H. 1993. *Multinational enterprises and the global economy.* Wokingham: Addison-Wesley

Duvivier, Florence, and Carine Peeters. 2011. The Use of Expatriates in the Offshoring of Services—Framework and Research Propositions. *Working Paper*, Solvay Brussels School 32 (0): 1–23.

Farrell, Diana. 2005. Offshoring: Value Creation through Economic Change. *Journal of Management Studies* 42 (3): 675–683.

Farrell, Diana, and Martha A. Laboissière. 2005. Sizing the Emerging Global Labor Market. *McKinsey Quarterly* 3: 92–103.

Gooris, Julien, and Carine Peeters. 2014. Home–Host Country Distance in Offshore Governance Choices. *Journal of International Management* 20 (1): 73–86.

Haslberger, Arno, Chris Brewster, and Thomas Hippler. 2013. The Dimensions of Expatriate Adjustment. *Human Resource Management* 52 (3): 333–351.

Hiltrop, Jean-Marie, and Maddy Janssens. 1990. Expatriation: Challenges and Recommendations. *European Management Journal* 8 (1): 19–26.

Howe-Walsh, Liza, and Birgit Schyns. 2010. Self-Initiated Expatriation: Implications for HRM. *The International Journal of Human Resource Management* 21 (2): 260–273.

Hutzschenreuter, Thomas, Arie Y. Lewin, and Stephan Dresel. 2011. Time to Success in Offshoring Business Processes a Multi Level Analysis. *Management International Review* 51 (1): 65–92.

Inkson, Kerr, Michael B. Arthur, Judith Pringle, and Sean Barry. 1997. Expatriate Assignment Versus Overseas Experience: Contrasting Models of International Human Resource Development. *Journal of World Business* 32 (4): 351–368.

James, Markusen. 2005. Modeling the Offshoring of White-Collar Services: From Comparative Advantage to the New Theories of Trade and FDI. *National Bureau of Economic Research, Working Paper No. 11827* (December).

Jennex, Murray E., and Olayele Adelakun. 2003. Success Factors for Offshore Information Systems Development. *Journal of Information Technology Cases and Applications* 5 (3): 12–31.

Kearney, A.T. 2004. *Making Offshore Decisions: AT Kearney's 2004 Offshore Location Attractiveness Index*. Chicago: AT Kearney.

Larsen, Marcus M., Stephan Manning, and Torben Pedersen. 2011. The Hidden Cost of Offshoring: The Impact of Complexity, Design Orientation and Experience. *Academy of Management Proceedings* 1: 1–6.

Lewin, Arie Y., Silvia Massini, and Carine Peeters. 2009. Why Are Companies Offshoring Innovation? The Emerging Global Race for Talent. *Journal of International Business Studies* 40 (8): 1406–1406.

Lewin, Arie Y., and Carine Peeters. 2006. Offshoring Work: Business Hype or the Onset of Fundamental Transformation? *Long Range Planning* 39 (3): 221–239.

Lewis, Morgan. 2009. Happy Returns. *Medical Economics* 86 (8): 14–16.

Mahoney, J.T. 2005. Resource-Based Theory, Dynamic Capabilities, and Real Options. In *Economic Foundations of Strategy: Foundations for Organizational Science*, 167–218. Thousand Oaks: Sage Publications.

Mahroum, Sami. 2000. Highly Skilled Globetrotters: Mapping the International Migration of Human Capital. *Research and Development Management* 30 (1): 23–31.

Manning, Stephan. 2014. Mitigate, Tolerate or Relocate? Offshoring Challenges, Strategic Imperatives and Resource Constraints. *Journal of World Business* 49 (4): 522–535.

Manning, S., A.Y. Lewin, and S. Massini. 2008. The Globalization of Innovation: A Dynamic Perspective on Offshoring. *Academy of Management Perspectives* 22 (3): 35–54.

Massini, Silvia, Nidthida Perm-Ajchariyawong, and Arie Y. Lewin. 2010. Role of Corporate-Wide Offshoring Strategy on Offshoring Drivers, Risks and Performance. *Industry and Innovation* 17 (4): 337–371.

Mayerhofer, Helene, Linley C. Hartmann, Gabriela Michelitsch-Riedl, and Iris Kollinger. 2004. Flexpatriate Assignments: A Neglected Issue in Global Staffing. *The International Journal of Human Resource Management* 15 (8): 1371–1389.

McDonnell, Anthony, Ryan Lamare, Patrick Gunnigle, and Jonathan Lavelle. 2010. Developing Tomorrow's Leaders—Evidence of Global Talent Management in Multinational Enterprises. *Journal of World Business* 45 (2): 150–160.

Mudambi, Ram, and Markus Venzin. 2010. The Strategic Nexus of Offshoring and Outsourcing Decisions. *Journal of Management Studies* 47 (8): 1510–1533.

Peiperl, Maury, Orly Levy, and Michael Sorell. 2014. Cross-Border Mobility of Self-Initiated and Organizational Expatriates. *International Studies of Management and Organization* 44 (3): 44–65.

Point, Sébastien, and Michael Dickmann. 2012. Branding International Careers: An Analysis of Multinational Corporations' Official Wording. *European Management Journal* 30 (1): 18–31.

Salt, John. 1988. Highly-Skilled International Migrants, Careers and Internal Labour Markets. *Geoforum* 19 (4): 387–399.

Stack, Martin, and Ricard Downing. 2005. Another Look at Offshoring: Which Jobs Are at Risk and Why? *Business Horizons* 48 (6): 513–523.

Stahl, Günter, Ingmar Björkman, Elaine Farndale, Shad S. Morris, Jaap Paauwe, Phlip Stiles, Jonathan Trevor, and Patrick Wright. 2007. Global Talent Management: How Leading Multinationals Build and Sustain Their Talent Pipeline. http://epub.wu.ac.at/3616/

Stroh, Linda K. 1995. Predicting Turnover Among Repatriates: Can Organizations Affect Retention Rates? *International Journal of Human Resource Management* 6 (2): 443–456.

Suutari, Vesa, and Chris Brewster. 2000. Making Their Own Way: Through Self-Initiated Foreign. *Journal of World Business* 35 (4): 417–436.

Suutari, Vesa, Chris Brewster, Liisa Mäkelä, Michael Dickmann, and Christelle Tornikoski. 2017. The Effect of International Work Experience on the Career Success of Expatriates: A Comparison of Assigned and Self-Initiated Expatriates. *Human Resource Management.* http://onlinelibrary.wiley.com/doi/10.1002/hrm.21827/abstract

Zetlin, Minda. 1994. Making Tracks. *The Journal of European Business* 5 (5): 40.

8

Inpatriate Career Profiles: A Historical Review and Future Outlook

Miriam Moeller and Michael Harvey

Introduction

The infectious need to globalize has ostensibly led firms to increasingly appoint inpatriates, although their defined value and impact across contexts such as country location and hierarchical levels remain largely unexplored (Maley and Kramar 2010; Moeller and Reiche 2017; Reiche et al. 2009). Recent research suggests that inpatriates are progressively used to a similar extent as expatriates (Collings et al. 2010; Harzing et al. 2016) as a way to achieve a global core competency at headquarter (HQ) locations (Harvey and Novicevic 2000b; Harvey and Buckley 1997; Tungli and Peiperl 2009). Mirroring the growth in corporate interest in inpatriate staffing is survey data which observes a relatively high percentage (57%) of employees being relocated either *to* or *from* the HQ country

---

M. Moeller (✉)
The University of Queensland, St Lucia, Australia
e-mail: m.moeller@business.uq.edu.au

M. Harvey
University of Arizona, Tucson, AZ, USA

© The Author(s) 2018
M. Dickmann et al. (eds.), *The Management of Global Careers*,
https://doi.org/10.1007/978-3-319-76529-7_8

201

(BGRS 2015), although this non-discerning relocation percentage includes estimated inpatriate (*to* HQ) and expatriate (*from* HQ) statistics. Parallel to the discussion of inpatriate value and impact at HQ and beyond, the pattern of inpatriate career lifecycles which could possibly impact their value proposition remains inconclusive at best.

At its core, the process of inpatriation is comprised of firms assigning subsidiary or third-country staff to operate in HQ locations (Cerdin and Sharma 2014; Harvey 1997; Harvey and Buckley 1997; Maley 2009, 2011; Moeller and Harvey 2011b; Reiche 2006, 2011), keeping in mind that assignments may vary relative to purpose, duration, country location and hierarchical levels (Moeller and Reiche 2017). A vast majority of research on inpatriation has described in detailed the characteristics of such assignments (see Table 8.1); we refer the reader to the most recent overview in Moeller and Reiche (2017: 220).

Interestingly, most literature appears to vehemently articulate the overarching benefits of inpatriation thereby largely excluding any concerted discussion around the contextualization of assignments. Shaped by the firm's strategic vision, the inpatriate's ascribed role and thus firm-determined purpose can manifest in one of two scenarios, either to act as a boundary spanner by contributing to knowledge transfer activities

Table 8.1 Inpatriate and expatriate differences

Characteristics	Inpatriate	Expatriate
Primary role/task/job	Boundary spanning	Control
Main strength of knowledge	Foreign market knowledge	Domestic/HQ market knowledge
Perceived status by locals	Peripheral member	HQ representative
Level of influence in host unit	Low	High
Focus of cross-cultural adjustment	Organizational and national culture	National culture
Goal congruency between HQ and subsidiary	High	Low
Value through diversity	High	Low
MNC staff composition	Geocentric	Ethnocentric
MNC stage of globalization (early vs mature)	Low vs high	High vs low

Source: The authors, adapted from Moeller and Reiche (2017)

(Azar 2012; Harvey et al. 2000a, b; Harzing et al. 2016; Kiessling et al. 2004; Kostova and Roth 2003; Reiche 2011, 2012), international management development (Bonache et al. 2001; Griffith et al. 2006; Kiessling and Harvey 2006), and creating an attitude that enables, in whatever form, increased diversity in management perspective (Harvey et al. 1999a, b, 2011a, b; Harvey and Novicevic 2000a; Moeller and Reiche 2017), or, to transfer expert knowledge in succinct short-term manner when needed (e.g. sending a product design specialist from the USA to the Netherlands for Phillips).

From a corporate view, firms seemingly find great value in the strategic utilization of inpatriates (Harvey et al. 2011a, b; Moeller and Harvey 2011b; Peterson 2003). To that extent, the inpatriate literature is replete with contrasts of inpatriates to other staffing options. It is filled with nuances about the purpose and manner in which to incorporate inpatriates at HQ. It contains some information about knowledge transfer capabilities and, albeit some, targeted efforts to accommodate this relatively embryonic staffing method in a strategic global human resource management (SGHRM) system (Collings et al. 2009; Maley 2009), what remains is an alarming shortage of evidence about the adaptation or evolution of existing policies and practices to fit inpatriates' needs. Likewise, it is imperative to understand how visible inpatriates are within organizations which has implications on how they are managed, likely through global mobility departments.

Moreover, we have not yet reached a palpable level of understanding relative to the return of inpatriates across any duration of assignment (for an exception, see Reiche 2012, on social capital and access to knowledge in host unit upon repatriation), should inpatriates return to their country of origin at all. Generally speaking, upon return assignees are placed in lower or equal positions, but the expectation is to get a promotion (BGRS 2015). The exception to this outcome is a shorter-term expert assignment. The general consensus as such remains that firms need to more carefully plan and deploy the types of support practices, particularly for longer-term assignments, extended to inpatriates (Lazarova and Caligiuri 2002; Reiche 2012) while balancing inpatriate expectations.

Expectations are a vital component of international assignments. Unfortunately from the inpatriate literature, we know virtually nothing about the assignment expectations or anticipated career moves of inpatriates. We observe that the literature has, by and large, practically aligned itself with what is observable and what we know to occur in the inpatriation process. If scholars continue to focus exclusively on maximizing the utility of inpatriation to firms, we run the risk of creating an even greater imbalance in the inpatriation literature by failing to consider the perspective of inpatriates relative to career lifecycles beyond the immediate relocation to HQ. While the expatriate manager can usually anticipate a 'return ticket' back to HQ at the end of their assignment (Bolino 2007), presumably with the predisposition to take on a new senior role at HQ (Judge et al. 1995; Ng et al. 2005) there is typically no 'return ticket' for the inpatriate manager; their ticket is 'one way' to HQ (exception: shorter-term expert assignments). Any subsequent relocation or pathway remains consistently undefined, or, at best, speculated by the firm and inpatriate alike.

This chapter supports the notion that even though research has identified career advancement as one of the most prominent individual expectations or motives for inpatriates to accept an assignment (Harvey et al. 1999a, b; Maley and Kramar 2007; Reiche 2007), the implementation of career development or career monitoring is severely lacking. In this vein, the chapter *does not* concentrate on suggestions for improvements underlying SGHRM processes to enable better career development; as highlighted, this has been far too prominent in extant works. Instead, we take a keen interest in the inpatriate as an individual agent by focusing on the inpatriate career profile which is encompassing of inpatriate-specific career experiences, movement, development and management aspects. The objectives in this chapter are twofold: (1) to identify and articulate the obvious agency problem in the inpatriate-firm relationship and (2) to explain 'what we know' and 'what we still need to know' about inpatriate career profiling. In-depth knowledge of these facets of inpatriation is most critical in order to achieve a more balanced scholarly inpatriate literature inventory that can in turn inform decisions about ongoing staff investments.

Given the lack of knowledge around how inpatriate career paths are managed within the firm, we suggest that, in agency terms, the inpatriate is incentivized to explore career opportunities beyond their assignment at HQ due to: (1) inherent uncertainty in career path options within the firm; (2) perceived inconsistent treatment relative to other staffing methods, which can lead to (3) perceptions of inadequate pay structure. The firm can help to eliminate the agency problem by altering the structure of the firm's career management support programme. In other words, greater clarity in how inpatriates are supposed to be incentivized and how career development and career choices must be delivered is important, which can, in turn, impact the motivation and contributions of inpatriates altogether. Arising from these circumstances is an explicit need for scholars to inform on the inpatriate-level perspectives.

For the most part, individual-level studies have remained disconnected from the macro-level implications of managing inpatriates. By portraying the inpatriate-firm relationship from an inpatriate's perspective, there is a flood of questions that remain unanswered. To illustrate the most obvious, they are: (1) How do inpatriates perceive their role in the firm? (2) What are inpatriates' career-related endeavours? (3) How do inpatriates perceive and evaluate their career lifecycles? (4) What are inpatriates' perceptions, expectations and actual career development opportunities? The answers to these questions deserve a nuanced approach, respecting the atypical nature of the inpatriate staffing method compared to other staffing methods.

In effect, the chapter proposes that mutual firm- and inpatriate individual-level outcomes are conditional upon an enriched understanding of the scope of inpatriate profiles, inpatriate career experiences and inpatriate family-career lifecycle pathways. We arrive at this conclusion by suggesting the inherent value behind company-level support systems sustaining inpatriation, yet, value is created only when there is a profuse repertoire of knowledge about inpatriates' experiences and how these underpin firm-level designs for career development and management. In this chapter, we take a major first step into the direction of understanding, at the individual level, inpatriate experiences and thus inpatriate career profiles.

In line with this charge, the chapter first provides a concise overview describing the present theoretical and empirical understanding of the inpatriate concept. Unambiguously, we highlight the deficiency in academic focus on the inpatriate career paths and career path prospects, given rise by an agency problem inherent in the observed inpatriate-firm relationship. The chapter then advances the inpatriate research agenda by presenting a thoughtful set of individual-level perspective research propositions linked to purposefully profiling inpatriate career paths. We anticipate this chapter will serve as the next wave of research in the inpatriate realm and make headway in understanding this phenomenon comprehensively.

The Inpatriate-Firm Relationship: An Agency Problem

This chapter's core foundation concerns a general theory of the principal-agent relationship, a theory that we apply to the employee-employer or inpatriate-firm relationships in this case (Harris and Raviv 1979). For all intents and purposes, the inpatriate and the firm are engaged in a ubiquitous agency relationship, in which one party (the principal—the firm from here onwards) delegates work to another party (the agent—the inpatriate from here onwards). This work engagement is, in agency-theory terms, a metaphorical contract (Jensen and Meckling 1976) between the firm and the inpatriate. But, contracts by nature are problematic as they negotiate the interests of parties and this can lead to challenges.

Agency theory suggests that an agency problem occurs when engaged cooperating parties, such as the firm and the inpatriate, have different goals and division of labour (Jensen and Meckling 1976; Ross 1973). The inpatriate-firm relationship hence transpires into an agency problem as the firm continuous to delegate or engage in a contract with the inpatriate, on the basis that the inpatriate carries a set of highly valuable tasks (e.g. boundary spanning through knowledge transfer or temporary expert support) and that the utility of these tasks are decidedly beneficial to the firm. The transfer of inpatriates to HQ is most commonly viewed as a status symbol or status move for inpatriates, yet firms do tend to underestimate the commitment to or under-resource the management of this type of staff member (Azar 2012; Harvey et al. 1999a, b, 2000a, b).

Agency theory is concerned with resolving two problems that can occur in agency relationships or agency contracts. First, an agency problem arises when (a) the desired goal of the principal or agent conflict, and (b) when it is difficult or expensive for the principal to verify what the agent is actually doing. The problem is that the principal cannot verify that the agent has behaved in accordance with the specified work engagement. In an inpatriate context this means that the firm does not always lend its efforts towards supporting the inpatriate's best career interest, in fact, it is inconclusive as to how firms think about inpatriate career management in the long term, or short term for that matter. On the other hand, the inpatriate may have career endeavours that lie outside the firm and therefore looks at the assignment as something temporary; meanwhile, the firm is unable to determine whether inpatriates in fact contribute to boundary spanning, for example, in an effective manner. For example, how do inpatriates contribute to building a global mindset and if so, how is this accomplished and what are the precise benefits for HQ?

The second layer of an agency problem arises when a problem of risk sharing occurs which happens when the principal and agent have different attitudes toward risk. The problem here is that the inpatriate, or agent in the relationship, is more risk averse due to the unique and relatively nascent nature of the assignment type. A lack of understanding of expectations, pathways and guidance to achieve firm-level goals can lead to greater inpatriate risk-averse attitudes and behaviour. The firm, knowing the added benefit and nature of inpatriates, is less hesitant about engaging in a contract with inpatriates as the goals of knowledge transfer and global mindset building are readily desired, albeit not concretely measurable. Accordingly, we assume the presence and pursuit of self-interest at the individual level and goal conflict at the organizational level (March 1962; Pfeffer 1981).

With the contextualization of the agency problem in mind, the goal then is to create the most efficient contract governing the principal-agent relationship given assumptions about individuals (i.e. self-interest, bounded rationality, risk aversion from both the principal and the agent), organizations (i.e. goal conflict among members), and information (i.e. information is a commodity which can be purchased) (March 1962, Pfeffer 1981). In this vein, the literature has made apparent the firm's intentions in employing inpatriates which makes their assumptions about the risk, or better yet, the certainty with which this staffing method is employed, slightly more visible. On the other side, we know virtually nothing about the assumptions around self-interest, risk and bounded rationality that the inpatriate fosters with regard to their role within the firm.

Indeed, the boundary-spanning task of the inpatriate is not yet precisely defined. The loosely delineated task of boundary spanning is based on idealism opposed to concrete value propositions. As a result, agent assumptions and behaviour are problematic to define, giving rise to opportunism on the agent's part. It is suggested by Eisenhardt (1989) that firms can invest in information systems in order to control agent opportunism. But, firms are presently not investing in inpatriates in that way, moreover, it is difficult to pinpoint the actual contributions inpatriates provide to the firm. Regardless of information systems, a dearth of knowledge remains on topics such as: What level of self-interest does exist? What level of bounded rationality does exist? How risk averse might the inpatriate actually be? Across what boundaries does this occur? Is risk aversion greater in the short term or the long term? We simply do not have answers to these questions yet. By profiling inpatriate careers, the literature can succumb to these deficiencies.

Inquiry into Inpatriate Career Profiles: A Brief Summary

Although previous work has at times suggested that international assignment experience might have career-enhancing effects (Ng et al. 2005), we argue that the relationship between inpatriates' perceptions and career pathways is not well acknowledged. Reiche's (2012) work defines career support in terms of the inpatriates' general beliefs about the extent to which the firm provides support for long-term career development.

The phrase 'general belief' is telling of the lack of consideration for the inpatriates' probable multifaceted perspective on the issue of career movements. The lack of information about inpatriate perceptions of career profiles is problematic, and contentiously, this circumstance will not lead firms to actively engage in long-lasting, sustainable inpatriate-firm relationships.

To that extent, work by Reiche et al. (2011) is informative in that it suggests that inpatriates' trusting ties with HQ staff and their fit with the HQ is positively related to inpatriates' firm-specific learning and their perceived career prospects. The latter predicts their retention two and four years later, although it remains inconclusive what the career intentions of the individual and firm are. Other firm-specific value propositions to the inpatriate career profiles and paths rely on proximity to influential senior managers at HQ who may offer mentorship and future career sponsorship (Reiche 2012), the ability to acquire valuable political skill, political and social capital (Harvey and Novicevic 2004; Reiche 2012) and provision of a firm-specific skill set (Moeller et al. 2010).

A more generic perspective of value propositions to the inpatriate is that of achieving a heightened level of cultural expertise or cultural mediation techniques (Gertsen and Søderberg 2012) which would help to develop their skill set for future assignments, within or external to the firm. Yet, the inherent characteristics of inpatriates may be what stifle the career advancement, particularly if the intention is to advance in hierarchy at HQ. Because of inpatriates' peripheral status at HQ, their career advancement intentions may not always be conveyed properly, moreover, their peripheral status may actively interfere with career advancement at HQ. Inpatriates' individual expectations for career advancement and retention at HQ may be thwarted, because it is generally more problematic for inpatriate managers to rise to senior positions at the global organization's HQ than it is for parent country nationals (Collings et al. 2009; Reiche et al. 2009).

Added to this institutional-like barrier is the fact that inpatriates' experience of performance appraisals frequently results in a perception of violation of psychological contract (Maley 2009). These firm-specific factors, generic factors and institutional challenges combined continue to highlight the disconnectedness between mutual firm-level and individual-level understandings of inpatriate assignments and inpatriate career profiles and pathways. The following section observes the inpatriate literature from three angles, whereby we are able to articulate how to overcome the dearth of information revealed about inpatriate career profiles.

Three Observations About Inpatriate Literature

By definition inpatriates lead global careers (Harvey 1989; Reiche 2012) and have cross-border responsibility (Cappellen and Janssens 2005; Harvey et al. 1999a, b). Yet, the global career paths look very different for inpatriates than they do for other staffing methods such as expatriate or flexpatriates (Harvey et al. 2010). For a full-fledged review on inpatriates over the last two decades, see Moeller and Reiche (2017). We observe, rather effortlessly, that the approach to studying inpatriates suffers from a blatantly apparent and proverbial organizational scientist-practitioner gap that calls for an intervention in how inpatriate research is carried out from today onwards. In this vein, we make a few general observations about the present inpatriate literature status that leads us to making our central point which is that the asymmetry found within inpatriate literature is influenced by a lack of consideration for the scope of inpatriate career profiles.

The First Observation admits a lack of knowledge about inpatriate boundaries. The inpatriate presents a relatively embryonic global employee when juxtaposed to the archetypal expatriate. Seminal works (Harvey 1997; Harvey and Buckley 1997) describe inpatriates as a pool of host or third-country international employees who are transferred to corporate HQ to serve as a linking pin across subsidiaries and HQ. In 2017, Moeller and Reiche tentatively concluded that inpatriates 'carry value whether engaged in a short- or long-term international assignment format, and whether they are semi-permanent, permanent or temporary, but that their utility must be gauged against a contextual backdrop' (pp. 4–5). In continuation of this idea, this chapter suggests that the profile and associated value of inpatriates in short- or longer-term formats is far from defined and seeks further refinement.

Refinement relies heavily on explaining the boundary conditions of the inpatriate experience as such boundary conditions can include, but are not limited to, investigating (1) the perceived purpose in their role at HQ; (2) how their role is linked to intended and realized performance variables such as knowledge transfer; (3) how the previously identified boundaries vary across contexts such as different hierarchical levels, assignment locations and assignment durations. For example, the longer-term view of inpatriation is described as a tool for developing a competitive edge through a sustainable pluralistic management perspective (Harvey and Buckley 1997), while the shorter-term view of inpatriation represents the value of developmental and knowledge transfer purposes and to train inpatriates to cope with management challenges beyond their stay at HQ (Peterson 2003; Reiche 2006). The argument is that shorter-term assignments would enable better maintenance of social ties at subsidiary levels while the longer-term inpatriation would enable sustainable relationships between two markets through the momentum of a consistent top management team perspective. Research has yet to envisage the actual processes and outcomes of these assignment duration circumstances, let alone in conjunction with other foreseeable boundary conditions.

We add to the mix of boundary conditions what is probably the most well-known set of criteria by which inpatriates differ to other staffing methods, namely (4) the implications of the inpatriate-specific characteristics (for a review see Reiche et al. 2009), and more recently, Moeller and Reiche 2017) on the aforementioned contexts, which have always presumed to interfere with inpatriate socialization (Moeller et al. 2010), integration (Guimaraes-Costa and Cunha 2009) and performance (Gong 2003; Maley 2009). It is suspected that the ownership exhibited by inpatriates of the assignment is greatly dependent upon the push and pull of adjustment factors like status differences, level of influence, corporate and cultural distances, goal alignment between HQ and subsidiaries and HQ staffing composition to name a few (Reiche et al. 2009; Moeller and Reiche 2017). An exploration of these undercurrents to this extent remains untouched in inpatriate literature.

Furthermore, the spectrum of possible inpatriate profiles may well vary from that of the typical expatriate, and as a result we envision inpatriates to perceive their roles according to their level of responsibility. To that extent it remains inconclusive as to how varying inpatriate profiles perceive their role relative to aiding the development of a strategic global mindset. How do inpatriates define success? To what extent are inpatriates aware of the distinguished set of characteristics (Reiche, et al. 2009; Moeller and Reiche 2017) and therefore challenges such as ownership of the assignment compared to the typical expatriate assignment? Are these challenges present to a greater extent at certain hierarchical levels or across other contexts? Likewise, over time, what does an inpatriate's contribution entail? As a result of this preliminary line of questioning, we offer the following research proposition:

Proposition 1: *Profiling inpatriate experiences will provoke the individual-level perspectives about inpatriate career profiles needed to generate a more balanced inventory of inpatriate literature.*

The Second Observation points to the skewed nature of chosen level of analysis. The approach to inpatriate research, as with any embryonic concept, can be patchy. Existing inpatriate works glorify the firm-level perspective (Collings et al. 2010; Harvey et al. 1999a, b; Peterson 2003; Solomon 1995; Tungli and Peiperl 2009). Previous work has primarily addressed the strategic and systemic use of inpatriation as a staffing option, in addition to articulating selection and integration undercurrents of inpatriates within host corporate and national settings (Moeller and Reiche 2017). To further promote the sporadic pool of inpatriate literature, few studies have attempted to examine issues across levels of analyses (for an exception see Collings et al. 2010). Individual-level studies therefore remain disconnected from the macro-level implications of managing inpatriates, contributing to an imbalance in familiarity with this topic. Resulting from this observation is an awkward indication that unless individual inpatriate perspectives are articulated and contextualized (Minbaeva 2016), it is unlikely that firms will succeed with their proposed set of intended HR solutions.

The fact that the inpatriate literature does not cover, in depth, multi-level viewpoints assumes that the inpatriate phenomenon is poorly understood. Inpatriates are noted to be critical firm-level strategic resources (Harvey and Buckley 1997; Linehan and Scullion 2001). It comes as no surprise then that our observation consists of noting the favouritism extended to addressing inpatriate assignments from a firm-level perspective. As an extension to the favouritism observation, it would be noteworthy to explore and explain the firm-level implications arising out of inpatriate hierarchical or lateral career moves (see Observation 1 on career profiles). We project that much like cultural chameleons blend in across cultural settings, inpatriates due to their uncertain career path structure have to entertain a spectrum of characteristics similar to that of the cultural chameleon to morph from inpatriate into a potentially very different staffing mechanism (i.e. flexpatriates perhaps). As a result of this preliminary line of questioning, we offer the following research proposition:

Proposition 2: *Increased attention to multilevel analysis will reinforce the inpatriate concept by exposing inpatriate career profiles while also generating a more balanced inventory of inpatriate literature.*

The Third Observation points to the skewed nature of extant inpatriate works whereby conceptual contributions starkly outpace empirical contributions. Conceptual contributions concentrate on themes such as the systematic integration of inpatriates (Collings et al. 2009; Harvey and Novicevic 2000b; Harvey et al. 2000a, b) through alignment of SGHRM systems specifically designed for inpatriate staff member needs, selection (Harvey et al. 2001, 2002, 2003, 2004, 2006; Harvey and Mejias 2002;) and integration mechanisms (Harvey 1997, inpatriate training; Harvey and Fung 2000, on realistic relocation previews; Novicevic et al. 2003, on ethical expectation management; Moeller and Harvey 2011a, on political skill and stigmatization; Moeller et al. 2010, on socialization patterns; Harvey et al. 2011a, b, on trust building).

The empirical high notes have focused on the strategic use of inpatriates (Peterson 2003, on joint ventures; Tungli and Peiperl 2009, on changes in staffing practices over time; Collings et al. 2010 and Harzing et al. 2016, on outward staffing flows), the development of an inpatriate competency (Harvey and Miceli 1999, on training programmes and acculturation processes; Tharenou and Harvey 2006, on management development; Peppas and Chang 1998, on managing cultural issues), the development of inpatriates' social capital (Reiche 2006, knowledge transfer; Reiche 2011, on boundary spanning; Reiche 2012, on repatriation; Gertsen and Søderberg 2012, on cultural mediators; Reiche et al. 2011, on firm-specific learning; Harzing et al. 2016, on function-specific knowledge transfer) and understanding the inpatriate psychological contract (Maley 2009, on the influence of performance appraisals; Maley and Kramar 2010, on structural variations; Maley 2011, on the HRM strategy type; Cerdin and Sharma 2014, on understanding global talent management).

Empirical works comprise of roughly one-fifth of all inpatriate-specific papers (Moeller and Reiche 2017). This percentage, interpreted jointly with the second observation about level of analysis concerns, prompts us to remark that further and targeted scrutiny is needed to establish a greater empirical scope of inpatriate literature. While empirical research has suggested that perceived career prospects are linked to short-term retention (Reiche et al. 2011), it only offers a single glimpse into the career lifecycle of inpatriates within and across firms. It may be appropriate to put into question the actual return of investment (ROI) of the inpatriate assignment, although any type of calculation is dependent precisely upon the career profile of the individual, the stakeholders surrounding the individual such as family and longevity of the assignment. While ROI has been philosophically addressed for expatriate assignments (McNulty and Inkson 2013), much remains to be done in the empirical space.

For example, uncertainty about the location and longevity of an existing or subsequent assignment can have immense implications on family lifecycles inclusive of the need for children's schooling arrangement, spousal job search and career development, stress management, adjustment to national cultures and religious support (if required). In analysing ROI, it is important for both the firm and the individual (inclusive of family) to engage in such an undertaking separately, contemplating the variable such as compensation packages, psychological contracts, family and career lifecycles and the extent of importance of each. As a result of this preliminary line of questioning, we offer the following research proposition:

Proposition 3: *Increased empirical research, both at and across firm and individual levels of analysis, will not only test existing conceptual ideas but also generate a more balanced inventory of inpatriate literature.*

Summary and Conclusion

Based on our review of the inpatriate-firm relationship, the inpatriate ostensibly has qualities that are difficult to emulate by expatriate or by any constellation of staffing methods outside of HQ. The technique of sending individuals from host or third-country locations to inform HQ of country-specific organizational and cultural dynamics present in the host countries is a vital component of running a successful business. The aforementioned three observations link back to an immense disconnectedness between understandings of the firm and the inpatriates it employs, leading us to believe that the dynamics of the inpatriate-firm relationship require further exploration. To summarize, we present the reader with a carefully chosen set of prominent and pressing future research (FR) ideas to engage in ongoing efforts in understanding the impact of inpatriate assignment:

Organizational Level

FR_1: Understanding of the intended career path structure for inpatriates to assess the support structure and fluidity of the assignment type.
FR_2: Understanding the inpatriate mindset and impact at varying hierarchical levels.

Individual Level

FR_3: Understanding the distinguished set of inpatriate characteristics and the challenges these provoke.
FR_4: Understanding the inpatriate career lifecycle and its return on investment to inpatriates and their families.

In addressing these primary challenges, we enhance the firm's capability to generate support systems contextualized to inpatriation. We explained herein that a pivotal factor of inpatriate-firm relationship transparency is that of an explicit understanding of inpatriate career profiles. The above-noted future research ideas help to address career profile mapping challenges.

By reviewing the literature on inpatriate since its inception in 1997, we are able to make three major observations relative to the state of research in this domain. First, there is a dearth of information about the inpatriate. Second, the nature of inpatriate literature is skewed towards firm-level analysis issues. Third, conceptual contributions outpace empirical contributions. The predominant goal of this chapter was not to address all aspects of these identified conundrums, but to initiate an awareness and discussion, for scholars and practitioners alike, of the slowly encroaching lopsidedness of inpatriate research. By outlining some of the focal areas of inpatriate career scholarship, we are hopeful that future work in this domain can carry the torch towards creating a more balanced, informed and transparent view.

References

Azar, Goudarz. 2012. Inpatriates and Expatriates: Sources of Strategic Human Capital for Multinational Food and Beverage Firms. *International Food and Agribusiness Management Review* 15 (7): 73–79.

Bolino, Mark C. 2007. Expatriate Assignments and Intra-Organizational Career Success: Implications for Individuals and Organizations. *Journal of International Business Studies* 38 (5): 819–835.

Bonache, Jaime, Chris Brewster, and Vesa Suutari. 2001. Expatriation: A Developing Research Agenda. *Thunderbird International Business Review* 43 (1): 3–20.

BGRS (Brookfield Global Relocation Services). 2015. *Global Relocation Trends Survey Report*. Woodridge, IL.

Cappellen, Tineke, and Maddy Janssens. 2005. Career Paths of Global Managers: Towards Future Research. *Journal of World Business* 40 (4): 348–360.

Cerdin, Jean-Luc, and Kushal Sharma. 2014. Inpatriation as a Key Component of Global Talent Management. In *Global Talent Management*, ed. Akram Al Ariss, 79–92. New York: Springer.

Collings, David G., Anthony McDonnell, Patrick Gunnigle, and Jonathan Lavelle. 2010. Swimming Against the Tide: Outward Staffing Flows from Multinational Subsidiaries. *Human Resource Management* 49 (4): 575–598.

Collings, David G., Hugh Scullion, and Peter J. Dowling. 2009. Global Staffing: A Review and Thematic Research Agenda. *The International Journal of Human Resource Management* 20 (6): 1253–1272.

Eisenhardt, Kathleen M. 1989. Agency Theory: An Assessment and Review. *Academy of Management Review* 14 (1): 57–74.

Gertsen, Martine C., and Anne-Marie Søderberg. 2012. Inpatriation in a Globalising MNC: Knowledge Exchange and Translation of Corporate Culture. *European Journal of International Management* 6 (1): 29–44.

Gong, Yaping. 2003. Subsidiary Staffing in Multinational Enterprises: Agency, Resources, and Performance. *Academy of Management Journal* 46 (6): 728–739.

Griffith, David A., Chun Zhang, and S. Tamer Cavusgil. 2006. Attributions of Noncooperative Incidents and Response Strategies: The Role of National Character. *Journal of World Business* 41 (4): 356–367.

Guimaraes-Costa, Nuno, and Miguel Pina E. Cunha. 2009. Foreign Locals: A Liminal Perspective of International Managers. *Organizational Dynamics* 38 (2): 158–166.

Harris, Milton, and Artur Raviv. 1979. Optimal Incentive Contracts With Imperfect Information. *Journal of Economic Theory* 20 (2): 231–259.

Harvey, Michael G. 1989. Repatriation of Corporate Executives: An Empirical Study. *Journal of International Business Studies* 20 (1): 131–144.

———. 1997. 'Inpatriation' Training: The Next Challenge for International Human Resource Management. *International Journal of Intercultural Relations* 21 (3): 393–428.

Harvey, Michael G., and M. Ronald Buckley. 1997. Managing Inpatriates: Building a Global Core Competency. *Journal of World Business* 32 (1): 35–52.

Harvey, Michael G., M. Ronald Buckley, and Milorad Novicevic. 2006. Addressing Ethical Issues Associated with the Inpatriation of Nursing Professionals. *Journal of Applied Management and Entrepreneurship* 11 (4): 18–32.

Harvey, Michael G., and Helan Fung. 2000. Inpatriate Managers: The Need for Realistic Relocation Reviews. *International Journal of Management* 17 (2): 151–159.

Harvey, Michael, Chad Hartnell, and Milorad Novicevic. 2004. The Inpatriation of Foreign Healthcare Workers: A Potential Remedy for the Chronic Shortage of Professional Staff. *International Journal of Intercultural Relations* 28 (2): 127–150.

Harvey, Michael G., Tim Kiessling, and Miriam Moeller. 2011a. Globalization and the Inward Flow of Immigrants: Issues Associated with the Inpatriation of Global Managers. *Human Resource Development Quarterly* 22 (2): 177–194.

Harvey, Michael G., Tim Kiessling, and Milorad Novicevic. 2003. Staffing Marketing Positions During Global Hyper-Competitiveness: A Market-Based Perspective. *International Journal of Human Resource Management* 14 (2): 223–245.

Harvey, Michael G., Helene Mayerhofer, Linley Hartmann, and Miriam Moeller. 2010. Corralling the "Horses" to Staff the Global Organization of 21st Century. *Organizational Dynamics* 39 (3): 258–268.

Harvey, Michael G., and Roberto Mejias. 2002. Addressing the US IT Manpower Shortage with Inpatriates and Technological Training. *Journal of Information Technology Management* 11 (3–4): 1–14.

Harvey, Michael G., and Nicholas Miceli. 1999. Exploring Inpatriate Manager Issues: An Exploratory Empirical Study. *International Journal of Intercultural Relations* 23 (3): 339–371.

Harvey, Michael G., and Milorad M. Novicevic. 2000a. The Influences of Inpatriation Practices on The Strategic Orientation of a Global Organization. *International Journal of Management* 17 (3): 362–371.

———. 2000b. Staffing Global Marketing Positions: What We Don't Know Can Make a Difference. *Journal of World Business* 35 (1): 80–94.

———. 2004. The Development of Political Skill and Political Capital by Global Leaders Through Global Assignments. *The International Journal of Human Resource Management* 15 (7): 1173–1188.

Harvey, Michael G., Milorad M. Novicevic, and Timothy Kiessling. 2002. Development of Multiple IQ Maps for Use in the Selection of Inpatriate Managers: A Practical Theory. *International Journal of Intercultural Relations* 26 (5): 493–524.

Harvey, Michael G., Milorad M. Novicevic, and Cheri Speier. 1999a. Inpatriate Managers: How to Increase the Probability of Success. *Human Resource Management Review* 9 (1): 51–81.

———. 2000a. An Innovative Global Management Staffing System: A Competency-Based Perspective. *Human Resource Management* 39 (4): 381–394.

Harvey, Michael G., B. Sebastian Reiche, and Miriam Moeller. 2011b. Developing Effective Global Relationships Through Staffing with Inpatriate Managers: The Role of Interpersonal Trust. *Journal of International Management* 17 (2): 150–161.

Harvey, Michael G., Cheri Speier, and Milorad M. Novicevic. 1999b. The Impact of Emerging Markets on Staffing the Global Organization: A Knowledge-Based View. *Journal of International Management* 5 (3): 167–186.

———. 2000b. Strategic Global Human Resource Management: The Role of Inpatriate Managers. *Human Resource Management Review* 10 (2): 153–175.

———. 2001. Strategic Human Resource Staffing of Foreign Subsidiaries. *Research and Practice in Human Resource Management* 9 (2): 27–56.

Harzing, Anne-Wil, Markus Pudelko, and B. Sebastian Reiche. 2016. The Bridging Role of Expatriates and Inpatriates in Knowledge Transfer in Multinational Corporations. *Human Resource Management* 55 (4): 679–695.

Jensen, Michael C., and William H. Meckling. 1976. Theory of the Firm: Managerial Behavior, Agency Costs and Ownership Structure. *Journal of Financial Economics* 3 (4): 305–360.

Judge, Timothy A., Daniel M. Cable, John W. Boudreau, and Robert D. Bretz. 1995. An Empirical Investigation of the Predictors of Executive Career Success. *Personnel Psychology* 48 (3): 485–519.

Kiessling, Timothy, and Michael Harvey. 2006. Global Organizational Control: A New Role by Inpatriates. *Multinational Business Review* 14 (2): 1–28.

Kiessling, Timothy, Michael Harvey, and Garry Garrison. 2004. The Importance of Boundary-Spanners in Global Supply Chains and Logistics Management in the 21st Century. *Journal of Global Marketing* 17 (4): 93–115.

Kostova, Tatiana, and Kendall Roth. 2003. Social Capital in Multinational Corporations and a Micro-Macro Model of its Formation. *Academy of Management Review* 28 (2): 297–317.

Lazarova, Mila, and Paula Caligiuri. 2002. Retaining Repatriates: The Role of Organizational Support Practices. *Journal of World Business* 36 (4): 389–401.

Linehan, Margaret, and Hugh Scullion. 2001. Challenges for Female International Managers: Evidence from Europe. *Journal of Managerial Psychology* 16 (3): 215–228.

Maley, Jane F. 2009. The Influence of Performance Appraisal on the Psychological Contract of the Inpatriate Manager. *South Asia Journal of Human Resource Management* 7 (1): 100–109.

———. 2011. The Influence of Various Human Resource Management Strategies on the Performance Management of Subsidiary Managers. *Asia-Pacific Journal of Business Administration* 3 (1): 28–46.

Maley, Jane, and Robin Kramar. 2007. International Performance Appraisal: Policies, Practices and Processes in Australian Subsidiaries of Healthcare MNCs. *Research and Practice in Human Resource Management* 15 (2): 21–40.

———. 2010. International Human Resource Management Structures and Their Effect on the Australian Subsidiary. *Asia Pacific Journal of Human Resources* 48 (1): 26–44.

March, James G. 1962. The Business Firm as a Political Coalition. *The Journal of Politics* 24 (04): 662–678.

McNulty, Yvonne, and Kerr Inkson. 2013. *Managing Expatriates: A Return on Investment Approach*. New York, NY: Business Expert Press.

Minbaeva, Dana. 2016. Contextualising the Individual in International Management Research: Black Boxes, Comfort Zones and a Future Research Agenda. *European Journal of International Management* 10 (1): 95–104.

Moeller, Miriam, and Michael Harvey. 2011a. The Influence of Political Skill on the Acceptance of Foreign Nationals at the Home Country Organization: An Examination of Cultural Stigmatization. *International Journal of Human Resource Management* 22 (12): 2593–2608.

———. 2011b. Inpatriate Marketing Managers: Issues Associated With Staffing Global Marketing Positions. *Journal of International Marketing* 19 (4): 1–16.

Moeller, Miriam, Michael Harvey, and Wallace Williams. 2010. Socialization of Inpatriate Managers to the Headquarters of Global Organizations: A Social Learning Perspective. *Human Resource Development Review* 9 (2): 169–193.

Moeller, Miriam, and B. Sebastian Reiche. 2017. Inpatriates—A Review, Synthesis and Outlook of Two Decades of Research. In *Research Handbook of Expatriates*, ed. Yvonne McNulty and Jan Selmer, 218–240. Cheltenham: Edward Elgar.

Ng, Thomas W., Lillian T. Eby, Kelly L. Sorensen, and Daniel C. Feldman. 2005. Predictors of Objective and Subjective Career Success: A Meta-Analysis. *Personnel Psychology* 58 (2): 367–408.

Novicevic, Milorad M., M. Ronald Buckley, Michael G. Harvey, Jonathon R.B. Halbesleben, and Susan Des Rosiers. 2003. Socializing Ethical Behavior of Foreign Employees in Multinational Corporations. *Business Ethics A European Review* 12 (3): 298–307.

Peppas, Spero C., and Lisa Chang. 1998. The Integration of Inpatriates Into Rural Communities. *Management Decision* 36 (6): 370–377.

Peterson, Richard B. 2003. The Use of Expatriates and Inpatriates in Central and Eastern Europe Since the Wall Came Down. *Journal of World Business* 38 (1): 55–69.

Pfeffer, Jeffrey. 1981. *Power in Organizations*. Marshfield, MA: Pitman.

Reiche, B. Sebastian. 2006. The Inpatriate Experience in Multinational Corporations: An Exploratory Case Study in Germany. *International Journal of Human Resource Management* 17 (9): 1572–1590.

———. 2007. The Effect of International Staffing Practices on Subsidiary Staff Retention in Multinational Corporations. *International Journal of Human Resource Management* 18 (4): 523–536.

———. 2011. Knowledge Transfer in Multinationals: The Role of Inpatriates' Boundary Spanning. *Human Resource Management* 50 (3): 365–389.

———. 2012. Knowledge Benefits of Social Capital Upon Repatriation: A Longitudinal Study of International Assignees. *Journal of Management Studies* 49 (6): 1052–1077.

Reiche, B. Sebastian, Maria L. Kraimer, and Anne-Wil Harzing. 2009. Inpatriates as Agents of Cross-Unit Knowledge Flows in Multinational Corporations. In *Handbook of International HR Research: Integrating People, Process and Context*, ed. Paul Sparrow, 151–170. Oxford: Blackwell.

Reiche, B. Sebastian, Maria L. Kraimer, and Anne-Wils Harzing. 2011. Why Do International Assignees Stay? An Organizational Embeddedness Perspective. *Journal of International Business Studies* 42 (4): 521–544.

Ross, Stephen A. 1973. The Economic Theory of Agency: The Principal's Problem. *The American Economic Review* 63 (2): 134–139.

Solomon, Charlene. 1995. HR's Helping Hand Pulls Global Inpatriates Onboard. *Personnel Journal-Baltimore Then Costa Mesa* 74 (11): 40–46.

Tharenou, Phyllis, and Michael Harvey. 2006. Examining the Overseas Staffing Options Utilized by Australian Headquartered Multinational Corporations. *International Journal of Human Resource Management* 17 (6): 1095–1114.

Tungli, Zsuzsanna, and Maury Peiperl. 2009. Expatriate Practices in German, Japanese, UK, and US Multinational Companies: A Comparative Survey of Changes. *Human Resource Management* 48 (1): 153–171.

9

The Role of Repatriation in and for Global Careers

Eren Akkan, Mila Lazarova, and B. Sebastian Reiche

Introduction

Repatriation encompasses the phase in which individuals return to their home countries from an international work experience (Herman and Tetrick 2009; Birur and Muthiah 2013; Feldman 1991). Regardless of whether the transition takes place within one organization or across organizations, returning home after working abroad constitutes a critical step for an individual's future career. The transition process between the expatriation and repatriation stages and the repatriation experience itself influence individual decisions of whether to continue to work in a global context or not. As such, repatriation plays a critical role in shaping future careers and some scholars consider it as the most challenging career step for individuals (Suutari and Mäkelä 2007).

E. Akkan (✉) • B. Sebastian Reiche
IESE Business School, University of Navarra, Madrid, Spain
e-mail: EAkkan@iese.edu; SReiche@iese.edu

M. Lazarova
Beedie School of Business, Simon Fraser University, Vancouver, BC, Canada
e-mail: mbl@sfu.ca

© The Author(s) 2018
M. Dickmann et al. (eds.), *The Management of Global Careers*,
https://doi.org/10.1007/978-3-319-76529-7_9

A global career can be defined as a career that "spans two or more countries" (Baruch and Reis 2015: 14), or one that "encompasses a succession or collection of multiple international assignments" (Suutari et al. 2012: 3456). In the context of these definitions, given that repatriates have worked both in their home country and at least one foreign country, they are people who have already embarked on a global career. As with all careers, global careers are a result of the interaction of organizations and individuals, as both parties are dependent on each other (Larsen 2004) and career decisions are influenced both by one's perceptions of oneself and by macro factors that reside outside the individual (Cappellen and Janssens 2005). Hence, repatriation is a time when people take into account a number of factors to reflect critically on what their international work experience might have added to or taken away from their careers and as a result try to envision what similar future international experiences may entail. Being back in the home country reality informs repatriates about what kind of implications further international moves may have on their careers.

For most people, repatriation is not an end in itself but a transition period. That is because a multitude of choices are available to individuals and the repatriation experience may help them make more informed decisions about their future careers. For example, a significant number of organizational repatriates consider leaving their organizations (Stahl et al. 2002), and some actually quit (Kraimer et al. 2012) due to various challenges faced during this period. Repatriate turnover arguably constitutes the primary focus of early academic research on repatriation (Lazarova and Caligiuri 2002). The underlying assumption behind this variable of interest has been that turnover is an undesirable outcome both for organizations and individuals. However, for people who see their careers as boundaryless (i.e. transcending physical and psychological boundaries), turnover is not necessarily dysfunctional (Lazarova and Cerdin 2007). To the contrary, from a global career perspective, turnover might aid repatriates in finding other organizations that value the international experience and help them pursue further work opportunities abroad (Olds and Howe-Walsh 2013).

Apart from turnover and seeking further international relocations in the current organization, repatriation may lead to an exploration of various other career options for individuals. The gamut of options of international work has greatly expanded in the last two decades (Shaffer et al. 2012). Beyond long-term relocations, global professionals may take part in global virtual teams or travel frequently to foreign destinations on a regular basis (Mayrhofer et al. 2004). Engaging in entrepreneurial activities outside the current organization in one's home country is another viable alternative career route for returnees (Valk et al. 2014; Lin et al. 2016). Although scholars have begun exploring the career implications of newer forms of global work, the predominant focus of international management research to date has been on global career decisions involving physical mobility, of which the decisions during repatriation remain critical. Therefore, we mainly concentrate on repatriates' decisions of whether to stay in the home country or take on further international relocations in the pursuit of future global career opportunities. Because the expatriation experience constitutes one step in the unfolding of global careers, and it may influence the repatriate experience itself, we first discuss how expatriation informs repatriation and its likely implications on career decisions during the repatriation period. Upon returning home, repatriate career choices are a function of the combined influence of the repatriate's agency, contextual factors (such as available employment opportunities) and macro variables such as the economic conditions in one's home country. Accordingly, our second emphasis is on the career-related challenges and opportunities that the repatriation experience entails and the obstacles or facilitators that repatriates perceive as, respectively, constraining or enabling their global career choices. Third, we discuss the different ways in which the international management literature has defined "career success" during repatriation. We also touch on findings on how self-initiated repatriation affects global career choices and conclude with various future research directions.

Several boundary conditions are worth noting. Returning home may take place with or without the help of the organizations that individuals are working for during their work experiences abroad. The international management literature has concentrated mainly on those who move back with the help of their organizations, that is, organizational repatriates. Due to the dearth of studies and a lack of paradigm development on self-initiated repatriates (SIRs), in this chapter we mainly concentrate on organizational repatriates and dedicate a short section for discussing the literature on SIRs. Further, we only consider repatriation-related concepts such as repatriation adjustment to the extent that they affect global career choices rather than provide a detailed review of all variables discussed in repatriation research. Finally, we constrain the content of this chapter to repatriates', rather than organizations', perceptions of the repatriation experience.

The Transition Between Expatriation and Repatriation

The repatriation experience is a function of both what happens during the repatriation stage and the expatriation period itself, as repatriation outcomes are often closely connected to one's previous international experience. Hence, international assignments and repatriation should be considered as one comprehensive experience (Altman and Baruch 2012; Hyder and Lövblad 2007; Yan et al. 2002). Scholars have underlined the links between international assignments and employees' broader career plans and have highlighted that when there is no fit between the two, repatriates may consider leaving the organization (Feldman 1991). The extent to which performance during expatriation predicts performance during repatriation depends on whether the subsequent position is related to the previous experience, that is, how consistent one's global career is and scholars have called for investigating this relationship in greater detail (Brewster et al. 2014; Cerdin and Le Pargneux 2009). However, various theoretical and empirical attempts have been made to associate the two periods of individuals' global careers. We focus on the role of one's proactivity during expatriation, the type of international assignment and the changes brought about by expatriation as the key themes that have been studied so far.

The international management literature has stressed the role of *proactivity* as an individual characteristic that aids in bridging the expatriation experience and repatriation outcomes. Leiba O'Sullivan (2002) highlighted that a proactive personality is related to higher levels of agentic control of career decisions upon repatriation. Hence, protean behaviours such as social networking and information seeking were suggested to mediate the relationship between having proactive personality traits and resultant career outcomes. Similarly, Lazarova and Cerdin (2007) proposed that career activism is an antecedent to turnover intentions upon repatriation. They showed that, after accounting for the role of organizational support, the more career initiatives individuals engage in prior to repatriation, the more they exert agency on their career choices upon return. This notion emphasized the idea that compared to structural constraints individual agency plays a more prominent role for career outcomes and can help repatriates overcome various career challenges. Another study showed that a substantial number of people were aware of the fact that they needed to be proactive and responsive to opportunities during their expatriation period so that they could minimize the challenges they typically face once they move back home (Altman and Baruch 2012).

As organizations have started to diversify their portfolio of international assignees with regard to their strategic importance (Lazarova and Caligiuri 2002), scholars have also shown interest in the difference between various *types of expatriates* and their implications for the repatriation experience. Notably, research suggests that the type of assignment (developmental v functional) may influence employees' repatriation concerns and their perceived career prospects with other employers, as developmental assignees perceive better career advancement opportunities in their organizations and are more confident that the assignment will enhance their career prospects upon repatriation (Stahl et al. 2009). Developmental assignees also tend to have higher levels of turnover intentions. However, regardless of the type of assignment, an employee's attitude towards developing competencies during the international work experience is thought to be more crucial in career-related repatriation outcomes than the type of assignment itself (Bolino 2007).

The *changes one goes through* during the international experience (we elaborate on this point in the sections to come), combined with changes in contextual factors in the home organization and changes in non-work life in the home country (Stroh et al. 2000), may result in perceiving repatriation as a career challenge or a career opportunity. Early research has found that many repatriates think of themselves as "organizational heroes" due to their accomplishments abroad (Osland 2000; Stroh et al. 1998). For an international assignee, working abroad means a period of intensive learning and building an international social network. Given that one's career capital, that is, one's career competencies consisting of knowing-how, knowing-whom and knowing-why, impacts global career behaviour (Mayrhofer et al. 2004), the perceptions of repatriates and other stakeholders regarding the learning taking place during the international work experience may affect the career choices available to the repatriate. Due to the "out of sight out of mind" effect, organizations however may not necessarily be cognizant of such accomplishments (Stroh et al. 1998). Returning home may also have a reputation-related effect in one's social circles in the home country. For example, in the case of repatriating from a developed to a developing country, it has been suggested that repatriates could suffer from "losing face" in the eyes of significant others, because moving back home may be perceived as a step-down in terms of one's career (Banai and Harry 2004).

Research has also pointed out that expatriation is a time during which individuals may question their *identities* (Kohonen 2008; Kraimer et al. 2012). The ways in which repatriates define their identities (Suutari and Mäkelä 2007) may complicate repatriates' career-related decision-making. Some individuals may build a balanced identity that bridges host and home country cultures, while others may hold all-inclusive global identities (Mao and Shen 2015). In contrast, for some individuals, expatriation is a period during which the home country identity is reinforced due to negative experiences abroad (Sussman 2002; Kohonen 2008). Research has found that those who were highly embedded in the host country before repatriation were more likely to develop an international employee identity, defined as the extent to which one's role as an international assignee has become central to one's self-concept, which in turn has implications for career choices upon return (Kraimer et al. 2012). These identity changes are particularly pronounced during one's first international assignment. This is attributed to individuals perceiving their first international work experience as a journey inwards, and it increases levels of "self-awareness, knowledge of one's own strengths, weaknesses, drives, and reactions to different situations" (Jokinen 2010).

Repatriation as a Challenge

Unmet Expectations

Perhaps the theme that emerges most frequently in organizational repatriate research is the mismatch between individuals' career prospects prior to repatriation and what they encounter upon returning home (Chiang et al. 2017). Organizational repatriates not only consider the presence of career prospects in the home country organization as an important input to their career decisions within the organization, but they also take into account the extent to which the organization can leverage the precious international work experience repatriates gained during their expatriation period (Szkudlarek 2010). Hence, repatriates usually have high expectations towards their organizations in terms of valuing the international knowledge, skills and abilities (KSAs) gained during their experiences abroad (Riusala and Suutari 2000).

One of the career outcomes that is generally sought after by repatriates is advancement within the organization (Stroh et al. 1998). In line with this, early research emphasized that employees expected organizations to consider repatriation as an integrated part of career management and incorporate the positive appraisal of international experience into a formal career development path, which would ultimately lead to a career progression within their organizations (Baruch and Altman 2002). Related to this, research has shown that a lack of perceived career prospects upon repatriation is associated with organizational turnover (Reiche et al. 2011). However, other research suggests that promotion upon repatriation is not necessarily an expected outcome of international assignments. Specifically, the lack of such promotion opportunities is considered to drive turnover intentions only if it leads to perceived underemployment from the repatriate's perspective (Kraimer et al. 2009). Hence, if repatriates feel that the developmental outcomes of international assignments are ignored by the organization, repatriation can become a challenging experience (Caligiuri and Bonache 2016).

Changes in one's financial compensation are another expected outcome of repatriation (Stroh et al. 1998). In one study that took a human capital perspective towards international work, the effect of financial concerns on career outcomes was found to be more prominent for first time repatriates, for those whose acquired skills have been less utilized and for those at a higher hierarchical level (Ramaswami et al. 2016). Another study pointed out that repatriates tend to select as reference group other current expatriates in their home country rather than local employees, which results in concerns that they are paid less than these expatriates (Banai and Harry 2004). In general, under-met financial expectations as an objective career success criteria have been shown to lead to career dissatisfaction for repatriates (Ren et al. 2013). Expanding this perspective, Tharenou and Seet (2014) suggested that inequitable salary during repatriation may even be a push factor away from the home country and result in being involved in further expatriation.

Beyond compensation, individuals' perceptions of how their organizations handle repatriation frequently involve unmet expectations. Research showed that repatriates' perceptions of an organization's lack of attention to repatriation policies and a lack of repatriation support may result in decreased commitment (Tung 1998; Lazarova and Caligiuri 2002). Repatriation support is crucial in terms of turnover, too, as the lack thereof may lead to an increase in a repatriate's intentions to quit the organization (Birur and Muthiah 2013).

In terms of unmet expectations, the role of significant others has also been considered critical, as long-term international work generally involves an individual's relocation with their family. Mäkelä and Suutari (2011) discussed that people whose careers involve frequent international relocations (i.e. global careerists) are usually aware of the challenges their families might face during repatriation and, as such, relocation decisions are taken into account with their potential negative effects on the family. Hence, trailing spouses and children play an important role for repatriates' future career choices. In particular, unmet expectations regarding family support might affect employee commitment to the organization (Stroh et al. 2000).

Regardless of whether the concern is career advancement, financial outcomes or non-work issues, the ways through which unmet expectations affect career decisions have often been subsumed under a breach of psychological contract (Yan et al. 2002). Specifically, the extent to which an individual's and the organization's perspectives are aligned likely influences repatriation outcomes. Lack of congruence between employee and organizational motivation and expectations may lead to repatriation failure (Paik et al. 2002; Tahir and Azhar 2013; Valk et al. 2015) and turnover intentions (Cesário et al. 2014). Moreover, studies have shown that unmet expectations lead to crucial outcomes such as weak commitment to the organization (Stroh et al. 2000), active job search (Lazarova and Caligiuri 2002) and turnover (Bossard and Peterson 2005).

Beyond Unmet Expectations

Apart from the organization and family, the repatriate literature has also considered other social actors. First, mentors and supervisors may have a role in the career choices of repatriates. The presence of formal hierarchical mentoring has been suggested to help the developmental needs of repatriates, reducing the challenges that repatriates might face upon return (Mezias and Scandura 2005). Some repatriates think that having a mentor with high levels of political power and emotional intelligence would aid them in ascending the corporate hierarchy and renewing the connections that could have been lost during the expatriation period (Jassawalla and Sashittal 2009). Moreover, individuals' relationships with their supervisors can influence career-related perceptions. In particular, goal incongruence between supervisors and repatriates in terms of fitting the assignment into the employee's career (i.e. having a reciprocal long-term relationship) influences turnover intentions (Pattie et al. 2013).

Second, how repatriates perceive their peers influences career choices upon repatriation. Repatriates who consider themselves international employees compare themselves to their colleagues without any prior international assignment experience. Their perceived lack of benefits received from the organization (compared to noninternational employees) may heighten the effect of identity strain that they feel. This in turn is likely to result in turnover (Kraimer et al. 2012). Further, not only peers without any international experience but also those who have worked abroad for the organization are influential for repatriate choices. Specifically, a repatriate's willingness to take on future relocations may be influenced by whether previously repatriated colleagues have experienced career success or not (Bolino 2007; Stroh et al. 1998). This suggests a contagion effect amongst repatriated employees in an organization.

More broadly, being away from home for long periods might have implications for repatriates' social capital. Having global careers could result in a higher number of weak ties in the organization, which may negatively impact the repatriation experience. While discussing the importance of international social capital on global careers, Mäkelä and Suutari (2009) emphasized how such social capital could also entail a paradox. That is, having a diverse external network that spreads across geographies might bear the risk of not being embedded in the home country. Given the importance of network position within the organization in terms of being visible inside the organization (Mäkelä et al. 2010), the insufficient social ties in one's own home country might result in not being recognized in the home country talent pool, thereby negatively affecting repatriation outcomes.

Repatriation as an Opportunity

The perceived developmental outcomes of international work experiences have been discussed prominently in the literature. Specifically, international work experiences imply changes in individuals, which in turn affect how they construe their future careers. From a career capital perspective, repatriates generally think that their prior international experiences possess great value, because these experiences add to their career capital of knowing-how, knowing-whom and knowing-why (Suutari and Mäkelä 2007; Dickmann and Harris 2005; Baruch et al. 2013). International assignees see their experiences abroad as a period in which they improve both their job-related and their intercultural skills (Stahl et al. 2002). As a result of such learning, they become more optimistic that their KSAs will not only help them advance inside their current organizations but will also be valued by other organizations (Stahl et al. 2009). This is also related to recent findings that international assignees usually consider the psychological contract as transactional (i.e. career oriented) and less dependent on one organization (Pate and Scullion 2009). Thus, even though some international assignees are aware of the likely negative outcomes of expatriation, they see the learning outcomes of the assignment as an opportunity for future careers either inside or outside the organization (Stahl et al. 2002; Tung 1998; Stahl and Cerdin 2004). In particular, those people who take on managerial roles during their expatriation perceive the learning outcomes of such assignments as highly transferrable amongst different international assignments by developing cultural metacognition (Jokinen 2010). Such competences, if not appreciated by the current organization, could be utilized by another multinational organization (Stahl et al. 2002). As a result, repatriates become more confident that they will have higher levels of mobility both within and between organizations, meaning their careers become more boundaryless (Lazarova and Cerdin 2007).

By the same token, the idea that new international relocations may provide similar development opportunities may be a pull force for employees to take on future international assignments (Suutari 2003), especially for those who were satisfied during their previous international assignment (Bossard and Peterson 2005). Indeed, managers who go through frequent international relocations are considered to have "global (aspatial) careers" and they build a deep understanding of global organizations (Roberts et al. 1998). Having worked abroad may turn out to be part of a lifestyle that embraces international working above other types of career opportunities (Suutari and Taka 2004). Related to this, researchers have identified an internationalism career anchor, indicating strong preferences to international work (Suutari and Taka 2004; Lazarova et al. 2014). Such an internationalism career anchor may be higher for "international itinerants" compared to "repeat expatriates" as international itinerants feel less bound to one place and are more motivated to integrate with locals (Näsholm 2014). Repatriates driven by the internationalism career anchor might be more willing to quit an organization which does not appreciate their international experience, motivated by the belief that the external labour market will provide more suitable opportunities for their international career aspirations (Suutari and Brewster 2003).

Furuya et al. (2008) offer an alternative perspective on the impact of learning stemming from international experiences on repatriates' future careers. Drawing on the concept of international careers as repositories of knowledge, the authors discuss that the KSAs gained during international work, once successfully transferred to the new position upon repatriation, may lead to higher levels of job motivation. This means that if recently acquired KSAs are successfully used in the home organization, the resulting self-efficacy could increase the intent to stay in the organization. Hence, the effects of international KSAs on global career-related outcomes are highly contingent on the extent to which such KSAs can be leveraged upon repatriation. However, an important blind spot of the current literature is that little detailed research has examined what type of KSAs individuals develop (Antal 2001; Dickmann et al. 2016).

Other Factors Influencing Global Careers

The Role of Social Resources and Embeddedness

The social resources one accumulates during an international experience may affect the career choices of a returnee in the context of inpatriation (Reiche 2012; Reiche et al. 2011). Reiche et al. (2011) used an organizational embeddedness perspective and showed that the social links created during inpatriation were related to perceived prospects in the organization upon return, which in turn increased the likelihood of retention. However, they also found that firm-specific learning during the assignment represented a significant investment in the organization, which further deterred the individual from quitting, as it increased the costs of leaving. This suggests that repatriates' career choices are also a function of the extent to which the KSAs they gained abroad can be leveraged by the current organization. Also relying on the embeddedness approach, Shen and Hall (2009) scrutinized career exploration outcomes as a function of job embeddedness. Their work suggests that higher levels of job embeddedness are related to internal career explorations. They also take a step further and posit that repatriation adjustment may be a crucial factor in deciding whether those who are embedded will want to embark on further international career roles within the organization. In other words, those who are highly embedded but not adjusted well during repatriation will seek to find subsequent international assignments within the organization. All in all, taking an embeddedness approach may bring a more detailed understanding of how leveraging the international experience is linked with career outcomes inside or outside the organization.

Identity Transformations

As discussed earlier, individuals may go through changes in identity during their work experience abroad. Recent research, which is anchored in the idea that individuals may go through various identity changes during expatriation, has shown that such transformations could also influence aspirations for further international relocation (Valk et al. 2013). On the one hand, people who were unhappy with their stay abroad and as a result had even higher levels of home country identity think of returning as an opportunity to build their careers back home, either inside or outside their current organizations. Valk et al. (2013) also found that this is particularly pronounced for those repatriating to booming economies. On the other hand, repatriates who feel they belong to the global community—that is, global identifiers—think that international experience leads to being culturally more independent and are more open-minded towards working abroad. Shen and Hall's (2009) work becomes relevant at this point again, in that those who have developed a global identity during prior experiences may have both less individual-organization fit and less individual-environment fit. It was also suggested that having both a global identity and a host country identity is positively related to repatriation adjustment (Mao and Shen 2015). While these arguments seem to imply challenges for individuals at first, they may also pave the way for individuals to identify opportunities that serve to gratify their identities in terms of career choices. Hence, similar to KSAs, changes in identity also influence mobility choices upon repatriation, resulting in perceptions of higher levels of boundarylessness in their careers.

Career Success and Global Careers

Career success upon repatriation has thus far been defined somewhat loosely. Because the career aspirations differ across individual repatriates, so does the definition of "success". A common distinction is to define success in objective and subjective terms. According to the literature, objective career success is defined in financial and hierarchical terms, whereas subjective career success is defined in more personal terms such as satisfaction (Judge et al. 1995).

Bolino (2007) took a within-organization approach and defined career success in terms of upward mobility, assuming that a key career focus of repatriates is moving up in the organizational hierarchy. He suggested that upward mobility within an organization upon return is affected by the amount of international experience the repatriate has, the strategic importance of the unit that the repatriate worked in during the assignment and the employee's performance during the assignment. Kraimer et al. (2009) found that the relationship between the number of international assignments and career advancement has an inverse-U shape. This means that prior international experiences influence organizational career outcomes upon repatriation in a complex fashion. On a more pessimistic note, Hamori and Koyuncu (2011) find that among a sample of CEOs, international experience (captured through a number of assignments and the length of international experiences) is positively related to the time individuals took to ascend to the CEO role of their respective organizations (in other words, international experience seemed to slow down one's path to the top). Another quantifiable success measure was considered in the work of Ramaswami et al. (2016). The authors conceptualize repatriation success in financial terms (i.e. cash compensation levels upon return) and find that financial success is influenced by the extent to which expatriate experience is utilized during repatriation, by the employee having served in a one-off or in multiple assignments and by the repatriate's hierarchical level.

Others have defined success in ways that do not emphasize hierarchical advancement. Thus, Yan et al. (2002) suggested that from the individuals' perspective, repatriation is successful to the extent that the expertise gained during international work is utilized and further development opportunities are offered by the organization. A common underlying assumption here is that successful repatriation entails retention in the organization. Lazarova and Cerdin (2007) brought a wider perspective to the debate and pointed out that success from the standpoint of the individual does not necessarily overlap with success from the standpoint of the organization. This perspective recognizes that, like boundaryless careers, global careers may unfold both within and between organizations (Bird 1994; Arthur et al. 2005). Related to this, Zikic et al. (2006) posited that repatriates' distal goal is to have career growth either inside or outside the organization. The authors also discussed that a sense of purpose serves as a critical reference point for career success and that purpose is subjective to the individual. This also brings our attention to the idea that individuals have higher levels of agency in the boundaryless world. In such a context, what we mean by being boundaryless also becomes more complicated than within or between organizations and could be extended to crossing international boundaries. Thus, linking the repatriation experience with psychological and physical mobility outcomes may provide a broader picture of how global careers can be shaped upon return.

However, it is difficult to judge which success criteria drives one to take on future international roles upon repatriation. From an objective career success perspective further expatriation usually entails financial compensation that one may not obtain in the home country organization (Toh and DeNisi 2003). In a similar vein, moving to a foreign operation that has a more strategic position in the multinational organization, either as a third-country national or inpatriate, may imply having career access to higher management levels within the organization (Reiche 2006). Such outcomes may act as a pull force for the individual towards retaking international roles. On the other hand, to the extent that repatriates consider having an international employee identity, a global identity or an international career anchor, being boundaryless may mean possessing a sense of purpose related to having a global career. In this case, the choice to embark on future global career roles may be fueled by subjective success criteria. Hence, both objective and subjective success criteria could be considered as variables of interest in linking repatriation and further global careers.

The Case of Self-Initiated Repatriates

The last few years have seen a surge in research on self-initiated expatriates (SIEs), or individuals who embark on an international work experience without the help of an organization (Selmer and Lauring 2011; Froese 2012; Chen and Shaffer 2016). Most SIE studies to date focus on what drives the decision to make that career move and on the various issues encountered once the individual relocates. In sharp contrast, repatriation has thus far received very little attention. Below we briefly touch on relevant SIE studies that have implications on repatriates' global careers and also discuss the very few studies that concentrate specifically on self-initiated repatriates (SIRs).

In terms of the reasons behind why individuals self-initiate their repatriation, arguably the most impactful study has been conducted by Tharenou and Caulfield (2010). Using a longitudinal design, the authors examine both pull forces towards the home country and push forces from the host country in their role as repatriation antecedents. Their findings suggest that repatriation is driven by the extent to which one is embedded both in his/her career and community network, as well as lifestyle benefits of returning to the home country, family encouragement to move back and by a national identity. While some of these findings are in line with the organizational repatriate literature, what is probably most salient to note from a global career perspective is that feeling embedded in the career circles in the host country may serve as an inertial force in the choice for repatriation. In particular, the negative relationship between host country career network embeddedness and the intention to repatriate highlights that SIRs may lose their host country career network once they move back home, making it more difficult to capitalize on this network upon return. A related finding was observed in another study that took place in the Chinese context, which showed that upon return SIRs often find they lack local career capital (Guo et al. 2013).

Career capital is another concept that recently caught the attention of international management scholars. In a research that compared the career capital of SIEs and organizational assignees, Dickmann et al. (2016) showed that organizational assignees acquire higher levels of knowing-whom competency and that the latter is perceived to be more beneficial in the long term after repatriating. The authors also found that organizational assignees tend to experience higher levels of change in their knowing-why career capital during their expatriation period compared to SIEs, which makes it likely that the repatriation experience is more impactful for them from a global career perspective.

The literature has also indicated that, in the broadest sense, SIRs, like their organizational counterparts, face various challenges in the home country. However, early research mentioned that as SIRs need to take care of their own employment upon repatriation, they face an extra layer of difficulty upon moving back. These individuals feel the need to get potential employers to recognize and appreciate their international experience on their own, which adds to the complexity of the career choices they face. Given organizations often undervalue international experience (Suutari and Brewster 2001), SIRs may need to settle for lower-level positions back in their home countries than expected (Begley et al. 2008), which implies a strong case of unmet expectations. Furthermore, SIRs' prior international experience may turn out to be a "double-edged sword" as it may tempt the employing organization to draw on the SIRs' international experience and send the individual abroad again, which runs counter to the self-initiated nature of repatriation (Begley et al. 2008). In terms of how SIR experience leads one to become involved in global careers after repatriation, Ho et al. (2015) used a similar approach to Tharenou and Caulfield (2010) and suggested that reverse culture shock upon repatriation and the perceived outcomes of career, family and quality of life in the anticipated host country are forces that lead people to intend to re-expatriate, that is, carrying on with their global careers.

Barely any research has examined how SIRs define career success. The only study that we are aware of has been conducted on a sample of Indian women academics. Valk et al. (2014) found that career success upon repatriation was related to the transferability of competencies to the home country, demonstrating one's value to others and recognition from peers in science. Thus, compared to organizational expatriates, having prosocial or altruistic motives may also be relevant in the definition of career success for SIRs. However, due to the specific characteristics of the sample, generalizations to the broader population of SIRs may not be appropriate.

Suggestions for Future Research

Research at the intersection between repatriation and global careers is still in its infancy, and there is a great deal of opportunities for scholars in this field. First, returning home is a step in one's global career for which the repatriation outcomes are affected by the returnee's experience of the transition between expatriation and repatriation. In order to unravel the temporal mechanisms that link pre-repatriation inputs to repatriation outcomes, we need more longitudinal research connecting individuals' perceptions of self, organization and more macro-level variables such as the economic and social welfare of the home country, at various stages of the repatriation process. This may help broaden our knowledge of the difference between short-term repatriation outcomes and long-term effects of the repatriation experience on global careers (Kraimer et al. 2016). Also, the choice of outcome variables should explicitly address the role of repatriation in global careers. A necessary step for studies of global careers is being explicit and precise about how each study defines "global career success". For instance, under which conditions could moving to a more strategic subsidiary of a MNC imply climbing up the ladder in the organizational hierarchy, hence enhancing an individual's objective global career success? Or in view of the presence of multiple levels of boundary crossing in which repatriates engage, how can we integrate the notion of boundarylessness into evaluations of subjective career success? In terms of career choices more generally, under which conditions does the internationalism career anchor lead individuals to quit organizations that do not offer promising opportunities for global work? For those who have the aspiration to work internationally, could the presence of alternative international work opportunities inside the organization act as a variable that deters turnover? Linking turnover intentions with the intentions to take on future international roles within the organization may help bridge repatriate retention research with the global career literature.

Second, there is a scarcity of research on alternative forms of global work. That is, having global careers may have different meanings for individuals and working internationally upon repatriation does not necessarily imply a new international relocation. Such careers may also take place within the boundaries of a home country, as in the case of global domestics (Shaffer et al. 2012). There are some attempts to initiate a scholarly conversation about alternative forms of global work (Tharenou 2003, 2005; Mayrhofer and Reiche 2014). In some emerging types of global work (e.g. working in virtual teams), repatriation is no longer a meaningful concept, whereas in others (e.g. short-term or project-based assignments), repatriation is likely quite different than that of "traditional"/long-term expatriates. This means that we should refocus our inquiries to address emerging issues. For example, one interesting question is whether alternative forms of international work generate unique forms of career capital and how such changes influence perceptions of career success in a global work environment. Thinking of boundarylessness in terms of crossing psychological and physical boundaries separately (Peiperl and Jonsen 2007) may help scholars define how individuals construe a subjective definition of global careers. It will also impact our conceptualization and study of embeddedness (e.g. when one is always at "home" but one's work is continuously crossing borders, what is the distinction between home and host country embeddedness?). One idea could be to consider the two-by-two matrix model of Sullivan and Arthur (2006), in which boundarylessness of individuals' careers is characterized by varying levels of physical and psychological mobility. Another theoretical route was proposed by Shaffer et al. (2012), who described global experiences as consisting of three dimensions: cognitive flexibility, physical mobility and non-work disruption. Conceptualizing the difference between working abroad and performing international work in domestic jobs in such terms may help scholars differentiate between types of global work, and this could pave the way for linking the repatriation experience with global career choices. This may also help scholars understand the extent to which the notion of repatriation is relevant to domestic global careers, that is, leveraging one's international career capital through exposure to international work in the home country (Dickmann and Cerdin 2014).

Third, more research is required on self-initiated repatriation. Once again, longitudinal studies that shed light on the SIR experience would be of particularly great value. One topic that has received almost no attention is the meaning of career success for SIRs. On the other hand, there are recent studies that discuss the role of the national economy for

SIRs' career choices (Valk et al. 2015). Similarly, as found in the work of Tharenou and colleagues (2010, Tharenou and Seet 2014), the role of family is salient in SIEs' decisions to repatriate. There is only one study that has delved into the role of families during SIE repatriation (Ho et al. 2015). Future research could also more explicitly account for the complex interplay between individuals' and their families' expectations, their newcomer status in a new organization and the macro context (Baruch et al. 2016), thereby contributing to our understanding of what can be considered SIR success.

International management research has widely concentrated on the individual-level outcomes of international experience and repatriation on global careers. While it is understandable that careers are foremost individual in nature, employees' careers have implications for organizational success (Judge et al. 1999). Accordingly, it would also be helpful to link the role of repatriation experience in one's global career to organizational outcomes. In order to accomplish this, macro-level organizational theories such as human capital theory (Becker 1994) could be utilized to integrate how organizational talent management systems may interact with employees' preferences in terms of career development. As for SIRs, it may be a useful idea to take into account the types of organizations (i.e. domestic v multinational) that individuals choose to work for upon repatriation and discuss whether or how their international orientations and career capital could be leveraged by the organization.

Finally, although a number of theories have been applied to understanding the repatriation experience and its outcomes, there still is room to integrate more theoretical approaches that help explain the mechanisms through which repatriation experiences relate to relevant outcomes. In terms of repatriation's effect on career success, psychological contract and agency theory (Yan et al. 2002) as well as boundaryless and protean career (Leiba O'Sullivan 2002; Lazarova and Cerdin 2007) perspectives have been discussed as possible underlying mechanisms. However, in terms of career choices upon repatriation, only a few studies are substantiated by existing theories. Organizational embeddedness (Ng and Feldman 2007) has been one theoretical approach that has been utilized in the literature (Reiche et al. 2011). In explaining self-initiated repatriation and re-expatriation, push and pull forces (Toren 1976) were mentioned in how choice behaviour takes place (Tharenou and Caulfield 2010). Another study has drawn on the theory of planned behaviour (Ajzen 1991) to explain intentions to move abroad (Ho et al. 2015). We suggest that, in order to complement the current state of research, anchoring the choices on motivation theories such as the theory of planned behaviour (Ajzen 1991) or the career motivation theory (London 1983) may help broaden the perspective of how repatriates choose to be involved in directing their careers towards the global arena. Similarly, process theories such as the expectancy theory (Vroom 1964) or the goal-setting theory (Locke and Latham 2002) could help scholars understand how the perceptions of individuals may lead to repatriation and global career choice outcomes.

In conclusion, repatriation could either be only a pit stop in one's global career or signal the end of the journey. Global career choices are likely influenced by how the returnee perceives the challenges and opportunities faced during expatriation and repatriation. Given the complexity of these experiences, more research needs to examine the role of repatriation in the unfolding of individuals' global careers. Having a more in-depth understanding of repatriation may help scholars, organizations and individuals to manage this complex period and help individuals steer through their global careers more effectively.

Home Soil or up in the Air: Fernando González at Biopharma*

[*Names have been changed to preserve anonymity]
Fernando González was sitting on his terrace, reflecting on his past 17 years at Biopharma that had carried him and his family across the globe and then back to Spain. After almost eight years of working as an R&D expatriate in Argentina, the USA and Poland, he had returned to Barcelona with his family two and a half years ago. He was certain that his professional experience thus far had equipped him well for his future career. However, he began to wonder where his logical next career step would carry him. As a senior manager in Global Clinical Development at

Biopharma, he was working in a global function and was part of the company's global talent pool, which meant that his future was more likely to be outside his home country, Spain. But he was unsure whether he could expect his family to agree to whatever move would present itself. He realized that his next career decisions were looming large on the horizon.

Embarking on a Career at Biopharma

Fernando and his wife Helen met at a university, when studying for a PhD in Biology. Fernando quickly realized that as a scientist couple it would be difficult to develop two academic careers in the same location. Helen continued to complete her PhD in Biology and strived to pursue an academic career that ultimately would lead her to become a professor at the University of Barcelona. However, towards the end of his studies, Fernando actively looked for career opportunities in industry. In December 1999, he decided to apply for a position at the Barcelona operations of Biopharma, a biopharmaceutical company, and immediately received an offer. Although his thesis defence was only scheduled for May 2000, he decided to discontinue his dissertation and embark on a corporate career in R&D.

Biopharma was a global company that employed over 60,000 people, generated worldwide sales of $45 billion and was active in more than 100 countries. Its R&D organization had an annual budget of over $5 billion and more than 10,000 employees.

A Global Career Path

After almost five years in his position, Fernando received a spontaneous offer to relocate to Argentina to initiate the R&D operations of Biopharma in Latin America. Fernando accepted the ten-month transfer because he thought that international relocations were an essential part of being employed by a multinational company and he was excited about getting to know a new culture and work environment. His assignment started in October 2004.

The Role of Repatriation in and for Global Careers   245

Since Helen was in her late stages of pregnancy with their first child, Fernando relocated alone. In the following months, he moved back and forth between Argentina and Spain as much as possible to see Helen and their newly born son Jaume. Soon after, Fernando experienced far-reaching changes also in his professional life. In July 2005, Fernando returned to Spain just to find out that due to reorganizations his previous department ceased to exist and his former boss had left the company. Given these changes, Fernando was not able to find an adequate position back in Barcelona.

He therefore spent his time on temporary project work while continuing to look for possible alternative positions within Biopharma. His direct boss' superior in the UK supported Fernando's cause and, in September 2006, offered him a position in Miami from where to develop the Latin American market. However, his direct boss himself did not back this move at all. Excited by the opportunities in Miami but frustrated by the inflexibility of his direct boss, Fernando decided to resign from the Spanish organization and sign a new employment contract with the UK organization of Biopharma. This meant that his Miami assignment would be managed from the UK. However, to maintain the possibility of returning to Spain in the future, Fernando also applied for a leave of absence without pay for a period of five years that would guarantee him some kind of job at the Spanish unit. Meanwhile, Helen was pregnant with their second son, and they considered relocating to Miami as a family.

Completing the employment contract in the UK organization was a rushed affair. As Fernando remembered:

> I literally received the new contract to sign when the whole family was in the hospital to welcome Xavier to the world. It was a bit of a joke to only have 48 hours to consider the contract. This was not a Spanish employment contract after all—I had to sign the contract neither knowing the labor conditions nor the tax system in the UK nor being able to read the fine print!

With the formalities clarified, Fernando moved to Miami to start his new position in January 2007. However, Helen continued to stay in Spain with their two children for the first year to follow through with her application for professorship at the University of Barcelona. Once she had succeeded with this process, she was granted maternity leave and the whole family joined Fernando in Miami. As part of his assignment in Miami, Fernando had to travel extensively throughout Latin America. He reflected on the demands his job entailed:

> In a sense, I was constantly straining the family by travelling so much and living apart. Even during our time in Miami where we were living together I had to travel a lot and often wouldn't see the family for several days. This was frustrating at times because I didn't always see enough support from the company for the personal sacrifices and stress that I took. Of course it is exciting to be able to travel around but there are also many personal challenges that people tend to forget about.

Still, he was happy that the whole family could be united. Partly to prolong Helen's maternity leave and hence the possibility to stay together in Miami, Fernando and Helen decided to have a third child, Pablo, who was born in May 2008. However, once again Fernando was concerned about his professional chances within the company upon return. He felt that Biopharma did not know what to do with him. More importantly, no hiring manager in Spain knew him anymore. With only a couple of months to go, he was eventually offered an opportunity to further expand the Eastern European market by moving to Warsaw, which he accepted.

The position in Poland started in January 2011 and so Fernando moved directly from Miami. Helen stayed on for another six months so their children could complete the school year at a US private school in Miami before following Fernando. Warsaw had an American School, which made the schooling transition for their children reasonably easy. However, a year later Helen had to return to Barcelona with the children to resume her job at the university or risk losing her professorship. While the transfer to the American School in Warsaw had been fairly smooth for the children, transitioning into a bilingual public school in Barcelona required a huge adjustment for them.

During his time in Warsaw, Fernando's boss in the UK organization changed. However, his new boss, Mike Gallagher, was supportive of Fernando's career and in 2012 pushed for Fernando to be included in the global talent pool at Biopharma. Fernando evaluated this as a positive sign yet also realized the professional implications:

The Role of Repatriation in and for Global Careers **247**

Becoming part of the global talent pool indicated to me that Biopharma had finally recognized my full potential for the company and started to take real ownership of my career development. But I also knew that by accepting I would indirectly commit myself to a global career at Biopharma.

Back on Spanish Soil

While he felt more taken care of by the company, his next career move was more up in the air than ever. Just as the last few months in Miami he experienced a very stressful time not knowing whether he would have to resign from Biopharma or whether an interesting alternative would open up.

In October 2013, with only three months to go in Warsaw, Fernando received two job offers for a subsequent position at Biopharma. The first opportunity involved running the regional R&D operations for Asia-Pacific from Hong Kong. Fernando considered this to be a very interesting position, but he knew that he would not be able to relocate with his whole family given they had just returned to Spain. In the end, he declined the offer for this very reason. Shortly afterwards, he learnt about an internal opening for a position with regional responsibilities in a research centre based in Manchester, UK. He applied for the position because he considered that a commute between the UK and Spain would be feasible. However, he did not get the job.

Just before his job ended in Warsaw, his boss helped Fernando to be contracted again by the Spanish subsidiary. While being a legal employee in Barcelona, he would assume a senior management position in Global Clinical Development and report to a global function based in the UK. Starting in January 2014, Fernando was happy to be back in Spain and close not only to his wife and children but also his extended family.

An Uncertain Future

As the sun set on his terrace, Fernando's mind was racing. After two and a half years back in Spain, he considered his options. Would there be sufficient opportunities for him in Spain? He knew that being in the global talent pool and working in a global function, future opportunities would be more abundant at one of Biopharma's main sites in the UK, the US or Asia. He also reflected on his career path so far. He looked back on very rich and interesting experiences in different cultures.

Would his family agree to relocate again if an appropriate opportunity arose? Fernando reminded himself that the support for international relocations had improved in the company over the past. He wondered whether it would be possible for Helen to stop working or take a prolonged sabbatical and live off a single salary. How important was it for his family to remain in Spain? Could he envision his family's future elsewhere? Another option for him was to commute, thereby agreeing to a life partially away from his family again. He knew there would soon be another large reorganization taking place at Biopharma, and he considered the scant possibility of having to change employers anyway. As the questions kept arising, he failed to notice how the last sun rays beautifully lit up the roofs around him.

References

Ajzen, Icek. 1991. The Theory of Planned Behavior. *Organizational Behavior and Human Decision Processes* 50 (2): 179–211.

Altman, Yochanan, and Yehuda Baruch. 2012. Global Self-Initiated Corporate Expatriate Careers: A New Era in International Assignments? *Personnel Review* 41 (2): 233–255.

Antal, Ariane B. 2001. Expatriates' Contributions to Organizational Learning. *Journal of General Management* 26 (4): 62–84.

Arthur, Michael B., Svetlana N. Khapova, and Celeste P.M. Wilderom. 2005. Career Success in a Boundaryless Career World. *Journal of Organizational Behavior* 26 (2): 177–202.

Banai, Moshe, and Wes Harry. 2004. Boundaryless Global Careers: The International Itinerants. *International Studies of Management & Organization* 34 (3): 96–120.

Baruch, Yehuda, and Yochanan Altman. 2002. Expatriation and Repatriation in MNCs: A Taxonomy. *Human Resource Management* 41 (2): 239–259.

Baruch, Yehuda, Yochanan Altman, and Rosalie L. Tung. 2016. Career Mobility in a Global Era: Advances in Managing Expatriation and Repatriation. *The Academy of Management Annals* 10 (1): 841–889.

Baruch, Yehuda, Michael Dickmann, Yochanan Altman, and Frank Bournois. 2013. Exploring International Work: Types and Dimensions of Global Careers. *The International Journal of Human Resource Management* 24 (12): 2369–2393.

Baruch, Yehuda, and Cristina Reis. 2015. How Global Are Boundaryless Careers and How Boundaryless Are Global Careers? Challenges and a Theoretical Perspective. *Thunderbird International Business Review* 58 (1): 13–27.

Becker, Gary S. 1994. Human Capital Revisited. In *Human Capital a Theoretical and Empirical Analysis*, 3rd ed., 15–28. Chicago: University of Chicago Press.

Begley, Annette, David G. Collings, and Hugh Scullion. 2008. The Cross-Cultural Adjustment Experiences of Self-Initiated Repatriates to the Republic of Ireland Labour Market. *Employee Relations* 30 (3): 264–282.

Bird, Allan. 1994. Careers as Repositories of Knowledge: A New Perspective on Boundaryless Careers. *Journal of Organizational Behavior* 15 (4): 325–344.

Birur, Santosh, and Krishnaveni Muthiah. 2013. Turnover Intentions Among Repatriated Employees in an Emerging Economy: The Indian Experience. *The International Journal of Human Resource Management* 24 (19): 3667–3680.

Bolino, Mark C. 2007. Expatriate Assignments and Intra-Organizational Career Success: Implications for Individuals and Organizations. *Journal of International Business Studies* 38 (5): 819–835.

Bossard, Annette B., and Richard B. Peterson. 2005. The Repatriate Experience as Seen by American Expatriates. *Journal of World Business* 40 (1): 9–28.

Brewster, Chris, Jaime Bonache, Jean-Luc Cerdin, and Vesa Suutari. 2014. Exploring Expatriate Outcomes. *The International Journal of Human Resource Management* 25 (14): 1921–1937.

Caligiuri, Paula, and Jaime Bonache. 2016. Evolving and Enduring Challenges in Global Mobility. *Journal of World Business* 51 (1): 127–141.

Cappellen, Tineke, and Maddy Janssens. 2005. Career Paths of Global Managers: Towards Future Research. *Journal of World Business* 40 (4): 348–360.

Cerdin, Jean-Luc, and Marie Le Pargneux. 2009. Career and International Assignment Fit: Toward an Integrative Model of Success. *Human Resource Management* 48 (1): 5–25.

Cesário, F. Santos, Maria José Chambel, and Carolos Guillen. 2014. What if Expatriates Decide to Leave? The Mediation Effect of the Psychological Contract Fulfilment. *The Journal of the Iberoamerican Academy of Management* 12 (2): 103–122.

Chen, Yu-Ping, and Margaret A. Shaffer. 2016. The Influences of Perceived Organizational Support and Motivation on Self-Initiated Expatriates' Organizational and Community Embeddedness. *Journal of World Business* 52 (2): 197–208.

Chiang, Flora F.T., Emmy van Esch, Thomas A. Birtch, and Margaret A. Shaffer. 2017. Repatriation: What Do We Know and Where Do We Go from Here. *The International Journal of Human Resource Management*: 1–39.

Dickmann, Michael, and Jean-Luc Cerdin. 2014. Boundaryless Career Drivers—Exploring Macro-Contextual Factors in Location Decisions. *Journal of Global Mobility* 2 (1): 26–52.

Dickmann, Michael, and Hilary Harris. 2005. Developing Career Capital for Global Careers: The Role of International Assignments. *Journal of World Business* 40 (4): 399–408.

Dickmann, Michael, Vesa Suutari, Chris Brewster, Liisa Mäkelä, Jussi Tanskanen, and Christelle Tornikoski. 2016. The Career Competencies of Self-Initiated and Assigned Expatriates: Assessing the Development of Career Capital Over Time. *The International Journal of Human Resource Management*: 1–25. Accessed May 2017. https://doi.org/10.1080/09585192.2016.1172657.

Feldman, Daniel C. 1991. Repatriate Moves as Career Transitions. *Human Resource Management Review* 1 (3): 163–178.

Froese, Fabian Jintae. 2012. Motivation and Adjustment of Self-Initiated Expatriates: The Case of Expatriate Academics in South Korea. *The International Journal of Human Resource Management* 23 (6): 1095–1112.

Furuya, Norihito, Michael J. Stevens, Allan Bird, Gary Oddou, and Mark Mendenhall. 2008. Managing the Learning and Transfer of Global Management Competence: Antecedents and Outcomes of Japanese Repatriation Effectiveness. *Journal of International Business Studies* 40 (2): 200–215.

Guo, Chun, Emily Porschitz, and Jose Alvez. 2013. Exploring Career Agency During Self-Initiated Repatriation: A Study of Chinese Sea Turtles. *Career Development International* 18 (1): 34–55.

Hamori, Monika, and Burak Koyuncu. 2011. Career Advancement in Large Organizations in Europe and the United States: Do International Assignments Add Value? *The International Journal of Human Resource Management* 22 (4): 843–862.

Herman, Jeffrey L., and Lois E. Tetrick. 2009. Problem-Focused Versus Emotion-Focused Coping Strategies and Repatriation Adjustment. *Human Resource Management* 48 (1): 69–88.

Ho, Nga Thi Thuy, Pi-Shen Seet, and Jane Jones. 2015. Understanding Re-Expatriation Intentions Among Overseas Returnees—An Emerging Economy Perspective. *The International Journal of Human Resource Management* 27 (17): 1938–1966.

Hyder, Akmal S., and Mikael Lövblad. 2007. The Repatriation Process—A Realistic Approach. *Career Development International* 12 (3): 264–281.

Jassawalla, Avan R., and Hemant C. Sashittal. 2009. Thinking Strategically About Integrating Repatriated Managers in MNCs. *Human Resource Management* 48 (5): 769–792.

Jokinen, Tiina. 2010. Development of Career Capital Through International Assignments and Its Transferability to New Contexts. *Thunderbird International Business Review* 52 (4): 325–336.

Judge, Timothy, Daniel M. Cable, John W. Boudreau, and Robert D. Bretz. 1995. An Empirical Investigation of the Predictors of Executive Career Success. *Personnel Psychology* 48 (3): 485–519.

Judge, Timothy A., Chad A. Higgins, Carl J. Thoresen, and Murray R. Barrick. 1999. The Big Five Personality Traits, General Mental Ability, and Career Success Across the Life Span. *Personnel Psychology* 52 (3): 621–652.

Kohonen, Eeva. 2008. The Impact of International Assignments on Expatriates' Identity and Career Aspirations: Reflections Upon Re-Entry. *Scandinavian Journal of Management* 24 (4): 320–329.

Kraimer, Maria, Mark Bolino, and Brandon Mead. 2016. Themes in Expatriate and Repatriate Research Over Four Decades: What Do We Know and What Do We Still Need to Learn? *Annual Review of Organizational Psychology and Organizational Behavior* 3 (1): 83–109.

Kraimer, Maria L., Margaret A. Shaffer, and Mark C. Bolino. 2009. The Influence of Expatriate and Repatriate Experiences on Career Advancement and Repatriate Retention. *Human Resource Management* 48 (1): 27–47.

Kraimer, Maria L., Margaret A. Shaffer, David A. Harrison, and Hong Ren. 2012. No Place Like Home? An Identity Strain Perspective on Repatriate Turnover. *Academy of Management Journal* 55 (2): 399–420.

Larsen, Henrik Holt. 2004. Global Career as Dual Dependency Between the Organization and the Individual. *Journal of Management Development* 23 (9): 860–869.

Lazarova, Mila, and Paula Caligiuri. 2002. Retaining Repatriates: The Role of Organizational Support Practices. *Journal of World Business* 36 (4): 389–401.

Lazarova, Mila B., and Jean-Luc Cerdin. 2007. Revisiting Repatriation Concerns: Organizational Support Versus Career and Contextual Influences. *Journal of International Business Studies* 38 (3): 404–429.

Lazarova, Mila, Jean-Luc Cerdin, and Yuan Liao. 2014. The Internationalism Career Anchor. *International Studies of Management and Organization* 44 (2): 9–33.

Leiba O'Sullivan, Sharon. 2002. The Protean Approach to Managing Repatriation Transitions. *International Journal of Manpower* 23 (7): 597–616.

Lin, Daomi, Jiangyong Lu, Xiaohui Liu, and Xiru Zhang. 2016. International Knowledge Brokerage and Returnees' Entrepreneurial Decisions. *Journal of International Business Studies* 47 (3): 295–318.

Locke, Edwin A., and Gary P. Latham. 2002. Building a Practically Useful Theory of Goal Setting and Task Motivation: A 35-Year Odyssey. *American Psychologist* 57 (9): 705–717.

London, Manuel. 1983. Toward a Theory of Career Motivation. *Academy of Management Review* 8 (4): 620–630.

Mäkelä, Kristiina, Ingmar Björkman, and Mats Ehrnrooth. 2010. How Do MNCs Establish Their Talent Pools? Influences on Individuals' Likelihood of Being Labeled as Talent. *Journal of World Business* 45 (2): 134–142.

Mäkelä, Kristiina, and Vesa Suutari. 2009. Global Careers: A Social Capital Paradox. *The International Journal of Human Resource Management* 20 (5): 992–1008.

Mäkelä, Liisa, and Vesa Suutari. 2011. Coping with Work-Family Conflicts in the Global Career Context. *Thunderbird International Business Review* 53 (3): 365–375.

Mao, Jina, and Yan Shen. 2015. Cultural Identity Change in Expatriates: A Social Network Perspective. *Human Relations* 68 (10): 1533–1556.

Mayrhofer, Wolfgang, Alexandre Iellatchitch, Michael Meyer, Johannes Steyrer, Michael Schiffinger, and Guido Strunk. 2004. Going Beyond the Individual. *Journal of Management Development* 23 (9): 870–884.

Mayrhofer, Wolfgang, and B. Sebastian Reiche. 2014. Guest Editorial: Context and Global Mobility: Diverse Global Work Arrangements. *Journal of Global Mobility* 2 (2).

Mezias, John M., and Terri A. Scandura. 2005. A Needs-Driven Approach to Expatriate Adjustment and Career Development: A Multiple Mentoring Perspective. *Journal of International Business Studies* 36 (5): 519–538.

Näsholm, Malin. 2014. A Comparison of Intra- and Inter-Organizational Global Careers. *Journal of Global Mobility* 2 (2): 183–202.

Ng, Thomas, and Daniel C. Feldman. 2007. Organizational Embeddedness and Occupational Embeddedness Across Career Stages. *Journal of Vocational Behavior* 70 (2): 336–351.

Olds, Dawn, and Liza Howe-Walsh. 2013. Why Repatriates Resign: Interviews with Those Who Left. *International Journal of Academic Research in Management* 3 (1): 11–30.

Osland, Joyce S. 2000. The Journey Inward: Expatriate Hero Tales and Paradoxes. *Human Resource Management* 39 (2/3): 227–238.

The Role of Repatriation in and for Global Careers 253

Paik, Yongsun, Barbara Segaud, and Christy Malinowski. 2002. How to Improve Repatriation Management. *International Journal of Manpower* 23 (7): 635–648.

Pate, Judy, and Hugh Scullion. 2009. The Changing Nature of the Traditional Expatriate Psychological Contract. *Employee Relations* 32 (1): 56–73.

Pattie, Marshall Wilson, George Benson, and Wendy Casper. 2013. Goal Congruence: Fitting International Assignment Into Employee Careers. *The International Journal of Human Resource Management* 24 (13): 2554–2570.

Peiperl, Maury, and Karsten Jonsen. 2007. Global Careers. In *Handbook of Career Studies*, ed. Hugh Gunz and Maury Peiperl, 350–371. Thousand Oaks: Sage Publications.

Ramaswami, Aarti, Nancy M. Carter, and George F. Dreher. 2016. Expatriation and Career Success: A Human Capital Perspective. *Human Relations* 69 (10): 1959–1987.

Reiche, B. Sebastian. 2006. The Inpatriate Experience in Multinational Corporations: An Exploratory Case Study in Germany. *The International Journal of Human Resource Management* 17 (9): 1572–1590.

Reiche, B. Sebastian. 2012. Knowledge Benefits of Social Capital Upon Repatriation: A Longitudinal Study of International Assignees. *Journal of Management Studies* 49 (6): 1052–1077.

Reiche, B. Sebastian, Maria L. Kraimer, and Anne-Wil Harzing. 2011. Why Do International Assignees Stay? An Organizational Embeddedness Perspective. *Journal of International Business Studies* 42 (4): 521–544.

Ren, Hong, Mark C. Bolino, Margaret A. Shaffer, and Maria L. Kraimer. 2013. The Influence of Job Demands and Resources on Repatriate Career Satisfaction: A Relative Deprivation Perspective. *Journal of World Business* 48 (1): 149–159.

Riusala, Kimmo, and Vesa Suutari. 2000. Expatriation and Careers: Perspectives of Expatriates and Spouses. *Career Development International* 5 (2): 81–90.

Roberts, Karen, Ellen Ernst Kossek, and Cynthia Ozeki. 1998. Managing the Global Workforce: Challenges and Strategies. *The Academy of Management Executive* 12 (4): 93–106.

Selmer, Jan, and Jakob Lauring. 2011. Acquired Demographics and Reasons to Relocate Among Self-Initiated Expatriates. *The International Journal of Human Resource Management* 22 (10): 2055–2070.

Shaffer, Margaret A., Maria L. Kraimer, Yu-Ping Chen, and Mark C. Bolino. 2012. Choices, Challenges, and Career Consequences of Global Work Experiences: A Review and Future Agenda. *Journal of Management* 38 (4): 1282–1327.

Shen, Yan, and Douglas T. Hall. 2009. When Expatriates Explore Other Options: Retaining Talent Through Greater Job Embeddedness and Repatriation Adjustment. *Human Resource Management* 48 (5): 793–816.

Stahl, Günter K., and Jean-Luc Cerdin. 2004. Global Careers in French and German Multinational Corporations. *Journal of Management Development* 23 (9): 885–902.

Stahl, Günter K., Chei Hwee Chua, Paula Caligiuri, Jean-Luc Cerdin, and Mami Taniguchi. 2009. Predictors of Turnover Intentions in Learning-Driven and Demand-Driven International Assignments: The Role of Repatriation Concerns, Satisfaction with Company Support, and Perceived Career Advancement Opportunities. *Human Resource Management* 48 (1): 89–109.

Stahl, Günter K., Edwin L. Miller, and Rosalie L. Tung. 2002. Toward the Boundaryless Career: A Closer Look at the Expatriate Career Concept and the Perceived Implications of an International Assignment. *Journal of World Business* 37 (3): 216–227.

Stroh, Linda K., Hal B. Gregersen, and J. Stewart Black. 1998. Closing the Gap: Expectations Versus Reality Among Repatriates. *Journal of World Business* 33 (2): 111–124.

Stroh, Linda K., Hal B. Gregersen, and J. Stewart Black. 2000. Triumphs and Tragedies: Expectations and Commitments Upon Repatriation. *The International Journal of Human Resource Management* 11 (4): 681–697.

Sullivan, Sherry E., and Michael B. Arthur. 2006. The Evolution of the Boundaryless Career Concept: Examining Physical and Psychological Mobility. *Journal of Vocational Behavior* 69 (1): 19–29.

Sussman, Nan M. 2002. Testing the Cultural Identity Model of the Cultural Transition Cycle: Sojourners Return Home. *International Journal of Intercultural Relations* 26 (4): 391–408.

Suutari, Vesa, and Brewster, Chris. 2003. Repatriation: Empirical Evidence From a Longitudinal Study of Careers and Expectations Among Finnish Expatriates. *The International Journal of Human Resource Management* 14 (7): 1132–1151.

Suutari, Vesa, and Chris Brewster. 2001. Making Their Own Way: International Experience Through Self-Initiated Foreign Assignments. *Journal of World Business* 35 (4): 417–436.

Suutari, Vesa, and Brewster, Chris. 2003. Repatriation: Empirical Evidence From a Longitudinal Study of Careers and Expectations Among Finnish Expatriates. *The International Journal of Human Resource Management* 14 (7): 1132–1151.

Suutari, Vesa, and Kristiina Mäkelä. 2007. The Career Capital of Managers with Global Careers. *Journal of Managerial Psychology* 22 (7): 628–648.

Suutari, Vesa, and Milla Taka. 2004. Career Anchors of Managers with Global Careers. *Journal of Management Development* 23 (9): 833–847.

Suutari, Vesa, Christelle Tornikoski, and Liisa Mäkelä. 2012. Career Decision Making of Global Careerists. *The International Journal of Human Resource Management* 23 (16): 3455–3478.

Szkudlarek, Betina. 2010. Reentry—A Review of the Literature. *International Journal of Intercultural Relations* 34 (1): 1–21.

Tahir, Rizwan, and Naheed Azhar. 2013. The Adjustment Process of Female Repatriate Managers in Australian and New Zealand (ANZ) Companies. *Global Business Review* 14 (1): 155–167.

Tharenou, Phyllis. 2003. The Initial Development of Receptivity to Working Abroad: Self-Initiated International Work Opportunities in Young Graduate Employees. *Journal of Occupational and Organizational Psychology* 76 (4): 489–515.

Tharenou, Phyllis. 2005. International Work in Domestic Jobs: An Individual Explanation. *The International Journal of Human Resource Management* 16 (4): 475–496.

Tharenou, Phyllis, and Natasha Caulfield. 2010. Will I Stay or Will I Go? Explaining Repatriation by Self-Initiated Expatriates. *Academy of Management Journal* 53 (5): 1009–1028.

Tharenou, Phyllis, and Pi-Shen Seet. 2014. China's Reverse Brain Drain. *International Studies of Management and Organization* 44 (2): 55–74.

Toh, Soo Min, and Angelo S. DeNisi. 2003. Host Country National Reactions to Expatriate Pay Policies: A Model and Implications. *Academy of Management Review* 28 (4): 606–621.

Toren, Nina. 1976. Return to Zion: Characteristics and Motivations of Returning Emigrants. *Social Forces* 54 (3): 546–558.

Tung, Rosalie L. 1998. American Expatriates Abroad: From Neophytes to Cosmopolitans. *Journal of World Business* 33 (2): 125–144.

Valk, Reimara, Mandy Van der Velde, Marloes Van Engen, and Rohini Godbole. 2014. International Career Motives, Repatriation and Career Success of Indian Women in Science & Technology. *Journal of Global Mobility* 2 (2): 203–233.

Valk, Reimara, Mandy Van der Velde, Marloes Van Engen, and Betina Szkudlarek. 2013. International Assignment and Repatriation Experiences of Indian International Assignees in the Netherlands. *International Journal of Organizational Analysis* 21 (3): 335–356.

Valk, Reimara, Mandy Van der Velde, Marloes Van Engen, and Betina Szkudlarek. 2015. Warm Welcome or Rude Awakening? *Journal of Indian Business Research* 7 (3): 243–270.

Vroom, Victor Harold. 1964. *Work and Motivation*. New York: John Wiley & Sons.

Yan, Aimin, Guorong Zhu, and Douglas T. Hall. 2002. International Assignments for Career Building: A Model of Agency Relationships and Psychological Contracts. *Academy of Management Review* 27 (3): 373–391.

Zikic, Jelena, Milorad M. Novicevic, Michael Harvey, and Jacob Breland. 2006. Repatriate Career Exploration: A Path to Career Growth and Success. *Career Development International* 11 (7): 633–649.

10

A Typology of Dual-Career Expatriate (Trailing) Spouses: The 'R' Profile

Yvonne McNulty and Miriam Moeller

Introduction

Dual-career expatriation has received increasing attention in the past two decades due mainly to a practical concern in terms of policy and practice to diminish the many barriers to international job mobility (Harvey 1995, 1996, 1998; Harvey et al. 2009b; Moore 2002). Consulting firms have provided much-needed evidence to suggest that, despite the growing demand for international talent, dual-career and spousal income concerns are frequently shown to be significant and insurmountable issues in global mobility (ORC Worldwide 2005; Permits Foundation 2012). These challenges arise, in part, because many expatriates who undertake

---

Y. McNulty (✉)
S R Nathan School of Human Development, Singapore University of Social Sciences, Clementi Road, Singapore
e-mail: yvonnemcnulty@suss.edu.sg

M. Moeller
The University of Queensland, St Lucia, QLD, Australia
e-mail: m.moeller@business.uq.edu.au

© The Author(s) 2018
M. Dickmann et al. (eds.), *The Management of Global Careers*,
https://doi.org/10.1007/978-3-319-76529-7_10

international work experiences do so with an accompanying spouse and/or partner (Brown 2008; Cole 2011; Lauring and Selmer 2010), of which a substantial number consist of families for whom *both* are psychologically committed to a career (Mäkelä et al. 2011). Furthermore, unlike their homemaker counterparts who may have little interest in professional pursuits, career-oriented spouses engaged in the decision whether to accept an international relocation bring to the negotiating table a bargaining chip that is often difficult for companies to placate with financial or other incentives—their career (Moore 2002).

There has been renewed interest in dual-career expatriation and its impact on 'expatriate success' particularly since Harvey's (1995, 1997, 1998) seminal work, as well as more recently among non-traditional expatriates (unmarried, homosexual or childless couples) and expatriates across communities (e.g. military) (McNulty and Hutchings 2016). While dual-career issues can manifest in a variety of situations that have nothing to do with mobility, the phenomenon is more critical in an international relocation context due to the high financial investment associated with moving families abroad and the widespread risks (to companies and individuals) associated with job failure. Not surprisingly, scholars have argued that organizations must attain a broader view of global talent management (GTM) in that talent begs the recruitment of not *one* individual but essentially the successful recruitment of *two* people disguised in the form of a dual-career couple (Harvey et al. 2009b; Mäkelä et al. 2011).

In this chapter, we provide an overview as to what is currently known about dual-career expatriates, including how they are defined and their challenges. Importantly, we broaden our literature review to include relevant industry articles, White Papers and consulting reports. In the section that follows, we then outline new empirical evidence about dual-career expatriates. Here, we build on and extend historical conceptualizations (Harvey et al. 1999, 2009a; Harvey and Wiese 1998) to develop a preliminary and empirically driven 'R' profile typology of dual-career expatriate (trailing) spouses. We conclude the chapter by discussing implications for practice arising from the typology, along with a detailed future research agenda for the next generation of dual-career expatriate research.

Status: What Do We Know?

The dual-career phenomenon was first introduced to the literature by Rapoport and Rapoport (1969) who were quick to construe it as a dilemma relative to work overload, personal norm behaviour, loss of individual identity and role cycling (who am I?). The dual-career phenomenon is defined as a situation where either spouse's partner has career responsibilities and aspirations (Rapoport and Rapoport 1969). These aspirations are expressed in a strong psychological commitment to a career as well as (personal) professional growth. Dual-career couples are further defined by a commitment to professional careers in combination with a commitment to the relationship *by both partners* (van Gus and Kraaykamp 2008).

In the context of international HRM and GTM, the relatively high refusal rate among expatriates and their families arising from dual-career issues is a major challenge (ORC Worldwide 2005; Permits Foundation 2009). In other words, the strong commitment by both partners to their separate careers can make it challenging for organizations to put forth convincing arguments for these families to engage in global mobility opportunities, particularly when one spouse is required to (potentially) put their career ambitions on hold as the 'trailing spouse' in order to help realize their partner's international career opportunity. A trailing spouse is defined as the partner for whom an international assignment or work experience is *not* offered, given that one spouse's job typically provides the opportunity to relocate internationally whereas the other's does not (Harvey 1998).

Defining Dual-Career Expatriates

Building on extant literature (Harvey et al. 1999; Harvey and Wiese 1998; Mäkelä et al. 2011), we define dual-career expatriates as:

> Individuals with an unyielding psychological commitment to their professional careers which requires relocation abroad, in combination with a commitment to a personal relationship that may or may not involve the relocation of their partner abroad, and that the commitment to career and personal relationship is extended by both adult partners.

Critical to our definition is that being a dual-career expatriate does not imply that the dual-career trailing spouse will necessarily work *during* an international relocation. Dual-career orientation for expatriates does not end due to temporary or long-term unemployment arising from an international relocation (Permits Foundation 2009, 2012; Vance and McNulty 2014). Equally important is that, even when both partners are employed abroad, it sometimes results in the trailing spouse being employed under different and less prestigious or status-driven employment conditions compared to what they had in their home country or in comparison to their partner's more lucrative job contract, for example, expatriate packages for the 'true expatriate' versus local employment terms and conditions for the trailing spouse. This increasingly leads to a situation where the trailing spouse can end up with a 'job' versus a 'career', even where paid employment is available (Vance and McNulty 2014). While consulting data does not distinguish paid employment according to whether a spouse continues in the same career, starts a new career or their employment is simply a 'job' as opposed to a 'career', McNulty (2012) alluded in her study to a substantial number of trailing spouses who overcame their employment challenges by embarking on a new 'portable' career that seemed to be a better fit with their unstable international lifestyle, although many suggested that their 'new' career was often a compromise, unsustainable over the long-term, underpaid and not ideally what they had in mind.

Challenges Associated with Dual-Career Expatriates

The dual-career expatriate dilemma remains an ongoing concern for companies with five main challenges. First, career-oriented spouses are often reluctant to give up their professional identity to assume the status of 'housewife', trailing spouse or 'corporate expatriate wife' (Rapoport and Rapoport 1969). Further problems can arise when a relocation abroad is instigated by a woman, and a male assumes the role of a trailing spouse 'house-husband' or 'stay-at-home dad' (Cole 2012; Moore 2002). Women have traditionally subordinated their careers for their husbands unhindered by the constraints of managing a dual-career family, and these gender-based decisions are more commonly accepted and supported in some cultures more than others (Stroh et al. 2000). Second, the Permits Foundation (2009) found in their study of 3300 expatriates and their spouses that nearly 60 per cent indicated that they would be unlikely in the future to relocate to a country where it is difficult for a spouse to get a work permit and to continue their career. Third, studies have found that organizational support for the trailing spouse is generally poor (Cole 2011; Shaffer and Harrison 2001), particularly among dual-career couples where assistance to find meaningful work opportunities is shown to be a 'major failing' on the part of companies (McNulty 2012; Moore 2002). Poor organizational support is likely to increase international assignment refusal rates at best and, at worst, to increase the likelihood of assignment failure in terms of premature return, refusal to re-assign or split families (i.e. the premature return of family members while an expatriate remains in situ to see out an assignment and then repatriate), thereby creating additional work-family stress (McNulty 2014). Lastly, relatively little research, if any, has examined the heightened dysfunctional family consequences arising from the challenges of dual-career expatriation, particularly in relation to marital stress. Of the few published studies we found, marital factors were found to be related to relocation adjustment for expatriates and their spouses (James et al. 2004). Scholars have found that powerlessness, a loss of identity and changes in relationship dynamics with their partner contribute to trailing spouses' feelings of isolation, frustration, disappointment and anger during international assignments (McNulty 2012; Shaffer and Harrison 2001).

Extant literature (Brown 2008; Harvey 1996; Mäkelä et al. 2011) summarizes the dual-career expatriate issue as being exacerbated by several factors including (1) the stage of one's partners' professional career, (2) the professional discipline in which each partner is engaged including professional licensing requirements to continue one's career in a new location and (3) the flexibility of each partner's career goals. There is also considerable evidence to suggest that while repatriation and career management support for expatriates is lacking in general (Lazarova and Cerdin 2007), there is even less support available to address the repatriation and re-engagement concerns of the dual-career-oriented trailing spouse (Harvey and Buckley 1998; ORC Worldwide 2005).

New Empirical Evidence: A Typology of Dual-Career Expatriate (Trailing) Spouses

In this chapter, so far, we have provided an overview of the status of extant literature about dual-career expatriates. As shown, most data about the topic stems from academic conceptualizations or empirical studies focused at the couple level of analysis. In this section, we build on this literature by reporting the findings of a very recent empirical study looking at the dual-career expatriate (trailing) spouse, from which we have developed the 'R' profile typology: *Ready, Reborn, Resentful* and *Resigned*. We use the term 'dual-career expatriate spouse' to refer to the trailing spouse during an international relocation (McNulty 2012), which is the phenomenon we explore in our study. We note, however, that other terms have been used to refer to the same phenomenon, with extant literature referring synonymously to the dual-career expatriate 'family' (Harvey 1995) and the dual-career expatriate 'couple' (Harvey 1998; Harvey et al. 2009a; Mäkelä et al. 2011; Moore 2002). Both imply that the dual-career expatriate issue is one that impacts adults (couples) as well as children (families), although for our purposes we feel more comfortable with the encompassing term 'dual-career expatriate family' because it includes the couple, even if the couple is childless.

Rationale for Our Study

In developing our typology, we attempted to overcome some concerns about prior conceptualizations of dual-career expatriates. First, in a departure from established thinking, we debunk the idea of a universal concept in which there is only one type of dual-career expatriate spouse. Rather, using a case study approach by drawing on interviews and 'thick description' with 46 dual-career expatriate spouses living and working in Asia Pacific, we conceptualize them as belonging to one of 4 distinct profiles that we term the 'R' profile. We developed the 'R' profile in an iterative manner from our data based on observation and interpretation of the findings (Rossman and Rallis 2003). For example, as the sample grew and the number of respondents increased, the capabilities and attitudes of one segment of the sample appeared to be different to other segments, and from this we developed four initial categories of dual-career success (or failure) that we then used as a preliminary conceptual framework as interviews progressed. When all the interviews were completed and full analysis conducted, clearer delineations between four types of dual-career trailing spouses became apparent, from which the *Ready, Reborn, Resentful* and *Resigned* categories emerged. The clearest delineation was between those spouses achieving dual-career success (employment: *Ready, Reborn*) v failure (no employment: *Resigned, Resentful*). We also found that membership to one category was not necessarily permanent, that is, the categories appeared to be fluid over a number of years (as trailing spouse/dual-career experience was gained) with bi-directional movement between them (see, for example, M#21's story below). Using a continuum approach, we were able to determine that some spouses who were originally *Resigned* were eventually able to move into the *Reborn* category, whereas others who were *Resigned* slipped further into the *Resentful* category. For the purposes of our study, however, we ignored fluidity during data collection and were careful to categorize respondents according to their current category and not a previous one, based on their answers to the interview questions and our interpretation. In developing our typology, we included dimensions (i.e. capabilities and attitudes) for each category as being typical and strongest for that category, noting that each dimension could also be found in other categories, albeit not as strongly (e.g. empowerment, resentment, identity, aggression and anger, acceptance of 'defeat', depression).

The purpose of the continuum is to help determine the likelihood of dual-career success for the expatriate family by developing a model that highlights how a core set of capabilities and attitudes acquired (or not acquired) by dual-career expatriate spouses determines how successful they will be while living abroad. These capabilities and attitudes, in turn, can contribute to a greater likelihood of expatriate success for the companies that employ their spouse. This then leads to a distinct competitive advantage for organizations that recruit and internationally deploy dual-career expatriate families. We also aimed to develop a typology that adequately captures the actual lived experiences of dual-career expatriate spouses from their point of view, rather than relying on anecdotal, secondary or aggregated data.

The rationale for the study upon which this chapter is based rests in taking a fresh look at the dual-career expatriate issue by examining the success factors of dual-career expatriate trailing spouses that have sustained a career while living abroad. Importantly, rather than examining the issue at the level of the couple (Harvey 1997; Mäkelä et al. 2011), employed spouse (Lauring and Selmer 2010) or the company (Moore 2002; ORC Worldwide 2005), or conceptually without empirically driven data (Harvey and Buckley 1998; Harvey et al. 2009a, b), we are interested in the challenges faced by a spouse when making the difficult personal decision, as well as private responsibility, to subordinate their career for their partner's international relocation. Furthermore, the specific purpose of this study is *not* to assume that failure or resistance among dual-career expatriates is high but to instead take the view that at least some dual-career expatriate spouses are successful in continuing their careers abroad (even if the number is small). We seek to understand how this has been achieved and why some dual-career expatriate spouses are more successful than others.

Our rationale is informed by two competing schools of thought. On the one hand scholars and other commentators are often quick to suggest that companies are not adequately invested in the jointly held career aspirations of dual-career couples, with insufficient support mechanisms in place to support their needs (Cole 2012; McNulty 2012; Moore 2002). This is then touted as the leading cause of poor dual-career expatriate success. We argue that this view is perhaps too simplistic and maybe even a 'cop out'; it is too easy to continually blame 'the company' and to expect that only companies need to be invested in resolving the dual-career expatriate dilemma. Instead, we argue that the dual-career issue is unavoidable in two-career families, particularly among expatriates who tend to be highly educated and career focused and who typically marry partners of a similar socio-economic background and professional standing (Permits Foundation 2009). In fact, because women have become more economically independent due to their increased participation in the labour force, they may be unwilling to give up their long-term independence for the international relocation of their spouse (Stroh et al. 2000). Our point is that the individual (in our case, the expatriate trailing spouse) has a role to play in dual-career expatriation success. We propose that it is the combination of support arising from the individual, the couple *and* the company that ultimately leads to dual-career expatriate spouse success.

Method

This study utilized a qualitative, inductive approach to draw on dual-career expatriate spouses lived experience (interviews). The approach was not limited to examining a priori (theoretical) variables but was intended to also uncover original themes to show how people make sense of relocating abroad in their daily lives (Lazarova et al. 2014). Our aim was to engage in the social construction of reality using narrative (Boje 2007), storytelling (Ochs and Capps 2001) and sense-making (i.e. 'turning circumstances into a situation that is comprehended explicitly in words and that serves as a springboard into action'; Weick et al. 2005: 409). Sense-making was an important lens through which we conducted the study as it allowed us to capture individuals at the precise point at which they were producing a sense of self and making sense of their lived experience.

Semi-structured interviews were conducted with 46 participants who identified as dual-career expatriate spouses (Table 10.1). Most interviews (n = 35) were conducted face-to-face in Singapore in settings that ranged from coffee shops, restaurants, their own home and place of work. The remaining 11 interviews were conducted via Skype (video). All the interviews took place over a two-year period from April 2014 to August 2016. Participants were invited to participate via personal invitation and/or being identified as a dual-career expatriate spouse through the first author's personal network. Interviews ranged from 30 minutes to 3 hours. At the time of data collection, all participants were still living abroad as a dual-career expatriate spouse, except for three that had recently repatriated

Table 10.1 Profile of participants (n = 46)

Name (pseudonym)	Gender/marital status	Home country	Currently living in	Partner living in	Lived in previously	Child	Employment status/industry	Same or new career	'R' profile
1. A#1	F/married	Australia	Singapore	Singapore	India	2	Self-employed/food and beverage	New	Reborn
2. B#2	F/married	Australia	Singapore	Singapore	Hong Kong	2	Employed/education	New	Reborn
3. C#3	F/married	Australia	Australia	Australia	Papua New Guinea	2	Employed/IT	New	Reborn
4. H#4	F/married	Canada	Singapore	Singapore	–	0	Employed/education	Same	Ready
5. H#5	F/married	USA	Singapore	Singapore	–	1	Self-employed/training	New	Reborn
6. H#6	F/de facto	USA	Hong Kong	Hong Kong	Italy, UK	2	Self-employed/training	New	Reborn
7. K#7[a]	F/separated	Australia	Singapore	Singapore	–	3	Self-employed/IT	Same	Ready
8. K#8	F/married	South Africa	Singapore	Singapore	UK	1	Self-employed/photography	New	Reborn
9. L#9	F/married	USA	Singapore	Singapore	UK, Hong Kong	3	Unemployed	–	Resigned
10. L#10	F/married	Australia	Singapore	Singapore	–	2	Employed/education	New	Reborn
11. L#11	F/married	Australia	Singapore	Maldives	Maldives	0	Self-employed/training	New	Reborn
12. M#12	F/married	USA	Singapore	Singapore	Italy, UK	1	Self-employed/coaching	New	Reborn

A Typology of Dual-Career Expatriate (Trailing) Spouses… 267

13. P#13[a]	F/married	UK	Singapore	Singapore	–	0	Employed/education	New	Reborn
14. K#14	F/married	France	Singapore	Singapore	Luxembourg	2	Self-employed/fashion	New	Reborn
15. T#15	F/married	Canada	Singapore	Singapore	–	2	Employed/education	Same	Ready
16. M#16[a]	M/married	Australia	Singapore	Singapore	–	3	Employed/banking	Same	Ready
17. C#17	F/married	France	Singapore	Singapore	Dubai, UK, USA	3	Unemployed	–	Resigned
18. D#18	F/separated	Australia	Singapore	Singapore	–	2	Unemployed	–	Resigned
19. P#19	F/separated	UK	Singapore	Singapore	–	1	Self-employed	New	Resentful
20. V#20	F/married	UK	Singapore	Singapore	–	2	Employed/education	Same	Ready
21. M#21	F/married	UK	Singapore	Singapore	France	1	Self-employed/coaching	New	Reborn
22. S#22	F/married	UK	Singapore	Singapore	Australia	2	Unemployed	–	Ready
23. M#23	F/married	UK	Singapore	Singapore	Australia	1	Unemployed	–	Resigned
24. R#24	F/married	Spain	Singapore	Singapore	USA	4	Unemployed	–	Ready
25. E#25	F/married	UK	Singapore	Singapore	–	2	Employed/education	New	Reborn
26. P#26	F/married	India	Singapore	Singapore	UK, Dubai	3	Employed/law	Same	Ready
27. B#27	F/married	UK	Singapore	Singapore	–	1	Self-employed/medical	New	Reborn
28. B#28[a]	M/married	USA	Singapore	Singapore	Vietnam	2	Self-employed/tourism	Same	Ready
29. G#29[a]	M/married	UK	Singapore	Singapore	India	1	Unemployed	–	Ready

(continued)

Table 10.1 (continued)

Name (pseudonym)	Gender/ marital status	Home country	Currently living in	Partner living in	Lived in previously	Child	Employment status/industry	Same or new career	'R' profile
30. S#30	F/married	UK	Singapore	Singapore	Australia	2	Unemployed	–	Reborn
31. A#31	F/married	UK	Singapore	Singapore	–	2	Unemployed	–	Reborn
32. S#32[a]	F/married	Australia	Singapore	Singapore	–	2	Employed/ finance	Same	Ready
33. K#33[a]	F/married	USA	Singapore	Singapore	–	1	Self-employed/ IT	Same	Ready
34. K#34	F/married	Denmark	Singapore	Singapore	Australia	3	Self-employed/ health	New	Reborn
35. D#35	F/married	USA	Singapore	Singapore	–	2	Self-employed/ insurance	Same	Ready
36. L#36	F/married	Australia	Australia	China	–	2	Unemployed	–	Resigned
37. L#37	F/married	Australia	Australia	Singapore	–	2	Employed/IT	Same	Ready
38. S#38	F/married	France	China	Argentina	UK, Dubai	2	Self-employed/ coaching	New	Reborn
39. A#39[a]	F/married	Canada	China	China	–	0	Unemployed	–	Resigned
40. S#40	F/ married	UK	Singapore	Singapore	–	1	Employed/ medical	New	Reborn
41. J#41	F/married	USA	Singapore	Singapore	Hong Kong	3	Self-employed/ training	New	Reborn
42. M#42	F/married	New Zealand	China	China	–	2	Unemployed	–	Resigned
43. R#43	F/married	USA	China	China	–	1	Unemployed	–	Resigned

44. J#44	F/married	UK	China	China	France	5	Employed/ education	Same	Ready
45. J#45[a]	F/married	South Africa	Hong Kong	Hong Kong	–	2	Employed/ consulting	Same	Ready
46. J#46	F/married	USA	China	China	–	0	Self-employed/ education	New	Reborn

Source: The authors

[a]Both = trailing spouse and lead expatriate; takes turn with spouse to have the lead career; at the time of interview, each was in the role of trailing spouse

(in the last three months). In this way the experiences of living abroad were fresh in their minds. Interview questions focused on participant's dual-career expatriate spouse 'journey' (see Appendix), including when they first moved abroad and why; how empowered they felt in the decision to expatriate; whether they were currently employed abroad and if so in the same career they had back home or a new one; challenges they faced (trying) to continue their career abroad; and success factors in their overall dual-career journey. We strived for openness and honesty with questions such as what was going well for them and why and what was a struggle. As points were raised, we probed for more detail. The advantage of our qualitative approach is that it concentrated only on the research theme (dual-career expatriate spouses), and it allowed us to probe to uncover new ideas and findings based on the participants own experiences (Rossman and Rallis 2003).

All interviews were recorded, transcribed and then manually coded. We compared the emerging salient themes and categories with prior literature and used representative quotes to convey the general experience of all the participants. We also engaged in member checking with the participants to allow them to verify and validate our interpretations. This was not just about authenticating the accounts given by allowing the participants' voices to be heard but about explicitly striving to understand the participants' different perspectives and experiences (sense-making). Hierarchical categories were used to reduce, sort and cluster the data and derive key themes (Denzin and Lincoln 2000), as well as content analysis to determine how strongly the themes are manifested (Miles and Huberman 1994). Although participants provided a single-rater response, they can be viewed as expert informants.

Data were collected from 46 participants ($n = 43$ females vs $n = 3$ males) that self-identified as being a dual-career expatriate spouse. Many participants lived in Singapore ($n = 35$), followed by Australia ($n = 3$), Hong Kong ($n = 2$) and China ($n = 6$). Nearly all were married ($n = 43$) versus separated/pending divorce ($n = 3$). Many participants ($n = 18$) were self-employed in businesses they had started themselves or employed by organizations in full-time or part-time jobs ($n = 15$), with a further 13 participants being unemployed at the time of the interview. Of those who were employed (n = 33), 20 were in a new career with only 13 continuing in the same career they had had before relocating abroad.

Expatriate Trailing Spouse Typology: The 'R' Profile

The findings of this empirical study showed that there are four types of dual-career expatriate (trailing) spouses: *Ready, Reborn, Resentful* and *Resigned* (Fig. 10.1). We categorize them per four character types based on their capabilities and attitudes towards solving their own dual-career expatriate challenge in terms of identity redevelopment, decision making, problem-solving abilities, initiative and resilience. Our analysis shows that 16 participants were in the *Ready* category, with a further 20 that were characterized as *Reborn*, 1 as *Resentful* and 9 as *Resigned*.

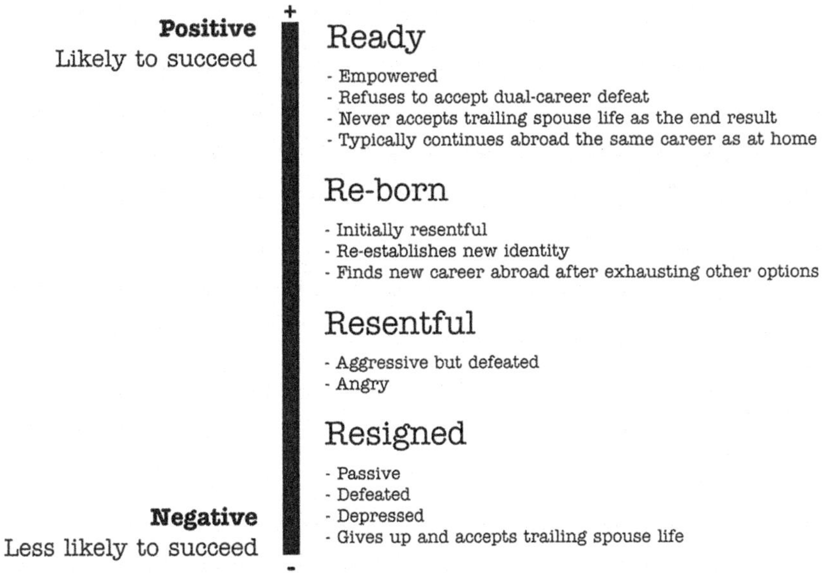

Positive
Likely to succeed

Ready
- Empowered
- Refuses to accept dual-career defeat
- Never accepts trailing spouse life as the end result
- Typically continues abroad the same career as at home

Re-born
- Initially resentful
- Re-establishes new identity
- Finds new career abroad after exhausting other options

Resentful
- Aggressive but defeated
- Angry

Resigned
- Passive
- Defeated
- Depressed
- Gives up and accepts trailing spouse life

Negative
Less likely to succeed

Fig. 10.1 A typology of dual-career expatriate (trailing) spouses—the 'R' profile. Source: The authors

Ready or Reborn

Those characterized as *Ready* or *Reborn* are considered more likely to succeed during international relocation (to find employment) because they are proactive in searching for career opportunities whilst living abroad. The defining characteristics of both character types are feeling empowered, (delayed) confidence, being realistic and having a pragmatic outlook. Both are also likely to be driven and single-minded individuals that are used to solving problems on their own. For those in the *Ready* category, key characteristics include (1) refusing to accept dual-career defeat, (2) never accepting the trailing spouse life as the end result and (3) typically continuing in the same career abroad as they had at home. For *Reborn* spouses, we determined their key characteristics as (a) being initially resentful about the dual-career challenge, (b) re-establishing a new identity and (c) finding a new career abroad after exhausting other options.

For some *Ready* spouses, we noted a reluctance to agree to relocate until they had secured a new job in the intended host location. For these spouses, proactivity in their job search occurred even before they had left the home-country or last location, with a small number starting new jobs immediately upon arrival. This was particularly the case for M#16, a father of three, with a CEO wife. When his wife was offered a promotion to the Hong Kong office of her company, he secured a new job for himself in the banking industry before the couple had even called the movers! As he recalled:

> Last time we moved eight years ago, from Melbourne to Singapore, it was for my job. This time it's for her job … As long as there's enough lead in time, we can usually make it happen for both our careers and we need that, otherwise it would be too hard. We're not stay-at-home type people, even with three kids … If I couldn't work, or she couldn't work, we wouldn't move. I know I wouldn't agree to go. Financially we need to work, for our own sanity we need to work.

For other *Ready* spouses, their job search began once they were in the new location, with a key success factor being a clear commitment to prioritize a lot of time in the early weeks and months of the relocation to networking, interviewing and partnering with recruitment firms to assist.

Understandably, those without children had more time to devote to job search activities, whereas those with children typically delayed their job search for three to six months until family members were settled in.

Reborn spouses are those that often intended to be a *Ready* spouse but for whom finding a satisfying job (i.e. avoiding underemployment) or continuing their career in the new location became extraordinarily difficult. Consequently, after a period of frustration, resentment and reflection over months (or sometimes even years), *Reborn* spouses began to search for new career opportunities different to those they may have had in their home country or elsewhere (McNulty 2012). Many of these spouses were self-employed in businesses they had set up that leveraged their skill set and expertise (coaching, training, IT), while others retrained for specific occupations (e.g. photographer, web designer, therapist) or moved into completely new occupations (education). We noted that success factors for *Reborn* spouses included an entrepreneurial and self-motivated character, with a 'never say die' attitude (J#41), 'being pragmatic', (H#6), having 'realistic expectations' (B#2) and the maturity to realize that 'there can be many paths to career success, not just one' (S#30) including 'sideways' and 'learner' career moves.

K#34 is a case in point: a mother of three with a law career that she found impossible to continue in Singapore due to licensing restrictions, she started her own health products business by importing vitamins and supplements from abroad. With a shop in one of Singapore's most prestigious malls, she works full-time in a new career that was facilitated by a long-held passion for healthy living, a supportive spouse, 'thinking outside the box' and a risk-taking mentality. For another spouse, M#21, the move to Singapore meant giving up a successful self-made educational practice in her home country with the hope that it could be rebuilt in the new location. When efforts to re-establish herself failed, she reinvented herself as a marriage therapist by undertaking post-graduate studies in counselling. Today, her new business is thriving in a location where Western marriage therapists are hard to find but sorely needed. In M#21's case, a key factor in her dual-career success was to 'fail quickly' (to recognize and acknowledge early after the move that she could not re-establish her old practice) and to then assess gaps in the market where newly acquired expertise and skills could be leveraged to earn a decent living. As she recalls:

I was very resentful about giving up my practice back home and coming here for his job. I really hated it and held out for a long time before finally agreeing to come, albeit with all sorts of 'conditions' attached to it (poor bloke!). Once I got here it became so obvious, as I'd expected, that all hope was lost for getting my practice back to what it was, so after spending a year feeling sorry for myself and angry about what I had given up, I blew it off and started again. I think that's all you can do. I couldn't just sit at home and mope. It's not who I am … This new career and practice is perfect for me. In a way, coming here created an opportunity I would probably never have pursued back home because the necessity to reinvent myself was not there.

Notable about M#21's story is that *Reborn* spouses, despite their success, are not immune to feelings of resentment, anger and frustration. Indeed, nearly all the *Reborn* spouses we interviewed characterized their dual-career journey as one that resembled a rollercoaster of positive and negative emotions ranging from fear, despair, sadness, worry, disappointment and hopelessness to feeling energized, empowered, grateful, motivated, refreshed and accomplished.

From a theoretical standpoint, both the *Ready* and *Reborn* character types are more likely to adopt change theory approaches to overcome their dual-career challenge. For example, *Ready* spouses are those that would likely emulate Shewhart's *plan-do-check-act* (PDCA) model (Ishikawa 1985) by adopting a structured, disciplined, logical and sequential approach to solving their dual-career situation. They are also likely to be 'change masters' (Kanter 1983) by adopting or already possessing several important characteristics such as perseverance, building coalitions and tuning into their environment that enables them to be successful in their job search. On the other hand, *Reborn* spouses are more likely to adapt Lewin's (1946) *unfreeze-change-freeze* approach to their dual-career situation, wherein they alter their attitude about conventional ways of getting things done (i.e. continuing in their existing career) to instead consider alternatives (i.e. a new career). The assumption is that the change process of moving into a new career requires them to first enter a state of disequilibrium and instability to allow the change to occur, after which they settle back into a state of equilibrium that resembles an ideal state of being (career success). In addition, both character types are inclined to follow Egan's (2014) *shadow-side theory* by surrounding themselves with people that will support them in their endeavours and who will be helpful to their quest (positive people, recruiters, networks, associations), that is, people who reinforce and validate their choice to have a career.

Resentful or Resigned

Dual-career expatriate spouses characterized as *Resentful* or *Resigned* represent the other end of the spectrum where dual-career success is less likely (Fig. 10.1). Neither of these character types are likely to overcome their dual-career challenge by gaining paid and/or fulfilling employment whilst living abroad. Instead, each is likely to be stuck in a place of denial for a long period, from which *Resigned* spouses may never escape.

Our data show that only one participant was categorized as *Resentful* at the time of being interviewed (P#19), which we characterize as (1) being aggressive but defeated and (2) living in a perpetual state of anger and frustration that dominates one's mood, behaviour and attitude. A self-confessed workaholic, P#19 acknowledged that her inability to continue her banking career had resulted in a lack of financial independence from her husband and an extended stay-at-home of more than three years while the family has been on their first relocation abroad to Singapore. Her passive availability to family members led her to see behavioural issues in her husband (heavy drinking, womanizing and depression) that has resulted in the couple temporarily separating:

> Anger doesn't begin to describe what I feel. I've been the biggest fool, I'm angry at myself mostly. I came here for his job, for him, for the money, career, blah blah, the usual stuff all trailing spouses do. I gave up a great life in the UK and a fantastic job, thinking we were moving forward into these amazing opportunities for all of us … I never thought I couldn't work here, I always thought something would come up eventually, but it just hasn't happened and maybe I sort of lost interest too along the way … being out of work is demoralizing, humiliating, embarrassing. You lose your mojo

after a while, you feel pathetic that you are groveling for a low paying job just to get your career back on track ... I've spent a lot of time lately crucifying myself for being such a bloody idiot because I didn't see it years ago ... Now I have all this frustration and anger at him and guilt about the kids and our future, and if I can even work here, or do I go home, can I even work there now that I've been gone over 3 years? And how do I even work when I am so upset about his behavior, the women, the booze, clinical depression he won't get help for, marriage counseling he won't go to ... I'm scared and I'm desperate ... I'm embarrassed.

The last category, *Resigned* spouses, are those that have given up and accepted their unemployed, stay-at-home trailing spouse life, typically after a long and exhaustive attempt at dual-career success but which has, in their mind, ended in failure (i.e. abandoning their career). Key characteristics of the *Resigned* category include being passive, defeated and depressed. We profiled nine participants as *Resigned*, noting that common to all was an underlying sense of miserableness and hopelessness expressed in statements such as, 'I hate my life' (L#36) and 'I'm the best housewife I never wanted to be' (M#42). For some, their *Resigned* state had been apparent for a long time (ten years or more) during which they had made small but lukewarm attempts to revive their careers but had quickly given up in self-fulfilling cycles of pity and despondency. Often, these attempts were sabotaged by a 'reluctance to trust the process' (D#18) and their inability to 'get everything about the job offer in writing' (A#39), especially when verbal promises were made by a potential employer or their partner's company about dual-career assistance. Notably, no spouse in this category recognized or acknowledged traits of the *Resigned* profile within themselves, believing instead that they were passive victims of others' wrongdoing, for example, 'my husband's ambition' (C#17), 'the company's ruthless pursuit of profits at the expense of people' (M#23), being 'lied to' (L#36), fed 'empty promises' (D#18) or 'constantly relocating every time I had a shot at a job' (L#9). Common to most *Resigned* spouses is the mistaken belief that having and raising children is going to make up for, or is to blame for, their dual-career failure; if they could not work, they filled up their time having babies and striving to be 'über' mothers, which for

A Typology of Dual-Career Expatriate (Trailing) Spouses...   277

some became their rationale for failing to continue their career.[1] As M#42 recounts, this led to deeper feelings of inadequacy, resentment and, in her case, clinical depression:

> Look, I love my boys, no doubt at all, but I only had them because I wasn't working and I couldn't work and my husband kind of looked at me with this expectation of "well, let's have kids, you have the time now". I didn't realize until my second son was born how boring it is to be at home all day, you know, the novelty wears off pretty fast. I spent every day of their lives until they were six wishing and praying for them to go to school so I didn't have to be their mum 24/7, so I could get my life back ... it's a pretty mean thing but that's how I still feel. I took anti-depressants for a long time ... it sounds awful, and I hate even admitting it ... I'm a chef and I loved my career, having money, being someone real ... now I'm nothing really. It's too late to get it back ... I wouldn't know where to even look and then I love my holidays with the kids, so work would interfere with that ... my life is dictated by when my husband's company will tell us we are moving home or going somewhere else or whatever it is they think is best. He controls everything, doesn't ask me anymore what I might want ... it's about him, kids, the paycheck ... I'm not in it anymore.

From a theoretical standpoint, the Kübler-Ross (1960) change cycle appropriately describes the challenges that *Resentful* and *Resigned* spouses face wherein their movement through the grief cycle of *denial-anger-bargaining-depression-acceptance* is one they are unlikely to ever emerge from in relation to the loss of their career. For example, *Resentful* spouses are likely to remain at the stage of anger, whereas *Resigned* spouses may process through all the stages to reach a point of acceptance, albeit having given up on their dual-career aspirations and mourning its loss in an endless cycle of self-pity and disdain. The grief cycle we observed during our interviews is consistent with McNulty's (2012) research on trailing spouses where respondents referred to being left to 'sink or swim' (p. 430) and 'being treated by the company as totally invisible' (p. 430). Others said 'I regret my life' (p. 63), 'this has caused intense bitterness' (p. 59) and 'I have ... become less of a person' (p. 65).

---

[1] While this comment may seem harsh, it is important to note that each participant in the study self-selected and identified as a *dual-career* expatriate spouse from which we then analysed success or failure in achieving their dual-career ambitions.

Discussion

What Price for Expatriate Dual-Career Success?

Our data show that attempts at dual-career success sometimes come at a heavy price, with three main themes emerging. First, in the case of three participants, their marriages were ending in divorce with each being separated from their partner, although still living together in Singapore for practical purposes. In K#7's case (*Ready*), she and her husband were self-employed entrepreneurs who found that the stress of financial pressures, business travel and raising three young children in a foreign location to be overwhelming. For D#18 (*Resigned*) and P#19 (*Resentful*), the stresses of their unemployment and financial dependence on their husbands led to changes in the dynamics of the relationship; each recounted a story of low self-esteem, addiction and extra marital affairs stemming from family dysfunction because of the relocation abroad.

Second, for other dual-career couples, career success was achieved by 'living together apart'. In these cases, four participants continued their career but only because they or their spouse lived in another country away from the family unit. For L#11 (*Ready*), living together apart has become a way of life for over a decade:

> We chose not to have children, so our careers became very important ... I met my Italian husband in the Maldives where he was working. He came back to Singapore to live with me, then we got married in Italy and we moved back to the Maldives. I hated it there. I'm a career woman so fishing all day made no sense. I was miserable ... We then tried moving to Australia, hoping to find a middle ground but my husband hated it as the only work he could get was as a waiter. I then came up with the unusual idea that I return to Singapore to a high paying job I'd been offered and he go to the Maldives in a self-funded deep-sea fishing business ... We make it work because we respect that each must be happy. We love each other and our marriage works because we enable each to 'be' who we need to be ... Personal happiness comes first and our marriage is strong because of the equality and respect. Never sacrifice your own personal happiness for

A Typology of Dual-Career Expatriate (Trailing) Spouses...   279

someone else—in the long run it's not worth it. I couldn't make him live in Singapore and work as a waiter any more than he could expect me to live in the Maldives gutting fish for a living.

For others, living together apart has required that the trailing spouse repatriate to continue their career, as is the case for L#36 (*Ready*) and L#37 (*Ready*) who both relocated back to Australia when job opportunities in China and Singapore, respectively, were no longer viable. For S#38 (*Reborn*), the situation was slightly more complicated:

We have been living abroad for about 15 years and I had already given up a career in France as a physical therapist to follow my husband to UK. I reinvent myself in London as a coach and I love it, working with universities and MBA students. This is my dream job and I earn good money and have independence, just for me. We then go to Dubai and I keep up the coaching business, starting all over with clients and it is hard, but I make it work. Then after three years his company move us again to Beijing ... I hated it and just wanted to go back to London, but my husband says we could stay five years here, so I think "ok, in five years I build up business again" and so I say yes. Then after only 2 years in Beijing his company tries to move us again to Indonesia and I refuse to go. I really put my foot down and say no way. After all these moves for him, I'm furious with his company and with him. They all expect me to be behind him saying yes, yes, yes to everything. Even if I like Indonesia, even if I think I can start my business again there, I am not going to say yes. This is for me, to say 'no, stop trying to upset my life and my career' ... So, he goes to Indonesia without us, and me and the children stay in Beijing and it has been now like this since two years. This is not even my home, but it is where I have decided to make home. I am earning so much money and am so happy to have a career that I love. This independence is important, to control things and my future. I don't care if he comes back or we divorce ... we are still married, but it is him that comes to see us, I don't go to see him with the kids ... he maybe doesn't like it but he really needs to start putting in some effort and not having it his way all the time.

Lastly, some dual-career expatriate couples achieved career success by taking the 'it's your turn' egalitarian approach. In other words, these couples routinely swapped the lead career role to accommodate job opportunities for their spouse. Of the 46 participants in our study, 9 took turns alternately as the trailing spouse, with a noticeable twist—every male in the study (n = 3, #16, #28, #29) actively engaged in this form of dual-career success, being categorized at the time of the interview as the trailing spouse. In another case, A#39 had reached the point of *Resigned* status and to save her marriage, insisted that she and her husband repatriate to Canada so that she could return to her career as a stockbroker with the same firm she had left three years earlier, to a position which had been put on hold for her as a long-term leave of absence. Her husband subsequently resigned from his job in China and, at the time of the interview, was jobless while preparing to return to Canada. A similar story emerged for K#33 whose husband had relocated their family to Singapore to begin a start-up venture, which then failed and necessitated that the couple return to their native USA to enable K#33 to resume her career as a professor of marketing at the university where she held tenure.

Adopting an 'R' Profile Mindset

Our study shows that dual-career expatriate spouses embark on unique journeys of identity redevelopment when they relocate internationally (Shaffer and Harrison 2001), from which emerges a range of psychological, emotional, career and job outcomes. The uniqueness of each journey results in a range of implications for sending companies, the most important of which is how best to manage a dual-career expatriate spouse 'type' based on their character profile. We note two relevant aspects in this regard. First, as alluded to earlier, our data allows us to reject the idea of there being only one type of dual-career expatriate spouse but instead four distinct profiles emerged. The likelihood of dual-career success is determined by the extent to which each character type is identified and then managed per their profile needs at a given point in time. For example, less emotional support and more practical support appears to be necessary for *Ready* and *Reborn* spouses, whereas more emotional and psychological support seems to be initially required for *Resigned* and *Resentful* spouses, after which practical support would be needed. The individualized approach to dual-career success we recommend here is in line with a broader family talent management perspective that extends a company's talent philosophy (Dries 2013) relative to the impact that families have on GTM practices.

A second aspect that is critical when implementing the R profile is to consider the temporal dimension, that is, that stage of life plays an important role in determining which R profile the expatriate trailing spouse adopts at a given point in time and that their profile is not fixed but is fluid as changes in their stage of life occur. The R profile is thus dynamic. The temporal dimension takes into account many aspects of stage of life including (1) dual-career lifecycle (whose turn is it? career seniority?), (2) birthing children, (3) raising children and (4) return to work mums. Critically, the dual-career journey is not linear; for women especially, it can stop and start according to family needs. For dual-career expatriate trailing spouses, dual-career success is made more difficult by living internationally and the unpredictability of the duration of the stay abroad: will it be short term (less than a year?); from one to five years; or much longer? The temporal dimension must also factor in settling in time in each new location (typically 6–12 months) and new challenges that might need to be overcome (language barriers, employment laws, professional licensing requirements). We recommend that when individuals make choices about expatriating, true success rests at the couple level of analysis in terms of how two partners combine to create, develop, become, implement or play out a dual-career expatriate character type that is geared for family talent management success.

Improve the Selection Process

In practical terms, the dual-career expatriate typology presented here can be a highly useful tool in the selection process of expatriate candidates and for improving GTM initiatives. While much research attention has been given to suggesting the inclusion of expatriate family members in the selection process and involving them in the decision to go (Harvey 1985; Mendenhall et al. 1987), including family interviews with HR, standardized and psychometric testing, adaptability screening and assessment centres to determine personality profiles, language skills, prior experience and expected adjustment difficulties (Caligiuri 2000; Harvey 1985), empirical research remains underdeveloped because studies have not explored the spouse's career orientation as a separate selection criteria. Instead, the inclusion of expatriate family members in selection decisions has for decades remained largely focused on (a) *process* issues such as host-location previews (familiarization trips), school and housing requirements and cost of living considerations (Caligiuri and Phillips 2003), (b) *informal* procedures such as the recommendations of peers and managers (Harris and Brewster 1999) and the candidate's overall self-selection and willingness to relocate (Hays 1974) and (c) *peripheral* issues such as the trailing spouse's general willingness to relocate and their ability to support the candidate in his/her new role largely as an 'unpaid social ambassador' for the company (Selmer 2001: 1228). An exception to the above is a very small body of research by Stephens and Black (1991) and Harvey (1995, 1996, 1998) whose early work on dual-career expatriate families brought to light for the first time the problematic nature of the trailing spouse's career orientation in relation to assignment expectations, adjustment and satisfaction (Harvey 1997) and on-assignment support (Harvey and Buckley 1998; Harvey et al. 1999; Harvey and Wiese 1998).

Very little academic research since these seminal studies has been conducted in relation to dual-career expatriates' refusal rates, selection or adjustment (Harvey et al. 2009b; Moore 2002). We propose using Lewin's (1951) *force field analysis* as a theoretical approach, wherein dual-career spouses can be considered suitable (or not suitable) for international relocation on the basis of their readiness to address their particular dual-career challenge. Those deemed *Ready* or with the capacity to be *Reborn* could be classified as a *done deal* (more likely to be successful) versus those characterized as *Resentful* or *Resigned* being viewed as a *dead duck* (where the resistors to adapt to the dual-career challenge far outweigh the drivers). The latter two character types may even be considered a *deadly disease* (Deming 1994), whose anticipated level of difficulty in addressing their dual-career challenge along with the expected severity of the impact on GTM programmes deems them to be sufficiently toxic that expatriating the family should be avoided at all costs. Other families, of course, may be borderline in which case the company is facing a 'difficult decision' (i.e. where an equal number of resistors and drivers exist).

A Typology of Dual-Career Expatriate (Trailing) Spouses... 283

Limitations and Future Research

While the sample of 46 respondents can be considered adequate, a larger sample would certainly provide more extensive data and perhaps allow quantitative analysis (e.g. factor analysis) from a wider population of survey respondents. Our study also does not account for the temporal dimension that we suggest is important in understanding the dynamic nature of the R profile for expatriate trailing spouses; we did not control for length of time on assignment at the time of the interview as it relates to achieving dual-career success. For instance, some participants had only been in the new location for a matter of months, whereas others had lived there for several years. Some had yet to encounter the brick walls that come from job (application) rejection and the associated resentment and anger and were still in the active hopeful phase of getting a job (with fewer or no rejections). Future research would do well to account for the temporal dimension in several ways, including time in the host location and prior relocations (i.e. personal experience overcoming dual-career issues), as well as stage of life considerations including no children/birthing children/raising children, seniority in their profession, professional licensing requirements, strict or lax employment laws and language barriers.

Another temporal dimension limitation is that we did not specifically study movement between the categories, that is, how trailing spouses move from one category to another. For example, although only one participant was categorized as currently being in a state of *resentment*, our data show that nearly every *Reborn* and *Resigned* participant displayed key characteristics of this category at some point during their dual-career journey, as each navigated career disappointments and rejection over a number of years (Lazarova et al. 2014; McNulty 2012). We conclude that there are two important aspects of the dual-career phenomenon that require further study. First, there can be movement between the categories in the R profile typology per varying degrees of career success and failure at any given point in time. Second, solving the dual-career dilemma is an ongoing process often over many months (or years) as opposed to a one-time event. We thus position dual-career expatriate spouse success as a dynamic construct impacted by a continuous and ongoing process of psychological changes, well-being, adjustment and sense-making. Research that explores movement between categories would allow for a more nuanced explanation of dual-career success than our exploratory study affords.

As one of the primary goals of this chapter is to develop a future research agenda that is focused on better understanding dual-career expatriate (trailing) spouse success, we raise some important research questions that require further study. First, in considering a four-character typology of dual-career expatriates:

RQ1: What are the success factors of each 'type' in the R profile in terms of

  (a) fundamental differences between each type (e.g. empowered vs unmotivated),
  (b) competencies held by each type (e.g. level of interest in addressing the dual-career challenge) and
  (c) characteristics of a successful dual-career expatriate (i.e. degree of personal investment in a successful outcome).

RQ2: To what extent is expatriate dual-career success impacted by (a) length of time abroad, (b) duration of stay in the host country and (c) prior experience with dual-career challenges?

RQ3: To what extent can (a) stage of life considerations including no children/birthing children/raising children, (b) seniority in one's profession, (c) professional licensing requirements, (d) strict or lax employment laws and (e) language barriers be considered antecedents of expatriate dual-career success?

Data in our study are cross-sectional and findings are somewhat limited by single-response bias (despite that the respondents can be viewed as expert informants). Future studies would do well to research matched samples of dual-career expatriate couples to track longitudinal changes in dual-career success, including why some trailing spouses go on to continue their career abroad while others fail in this endeavour.

This could lead to important insights as to how couples develop strong dual-career competencies to enhance overall GTM success. In terms of coping mechanisms that dual-career expatriates use, it would be useful to explore whether coping behaviours and skills are different for males versus female trailing spouses (Selmer and Leung 2003) and whether personality characteristics play a role in dual-career success (Caligiuri 2000). This might then facilitate better organizational support for the trailing spouse.

RQ4: To what extent do the development of dual-career competencies among expatriate couples impact on dual-career success for the trailing spouse?

RQ5: Can the following be considered antecedents of expatriate dual-career success: (a) gender and (b) personality characteristics of the trailing spouse?

Conclusion

There is strong evidence suggesting that dual-career expatriation remains a challenge and a top concern for most companies. Yet, despite decades of research and reports, few solutions have been developed to adequately address it. While prior research has pointed to gaps in identifying appropriate selection processes for dual-career expatriate families, efforts to create a holistic view of dual-career expatriate management have remained limited. Our study provides evidence that managing dual-career expatriates according to an R profile of character types may lead to a competitive advantage, not just for multinational corporations that engage in global mobility but also for the expatriates they employ. We further argue that awareness of the R profile can potentially lower international assignment refusal rates and improve individuals' expectations about dual-career expatriation. Our goal in this chapter has been to facilitate a new research agenda about dual-career expatriation that requires further study.

Appendix

Interview Questions

1. Tell me about your expat journey—when you first moved abroad and the reasons for the move and where you have lived/travelled since then?
2. Whose decision was it to expatriate—your partner's, yours or both?
3. How empowered did you feel in the decision to expatriate?
4. Tell me about your career—is it the one you had before expatriating or a new one?
5. Did you intend to continue your career once you had relocated abroad?
6. What challenges did you face in continuing your career abroad (personal, professional, institutional, environmental)?
7. Or, what prompted the 'new' career you have now?
8. Or, why are you taking a break from your career? Do you think you will go back to your career or embark on a new one?
9. What do you think it takes to be successful as a dual-career family? Is it up to the individual? Or is it more than that? Why?
10. Knowing what you know now about dual-career challenges, would you expatriate again? Why or why not?
11. What advice do you have for other dual-career families considering an international relocation?

References

Boje, David. 2007. From Wilda to Disney: Living Stories in Family and Organization Research. In *Handbook of Narrative Inquiry: Mapping a Methodology*, ed. D. Jean Clandinin, 330–353. Thousand Oaks, CA: Sage.

Brown, Robert J. 2008. Dominant Stressors on Expatriate Couples During International Assignments. *International Journal of Human Resource Management* 19 (6): 1018–1034.

Caligiuri, Paula. 2000. Selecting Expatriates for Personality Characteristics: A Moderating Effect of Personality on the Relationship Between Host National Contact and Cross-Cultural Adjustment. *Management International Review* 40 (1): 61–80.

Caligiuri, Paula M., and Jean N. Phillips. 2003. An Application of Self-Assessment Realistic Job Previews to Expatriate Assignments. *International Journal of Human Resource Management* 14 (7): 1102–1116.

Cole, Nina. 2011. Managing Global Talent: Solving the Spousal Adjustment Problem. *International Journal of Human Resource Management* 22 (7): 1504–1530.

———. 2012. Expatriate Accompanying Partners: The Males Speak. *Asia Pacific Journal of Human Resources* 50 (3): 308–326.

Deming, W. Edwards. 1994. *The New Economics for Industry, Government and Education*. 2nd ed. Massachusetts, MA: MIT.

Denzin, Norman K., and Yvonna S. Lincoln. 2000. *Qualitative Research*. Thousand Oaks: Sage Publications.

Dries, Nicky. 2013. The Psychology of Talent Management: A Review and Research Agenda. *Human Resource Management Review* 23 (4): 272–285.

Egan, Gerard. 2014. *The Skilled Helper: A Problem-Management and Opportunity-Development Approach to Helping*. Belmont, CA: Cengage Learning.

Harris, Hilary, and Chris Brewster. 1999. The Coffee-Machine System: How International Selection Really Works. *International Journal of Human Resource Management* 10 (3): 488–500.

Harvey, Michael. 1985. The Executive Family: An Overlooked Variable in International Assignments. *Columbia Journal of World Business* 20 (2): 84–92.

———. 1995. The Impact of Dual-Career Families on International Relocations. *Human Resource Management Review* 5 (3): 223–234.

———. 1996. Addressing the Dual-Career Expatriation Dilemma in International Relocations. *Human Resource Planning* 19 (4): 18–39.

———. 1997. Dual-Career Expatriates: Expectations, Adjustment, and Satisfaction with International Relocation. *Journal of International Business Studies* 28 (3): 627–658.

———. 1998. Dual-Career Couples During International Relocation: The Trailing Spouse. *International Journal of Human Resource Management* 9 (2): 309–331.

Harvey, Michael, and M. Ronald Buckley. 1998. The Process for Developing an International Program for Dual-Career Couples. *Human Resource Management Review* 8 (1): 99–123.

Harvey, Michael, M. Ronald Buckley, Milorad M. Novicevic, and Danielle Wiese. 1999. Mentoring Dual-Career Expatriates: A Sense-Making And Sense-Giving Social Support Process. *International Journal of Human Resource Management* 10 (5): 808–827.

Harvey, Michael, Nancy Napier, and Miriam Moeller. 2009a. Interpreting Dual-Career Couples' Family Life-Cycles: Identifying Strategic Windows of Global Career Opportunity. *Research and Practice in Human Resource Management* 17 (2): 14–35.

Harvey, Michael, Milorad Novicevic, and Jacob W. Breland. 2009b. Global Dual-Career Exploration and the Role of Hope and Curiosity During the Process. *Journal of Managerial Psychology* 24 (2): 178–197.

Harvey, Michael, and Danielle Wiese. 1998. Global Dual-Career Couple Mentoring: A Phase Model Approach. *Human Resource Planning* 21 (2): 33–48.

Hays, Richard D. 1974. Expatriate Selection: Insuring Success and Avoiding Failure. *Journal of International Business Studies* 5 (1): 25–38.

Ishikawa, Kaoru. 1985. *What is Total Quality Control? The Japanese Way*. Englewood Cliffs, NJ: Prentice-Hall.

James, Susan, John Hunsley, Geoffrey S. Navara, and Melanie Alles. 2004. Marital, Psychological, and Sociocultural Aspects of Sojourner Adjustment: Expanding the Field of Enquiry. *International Journal of Intercultural Relations* 28 (2): 111–126.

Kanter, Rosabeth Moss. 1983. *The Change Masters: Innovation and Entrepreneurship in the American Corporation*. New York, NY: Simon and Schuster, Inc.

Kübler-Ross, Elizabeth. 1960. *On Death and Dying*. New York, NY: Touchstone.

Lauring, Jakob, and Jan Selmer. 2010. The Supportive Expatriate Partner: An Ethnographic Study of Partner Involvement in Expatriate Careers. *International Business Review* 19 (1): 59–69.

Lazarova, Mila B., and Jean-Luc Cerdin. 2007. Revisiting Repatriation Concerns: Organizational Support Versus Career and Contextual Influences. *Journal of International Business Studies* 38 (3): 404–429.

Lazarova, Mila B., Yvonne McNulty, and Monica Semeniuk. 2014. Expatriate Family Narratives on International Mobility: Key Characteristics of the Successful Moveable Family. In *Work and Personal Life Interface of International Career Contexts*, ed. Vesa Suutari and Liisa Makela. Heidelberg: Springer.

Lewin, Kurt. 1946. Action Research and Minority Problems. *Journal of Social Issues* 2 (4): 34–46.

—————. 1951. *Field Theory in Social Science.* New York, NY: Harper Row.

Mäkelä, Liisa, Marja Känsälä, and Vesa Suutari. 2011. The Roles of Expatriates' Spouses Among Dual Career Couples. *Cross Cultural Management: An International Journal* 18 (2): 185–197.

Mendenhall, Mark, Edward Dunbar, and Gary R. Oddou. 1987. Expatriate Selection, Training and Career-Pathing: A Review and Critique. *Human Resource Management* 26 (3): 331–345.

McNulty, Yvonne. 2012. 'Being Dumped in to Sink or Swim': An Empirical Study of Organizational Support for the Trailing Spouse. *Human Resource Development International* 15 (4): 417–434.

—————. 2014. Women in Non-Traditional Expatriate Families as a Source of Global Talent: Female Breadwinners, Single Parents, Split Families, and Lesbian Partnerships. In *Research Handbook on Women in International Management*, ed. Kate Hutchings and Snejina Michailova. Cheltenham: Edward Elgar.

McNulty, Yvonne, and Kate Hutchings. 2016. Looking for Global Talent in all the Right Places: A Critical Literature Review of Non-Traditional Expatriates. *The International Journal of Human Resource Management* 27 (6): 699–728.

Miles, Matthew B., and Michael A. Huberman. 1994. *Qualitative Data Analysis: An Expanded Sourcebook.* Thousand Oaks: Sage Publications.

Moore, Meredith. 2002. Same Ticket, Different Trip: Supporting Dual-Career Couples on Global Assignments. *Women in Management Review* 17 (2): 61–67.

Ochs, Elinor, and Lisa Capps. 2001. *Living Narrative: Creating Lives in Everyday Storytelling.* Cambridge, MA: Harvard University Press.

ORC Worldwide. 2005. *Dual Careers and International Assignments Survey.* New York: ORC Worldwide.

Permits Foundation. 2009. *Employment, Work Permits, and International Mobility.* The Hague, The Netherlands: Permits Foundation.

—————. 2012. *International Mobility and Dual Career Survey of International Employers.* The Hague, The Netherlands: Permits Foundation.

Rapoport, Rhona, and Robert N. Rapoport. 1969. The Dual-Career Family: A Variant Pattern and Social Change. *Human Relations* 22 (1): 3–30.

Rossman, Gretchen B., and Sharon F. Rallis. 2003. *Learning in the Field: An Introduction to Qualitative Research.* 2nd ed. Thousand Oaks, CA: Sage.

Selmer, Jan. 2001. Expatriate Selection: Back to Basics? *International Journal of Human Resource Management* 12 (8): 1219–1233.

Selmer, Jan, and Alicia S.M. Leung. 2003. Personal Characteristics of Female Versus Male Business Expatriates. *International Journal of Cross Cultural Management* 3 (2): 195–212.

Shaffer, Margaret, and David Harrison. 2001. Forgotten Partners of International Assignments: Development and Test of a Model of Spouse Adjustment. *Journal of Applied Psychology* 86 (2): 238–254.

Stephens, Gregory, and Stewart Black. 1991. The Impact of Spouse's Career-Orientation on Managers During International Transfers. *Journal of Management Studies* 28 (4): 417–428.

Stroh, Linda, Arup Varma, and Stacey J. Valy-Durbin. 2000. Why Are Women Left at Home: Are They Unwilling to go on International Assignments? *Journal of World Business* 35 (3): 241–255.

van Gus, Wouter, and Gerbert Kraaykamp. 2008. The Emergence of Dual-Career Couples: A Longitudinal Study of the Netherlands. *International Sociology* 23 (3): 345–366.

Vance, Charles M., and Yvonne McNulty. 2014. Why and How Women and Men Acquire Global Career Experience: A Study of American Expatriates In Europe. *International Studies of Management and Organization* 44 (2): 34–54.

Weick, Karl E., Kathleen M. Sutcliffe, and David Obstfeld. 2005. Organizing and the Process of Sensemaking. *Organization Science* 16 (4): 409–421.

11

Management of Work-Life Interface of Global Careerists: Experiences Among Different Types of International Professionals

Vesa Suutari, Liisa Mäkelä, and Olivier Wurtz

Introduction

International work appears in various forms spanning long-term assignments lasting several years, short-term assignments and frequent international travelling (Collings et al. 2007; Suutari and Brewster 2009; Caligiuri and Bonache 2016). While the main focus of expatriation research has traditionally been on international assignments within multinational companies (MNCs) involving a company sending an employee abroad for several years, the latest research investigates different types of international professionals. The shift in focus is important because, for example, experts predict self-initiated expatriates will become the largest group of internationally mobile managers (Tharenou and Caulfield 2010). Similarly, MNCs are increasingly using short-term assignments and international job-related travel is becoming a common part of the

---

V. Suutari (✉) • L. Mäkelä • O. Wurtz
School of Management, University of Vaasa, Vaasa, Finland
e-mail: vsu@uva.fi; liisa.makela@uwasa.fi; owurtz@uva.fi

© The Author(s) 2018   **291**
M. Dickmann et al. (eds.), *The Management of Global Careers*,
https://doi.org/10.1007/978-3-319-76529-7_11

lives of business professionals (Collings et al. 2015; Suutari et al. 2013; Caligiuri and Bonache 2016).

Such international work also challenges business professionals who have to adjust to working in a new organizational unit abroad, face new and often challenging jobs and also adapt to a new living environment and culture. Given that assignees often have families, it is important to note that moving and living abroad is at least as challenging for their partners and children as it is for the expatriates themselves (Shaffer et al. 2001; Richardson 2006). Such challenges have attracted scholars to investigate the work-life interface of international professionals. MNCs have also faced challenges when trying to recruit expatriates (Dickmann et al. 2008). Indeed, family-related issues are often among the main reasons offered for refusing expatriate assignments, but the same reason appears in justifications for the premature termination of international assignments, suggesting that family issues affect expatriate adjustment and performance (Cole 2011; Takeuchi 2010). Similarly, the major negative characteristics stated of short-term assignments typically include work-life balance issues (Collings et al. 2007; Suutari et al. 2013). These observations indicate that work-family issues should be high on the agenda of a company aiming to recruit and support international talent.

Owing to the increasing number of studies on expatriates, their partners and families, we are starting to understand the main challenges related to work and personal life interaction involved with international mobility. Moreover, the first edited book on the work-life interface (WLI) in the context of international careers has recently been published (Mäkelä and Suutari 2015). In this chapter, we aim to draw together what is known about the interaction between working life and personal life (including family) in regard to the spheres of different types of internationally mobile professionals.

We start from the discussion on negative interactions between these two life spheres—the issue that has attracted most attention in the literature. Next, we will complement the picture by discussing the often forgotten side of these experiences—the positive experiences of international professionals and their families. Given the large amount of transference between the work and non-work spheres of families during international assignments, it is also important to understand the ways in which organizations can help expatriates and their families (Lazarova et al. 2015). There is some research evidence on which aspects of support are most useful, and there is a growing discussion of how organizations can improve how non-work aspects affect the work-life balance and well-being of assignees and their families (Caligiuri and Lazarova 2005). We will also discuss how firms can manage the WLI issues of their internationally mobile staff.

The Work-Life Interface of Different Types of Global Careerists

In line with the discussion in Chap. 3, we address these issues separately as they affect international business travellers, short-term assignees, assigned expatriates, self-initiated expatriates and internationally more experienced global careerists.

The Work-Life Interface of International Business Travellers

International travel to fulfil work requirements (e.g. meeting customers, coordinating international operations or transferring knowledge across borders) has long been a common activity for many specialists and managers. It is also very common that expatriate jobs require international travel in their business arena. International travel means the traveller is absent from home, and travel thus typically has a negative impact on the work-family balance of travellers (DeFrank et al. 2000; Jensen 2013). While away, travellers cannot participate in the everyday lives of their families and share family responsibilities as a parent or partner usually would (Mayerhofer et al. 2004; Mäkelä et al. 2012; Welch and Worm 2006). Frequent travel absorbs considerable time and energy, and extensive travel may not permit travellers to spend enough time with their families or to participate in social activities (Shaffer et al. 2012). The family situation makes a difference because travelling parents naturally face a higher level of work-life conflict than those without children, particularly in the case of a traveller who is a mother of dependent children and who travels frequently (Mäkelä et al. 2015a). The family members can also experience role confusion associated with separations and reunions that necessitates continual adjustments (Orthner and Rose 2009).

In addition, health-related problems are reported to be common among international workers (Patel 2011). International travel may cause psychological stress, strain and burnout (Westman and Etzion 2002; Jensen 2013). Increasing the frequency and duration of trips is also connected with symptoms such as jet lag, increased alcohol consumption, sleep deprivation and feeling insecure about the ability to keep abreast of the workload (Burkholder et al. 2010). These health and well-being problems in turn have spillover effects on the work and personal life interface (Burkholder et al. 2010). Additionally, work-family conflict (WFC) triggered by international business travel may also lead to health problems, for instance, a high number of days spent on business travel has been linked to sleeping problems, as mediated by work-to-family conflict (Mäkelä et al. 2014a).

It is also important to note that it is not only the time on a business trip that causes stress. In fact, stress levels are even higher before the trip and the level of stress continues to rise after the trip as the traveller integrates back into daily family life and job responsibilities, which may have increased due to a partner's absence (DeFrank et al. 2000). For example, Saarenpää (2016) found that there was an imbalance between work and family life both when a traveller was on a business trip and when that traveller was at home. An imbalance between work and family spheres produced negative outcomes for the travellers themselves and also for their partners. Those outcomes can be divided into mental and practical forms. The former would include feelings of uncertainty, guilt or inadequacy; and the latter arguments between couples, a lack of personal time, difficulty with managing the demands of the job and so on. The awareness that a forthcoming trip would again interrupt the family's routine prompted feelings of uncertainty. Such uncertainty often necessitates childcare arrangements and often also interferes with the partner's work. For an international business traveller (IBT), travel thus influences not only the person's stress levels and health but also the stress level of the partner and any children (Espino et al. 2002; Saarenpää 2016). For example, partners who experience frequent travel-related separation are at greater risk of poor psychological well-being than partners generally (Orthner and Rose 2009). The extent to which travellers have control over their trips has been found to be one of the primary factors affecting stress for people who travel frequently on business: it contributes to the reduction in work-family conflict (Jensen 2013).

Sometimes a short business trip is not long enough to handle the required job and an international trip has to span several months. Such jobs are typically referred to in companies as short-term assignments, the effects of which we will discuss next.

The Work-Life Interface of Short-Term Assignees

Short-term assignments typically last from three months up to one year and clearly less is known about the experiences of assignees on them (Baker and Ciuk 2015). Such assignments are easier to arrange than long-term moves, can be less costly for companies (Collings et al. 2015) and can be used when the need for the assignee is more temporary. Typical tasks can relate to construction, repairs, dissipating IT changes, expanding the company's market and managing major projects (Salleh and Koh 2013). Short-term assignments are generally useful when transferring knowledge across borders or different processes within an MNC (Minbaeva and Michailova 2004). Such assignments also have considerable management development potential (Salleh and Koh 2013).

Our knowledge of the WLI of short-term assignees and their families is very limited. Starr and Currie (2009) analyse the role of the family in the assignment process from the perspective of the assignee. Other studies discuss family issues among the typical challenges faced by short-term assignees and their families (Tahvanainen et al. 2005; Suutari et al. 2013). Baker and Ciuk (2015) in turn study business people with many short-term assignments to call upon. The main difference in comparison with a person on a long-term assignment is that the short-term assignee's family usually stays in the home country and thus their daily life (e.g. the career of the partner, school or day-care arrangements of the children or social connections of the family members) is less affected. Although the direct impacts of the assignment on the family may be smaller, the fact that the assignee is away from home over quite a long period may cause as many or even more problems than moving with the family abroad; especially, if such assignments involve more frequent and often unplanned periods of separation to engage in international project work (Meyskens et al. 2009). The WLI challenges short-term assignees face share similarities with those of international travellers. International travel of any duration requires travel preparations, causes a person to be absent from family life and makes it necessary to integrate back into family life after the assignment.

The existing research also indicates that short-term assignees receive less support from their employers than their long-term assignee counterparts do. Short-term assignments are often managed by line managers and thus garner less support from the firm's HR department than a longer-term assignment would (Dickmann 2016). This supervisory issue might also explain why assignees working for the same organization can be treated differently with regard to their home leave arrangements, accommodation, expenses and travel time allowances. Short-term assignees are often expected to be able to fulfil their information needs themselves and find the necessary operational support. That situation can cause problems for assignees, particularly the less experienced ones, and can cause dissatisfaction among them.

In a single case study, Suutari et al. (2013) establish that short-term assignments such as project assignments have implications for the work-life interface. The main challenge faced by project assignees was the distance from their family. While on assignment, the family had to arrange daily life without the assignee. Even opportunities to communicate with families could sometimes be restricted by working in difficult environments, or different time zones, but also by the intensive nature of project work. The well-being of groups of people living and working together closely is prone to be affected by challenges besetting individuals. Sometimes international travel/assignments might resemble a form of semi-permanent commuting, a situation in which the assignee lives in one country and works in another during the week or works in two locations in different countries. If a longer-term permanent presence is not needed in some location, long-term or project assignments could be replaced by commuting, especially when the distance involved is not too far. Sometimes commuting can be an option if the family does not wish to leave its home country (Mäkelä et al. 2017). The most challenging issues appear to be a lack of free time owing to long and intensive working weeks combined with extensive travelling and the consequent lack of time with the family. These issues can easily lead to burnout and family problems in the longer term (Suutari et al. 2013).

Baker and Ciuk (2015) report on rotational assignees—short-term assignees who regularly go on assignment in the course of various international projects. Their interviews revealed that the overall amount of time spent on assignment, the unpredictability of the work schedule and the lack of control the assignees had over it combined to create work-life conflict (WLC). The same study indicates company support was often missing as workers faced these challenges. The assignees described that their extensive stays away from home sometimes meant they felt they were abandoning their children. Such periods of absence naturally strained relationships with the children. Overall, the assignees felt that their absence had major impacts on their family life.

While the work-life challenges of short-term assignees are not yet well reported, more evidence can be found among long-term expatriates.

The Work-Life Interface of Assigned Expatriates

The issues related to WLI and work-life balance are also often very salient with long-term international assignments that typically last for a few years. It should first be noted that an international assignment per se is a major disruption stemming from working life and impacting the private life. Relocation and adapting to life in a foreign country themselves have major effects on the private life of the assignee and to his/her family. Most international assignees mention that work regularly interferes with their private life (Grant-Vallone and Ensher 2001). It appears that work causes more disruption in the private life of expatriates than it does for domestic employees (IRC/ORC 2006/2007; Shortland and Cummins 2007). Moreover, these disruptions can be more detrimental in the expatriation context because the status quo between couples and families is already affected by the move (Caligiuri et al. 1998; Lazarova et al. 2010). Indeed, the Global Mobility Trends report of 2016 shows that assigned expatriates see family issues as the biggest cause of a premature departure from an assignment (Brookfield Global Relocation Services 2016). Moreover the Global Relocation Trends report (Brookfield Global Relocation Services 2012) reveals that the main reasons to turn down an international assignment are family-related: such issues account for more than half of the reasons for refusal (34 per cent of them are related to family concerns and 17 per cent due to a partner's career).

One of the main reasons for these issues is that boundaries between work and family (or more generally, the private life) are weaker and more permeable in the expatriation context (Caligiuri and Lazarova 2005). Therefore, problems in one area, such as stress at work, are more likely to affect other areas than they would in the country of origin. The conjunction of the increased work responsibilities that often happen in expatriation scenarios, with the isolation felt owing to entering a new environment, are likely to compel the expatriate to increase the hours and energy dedicated to work. These elements also suggest an imbalance between expatriates busy with often challenging and time-consuming work tasks and responsibilities and the lesser extent of the private network and activities of non-working partners in the case of the expatriate families. While expatriates have their corporate networks, daily activities and support networks, partners and families can feel more isolated and struggle to integrate into the local community (Wurtz and Suutari 2015).

It has also been found that gender issues have an impact on expatriation decisions and also on the interaction between working life and personal/family life. Alongside the debate on corporate barriers that hinder appointing women to senior roles (Adler 1987), there has been some discussion on why women are less likely to work abroad, which has in turn led to consideration of individual and family barriers to expatriation. For example, Tharenou (2008) reports that having a family restricted women's ability to transform their willingness to expatriate into an international job search more than it did for men. In line with this, Rusconi et al. (2013) state that in general, decisions among dual career couples around work and family priorities are often gendered. Only a few studies investigate the work-life interface of female expatriates and their families (Linehan and Walsh 2000; Mäkelä et al. 2011). Those studies report that despite having to work, female expatriates are responsible for taking care of the home and children and are also mainly responsible for very practical issues such as shopping. Even without children, managing relationships with partners can be a challenge, especially in terms of prioritizing careers and the required job responsibilities (Linehan and Walsh 2000). In line with this, Mäkelä et al. (2011) report that their demanding expatriate jobs mean it is not easy for female expatriates to find time for themselves and their families. The lack of relatives and long-term friends close by mean family support networks are not available when needed (e.g. in case of sickness, travel or overtime work demands). It was also recognized that it may be culturally more difficult for male partners to be "trailing partners" and to take the primary responsibility for domestic chores. Such challenges mean it is quite common that women on assignment will have no dependents, while, in contrast, studies of expatriates reported that a clear majority of male expatriates have families with them abroad.

WLC has multiple consequences for expatriates and for families. First, it affects individual well-being. Research shows that WLC fosters anxiety and depression among international assignees (Grant-Vallone and Ensher 2001). Second, WLC has family outcomes, in that it reduces satisfaction with family relationships (Andres et al. 2012). Third, work-related attitudes and behaviours are also influenced by WLC. Expatriates experiencing higher levels of WLC are less satisfied with their working life and perform less well at work than they might (Shih et al. 2010). Professionals turn down career opportunities requiring expatriation because they anticipate WLC (Dickmann et al. 2008), and WLC is associated with increased turnover intention among expatriates (Andres et al. 2012; Shaffer et al. 2001).

Besides those assignees sent abroad by their employers, increasing numbers of professionals head abroad on their own initiative and without corporate support in the process. The specific challenges faced by these self-initiated expatriates will be discussed next.

The Work-Life Interface of Self-Initiated Expatriates

While research has traditionally focused on assigned expatriates, researchers have recently become interested in understanding the nature of self-initiated expatriation, a situation where the expatriate seeks a job abroad on his or her own initiative (Suutari and Brewster 2000). While all expatriates face fairly similar adjustment and work-life interface challenges when moving abroad, the situation of specific types of expatriates may also differ to some extent. Accordingly, this chapter describes how the situations of assigned expatriates and self-initiated expatriates differ.

One of the main differences between assigned and self-initiated expatriates is the level of control over the decision making around going to work abroad (Mäkelä and Suutari 2013). Assigned expatriates have to follow the corporate logic when accepting the assignments and thus cannot exert much influence on the location or timing of the assignment. Accordingly, there is less room to take family perspectives into account in the decision making. Self-initiated assignees, in turn, can take greater account of such family interests (Richardson 2006). For example, families typically consider the age of the children and related needs for day care or schooling to assess the optimal timing of an assignment for the whole family. Moreover, assigned expatriates may have to go where their employer needs them and, if the firm is expanding internationally, that might involve relocating to countries with a very challenging living environment. Self-initiated expatriates, in contrast, can more often choose locations offering an easier living environment, higher standard of living, better climate and a better country reputation overall (Doherty et al. 2011). By staying in developed economies and in major cities, they can choose locations with better education or day-care options for children or better job opportunities for the partner (Dickmann 2013). They can also be more flexible in choosing the type of jobs they want to take abroad, although such freedom is naturally limited by the options available. These starting points of self-initiated expatriation do still improve the options and foster a beneficial overall work-life balance.

While greater freedom to make family-friendly decisions might ease the adjustment process and help establish an acceptable work-life balance, the price of that benefit is often the lack of corporate support in the expatriation process in comparison with international assignees (Richardson 2006). Companies typically provide some support for the employees they send abroad, although that might often be less than the expatriates hope for. Such support might cover help with travel and practical arrangements such as housing, day care, insurance, health care, dealing with local authorities and so on. Language training and cross-cultural training have become quite common support practices either prior to departure or while abroad (Wurtz 2014). Some firms go further and extend cross-cultural and language training to families and might help partners into employment abroad. However, self-initiated expatriates and their families do not usually benefit from such arrangements and thus can face greater adjustment issues than their assigned counterparts. Assigned expatriates can often also access a support network revolving around the organization. They are probably already familiar with many organizational practices, know people within the organization and who to contact if they need help, although practice may well vary to some extent across countries. Assigned expatriates also often have more generous compensation packages than self-initiated expatriates. That compensation might include a range of allowances and health insurance that offer affordable access to external services that smooth daily life and adjustment. Self-initiated expatriates typically have local contracts that lack such additional benefits. Private schools, higher quality day care, private health and apartments in nicer areas of a city are available only for those with a sufficiently high income.

While expatriation experiences are typically analysed as once in a lifetime experiences, in reality, a growing number of expatriates have longer-term international careers punctuated by various assignments. We thus next discuss the WLI issues faced by such experienced global careerists.

The Work-Life Interface of Experienced Global Careerists

The globalization of business and the related growth of careers for internationally oriented business professionals have spawned interest in understanding the specific features of global careers involving frequent moves across borders during a career (Cappellen and Janssens 2005; Suutari 2003; Suutari et al. 2012). In some European studies, it has been reported that 64 per cent of French expatriates, 41 per cent of German expatriates and 55 per cent of Finnish expatriates had already gained prior international assignment experience before their current role (Stahl and Cerdin 2004; Jokinen et al. 2008).

Studies of this group of the most internationally experienced professionals cite work-life balance issues among their main challenges (Suutari 2003). It is also argued that the rigours of a global career would be too challenging for most individuals and their families (Forster 2000). There are several reasons why this is the case. Given that international assignments always have a considerable impact on the whole family, it is of no surprise that a collection of moves during a career makes life even more challenging for the whole family. All family members have to constantly adjust to a new living environment and create new social connections. The experience of having gone through such adjustment processes before helps but cannot fully prepare families for changes in their situation such as adding new family members or children becoming teenagers. Each context also inevitably brings unexpected challenges of which the family has no previous experience. Owing to their international experience gained in different locations and jobs, global careerists often have senior jobs with burdensome responsibilities that demand extensive travel. These requirements often mean working long days, being absent from home and being preoccupied by job responsibilities even during free time.

Mäkelä and Suutari (2011) grouped the work-family conflicts faced by global careerists and their families into three main categories: time-based conflicts, strain-based conflicts and mobility-based conflicts. Time-based conflicts appear when expatriates work in very challenging jobs often requiring long working hours, travelling and full-time availability. The situation leaves little time for family issues and increases the demands on the partner to handle such family issues. Strain-based conflicts similarly reflect the high level of responsibility, autonomy and the challenging nature of the assignments. This means that expatriates often find themselves exhausted by their work load and thus the work follows them home. The mobility-based conflicts do not relate to the expatriate job responsibilities but the overall adjustment challenges related to international moves. When global careerists and their families make such a move several times, they experience discontinuity and uncertainty-based stress that affects both their work and private lives. Given that international assignments are typically fixed-term arrangements, subsequent career moves need to be planned, often in the face of information on the next career move becoming available quite late. The effect is that decisions on the whole family's future might be rushed. In addition, social connections need to be rebuilt in each context and the distance from the home country (or the third country) makes it difficult to stay in touch with friends and relatives. If repatriation, whether temporary or permanent, was planned at a certain stage of the career, that repatriation was reported to be, or expected to be, very challenging because of the long stays abroad. In many cases the internationally experienced children of global careerists were also studying or working abroad, which impacted on the family situation and related future decisions.

While our discussion has thus far focused on the challenges faced by global careerists, the following section focuses on the positive side of the interaction between the international work and personal life spheres.

Positive Interactions Between Work and Personal Life in the Context of International Careers

In general, expectations related to individuals' different roles in different life spheres, such as being a competent employee in working life and at the same time being a partner, parent or a friend in the personal life sphere, deplete an individual's resources. However, these different roles can also provide opportunities for the renewal of resources through activities in different life domains (Fisher et al. 2009). Therefore, it is important to discuss the positive side of work and life sphere interaction. These are phenomena that have been studied using concepts such as positive spillover, facilitation and enrichment in prior literature (Fisher et al.

2009; Frone 2003; Wayne et al. 2007). Because very little empirical research is done on the positive interactions between the work and personal or family lives of different types of international professionals, they are not all discussed separately. We will start our discussion on these positive interactions with the analysis of the effects that international work has on the personal life sphere and follow that with a section focusing on effects flowing from the personal life sphere to the working life sphere of international professionals.

International Work Enriching the Personal Life

International work involving relocation is seen to offer interesting, stimulating and developmental aspects for the personal life of both international professionals themselves and for those of their families (Suutari 2003). Sometimes relocation enables a couple or family to live together, especially in the situation of cross-cultural relationships (Mäkelä and Suutari 2013), thus providing an opportunity to spend more time together and enjoy each other's company.

The experience of living in an unfamiliar environment and learning about a new culture has been found to develop expatriates' sense of self and affect their self-identity (Kohonen 2004, 2007). It has also been found to increase their empathy for others and tolerance for diversity (Lovvorn and Chen 2011). Thus, living away from one's home country for a longer period might offer an opportunity to grow as a person; be that as an international professional or a following family member. Such growth can be seen as an enrichment caused by working life affecting the personal and/or family life. In the case of international professionals who do not relocate abroad for a longer period of time, namely, IBTs and short-term assignees, the effects affect those international professionals' families but are primarily important for the travellers themselves. First, it has been suggested that international business trips are enriching because they provide opportunities to learn of new countries and cultures (Stahl and Björkman 2006; Westman et al. 2009). However, it can be assumed that staying for only a short period in the same location does not have as

Management of Work-Life Interface of Global Careerists... **305**

strong an effect on personal development as a longer stay or relocation would. An alternative viewpoint is that IBTs and short-term assignees might work in several different countries, and thus perhaps gain a broad range of developmental cultural experiences (Harvey et al. 2010).

Working as an international professional can also provide material benefits and therefore positively affect the personal life sphere. For instance, living abroad as an expatriate may offer a higher salary, life in a country with lower living costs or a more developed infrastructure than available in the country of origin (Bonache 2006; Suutari et al. 2012; Shaffer et al. 2012; Richardson et al. 2015). Therefore, international professionals and their families who move abroad might enjoy higher standards of living due to the relocation (Mäkelä and Suutari 2013). Material benefits may affect international professionals' and their families' everyday lives, for instance, living in a high-standard apartment or being able to employ a domestic help. Some of these benefits are also relevant to IBTs and short-term assignees, for instance, when they too benefit from good salaries and other allowances (e.g. a tax-free daily allowance) (Tahvanainen et al. 2005) that provide an opportunity to live comfortably and therefore also benefit his/her family.

Living abroad may also have a positive effect on leisure activities. Material resources and also the location of the host country can improve leisure time options for global careerists. Earning a higher salary than at home might enable them to travel more often and more easily (Mäkelä et al. 2014b). For IBTs and short-term assignees, the travel or assignment itself may provide an opportunity to see interesting places and cities and sometimes a chance to spend some extra time in the location before or after working days (Mayerhofer et al. 2011). The climate of the host/destination country may provide an opportunity to cultivate hobbies that are not possible in the home country or are possible for only a short period during the year. For instance, an international professional from Finland who plays golf may enjoy living in or having a business trip to Spain in January when Finnish golf courses are shut. However, the families of IBTs or short-term assignees do not typically benefit from these positive aspects for the personal life sphere provided by the location (unless the family can travel with or visit a short-term assignee).

Personal Life Enriching the Working Life of the International Professional

Positive effects flowing from the personal life sphere to the working life sphere of international professionals have rarely been researched, but some studies shedding light on the topic are available. First, positive links between the social support offered by a partner and/or family to an international professional and his/her working life sphere can be found. In the context of international work involving relocation, it has been reported that spending time with one's family or drawing support from a partner are important factors supporting the adjustment of the expatriate (Lauring and Selmer 2010). Support from a partner has also been linked to expatriates' performance and the successful completion of international assignments (Lauring and Selmer 2010). It has also been reported that support from the family reduces stress among IBTs (DeFrank et al. 2000) and that the support of a family increases IBTs' satisfaction with their work-related international travel (Mäkelä et al. 2015b).

More precisely, partners can provide very concrete support. It has been found that sometimes partners postpone or abandon their own careers to fit with the trailing partner role and thus make an international career possible for their partner (Lauring and Selmer 2010; Mäkelä et al. 2012). The same has been shown to apply in the context of international business travel (Saarenpää 2016). Partners willing to suspend or abandon their own careers might become more focused on the family and take a greater role in family affairs than would otherwise be the case, in order to allow their international professional partner to handle a challenging job (Mäkelä et al. 2012; Saarenpää 2016). Evidence on IBTs suggests support from other relatives can be significant too, for instance, grandparents seem to be crucial in helping to successfully combine family obligations and work involving travel (Mäkelä et al. 2012).

Having a partner from the destination country can benefit the adjustment of the expatriate (Davies et al. 2015). In addition to the fact that a local partner introduces the local way of life and thus eases the adjustment, he/she provides access to his/her social network, which may also be beneficial for career purposes. A local partner may also support an expatriate in acquiring skills needed in working life, for instance, learning the local language (Mäkelä and Suutari 2013).

In addition, other aspects of the personal life sphere than those related to the family or partner may have positive effects on the working life of international professionals. For instance, having hobbies or participating in sports in a host country is likely to broaden social contacts and enhance well-being, which may be beneficial for working life. It has also been found that physical exercise decreases levels of work-to-family conflict among IBTs and relatedly that the higher their level of alcohol consumption, the more likely IBTs are to have problems sleeping (Mäkelä et al. 2014a), thus providing support for the idea that cultivating a healthy lifestyle is linked to the improved well-being of international professionals. Therefore, what a person does in his/her personal life sphere during leisure time is very likely to have an effect on the well-being of the international professional and, through that, affect his/her performance in the working life sphere.

After discussing the work-life experiences of different types of global careerists, we will now focus on how companies can support their travellers and assignees in achieving a good work-life balance.

Management of the WLI Within MNCs

International employees can be strongly affected by work-life issues occasioned by their cross-border experiences. Fortunately, different forms of support can be provided by companies to limit the negative impacts of work on the private-life sphere and to lessen these impacts. First, an important step is the *decision to accept an international job* and that is the case even more so for families. The first major way in which work can affect the private life is the working arrangements and the related relocation and international travel per se. It is, therefore, key that the employee is provided with a real, not merely a theoretical, opportunity to refuse such a job offer without there being any impact on his/her career. If the expatriate has a partner or a family, the company should strongly recommend the decision on whether to accept such a job be made jointly as a family. International experiences also affect partners and families in major ways, so they should, therefore, be consulted and have the opportunity to accept or decline the offer. Finally, the decision needs to be an informed decision. Employees, partners and maybe children should be advised of the challenges and the hardships of international postings in general and those of the host country in particular; one of the elements being the difficulty of finding a job for a partner abroad. That issue can be a serious one in some countries where legislation makes it almost impossible. A pre-decision trip to the host country can give the expatriate and his or her partner an accurate impression of the host country. Not following these steps and respecting these guidelines is to risk making employees, partners and families more sensitive to WLC during expatriation and make these issues more difficult to manage in a harmonious way.

Second, companies can provide various types of *practical support* to mitigate WLC (Suutari 2003; Mäkelä and Suutari 2011; Mäkelä et al. 2012; Wurtz and Suutari 2015). Assistance concerning the search for and financing of housing, schools, childcare and housework are appreciated and are often needed because of a lack of knowledge of the host country. Settling-in programmes that can include these elements, help with transportation, communications (phone and internet), social security and administration are valued by international employees. Moreover, international professionals often find themselves in complex situations that require assistance from legal counsellors, pension specialists, insurance advisors and investment and tax consultants that could be provided or financed by the employer organization. The company might also support expatriates and their families in re-creating networks, building relationships and integrating into some communities. It may, for instance, pay for membership of clubs or organize events for partners or families, as well as provide coaching and advice (Wurtz and Suutari 2015).

Third, concerning expatriate' partners; there is strong evidence that for those that worked before expatriating, having to stop working strongly affects not only the partner but also the whole family and the expatriate. This is likely to exacerbate any WLC. Therefore, providing partners with *career-oriented support* to possibly help find a job or support to develop new activities, such as entrepreneurship, studying or volunteering (Lazarova et al. 2015), can be productive options for an employer.

Fourth, companies can take various *specific measures to reduce the impact of work on private life* (Grant-Vallone and Ensher 2001). Reducing work demands is the first option. This includes limiting working hours as well as the workload, number of responsibilities and possibly the number of business trips. Global employees often work long hours and have challenging responsibilities, and keeping them at an acceptable level can limit WLC. Care should thus be taken to ensure the sustainability of the staffing practices in order to ensure that satisfying customer demands does not take place at the expense of the well-being of assignees (Baker and Ciuk 2015). In addition, work resources can be improved: researchers have shown that increasing organizational social support, job control and job clarity help an individual handle work better and reduces conflicts (Kinnunen and Mauno 2008; Michel et al. 2011). Moreover, companies should enable assignees and travellers to exercise greater control over assignment timing and duration (Baker and Ciuk 2015). In addition, flexibility regarding work arrangements facilitates the management of the demands of the private life. Such flexibility might encompass being allowed to work from home at times and having a flexible working schedule in order to attend to domestic issues. Furthermore, providing expatriates with additional leave to travel back to their home country (and possibly supporting them financially by paying some of the associated fares) might also be offered. Allowing an IBT time for recovery after a business trip can be a great help to the employee too. These measures help to maintain relationships with the extended family back in the home country, and it is clear that doing so can, to some extent, reduce the disruption caused by international work. In addition, a supportive work-family culture within the organization should also be promoted (Allen 2001; Anderson et al. 2002; Mauno et al. 2006), lest employees refrain from using the previously mentioned family-friendly arrangements (Anderson et al. 2002). It even appears that "informal workplace practices are more strongly related to worker outcomes than formal policies" (MacDermid and Wittenborn 2007: 566).

Another tool companies can use to help expatriate families abroad is *training on how to manage WLC* and how to limit its detrimental effects. Companies could also utilize stress management policies that acknowledge the importance of identifying and reducing assignment stressors and emphasize the manager's role in implementation (Baker and Ciuk 2015). Finally, expatriate employees and families have very different experiences, different needs and they face different issues. Therefore, companies should customize the support provided to them in order to accurately address their specific needs (Fischlmayr and Kollinger 2010).

Conclusions

As our discussion above indicates, work-life conflict is very common in an international career context. Many of the challenges are quite similar for the different groups of international professionals and their families. At the same time, such challenges appear in slightly different forms in different situations and each type of international work involves certain specific challenges.

In order to avoid building too negative a view of the international career context, it is also good to remember that such careers involve positive WLI experiences. It should be emphasized that the challenges involved can be reduced by carefully planning the jobs and assignments of international professionals and by providing adequate organizational support and training to handle such challenges.

Our review indicates that knowledge of the WLI of global careerists is increasing but we know more about some types of careerist than others. There is more evidence available on the problems affecting assigned expatriates and also on their potential solutions, while other groups such as short-term assignees have received less attention, despite such alternative forms of assignment becoming increasingly common. Similarly, research among self-initiated expatriates is still fairly limited with regard to WLI, although some progress has been made. We could also conclude that, as is typical in international career research, problems have received far more attention than positive aspects such as enrichment in the context of WLI.

References

Adler, Nancy J. 1987. Pacific Basin Managers: A Gaijin, Not a Woman. *Human Resource Management* 26 (2): 169–191.

Allen, Tammy D. 2001. Family-Supportive Work Environments: The Role of Organizational Perceptions. *Journal of Vocational Behavior* 58 (3): 414–435.

Anderson, Stella E., Betty S. Coffey, and Robin T. Byerly. 2002. Formal Organizational Initiatives and Informal Workplace Practices: Links to Work-Family Conflict and Job-Related Outcomes. *Journal of Management* 28 (6): 787–810.

Andres, Manon, René Moelker, and Joseph Soeters. 2012. The Work–Family Interface and Turnover Intentions over the Course of Project-Oriented Assignments Abroad. *International Journal of Project Management* 30 (7): 752–759.

Baker, Charlotte, and Sylwia Ciuk. 2015. "Keeping the Family Side Ticking Along" an Exploratory Study of the Work-Family Interface in the Experiences of Rotational Assignees and Frequent Business Travellers. *Journal of Global Mobility* 3 (2): 137–154.

Bonache, Jaime. 2006. The Compensation of Expatriates: A Review and a Future Research Agenda. In *Handbook of Research in International Human Resource Management*, ed. Gunther Stahl and Ingmar Björkman, 158–175. Cheltenham: Edward Elgar Publishing Limited.

Brookfield Global Relocation Services. 2012. *Global Relocation Trends Survey Report*. Woodridge, IL.

Brookfield Global Relocation Services. 2016. *Global Relocation Trends Survey Report*. Woodridge, IL.

Burkholder, Justin, Ron Joines, Mark Cunningham-Hill, and Xu Baowei. 2010. Health and Well-Being Factors, Associated with International Business Travel. *Journal of Travel Medicine* 17 (5): 329–333.

Caligiuri, Paula, and Jaime Bonache. 2016. Evolving and Enduring Challenges in Global Mobility. *Journal of World Business* 51 (1): 127–141.

Caligiuri, Paula M., Mary Anne M. Hyland, Aparna Joshi, and Allon S. Bross. 1998. Testing a Theoretical Model for Examining the Relationship Between Family Adjustment and Expatriates' Work Adjustment. *Journal of Applied Psychology* 83 (4): 598–614.

Caligiuri, Paula M., and Mila Lazarova. 2005. Expatriate Assignments and Work-Family Conflict. In *International Research in Work and Family*, ed. Steven A.Y. Poelmans, 121–146. Mahwah, NJ: Lawrence Erlbaum Associates.

Cappellen, T. and T. Janssens (2005). Career paths of global managers: Towards future research. *Journal of World Business* 40, 348–360.

Cole, Nina D. 2011. Managing Global Talent: Solving the Partner Adjustment Problem. *The International Journal of Human Resource Management* 22 (7): 1504–1530.

Collings, David G., Anthony McDonnell, and Amy McCarter. 2015. Types of International Assignees. In *The Routledge Companion to International Human Resource Management*, ed. David G. Collings, Goff Wood, and Paula Caligiuri, 259–275. London: Routledge.

Collings, David G., Hugh Scullion, and Michael J. Morley. 2007. Changing Patterns of Global Staffing in the Multinational Enterprise: Challenges to the Conventional Expatriate Assignment and Emerging Alternatives. *Journal of World Business* 42 (2): 198–213.

Davies, Samuel, Albert Kraeh, and Fabian Froese. 2015. Burden or Support? The Influence of Partner Nationality on Expatriate Cross-Cultural Adjustment. *Journal of Global Mobility* 3 (2): 169–182.

DeFrank, Richard S., Robert Konopaske, and John M. Ivancevich. 2000. Executive Travel Stress: Perils of the Road Warrior. *The Academy of Management Executive* 14 (2): 58–71.

Dickmann, Michael. 2013. Why Do They Come to London? Exploring the Motivations of Expatriates to Work in the British Capital. *Journal of Management Development* 31 (8): 783–800.

———. 2016. *The RES Forum Annual Report 2016: Beyond Uniformity—A World of Opportunity*. RES Forum, Harmony Relocation Network and Equus Software, 116 pages, London.

Dickmann, Michael, Noeleen Doherty, Timothy Mills, and Chris Brewster. 2008. Why Do They Go? Individual and Corporate Perspectives on the Factors Influencing the Decision to Accept an International Assignment. *The International Journal of Human Resource Management* 19 (4): 731–751.

Doherty, Noeleen, Michael Dickmann, and Timothy Mills. 2011. Exploring the Motives of Company-Backed and Self-Initiated Expatriates. *The International Journal of Human Resource Management* 22 (3): 595–611.

Espino, C.M., S.M. Sundstrom, H.L. Frick, M. Jacobs, and M. Peters. 2002. International Business Travel: Impact on Families and Travellers. *Occupational and Environmental Medicine* 59 (5): 309–322.

Fischlmayr, Iris C., and Iris Kollinger. 2010. Work-Life Balance—A Neglected Issue Among Austrian Female Expatriates. *The International Journal of Human Resource Management* 21 (4): 455–487.

Fisher, Gwenith G., Carrie A. Bulger, and Carlla S. Smith. 2009. Beyond Work and Family: A Measure of Work/Nonwork Interference and Enhancement. *Journal of Occupational Health Psychology* 14 (4): 441–456.

Forster, Nick. 2000. The Myth of the 'International Manager'. *International Journal of Human Resource Management* 11 (1): 126–142.

Frone, M.R. 2003. Work-Family Balance. In *Handbook of Occupational Health Psychology*, ed. James Campbell Quick and Lois E. Tetrick, 143–162. Washington, DC: American Psychological Association.

Grant-Vallone, Elisa J., and Ellen A. Ensher. 2001. An Examination of Work and Personal Life Conflict, Organizational Support, and Employee Health Among International Expatriates. *International Journal of Intercultural Relations* 25 (3): 261–278.

Harvey, Michael, Helene Mayerhofer, and Linley Hartmann. 2010. Corralling the 'Horses' to Staff the Global Organization of 21st Century. *Organizational Dynamics* 39 (3): 258–268.

IRC/ORC. 2007. *2006/2007 IRC/ORC Expatriate Work-Life Balance Survey.* New York: Industrial Relations Counselors and Organization Resources Counselors, Inc.

Jensen, Marie T. 2013. Exploring Business Travel with Work-Family Conflict and the Emotional Exhaustion Component of Burnout as Outcome Variables: The Job Demands-Resources Perspective. *European Journal of Work and Organizational Psychology* 23 (4): 497–510.

Jokinen, Tiina, Chris Brewster, and Vesa Suutari. 2008. Career Capital during International Work Experiences: Contrasting Self-Initiated Expatriate Experiences and Assigned Expatriation. *International Journal of Human Resource Management* 19 (6): 979–998.

Kinnunen, Ulla, and Saija Mauno. 2008. Work-Family Conflict in Individuals' Lives: Prevalence, Antecedents and Outcomes. In *The Individual in the Changing Working Life*, ed. Katharina Naswall, Johnny Hellgren, and Magnus Sverke, 126–146. Cambridge: Cambridge University Press.

Kohonen, Eeva. 2004. Learning Through Narratives About the Impact of International Assignments on Identity. *International Studies of Management & Organization* 34 (3): 27–45.

———. 2007. *Essays on the Consequences of International Assignments on Expatriates' Identity and Career Aspirations.* Universitas Wasaensis.

Lauring, Jakob, and Jan Selmer. 2010. The Supportive Expatriate Spouse: An Ethnographic Study of Spouse Involvement in Expatriate Careers. *International Business Review* 19 (1): 59–69.

Lazarova, Mila, Yvonne McNulty, and Monika Semeniuk. 2015. Expatriate Family Narratives on International Mobility: Key Characteristics of the Successful Moveable Family. In *Work and Family Interface in the International Career Context*, ed. Liisa Mäkelä and Vesa Suutari, 29–51. New York: Springer.

Lazarova, Mila, Mina Westman, and Margaret A. Shaffer. 2010. Elucidating the Positive Side of the Work-Family Interface on International Assignments: A Model of Expatriate Work and Family Performance. *Academy of Management Review* 35 (1): 93–117.

Linehan, Margaret, and James S. Walsh. 2000. Beyond the Traditional Linear View of International Managerial Careers: A New Model of the Senior Female Career in an International Context. *Journal of European Industrial Training* 24 (2/3/4): 178–189.

Lovvorn, Al S., and Jiun-Shiu Chen. 2011. Developing a Global Mindset: The Relationship Between an International Assignment and Cultural Intelligence. *International Journal of Business and Social Science, Special Issue* 2 (9): 275–283.

MacDermid, Shelley M., and Andrea K. Wittenborn. 2007. Lessons from Work-Life Research for Developing Human Resources. *Advances in Developing Human Resources* 9 (4): 556–568.

Mäkelä, Liisa, Barbara Bergbom, Kati Saarenpää, and Vesa Suutari. 2015a. Work-Family Conflict Faced by International Business Travelers: Do Gender and Parental Status Make a Difference? *Journal of Global Mobility* 3 (2): 155–168.

Mäkelä, Liisa, Barbara Bergbom, Jussi Tanskanen, and Ulla Kinnunen. 2014a. The Relationship between International Business Travel and Sleep Problems Via Work-Family Conflict. *Career Development International* 19 (7): 794–812.

Mäkelä, Liisa, Helen De Cieri, and Audra Mockaitis. 2015b. International Business Traveler, Is Work Always on Your Mind? An Investigation of the Relationship Between Sources of Social Support and Satisfaction with Work-Related International Travel: The Moderating Role of Over-Commitment. In *Work and Family Interface in the International Career Context*, ed. Liisa Mäkelä and Vesa Suutari, 181–195. Hamburg: Springer International Publishing.

Mäkelä, Liisa, Kati Saarenpää, and Yvonne McNulty. 2017. Flexpatriates, Short-Term Assignees and International Commuters. In *Research Handbook of Expatriates*, ed. Yvonne McNulty and Jan Selmer, 276–296. Cheltenham: Edward Elgar.

Mäkelä, Liisa, Kati Saarenpää, Vesa Suutari, and Olivier Wurtz. 2012. How to Cope with Work-Family Conflicts in International Career Context. In *Handbook of the Psychology of Coping: New Research*, ed. Bernando Molinelli and Valentino Grmaldo, 151–168. New York: Nova Science Publishers Ltd.

Mäkelä, Liisa, and Vesa Suutari. 2011. Coping with Work-Family Conflicts in the Global Career Context. *Thunderbird International Business Review* 53 (3): 365–375.

———. 2013. The Work-Life Interface of Self-Initiated Expatriates: Conflicts and Enrichment. In *Talent Management of Self-Initiated Expatriates*, ed. Vlad Vaiman and Arno Haslberger, 278–303. Hampshire: Palgrave Macmillan UK.

———. 2015. *Work and Family Interface in the International Career Context*. Hamburg: Springer International Publishing.

Mäkelä, Liisa, Vesa Suutari, and Chris Brewster. 2014b. The Factors Contributing to Work/Life Conflicts and Enrichment Among Finnish Global Careerists. *Journal of Finnish Studies* 17 (1/2): 225–248.

Mäkelä, Liisa, Vesa Suutari, and Helene Mayerhofer. 2011. Lives of Female Expatriates: Work-Life Balance Concerns. *Gender in Management: An International Journal* 26 (4): 256–274.

Mauno, Saija, Ulla Kinnunen, and Mervi Ruokolainen. 2006. Exploring Work- and Organization-Based Resources as Moderators between Work–Family Conflict, Well-Being, and Job Attitudes. *Work & Stress* 20 (3): 210–233.

Mayerhofer, Helene, Linley C. Hartmann, Gabriela Michelitsch-Riedl, and Iris Kollinger. 2004. Flexpatriate Assignments: A Neglected Issue in Global Staffing. *The International Journal of Human Resource Management* 15 (8): 1371–1389.

Mayerhofer, Helene, Angelika Schmidt, Linley Hartmann, and Regine Bendl. 2011. Recognising Diversity in Managing Work Life Issues of Flexpatriates. *Equality, Diversity and Inclusion: An International Journal* 30 (7): 589–609.

Meyskens, Moriah, Mary Ann Von Glinow, William B. Werther Jr., and Linda Clarke. 2009. The Paradox of International Talent: Alternative Forms of International Assignments. *The International Journal of Human Resource Management* 20 (6): 1439–1450.

Michel, Jesse S., Lindsey M. Kotrba, Jacqueline K. Mitchelson, Malissa A. Clark, and Boris B. Baltes. 2011. Antecedents of Work–Family Conflict: A Meta-Analytic Review. *Journal of Organizational Behavior* 32 (5): 689–725.

Minbaeva, Dana B., and Snejina Michailova. 2004. Knowledge Transfer and Expatriation in Multinational Corporations: The Role of Disseminative Capacity. *Employee Relations* 26 (6): 663–679.

Orthner, Dennis K., and Roderick Rose. 2009. Work Separation Demands and Spouse Psychological Well Being. *Family Relations* 58 (4): 392–403.

Patel, D. 2011. Occupational Travel. *Occupational Medicine* 61 (1): 6–18.

Richardson, Julia. 2006. Self-Directed Expatriation: Family Matters. *Personnel Review* 35 (4): 469–486.

Richardson, Julia, Steve McKenna, Carolyn Dickie, and Clare Kelliher. 2015. Integrating the Work-Life Interface During Expatriation: A Case Study of Expatriate Mining Professionals. In *Work and Family Interface in the International Career Context*, ed. Liisa Mäkelä and Vesa Suutari, 11–28. Hamburg: Springer International Publishing.

Rusconi, Alessandra, Phyllis Moen, and Anna Kaduk. 2013. Career Priorities and Pathways Across the (Gendered) Life Course. In *Handbook of Work-Life Integration among Professionals: Challenges and Opportunities*, ed. Debra Major and Ronald Burke, 95–119. Cheltenham: Edward Elgar.

Saarenpää, Kati. 2016. Stretching the Borders: How International Business Travel Affects the Work–Family Balance. *Community, Work & Family* 21 (1): 1–16. https://doi.org/10.1080/13668803.2016.1170666.

Salleh, Noorziah Mohd, and Jacqueline Koh. 2013. Analysing the Functions of Short-Term Expatriate Assignments. *Procedia-Social and Behavioral Sciences* 107: 34–42.

Shaffer, Margaret A., David A. Harrison, K. Matthew Gilley, and Dora M. Luk. 2001. Struggling for Balance amid Turbulence on International Assignments: Work–Family Conflict, Support and Commitment. *Journal of Management* 27 (1): 99–121.

Shaffer, Margaret A., Maria L. Kraimer, Yu-Ping Chen, and Mark C. Bolino. 2012. Choices, Challenges, and Career Consequences of Global Work Experiences: A Review and Future Agenda. *Journal of Management* 38 (4): 1282–1327.

Shih, Hsi-An, Yun-Hwa Chiang, and Chu-Chun Hsu. 2010. High Involvement Work System, Work–Family Conflict, and Expatriate Performance– Examining Taiwanese Expatriates in China. *The International Journal of Human Resource Management* 21 (11): 2013–2030.

Shortland, Sue, and Siobhan Cummins. 2007. Work-Life Balance: Expatriates Reflect the International Dimension. *Global Business and Organizational Excellence* 26 (6): 28–42.

Stahl, Günter K., and Ingmar Björkman, eds. 2006. *Handbook of Research in International Human Resource Management*. Cheltenham, UK: Edward Elgar Publishing.

Stahl, Gunter, and Jean-Luc Cerdin. 2004. Global Careers in French and German Multinational Corporations. *Journal of Management Development* 23 (9): 885–902.

Starr, Tina L., and Graeme Currie. 2009. Out of Sight but Still in the Picture': Short-Term International Assignments and the Influential Role of Family. *The International Journal of Human Resource Management* 20 (6): 1421–1438.

Suutari, Vesa. 2003. Global Managers: Career Orientation, Career Tracks, Life-Style Implications and Career Commitment. *Journal of Managerial Psychology* 18 (3): 185–207.

Suutari, Vesa, and Chris Brewster. 2000. Making Their Own Way: International Experience Through Self-Initiated Foreign Assignments. *Journal of World Business* 35 (4): 417–436.

———. 2009. Beyond Expatriation: Different Forms of International Employment. In *Handbook of International Human Resource Management: Integrating People, Process and Context*, ed. Paul Sparrow, 131–150. Oxford: John Wiley & Sons.

Suutari, Vesa, Chris Brewster, Kimmo Riusala, and Salla Syrjäkari. 2013. Managing Non-Standard International Experience: Evidence from a Finnish Company. *Journal of Global Mobility* 1 (2): 118–138.

Suutari, Vesa, Christelle Tornikoski, and Liisa Mäkelä. 2012. Career Decision Making of Global Careerists. *The International Journal of Human Resource Management* 23 (16): 3455–3478.

Tahvanainen, Marja, Denice Welch, and Verner Worm. 2005. Implications of Short-Term International Assignments. *European Management Journal* 23 (6): 663–673.

Takeuchi, Riki. 2010. A Critical Review of Expatriate Adjustment Research Through a Multiple Stakeholder View: Progress, Emerging Trends, and Prospects. *Journal of Management* 36 (4): 1040–1064.

Tharenou, Phyllis. 2008. Disruptive Decisions to Leave Home: Gender and Family Differences in Expatriation Choices. *Organizational Behavior and Human Decision Processes* 105 (2): 183–200.

Tharenou, Phyllis, and Natasha Caulfield. 2010. Will I Stay or Will I Go? Explaining Repatriation by Self-Initiated Expatriates. *Academy of Management Journal* 53 (5): 1009–1028.

Wayne, Julie Holliday, Joseph G. Grzywacz, Dawn S. Carlson, and K. Michele Kacmar. 2007. Work-Family Facilitation: A Theoretical Explanation and Model of Primary Antecedents and Consequences. *Human Resource Management Review* 17 (1): 63–76.

Welch, Denice E., and Verner Worm. 2006. International Business Travellers: A Challenge for IHRM. In *Handbook of Research in International Human Resource Management*, ed. Günther K. Stahl and Ingmar Björkman, 283–301. Cheltenham: Edward Elgar Publishing Ltd.

Westman, Mina, and Dalia Etzion. 2002. The Impact of Short Overseas Business Trips on Job Stress and Burnout. *Applied Psychology* 51 (4): 582–592.

Westman, Mina, Dalia Etzion, and Shoshi Chen. 2009. Crossover of Positive Experiences from Business Travelers to Their Spouses. *Journal of Managerial Psychology* 24 (3): 269–284.

Wurtz, Olivier. 2014. An Empirical Investigation of the Effectiveness of Pre-Departure and in-Country Cross-Cultural Training. *The International Journal of Human Resource Management* 25 (14): 2088–2101.

Wurtz, Olivier, and Vesa Suutari. 2015. Work–Life Balance and Coping of International Assignees. In *The Routledge Companion to International Human Resource Management*, ed. David G. Collings, Goff Wood, and Paula Caligiuri, 363–377. London: Routledge.

12

Compensating Global Careerists

Celia Zárraga-Oberty and Jaime Bonache

Introduction

Compensation is a key strategic component of the management of international assignments. It is, nonetheless, the area to which the academic literature has paid the least attention, focusing instead almost exclusively on business practice. Over these first years of the twenty-first century, the compensation of international assignees has undergone numerous changes, although there still lacks a holistic proposal that addresses all the challenges and difficulties present in this field (McNulty 2014; Caligiuri and Bonache 2016).

This chapter sets out to lay the foundations for this holistic proposal. We shall begin by analysing the traditional systems of expatriate

---

This work was supported by the Spanish Ministry of Economy: Grant Number: ECO2015-68343-R.

C. Zárraga-Oberty (✉) • J. Bonache
Department of Business Administration, Carlos III University of Madrid, Madrid, Spain
e-mail: czarraga@emp.uc3m.es; bonache@emp.uc3m.es

© The Author(s) 2018   **319**
M. Dickmann et al. (eds.), *The Management of Global Careers*,
https://doi.org/10.1007/978-3-319-76529-7_12

compensation, explaining how they work, while at the same time singling out the problems they generate. We shall continue by describing today's new compensation trends and arrangements, studying the extent to which they resolve the issues surrounding traditional systems. Once the traditional and the new in this field have been analysed, we shall propose the approach according to which, in our view, the compensation of international assignees should be considered within today's context.

The Traditional Arrangement for Compensating Expatriates

The traditional arrangement for compensating expatriates is referred to as the balance sheet approach (Solomon 1995). This system, for which we shall be providing a detailed explanation in due course, was designed with the classic figure of an expatriate in mind, namely, an employee from a multinational's country of origin or from one of its subsidiaries that is posted abroad to take up a management position for a relatively long period of time (Phillips and Fox 2003).

The overall strategy of the balance sheet system involves attracting, retaining and motivating employees to accept a posting anywhere in the world, whereby such assignments, compared to the terms and conditions of employment in the assignee's home country, are at least equally attractive. In operational terms, this is achieved by raising the basic salary in the country of origin through a series of allowances that enable expatriates to maintain their purchasing power in the home country, pay no more taxes or contributions than they would at home and be rewarded for "the sacrifice" they are making when accepting an international posting.

These allowances are always made in terms of the following items:

- *Goods and services*: making up for the cost differentials between home and host countries (food, clothing, leisure, health, transport and children's schooling).
- *Housing*: compensating the expatriate for the need to rent a new home.
- *Taxes and contributions* (social security contributions and income tax): expatriates are compensated for any differences in taxation, whereby

they never pay more than they would if they had remained in their home country, also referred to as tax equalization.

- *Incentives or assignment premium*: typically a percentage of the salary. This percentage has been steadily reduced over time. At the end of the twentieth century, this could be as much as 50 per cent of the salary (Hodgetts and Luthans 1997), whereas now it is almost never more than 15 per cent (Phillips and Fox 2003).
- *Performance* bonuses.
- *Others*: such as reimbursement for lost income for the "trailing" spouse/significant other (Reynolds and Bennett 1995).

Thus defined, this compensation system is referred to as the home-country balance sheet approach. In other words, the basic salary the expatriate would receive in their home country is paid and the above allowances are added on.

In some cases, the levels of compensation are significantly higher in the host country, which means the salary there is the one used for reference purposes. In this case, only a housing allowance is paid, along with an additional amount under the item of an assignment premium. We are therefore referring to a system called the host-country balance sheet approach.

Finally, there is the case of the global balance sheet approach, which is used by multinational corporations (MNCs) with numerous employees in different countries, who in turn plan to move between countries, that is, forgoing any direct link to the salary structure in both the home and host countries (O'Really 1996). This means salaries are paid according to an international scale with allowances added onto the base. An international shopping basket of goods and services is used for all expatriates, regardless of their country of origin (Bonache and Stirpe 2012).

Nevertheless, despite firms' overwhelming use of the home-country balance sheet approach, as shown in Table 12.1, it is not without its criticisms and difficulties (Bonache and Zárraga-Oberty 2016). There now follows an analysis of the main shortfalls and drawbacks of this very widely used compensation system.

322   C. Zárraga-Oberty and J. Bonache

Table 12.1 Traditional expatriate compensation systems

	Home-country balance sheet	Host-country balance sheet	Global balance sheet
Reference	Basic salary at origin	Basic salary at destination	International standard
Allowances	Cost of living Housing Taxes and contributions Incentives Performance bonuses Others…	Housing Assignment premium	–
Level of use (Mercer 2015)	74%	17%	13%

Source: The authors

Main Drawbacks of the Traditional Expatriate Compensation System

The system was introduced with a series of clearly defined objectives: to be cost-effective, uphold fairness and to satisfy expatriates with a view to attracting, retaining and motivating them in the direction intended by the MNC (Reynolds 1997). However, when judged in the light of these same objectives, the home-country balance sheet approach faces a number of issues. Drawing on the study by Bonache and Zárraga-Oberty (2016), these may be summarized as follows:

- *The system incurs high costs for the firm in both gross and management terms.* This is the most frequent criticism of this compensation system, as it is well known to make international assignments a very expensive option. Indeed, according to the Mercer report (2015), the cost of international staff when compared to their domestic counterparts (same level and category) when using this system is 2.4 times higher. Apart from the direct costs, there are certain indirect costs associated with this compensation system that should not be dismissed (Nowak and Linder 2016). Specifically, it is a system that its implementation requires constant supervision by experts, with the additional costs this implies.

- *Perception of injustice among host-country nationals.* As noted earlier, the system aims to ensure an expatriate retains the purchasing power they would have had at home, which is used as the basis for building up the overall pay package. This means disregarding host-country nationals (HCNs), who are very likely to receive a lower remuneration than the expatriate (as their salary will normally be set according to the scale in force in the host country) while often performing almost the same tasks as the expatriate. In the light of equity or fairness theory (Adams 1963, 1965; Mowday 1991), this will lead to a perception of injustice among HCNs, which will undoubtedly impact negatively on business performance.

  Equity theory is based on two key issues: the ratio of contributions (inputs) to rewards (outputs) and reference groups. The value of the exchange to the individual depends on the output/input ratio, where inputs include comprehensive investments (i.e., intelligence, education, skills, experience) and outputs refer to the inducements (i.e., money, esteem and status) that an employee receives from the organization. Additionally, the value of those exchanges is not created in a vacuum. Individuals judge the fairness of their exchange relationships within the organization by comparing the balance between their output/input ratio and their reference groups. The norm of equity is defined as balanced outcome/input ratios (Carrell and Dittrich 1978). In our case, HCNs will perceive unfairness because their output/input ratio is lower than the expatriates', with expatriates constituting their reference group. This problem of perceived injustice is so important that several studies have set out to identify the factors that may remove, or at least mitigate, such a perception (Chen et al. 2002; Paik et al. 2007; Bonache et al. 2009; Leung et al. 2009).

- *The system provides no assurance of expatriate satisfaction.* Just like any other employee, in most cases expatriates are dissatisfied with their salaries (Black et al. 1992; Bonache 2005; Gomez-Mejia et al. 2006). Furthermore, the analyses conducted on the sources of this dissatisfaction (Phillips and Fox 2003) single out issues involving the assessment they make of their allowances: they are considered factors of hygiene in the sense propounded by Herzberg (1968), whereby they do not heighten satisfaction when granted, yet they lead to dissatisfaction when not.

- *The system does not guarantee the retention of expatriates.* Repatriation is one of the classic and as-yet pending issues of international assignments (Caligiuri and Bonache 2016). One of the aims of the home-country balance sheet compensation system is precisely to retain expatriates when they return home. However, research has reported high rates of turnover among repatriates (Adler 1984; Black 1988; Black et al. 1992; Stahl et al. 2009). In fact, past research on US companies suggests that between 20 and 25 per cent of repatriated employees leave their firms within a year after their return (Black et al. 1992). More recent studies have found that repatriate turnover is twice as high compared to non-expatriated peers (Doherty and Dickmann 2012). Some companies have reported losing as many as half of their repatriates through voluntary turnover within three years after repatriation (Black et al. 1999).

Taking this evidence into account, it is clear that the problem does not appear to be easy to solve. Numerous explanations have been proposed for this situation, mostly seeking to shed light on the "reverse culture shock" that expatriates experience upon returning to their home country (Selmer 1999; Bonache and Brewster 2001). It is clear that compensation is not everything, but it has a role to play. The incentives and allowances designed to encourage employees to take up a foreign assignment are not sustained when the expatriate returns home, leading to a substantial loss of income (Harvey 1993). In the light of the prospect theory (Kahneman and Tversky 1984), this situation becomes the trigger of turnover intention. This theory is based on the principle that we hate losing more than we love winning.

Let us consider two expatriates that at the time of their repatriation have the same degree of satisfaction with their salary, although one has a higher salary than the other one (one has been compensated with a traditional expatriate salary, while the other has been hired according to local terms and conditions). Upon their return, they are both offered a new salary package, which in the first of these two cases means, for example, a 10 per cent reduction, while for the second it means a 10 per cent increase on their host-country income. The first will experience a sharp drop in their satisfaction with their salary that will prompt them to look for an opening elsewhere, in another company. By contrast, the second one will experience a certain degree of satisfaction, but not overly so, as they will consider it is no more than they deserve. In short, we contend that generous expatriate salary packages drive high expatriate turnover (Bonache and Zárraga-Oberty 2016).

* *The compensation system blocks an expatriate's cultural integration.* An international experience is said to be the main way of shaping the outlook and capabilities of true global leaders (Black, et al. 1999). Furthermore, 23 per cent of firms now single out management development as one of the main goals of international assignments (Brookfield 2015). Nevertheless, it is well known that simply breathing the air of a foreign country is not enough for this development (Caligiuri and Bonache 2016). Precisely because of its purpose of maintaining expatriate purchasing power in the country of origin, the home-country balance sheet compensation system does not mean that expatriates fully understand the reality of the environment in which they are living and working and do not develop true intercultural skills and capabilities.

Besides all these drawbacks of the compensation system, the context of this highly globalized twenty-first century has shaped a new scenario for global mobility, with profiles for international assignments that have little to do with traditional expatriates. Let us now review these profiles and then analyse how the compensation system has changed to integrate the new forms of international mobility.

Compensating New Global Careerists

The traditional expatriate compensation system (home-country balance sheet) assumes that expatriates are parent company employees, generally top managers, who will return home after one or more assignments lasting between three and five years. This means that upholding internal fairness with their peers back home is one of the inescapable premises of the compensation system. Nevertheless, this is no longer such a common occurrence in the world of international assignments. The environment has changed and with it, the expatriate profile. In today's globalized world, in which transport and communications have ceased to be an issue, traditional expatriates are being replaced by other forms of international assignment that are less costly for firms and more project based.

Globalization has brought greater flexibility (geographical and temporal) and a broader range of contractual relationships (Banai and Harry 2004). In particular, contractual relationships (based on long-term service and loyalty) have been replaced by transactional ones (project based) (Herriot and Pemberton 1995).

In turn, careers are more self-managed than guided by the organization and thus more defined by greater inter-organizational mobility. This change has also been seen in the expatriate field. Specifically, there has been a rise in the number of self-initiated expatriates who follow a different logic to that of their traditional counterparts. Their reasons for being attracted by an international assignment extend beyond the boundaries of the organization employing them, often being rooted in their personal and family life. Moreover, employees deliberately seek permanent international transfers as a step forward in their professional careers, even though this might not mean more pay (Collings et al. 2007). In fact, the Brookfield Global Mobility Trends (2016) survey reports that 61 per cent of those surveyed acknowledged that their firms have explicitly told them that accepting an international assignment is an important career move.

Finally, one should mention the increased delocalization of business operations through offshoring and other international management initiatives (Caligiuri et al. 2010; Creven Fourrier and Point, Chap. 7 in this book). As a result of this tendency, many people are forced to work abroad if they want to keep their job at the firm, yet the posting may be for an indefinite period of time and often with no possibility of returning home. According to Mercer (2015), these so-called one-way transfers are used in 63 per cent of firms, and 54 per cent expect their use to increase over the next two years.

The following figure shows the current percentages of use of the different types of international assignments we are dealing with. In this figure, the authors considered more than one year to be a "long-term assignment" and, accordingly, they mapped the different profiles of international assignments in the highly globalized twenty-first century.

Like the research findings in the field of international assignments, they cannot be wholly understood without clearly delimiting the nature of the international assignment we are referring to (Tharenou 2015) or the compensation system being applied. Therefore, in the light of the range of situations described in Fig. 12.1, new compensation systems have emerged that we shall describe in more detail.

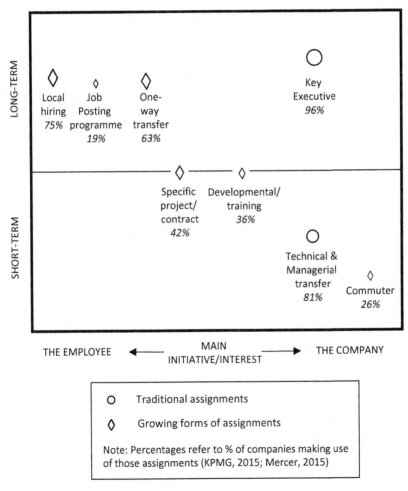

Fig. 12.1 Current types of global mobility within MNCs. Source: The authors (Bonache and Zárraga-Oberty 2016)

Increasingly Popular Compensation Arrangements: Local-Plus and Localization

The compensation systems that have emerged as an alternative to the traditional home-country balance sheet arrangement are referred to as local-plus and localization (McNulty 2014). We shall now describe how they work and then analyse the extent to which these systems resolve the traditional system's aforementioned drawbacks and shortfalls.

Description

With the local-plus system, an expatriate receives a salary that is consistent with the pay scales in the host country, but it is raised by a series of allowances, such as those for transport, housing and their children's schooling. The package of allowances is not the same for all expatriates. The decision is made by the firm, being determined largely by the assignment's location (i.e., the location's degree of hardship), among other factors (Stanley 2009).

It is clear that the workings of the local-plus compensation system are the same as those of the host-country balance sheet. We might therefore infer that local-plus is not an innovative compensation system. Yet in fact, given that the change involves the reasons for its application, that is, while the host-country balance sheet was used as a system for traditional expatriates when levels of compensation were significantly higher in the host country than in the home one, local-plus is currently being applied independently of the differences in the level of compensation between home and host countries.

The localization system simply means that the expatriate receives a salary that is consistent with the salary levels in their posting destination or where they were already living and working. In short, localization for the person involved implies the removal or absence of "expatriate" status in terms of company policy, which includes allowances and premiums (McNulty 2014).

When referring to a localization system, it is important to avoid any possible confusion stemming from the term's use in other areas of international assignments. We sometimes use localization to refer to the replacement of expatriates by local talent (i.e., HCNs). This use of localization is not the one applicable within the scope of compensation. In this last case, localized employees may therefore be HCNs or involve postings from other countries. This means that localization does not involve replacing expatriates with HCNs but instead the transition of assignees to local salary terms and conditions, whereby they blend into the local workforce.

The local-plus and localization remuneration systems can be applied in the following two ways:

- *From the start of the employee's assignment.* The employee is aware from the start that they will be paid according to the local-plus system, or directly "localized", and so the company has no responsibility regarding their repatriation or reassignment. This avoids the problems the traditional system posed in terms of repatriation, although as we shall argue in due course, it may lead to problems of a different kind.

  A local-plus compensation package is sometimes offered to a "one-way transfer" during the initial settling-in period (no more than two years) to ease the transition to the localized compensation system. This means that staff posted abroad are seen as expatriates upon arrival, as they are neither "immigrants" nor HCNs.

- *After a period of time as an expatriate paid according to the traditional balance sheet system.* Consider the following case: an expatriate begins an international assignment according to the balance sheet system and then, after a period of between three and five years, they transition to local-plus or directly become localized. This has sometimes been preordained in the initial contract on the international assignment, whereby the employee already knew that this change would be applied to them; but on other occasions the situation arises once the posting has concluded, as a means of extending it. This change obviously involves a reduction in the compensation package, which explains why transition periods tend to be used during which the special allowances typically granted to expatriates (e.g., transport, housing, health insurance and children's schooling) are gradually reduced. Nevertheless, it should be noted that reducing this compensation leads to problems, as it affects the "psychological contract" entered into with the employee (McNulty 2014). This may logically have negative repercussions for the firm.

Assessment of New Proposals

The local-plus and localization compensation systems are an alternative to the balance sheet arrangement. Their advocates contend that they adapt better to the new scenario for global mobility in the highly globalized twenty-first century. Whether this is true or not, it is important to assess the extent to which they manage to redress the traditional system's drawbacks as described earlier.

- *Impact on costs.* The local-plus and localization systems clearly reduce the firm's costs, in both gross and management terms. In fact, the 2012 Brookfield Global Relocation Services study, for example, reported that one-third of the 123 companies in their study used "one-way moves", considering them to be an effective cost-reducing tool compared to traditional international assignments (balance sheet).
- *Are they fairer?* The new compensation systems do not appear to generate problems of fairness among HCNs, as the expatriates ultimately end up blending in with local staff as just another employee (McNulty 2014). Nevertheless, some additional reward components, such as many companies paying private education for localized staff's children or, albeit rarely, some return travel, may still lead to some feeling of unfairness by host employees (Dickmann 2017).

  Nevertheless, if the firm uses the local-plus or localization systems in parallel with the balance sheet arrangement, the issue of the perception of injustice shifts onto new incoming employees from abroad when they compare themselves to the expatriates that continue to be paid according to the traditional arrangement. This perception may be a cause of greater staff turnover. Furthermore, we lack the evidence to know the extent to which the new systems may lead, from the perspective of the expatriates themselves to problems of unfairness with other groups (e.g., expatriates in more or less attractive postings, HCNs with local allowances that are not granted to international staff).

Compensating Global Careerists 331

- *Do they generate greater satisfaction?* When we consider the triggers of expatriates' dissatisfaction with the traditional system described here, there is nothing to suggest that these new systems will sweep them away. In fact, they may even make them worse in certain cases. The debate over the allowances to be included will likewise continue with a local-plus compensation system. It is obvious that reaching an agreement on the nature and amount of those allowances is no easy matter to manage. Moreover, the problem of perceiving these allowances as a factor of hygiene is especially important with the local-plus system. The premium the firm pays to compensate the person assigned abroad is not seen as a motivating factor when it is received, but it does lead to considerable dissatisfaction when not (Herzberg 1968). This dissatisfaction may therefore be expected to increase when the posting is subject to the local-plus system for a period of time and then transitions to a localization arrangement.
- *Does this help to retain international staff?* As we have already mentioned, the new compensation system eliminates the repatriation stage. We may therefore assume that it removes a problem. But this is not the case. Although there is no longer an issue of retaining international staff when they return from their posting (unless they return to a comparatively less attractive context), the problem of retaining staff while they are actually on their international assignment is aggravated. Throughout the entire posting the firm has to deal with local competition. These new compensation systems mean that employees' opportunity cost is greatly reduced and they will therefore be more willing to swap their allegiance more readily than if they were subject to the traditional balance sheet system. This therefore clearly increases the firm's risk of losing employees with a high overall potential (McNulty 2014). The Brookfield Global Relocation Trends study (2012) has indicated that the retention of international staff is a problem because 22 per cent of expatriates now leave their jobs before the assignment period is over. It stands to reason that if ever greater use has been made in recent years of the local-plus and localization compensation systems, this percentage will only increase. As McNulty (2014: 10) affirms: "assignees that perceive they are not sufficiently supported or 'valued' by a company, in comparison to other types of expatriates, are at risk of

looking for job opportunities with competitors because they are working in a business environment where there are lucrative career opportunities available elsewhere".

- *Do they foster cultural integration?* We should remember that the traditional system was an obstacle to the cultural integration of expatriates. The new compensation systems will clearly mean diminishing this obstacle, as international assignees are less likely to be considered expatriates and may be blending in more with the local workforce.

Overall, the new systems for compensating international assignees have some advantages (e.g., they foster cultural integration and reduce costs), but they are not without their drawbacks. Out of all of these, we would like to highlight the one involving the risk of a larger turnover of high value-added staff (qualified personnel that accept an international posting). The opportunity cost of leaving the firm for international staff is very low both in terms of salary (they do not receive the traditionally high pay packages) and emotionally (psychological contract) as they do not generate an employment relationship whereby they are obliged to give more because they receive more.

The problem we are referring to is consistent with a topic that is receiving growing attention in the specialized literature: the problem of critical talent retention in a firm (McNulty 2014; Cerdin and Brewster 2014). The next section develops this notion, which we consider to be the foundation upon which to build a new twenty-first-century model for the compensation of international staff.

Costs and Competitive Advantage in the Compensation of New Global Careerists

From a costing perspective, the shift from the traditional expatriate compensation system (home-country balance sheet) to today's local-plus and localization arrangements is a major step forward. The latter arrangements obviously reduce a firm's costs. Furthermore, it is to be assumed that these new pay policies mean that those subsidiaries unable to deal with major expenses (as incurred by traditional expatriates) will be able to deploy qualified staff of this kind. What's more, within such a global

Compensating Global Careerists 333

scenario as the one we are in today, it should not be difficult to find talented young people seeking to enrich their career with international experience. There will also be former expatriates that are unable to happily resettle in their home country and will prefer to continue living abroad. There will also be employees that for different reasons (e.g., assignment of their life partner, experience for their children) will apply for a foreign posting (Mercer 2015). With these three groups of employees, it does not appear likely that a firm will find it difficult to cover its international assignments.

Let us now focus on the first group: the international assignee accepts the posting for reasons of their own professional development. The employee in this case is not expected to be highly committed to the firm. As soon as they receive a better offer (in order to further their professional career), they will take it and leave the company at the drop of a hat. This makes it very difficult for the firm to retain talent. In other words, international assignees have become what the resource-based view of the firm refers to as an "easily transferable" resource, which can never be the source of a sustainable competitive advantage[1].

Costing can therefore be used to justify the developments affecting the compensation system applied to international assignees, but, from a perspective more focused on strategic human resources, this solution does not seem quite so satisfactory. As Collings and Mellahi (2009: 305) note, talent management involves identifying key positions that "differentially contribute to the organization's sustainable competitive advantage". A local-plus or localization compensation policy for international assignments does not clarify the extent to which it responds to an action.

It is clear that up to now the research into expatriation has been and continues to be conducted without a clear link to talent management. This needs to start changing. Nevertheless, integrating expatriate management into broader HRM policies, with particular stress on career management, requires a change of mindset in organizations, shifting from a basically administrative approach (salary and conditions) to another more strategic one (Cerdin and Brewster 2014). Not all international

---

[1] Grant (1991:112) states that a firm's "crown jewels" are its "most important resources and capabilities [...] which are durable, difficult to identify and understand, imperfectly transferable, not easily replicated, and in which the firm possesses clear ownership and control".

assignments have the same strategic value for a firm. The lesser ones could be addressed with compensation systems in which costs take centre stage. By contrast, when the international assignment has a strategic value for the firm, the compensation system should reflect this. To date, the expatriate compensation system that actually does so is the home-country balance sheet. Nonetheless, this need not be the only system. Scholars such as McNulty (2014) posit the need to continue advancing towards a change of mentality that will lead us to devise a global compensation system based on a psychological contract to stimulate the retention of those employees that guarantee the firm's competitive present and future.

To conclude, Table 12.2 provides an overview of the main learning points addressed here.

Table 12.2 Summary

Learning points	IHRM pract.	IHRM resear.
Traditional expatriate compensation system: *balance sheet*	X	
• Home-country balance sheet approach		
• Host-country balance sheet approach		
• Global balance sheet approach		
Drawbacks of traditional expatriate compensation system:		X
• High costs for the firms		
• Perception of injustice among HCNs (equity theory)		
• No assurance of expatriate satisfaction (Herzberg theory)		
• No guarantee of retention of repatriates (prospect theory)		
• Block an expat's cultural integration		
New global careerist: *new profiles of IAs*	X	X
• Transactional relationships (no contractual ones)		
• Project based (no long-term service and loyalty)		
• Short-term assignees		
• Self-managed careers (SIEs)		
• Inter-organizational mobility		
• One-way transfers (consequence of offshoring)		
New compensation system:	X	
• *Local-plus*		
• *Localization* (no expat status!)		
Application methods:		
• From the start of the IA		
• After a period as a traditional expat		

(continued)

Compensating Global Careerists   335

Table 12.2 (continued)

Learning points	IHRM pract.	IHRM resear.
Assessment of new compensation system: • Low costs • Fairness with HCNs, but not among expatriates • No assurance of expatriate satisfaction (Herzberg) • No guarantee of the retention of expatriates (during the IA) • Favourable to cultural integration		X

Implications:
• New source of IAs:
  – Young people seeking to enrich their career with low commitment to the firm
    – Former expats. Want to continue living abroad
    – No professional reason to live abroad
• Problems of talent retention
• Difference to psychological contract
		X

Source: The authors

Although all the points are of interest to the IHRM community, we distinguish between those of greater relevance for practitioners and those more pertinent for researchers. In the latter case, new research streams are prompted, especially regarding the implications of new compensation systems for international staff. The traditional lack of attention academia has paid to the issue of compensating international staff should be redressed. Empirical research is required to provide valid and reliable conclusions for improving management practice.

Practical Case[2]

Lena Schweizer, the HR manager of an MNC providing industrial services, is slightly concerned and somewhat confused, as she has long been exploring the possibility of moving away from the balance sheet approach to compensate international assignees. She now has to design the compensation package for a senior industrial engineer called Peter

---

[2] This practical case is a wholly fictional work by the authors, for example, purposes only. The names are pseudonyms and do not refer to anyone.

336 C. Zárraga-Oberty and J. Bonache

Becker. Peter has six years' experience in the firm; he is 42 years old, married and has two children (aged 6 and 8 years, respectively). The company headquarters is in *Alfa*, but Peter is going to be posted to *Beta*. *Beta* is a country with a higher standard of living than *Alfa*, which is proven by a goods and services index of 139 points (i.e., the cost of living (G&S) in *Beta* is 39 per cent higher than in *Alfa*). Peter's job in *Alfa* would be to provide engineering services, advice on industrial engineering activities and prepare reports reviewing production methods, equipment layout, and equipment and material utilization.

As mentioned, the company applies the balance sheet approach to calculate the compensation for an international assignment and, in particular, the home-country balance sheet approach. However, Lena is thinking about changing the system. The company's competitors in the industry

Table 12.3 The case of an assignee posted from *Alfa* to *Beta*

	A	B	C	D	E	F
1			Name	*Peter*	*Becker*	
2			Home country	*Alfa*	Host country	*Beta*
3			Family size	*4*	G&S index	*135*
4	Annual base pay	*48081*				
5	Goods and services spendable	*21035*				
6	Goods and services differential					
7	Foreign housing cost	*10818*				
8	Home-country housing norm	*4357*				
9	Foreign service premium (15%)					
10	Hardship allowance					
11	Other premiums					
12	Hypothetical tax					
13	*Net compensation*					
14	Portion paid in host country					
15	Portion paid in home country					

Source: The authors

Compensating Global Careerists   **337**

are starting to compensate according to the "local-plus" system. She therefore thinks that the time may have come to change.

In order to make an informed decision, Lena wants to know the figures in order to understand the real impact of the decision made.

You can help her by answering the following questions:

1. Table 12.3 provides some data for the case of an assignee posted from *Alfa* to *Beta*. Complete this sheet by assuming that you are not paying any amount for a hardship allowance or any other premiums.

2. If Lena, the HR Manager wants to use the "local-plus" approach:

   (a) What information does she need?
   (b) What key decisions does she have to make?
   (c) What challenges, advantages and difficulties will she have to face if she finally opts for a different compensation system for Peter and newly appointed international assignees?

References

Adams, J. Stacy. 1963. Wage Inequities, Productivity and Work Quality. *Industrial Relations* 3 (1): 9–39.

———. 1965. Inequity in Social Exchange. In *Advances in Experimental Social Psychology*, ed. Leonard Berkowitz, 267–299. New York: Academic Press.

Adler, Nancy J. 1984. Expecting International Success: Female Managers Overseas. *Columbia Journal of World Business* 19 (3): 79–85.

Banai, Moshe, and Wes Harry. 2004. Boundaryless Global Careers: The International Itinerants. *International Studies of Management and Organization* 34 (3): 96–120.

Black, J. Stewart. 1988. Work Role Transitions: A Study of American Expatriate Managers in Japan. *Journal of International Business Studies* 19 (2): 277–294.

Black, J. Stewart, Hal B. Gregersen, and Mark E. Mendenhall. 1992. Toward a Theoretical Framework of Repatriation Adjustment. *Journal of International Business Studies* 23 (4): 737–760.

Black, J. Stewart, Hal B. Gregersen, Mark E. Mendenhall, and Linda K. Stroh. 1999. *Globalizing People through International Assignment*. Reading, MA: Addison-Wesley.

Bonache, Jaime. 2005. Job Satisfaction Among Expatriates, Repatriates and Domestic Employees: The Perceived Impact of International Assignments on Work-Related Variables. *Personnel Review* 34 (1): 110–124.

Bonache, Jaime, and Chris Brewster. 2001. Knowledge Transfer and the Management of Expatriation. *Thunderbird International Business Review* 43 (1): 145–168.

Bonache, Jaime, J.I. Sánchez, and Celia Zárraga-Oberty. 2009. The Interaction of Expatriate Pay Differential and Expatriate Inputs on Host Country Nationals' Pay Unfairness. *The International Journal of Human Resource Management* 20 (10): 2135–2149.

Bonache, Jaime, and Luigi Stirpe. 2012. Compensating Global Employees. In *Handbook of Research in International Human Resource Management*, ed. Günter Stahl and Ingmar Bjökman, 162–182. Cheltenham, UK: Edward Elgar.

Bonache, Jaime, and Celia Zárraga-Oberty. 2016. The Traditional Approach to Compensating Global Mobility: Criticisms and Alternatives. *The International Journal of Human Resource Management* 28 (1): 1–21.

Brookfield Global Relocation Services. 2012. *Global Relocation Trends Survey Report*. Woodridge, IL: Brookfield Global Relocation Services.

———. 2015. *Global Relocation Trends Survey Report*. Woodridge, IL: Brookfield Global Relocation Services.

Brookfield Global Mobility Trends. 2016. *Global Mobility Trends Survey*. Woodridge, IL: Brookfield Global Relocation Services.

Caligiuri, Paula, and Jaime Bonache. 2016. Evolving and Enduring Challenges in Global Mobility. *Journal of World Business* 51 (1): 127–141.

Caligiuri, Paula, David Lepak, and Jaime Bonache. 2010. *Managing the Global Workforce*. Chichester: John Wiley and Sons.

Carrell, Michael R., and John E. Dittrich. 1978. Equity Theory: The Recent Literature, Methodological Considerations and New Directions. *Academy of Management Review* 3 (2): 202–210.

Cerdin, Jean-Luc, and Chris Brewster. 2014. Talent Management and Expatriation: Bridging Two Streams of Research and Practice. *Journal of World Business* 49 (2): 245–252.

Chen, Chao C., Jaepil Choi, and Shu-Cheng Chi. 2002. Making Justice Sense of Local-Expatriate Compensation Disparity: Mitigation by Local Referents, Ideological Explanations, and Interpersonal Sensitivity in China-Foreign Joint Ventures. *Academy of Management Journal* 45 (4): 807–817.

Collings, David G., and Kamel Mellahi. 2009. Strategic Talent Management: A Review and Research Agenda. *Human Resource Management Review* 19 (4): 304–313.

Collings, David G., Hugh Scullion, and Michael J. Morley. 2007. Changing Patterns of Global Staffing in the Multinational Enterprise: Challenges to the Conventional Expatriate Assignment and Emerging Alternatives. *Journal of World Business* 42 (2): 198–213.

Dickmann, Michael. 2017. *The RES Forum Annual Report 2017: The New Normal of Global Mobility—Flexibility, Diversity & Data Mastery*. RES Forum, Harmony Relocation Network and Equus Software, London.

Doherty, Noeleen, and Michael Dickmann. 2012. Measuring the Return on Investment in International Assignments: An Action Research Approach. *International Journal of Human Resource Management* 23 (16): 3434–3454.

Gomez-Mejia, Luis R., David B. Balkin, and Robert L. Cardy. 2006. *Management: People, Performance, Change*. Boston: McGraw-Hill Irwin.

Grant, Robert M. 1991. The Resource-Based Theory of Competitive Advantage: Implications for Strategy Formulation. *California Management Review* 33 (3): 114–135.

Harvey, Michael G. 1993. Empirical Evidence of Recurring International Compensation Problems. *Journal of International Business Studies* 24 (4): 785–799.

Herriot, Peter, and Carole Pemberton. 1995. *Competitive Advantage through Diversity: Organizational Learning from Difference*. Thousand Oaks: Sage Publications, Inc.

Herzberg, Frederick. 1968. *One More Time: How Do You Motivate Employees?* 46–57. Boston, MA: Harvard Business Review.

Hodgetts, Richard, and Fred Luthans. 1997. Managing Organizational Culture and Diversity. *International Management*, McGraw-Hill.

Kahneman, Daniel, and Amos Tversky. 1984. Choices, Values, and Frames. *American Psychologist* 39 (4): 341–350.

Leung, Kwok, Yongxin Zhu, and Cungen Ge. 2009. Compensation Disparity Between Locals and Expatriates: Moderating the Effects of Perceived Injustice in Foreign Multinationals in China. *Journal of World Business* 44 (1): 85–93.

McNulty, Yvonne. 2014. The Opportunity Costs of Local-Plus and Localization Approaches to Expatriate Compensation. In *The Compensation Handbook*, ed. Lance Berger and Dorothy Berger, 6th ed. Columbus, OH: McGraw-Hill Education.

Mercer. 2015. *Worldwide Survey of International Assignment Policies and Practices.* Geneva: Mercer.

Mowday, Richard T. 1991. Equity Theory Perceptions of Behavior in Organizations. In *Motivation and Work Behavior*, ed. Richard M. Steers and Lyman W. Porter, 111–131. New York: McGraw-Hill Publishers.

Nowak, Christian, and Christian Linder. 2016. Do You Know How Much Your Expatriate Costs? An Activity-Based Cost Analysis of Expatriation. *Journal of Global Mobility* 4 (1): 88–107.

O'Really, M. 1996. Expatriate Pay: The State of the Art. *Compensation and Benefits Review* 12 (1): 54–60.

Paik, Yongsun, K. Praveen Parboteeah, and Wonshul Shim. 2007. The Relationship between Perceived Compensation, Organizational Commitment and Job Satisfaction: The Case of Mexican Workers in the Korean Maquiladoras. *The International Journal of Human Resource Management* 18 (10): 1768–1781.

Phillips, Larry, and Mark A. Fox. 2003. Compensation Strategy in Transnational Corporations. *Management Decision* 41 (5): 465–476.

Reynolds, Calvin. 1997. Expatriate Compensation in Historical Perspective. *Journal of World Business* 32 (2): 118–132.

Reynolds, Calvin, and Rita Bennett. 1995. The Career Couple Challenge. *Personnel Journal* 74 (9): 1–4.

Selmer, Jan. 1999. Effects of Coping Strategies on Sociocultural and Psychological Adjustment of Western Expatriate Managers in the PRC. *Journal of World Business* 34 (1): 41–51.

Solomon, Robert C. 1995. *A Passion for Justice: Emotions and the Origins of the Social Contract.* Lanham, MA: Rowman and Littlefield.

Stahl, Günter K., Chei Hwee Chua, Paula Caligiuri, Jean-Luc Cerdin, and Mami Taniguchi. 2009. Predictors of Turnover Intentions in Learning-Driven and Demand-Driven International Assignments: The Role of Repatriation Concerns, Satisfaction with Company Support, and Perceived Career Advancement Opportunities. *Human Resource Management* 48 (1): 89–109.

Stanley, Phil. 2009. Local-Plus Packages for Expatriates in Asia: A Viable Alternative. *International HR Journal* 3: 9–11.

Tharenou, Phyllis. 2015. Chinese International Business Graduates: A Career Dilemma: Repatriate or Stay? *Journal of Management and Organization* 21 (1): 37–59.

Index[1]

A

Adjustment, 7, 11, 12, 65, 76, 96, 100, 103, 158–163, 174, 202, 211, 214, 226, 234, 235, 246, 261, 282, 284, 292, 294, 300–303, 306

Advancement, 97, 139, 151, 204, 209, 227, 229, 230, 236

Allowance, 11, 15, 76, 171, 184, 296, 301, 305, 320–324, 328–331, 336, 337

Assigned expatriate (AEs), 3–5, 7, 10, 18, 20, 23, 34, 36, 46, 48, 63–80, 151, 187, 188, 293, 297–301, 310

Assignment, 2, 39, 66, 92, 150, 185, 190, 202, 226, 259, 291, 319

B

Balance sheet, 23, 320–322, 324, 325, 328–332, 334–336

Benefits, 5, 6, 12, 16, 46, 54, 67, 68, 72, 74, 76, 77, 92, 100, 103, 109, 110, 139–141, 163, 165, 166, 168, 170, 171, 185, 185n1, 188, 191, 192, 196, 202, 207, 231, 238, 300, 301, 305, 306

Bonus, 321, 322

Boundaryless career, 150, 151, 153, 155, 156, 162, 164, 175, 190, 195, 237

Boundary-spanning, 202, 206–208, 214

Burnout, 14, 17, 294, 297

---

[1] Note: Page numbers followed by 'n' refer to notes.

© The Author(s) 2018

M. Dickmann et al. (eds.), *The Management of Global Careers*,

https://doi.org/10.1007/978-3-319-76529-7

342 Index

C

Care, 4, 162–164, 175, 239, 247, 279, 299–301, 309

Career, 1, 40, 65, 92, 117, 149, 186, 201–216, 223, 258, 292, 326

Career anchor, 69, 124, 233, 237, 240

Career capital, 7, 18, 23, 72, 77, 79, 102, 103, 167, 169, 228, 232, 238, 239, 241, 242

Career choice, 9, 205, 225–228, 230, 231, 234, 235, 239–243

Career path, 70, 124, 150, 153, 158, 161, 164, 174, 205, 206, 210, 213, 215, 244–248

Career planning, 5, 138–140, 150, 169

Career progression, 6, 73, 75, 167, 229

Career stage, 68, 71, 79, 121

Career success, 20, 22, 23, 73, 117–143, 151, 152, 225, 230, 232, 236–237, 239–242, 273, 275, 278, 279, 283

Challenge, 14–19, 47–49, 65, 67, 72, 75, 93, 95–98, 100, 102, 104, 109, 127, 150, 152, 162, 163, 166, 167, 185, 187, 192–193, 206, 209, 211, 212, 215, 216, 224, 225, 227–232, 235, 239, 243, 246, 257–261, 264, 270–272, 274, 275, 277, 281, 282, 284–286, 292, 295–297, 299, 300, 302, 303, 308, 310, 319, 337

Children, 4, 13–16, 38, 76, 162, 163, 165, 214, 230, 245–247, 262, 273, 276, 278, 279, 281, 283, 284, 292, 294, 295, 297, 299, 300, 302, 303, 308, 320, 328–330, 333, 336

Coaching, 21, 76, 91–110, 134, 273, 279, 308

Commitment, 20, 46, 103, 190, 207, 230, 231, 259, 272, 335

Commuter, 3, 15–16, 20, 46, 47

Compensations, 9, 12, 23, 47, 65, 163, 170, 171, 184, 194, 214, 229, 230, 236, 237, 301, 319–325, 327–337

Competency, 3, 12, 45, 72, 76, 93, 96, 97, 101, 109, 165, 167, 174, 201, 214, 227, 228, 238, 239, 284, 285

Competitive advantage, 263, 285, 332–335

Competitor, 3, 22, 164–174, 332, 336

Compliance, 4, 5, 8, 9, 14, 156–158, 165, 166

Contract, 10–12, 15, 18, 33, 40, 46, 71, 74–76, 92, 102, 154, 162, 174, 185, 185n1, 190, 192, 193, 196, 206, 207, 209, 214, 230, 232, 242, 245, 260, 301, 329, 335

Control, 7, 15–17, 44, 47, 101, 122, 170, 188, 195, 202, 208, 227, 277, 279, 283, 295, 297, 300, 309, 333n1

Coping, 79, 109, 162, 285

Corporate expatriate, 20, 92, 104, 260

Cost, 2, 8, 11, 13, 15, 17, 35, 46, 75, 103, 151, 165, 174, 183, 184, 186, 187, 190, 191, 193, 196, 234, 282, 305, 320, 322, 330–336

Culture, 14, 16, 22, 70, 76, 96–100, 102–105, 109, 118–120, 124, 126, 135, 137, 159–161, 185, 188, 194, 195, 202, 214, 228, 239, 244, 248, 261, 292, 304, 309

D

Data analytics, 5, 9–10, 165
Decision, 2, 9, 10, 14, 19, 23, 40, 45, 68, 139, 140, 161, 162, 164–167, 175, 176, 183, 184, 196, 204, 223–225, 227, 229, 230, 238, 242, 244, 258, 261, 264, 270, 271, 281, 282, 298, 300, 303, 308, 328, 337
Demand, 6, 47, 136, 156–158, 167, 168, 246, 257, 294, 299, 302, 309
Development, 3, 34, 67, 92, 119, 164, 186, 203, 226, 285, 295, 325
Diversity, 2, 70, 79, 91, 120, 126, 157, 160, 163, 165, 166, 173, 202, 203, 304
Driver, 1–4, 9, 12, 34, 45, 47, 49, 68, 75–79, 165–167, 171, 193, 195, 282
Dual career, 23, 69, 162–164, 257–286, 277n1, 298–299

E

Education, 17, 68, 120, 122, 128, 159, 162, 163, 184, 185, 192, 196, 273, 300, 323, 330
Employability, 18, 140, 142
Engagement, 76, 99, 124, 138–140, 206, 207

Expatriate cycle, 4, 74
Expectations, 2, 6, 23, 105, 149, 167, 175, 203–205, 207, 209, 213, 229–232, 239, 242, 277, 282, 285, 303
Experienced global careerist, 23, 293, 301–303

F

Failure, 65, 97, 191–193, 231, 258, 261, 263, 264, 276, 277n1, 283
Family, 2, 34, 68, 97, 141, 150, 184, 214, 230, 258, 292, 326
Foreign market, 14, 202

G

Gender, 22, 66, 79, 96, 121, 122, 124, 128, 132–133, 140, 143, 166, 266, 285, 298
Global career, 1–24, 44, 48, 71, 75, 79, 92, 109, 117, 149, 152, 153, 155, 158, 165, 174–175, 185–188, 190–196, 210, 223, 301, 302
Global careerist, 2, 17, 21–23, 44, 45, 47, 48, 91–110, 149–176, 230, 291, 319–335
Globalization, 2, 10, 91, 193, 202, 301, 326
Global mobility department/ manager, 14, 18, 44, 96, 150, 203
Global work, 12, 20, 46–49, 79, 165, 196, 225, 240, 241
Government, 22, 140, 141, 143, 153, 155–158, 161, 166

344   **Index**

H

Headquarters (HQ), 73, 96, 151, 154, 155, 174–176, 183, 201–205, 207, 209–211, 215, 248, 336

Health, 4, 8, 14, 17, 46, 159, 162, 170–172, 184, 192, 273, 294, 301, 320, 329

History, 63, 64, 68, 123, 159, 161

Home country, 10, 15, 16, 18–20, 23, 40, 45, 67–71, 73, 75, 78, 96, 141, 151, 153, 155, 163, 167, 175, 183, 191, 192, 223–225, 227–230, 232, 235, 237–241, 244, 260, 266, 273, 295, 297, 303–305, 309, 320–322, 324, 325, 328, 332–334, 336

Home-country balance sheet, 23, 321, 322, 325, 328, 332, 334, 336

Host country, 7, 8, 10, 12, 15, 18, 19, 43, 68, 69, 76, 77, 79, 80, 101–103, 155, 157, 163, 166, 170, 176, 185, 189, 190, 195, 215, 228, 235, 238, 239, 241, 284, 305, 307, 308, 320–324, 328, 334, 336

Host unit, 7, 161, 202, 203

Housing, 4, 76, 170, 194, 282, 301, 308, 320–322, 328, 329, 336

Human resource management (HRM), 11, 14, 18, 66, 67, 70, 77, 78, 119, 134, 136, 137, 175, 214, 333

I

Identity, 16, 18, 97, 98, 102, 105, 108, 109, 142, 143, 228, 231, 235, 237, 238, 259–261, 263, 271, 272, 280

Incentives, 46, 68, 75, 76, 165, 171, 258, 321, 322, 324

Individual needs, 149, 239

Initiation, 194

Inpatriate, 22, 201, 202, 204–216, 237

Inpatriation, 22, 202, 204, 205, 211, 212, 216, 234

International assignee, 74, 92, 96, 97, 100, 157, 163, 164, 190, 191, 227, 228, 232, 297, 299, 301, 319, 332, 333, 335, 337

International business traveller (IBTs), 16, 17, 23, 293–295, 304–307, 309

International career, 17–20, 22, 23, 70, 71, 150–153, 161, 164, 174, 175, 233, 235, 237, 241, 259, 292, 301, 303–304, 306, 310

International HRM, 123, 259

International mobile employee (IMEs), 34–36, 39–44, 46, 48, 49

International work, 1–3, 6, 8, 16, 18, 19, 33, 47, 67–69, 72–74, 78, 79, 92, 100, 117–119, 149, 153, 166, 167, 169, 174, 223–225, 227–230, 232–234, 236, 238, 240, 241, 258, 291, 292, 294, 303–306, 309, 310

L

Language, 12, 13, 70, 75, 76, 100, 102, 103, 105, 110, 159, 161, 168, 194, 281, 283, 284, 301, 307

Leader, 33, 93, 96, 105, 139, 325

Index **345**

Leadership, 3, 5, 92, 96, 99–102, 104–106, 109, 126, 168, 172
Learning, 1, 8, 19, 20, 76, 77, 94, 95, 105, 107, 109, 122, 123, 126, 132, 136, 138, 140, 142, 169, 173, 174, 188, 195, 209, 214, 228, 232–234, 304, 307, 334
Local, 2, 3, 8, 9, 12, 14, 18, 23, 47, 65, 67, 71–73, 75–77, 92, 96, 97, 100, 101, 103, 105, 119, 123, 139, 150, 154, 157, 158, 160–162, 164, 167–171, 175, 176, 188–190, 192, 193, 195, 202, 233, 238, 260, 298, 301, 306, 324, 329–332
Local contract, 11, 12, 18, 71, 74–76, 162, 185, 190, 301
Localization, 18, 161, 328–334
Localized, 329, 330
Local plus, 8, 23, 46, 76, 328–334, 337

M

Mentor, 7, 76, 94, 169, 171, 231
Migrant, 34, 36–40, 43, 49, 53, 54, 64, 79
Migration, 2, 49, 54, 56, 118
Mobility, 3–6, 8, 13, 18, 22, 34, 36–38, 40–42, 47–51, 55, 56, 69, 74, 80, 92, 93, 95–98, 143, 150, 152, 153, 156, 157, 159–160, 163, 165, 167, 170, 173, 175, 176, 188, 203, 225, 233, 236, 237, 241, 257–259, 285, 292, 298, 325–327, 330, 334

Move, 1–4, 8, 11, 13, 15, 37, 38, 40, 67, 70, 71, 75, 77, 105, 142, 143, 149, 150, 153–174, 184, 185, 187, 189, 191–192, 204, 207, 213, 224, 225, 227, 238, 243–245, 247, 263, 272, 273, 279, 283, 286, 295, 298, 302, 303, 305, 321, 326, 330
Multinational corporation (MNC), 2, 3, 5, 8, 9, 11, 47, 65, 70–72, 77, 78, 80, 139, 156, 158, 159, 185, 202, 240, 285, 291, 292, 295, 307–310, 321, 322, 327, 335

N

Needs, 2, 5, 9, 11, 15, 17, 18, 22, 33, 34, 36, 39, 40, 42, 44, 47, 49, 50, 64, 66, 67, 95, 97, 98, 100, 102, 104, 106, 109, 110, 139, 141–143, 149, 152–156, 163, 174, 175, 188, 191, 193, 201, 203–205, 213, 214, 231, 239, 240, 243, 264, 272, 278–281, 295, 296, 300, 301, 303, 308, 310, 320, 333, 334, 337
Network, 13, 73, 75, 76, 79, 108, 160, 163, 166, 169, 171–173, 175, 228, 232, 238, 265, 275, 298, 299, 301, 306, 308

O

Objective career success, 124, 139, 151, 152, 230, 236, 237
Off-shoring, 22, 183–196, 326, 334

346 Index

Openness, 102, 159, 160, 270
Organizational expatriate,
  51, 109, 239
Organizational needs, 149–176
Outsourcing, 8, 9, 186, 187

P

Partner, 6, 8, 10, 13, 14, 16, 23, 40,
  55, 70, 162–164, 166–168,
  172, 258–261, 264, 276, 278,
  281, 286, 292–295, 298–303,
  306–308, 333
Peer, 71, 75, 95, 231, 239, 282,
  324, 325
Performance, 4–6, 45, 47, 53, 77,
  78, 92, 94, 95, 98, 101, 102,
  122, 140, 155, 164, 167, 170,
  175, 191, 209, 211, 214, 226,
  236, 292, 306, 307, 321–323
Personal development, 69, 72,
  96, 305
Physical mobility, 55, 225, 237, 241
Planning, 3, 5, 7, 55, 138–140, 143,
  150, 155, 161, 163, 168–170,
  172, 174–176, 310
Policy, 9, 78, 134, 137–141, 143,
  167, 257, 328, 333
Premium, 75, 321, 322, 328, 331,
  336, 337
Preparation, 4, 11, 14, 15, 45–46,
  55, 154, 161, 191, 194, 296
Profile, 6, 12, 22, 23, 167, 190,
  201, 202, 204–216, 257,
  325, 326, 334
Promotion, 4, 73, 124, 151, 154,
  172, 203, 229, 272

Protean career, 71, 120, 124, 152,
  173, 242
Psychological contract, 46, 154, 174,
  209, 214, 230, 232, 242, 330,
  332, 334, 335

R

Re-entry, 155, 169
Relocation, 15, 41–43, 55, 56, 92,
  150, 154, 157, 160, 163, 166,
  170, 172–174, 183–189,
  185n1, 192, 193, 196, 202,
  204, 213, 225, 230, 231, 233,
  235, 240, 244, 248, 258–262,
  264, 265, 272, 275, 278, 282,
  283, 286, 297, 298,
  304–307, 330, 331
Repatriation, 13, 47–48, 65, 96,
  152, 164, 185, 203,
  223–243, 261, 303, 324
Resources, 66, 67, 91, 93, 102, 106,
  108, 119, 154, 165, 186,
  213, 234–235, 303, 305,
  309, 333, 333n1
Retention, 5, 12, 20, 71, 80, 92,
  185, 189, 190, 193, 195, 196,
  209, 214, 234, 237, 240, 324,
  331, 332, 334, 335
Reward, 5, 6, 8–9, 20, 45, 46, 53,
  56, 139, 140, 164–167, 171,
  323, 330
Reward package, 8, 12, 45, 162
Risk, 16, 37, 38, 41–43, 96, 103, 142,
  156, 161, 165, 167, 173, 184,
  189, 195, 204, 207, 208, 232,
  246, 258, 295, 308, 331, 332

Index   **347**

S

Safety, 14

Satisfaction, 65, 79, 101, 123, 124, 126, 140, 236, 282, 299, 306, 323–325, 331, 334, 335

School, 118, 163, 185, 246, 277, 282, 295

Security, 4, 8, 9, 13, 47, 68, 76, 80, 123, 126, 127, 129, 130, 132, 136, 138, 140, 141, 156–162, 165, 171, 192, 194, 320

Selection, 6, 14, 35, 36, 45–46, 65, 75, 78, 106, 140, 167, 169, 212, 213, 281–282, 285

Self-initiated repatriates (SIRs), 23, 226, 238–239

Sense-making, 265, 270

Short-term assignee, 18, 23, 293, 295–297, 304, 305, 310, 334

Skill, 6, 12, 13, 15, 47, 67, 75, 77, 79, 92, 94, 96–98, 104–109, 140, 142, 168–171, 174, 188, 194, 209, 213, 229, 230, 232, 273, 281, 285, 307, 323, 325

Social capital, 20, 203, 209, 214, 232

Social security, 4, 8, 13, 76, 141, 156, 157, 171, 308, 320

Societal needs, 149–176

Society, 22, 118, 150, 158–160, 162

Spouse, 20, 53, 56, 69, 97, 168, 194, 257, 277n1

Staffing, 56, 201, 203, 205, 208, 210–213, 215, 309

Stakeholder, 2, 9, 22, 92, 94, 149, 165, 176, 214, 228

Status, 16, 18, 39, 48, 53, 55, 56, 72, 98, 122, 137, 151, 202,

207, 209–211, 242, 259, 260, 262, 266, 280, 298, 323, 328, 334

Strategic HRM, 123, 214

Strategy, 5, 46, 93, 140, 165, 174, 183–187, 190, 320

Stress, 14, 17, 69, 75, 96, 101, 109, 214, 246, 261, 278, 294, 295, 298, 303, 306, 310, 333

Subjective career success, 134, 151, 152, 236, 240

Supervisor, 17, 95, 127, 231, 296

Support, 3, 34, 51, 70, 92, 150, 183, 203, 227, 246, 292

Sustainability, 108, 187, 309

T

Talent, 2, 3, 5–7, 20, 74, 92, 93, 139, 143, 153, 184, 185, 193, 196, 232, 244, 246–248, 257, 258, 281, 292, 329, 332, 333, 335

Talent management, 1, 5, 9, 74, 93, 168, 188, 190, 214, 242, 281, 333

Tax, 4, 8, 13, 16, 141, 157, 158, 171, 184, 190, 245, 308, 320–322, 336

Taxation, 8, 14, 56, 156–158, 161, 320

Theory, 22, 34–36, 39, 50, 94, 99, 120, 137, 206, 207, 242, 243, 274, 275, 323, 324, 334

Third country national (TCN), 56, 237

Trailing spouse, 23, 39, 230, 257–286, 321

348 Index

Training, 6, 11, 12, 14, 15, 66,
76–78, 100, 101, 103, 106,
142, 155, 160, 161, 164,
168, 175, 176, 185, 213,
214, 273, 301, 310
Transition, 21, 39, 93, 96–98, 109,
119–122, 129, 191, 223, 224,
226–228, 240, 246, 329, 331
Transnational career,
150, 153–155, 158
Travel, 1, 2, 9, 11, 13–18, 46, 51,
52, 64, 66, 68, 96, 163, 171,
225, 246, 278, 291, 293–296,
299, 301, 302, 305–307,
309, 330
Turnover, 19, 20, 192, 224, 225,
227, 229–231, 240, 299,
324, 325, 330, 332
Typology, 23, 35–37, 40, 41, 43, 44,
49, 50, 257–286

U
Uncertainty, 2, 47, 79, 96, 122,
161, 205, 214, 294, 303

W
Well-being, 17, 79, 92, 284,
293–296, 299, 307, 309
Workforce, 14, 143, 184, 329, 332
Work-life balance, 122, 126, 127,
130, 132, 133, 136, 138–141,
173, 292, 293, 297, 300,
302, 307
Work-life conflicts (WLC),
294, 297, 299, 308–310
Work-life enrichment, 304, 306–307
Work-life interface (WLI),
20, 23, 291–310
Work permit, 69, 96, 156,
157, 261

CPSIA information can be obtained
at www.ICGtesting.com
Printed in the USA
LVOW13*2107310518
578995LV00020BA/308/P